Portraits of Literacy Development

Instruction and Assessment in a Well-Balanced Literacy Program, K–3

Portraits of Literacy Development

Instruction and Assessment in a Well-Balanced Literacy Program, K–3

Patricia A. Antonacci
Iona College

Catherine M. O'Callaghan
Iona College

Upper Saddle River, New Jersey
Columbus, Ohio

Library of Congress Cataloging-in-Publication Data
Antonacci, Patricia.
Portraits of literacy development : instruction and assessment in a well-balanced literacy program, K-3 / Patricia A. Antonacci, Catherine M. O'Callaghan.– 1st ed.
p. cm.
ISBN 0-13-094314-2
1. Language arts (Primary) 2. Language arts (Primary)—Ability testing. I. O'Callaghan, Catherine M. II. Title.
LB1528.A48 2004
372.6--dc22
2003018024

Vice President and Executive Publisher: Jeffery W. Johnston
Publisher: Kevin M. Davis
Editorial Assistant: Autumn Crisp
Production Editor: Linda Hillis Bayma
Production Coordination: Cindy Miller, Carlisle Publishers Services
Design Coordinator: Diane C. Lorenzo
Photo Coordinator: Valerie Schultz
Text Design and Illustrations: Carlisle Publishers Services
Cover Designer: Jim Hunter
Cover image: Corbis
Production Manager: Laura Messerly
Director of Marketing: Ann Castel Davis
Marketing Manager: Autumn Purdy
Marketing Coordinator: Tyra Poole

This book was set in Century Light by Carlisle Communications, Ltd. It was printed and bound by R.R. Donnelley & Sons Company. The cover was printed by Phoenix Color Corp.

Photo Credits: pp. 22, 84, 145 by Laima Druskis/PH College; pp. 27, 51, 88, 101 (bottom), 224, 251, 330, 368 by Anthony Magnacca/Merrill; pp. 29, 108, 150, 202, 406, 408 by Anne Vega/Merrill; pp. 39, 101 (top), 206, 366 by Barbara Schwartz/ Merrill; p. 55 by KS Studios/Merrill; p. 83 by Shirley Zeiberg/PH College; pp. 92, 109, 248 by Todd Yarrington/Merrill; p. 99 by Dan Floss/Merrill; pp. 112, 168, 225, 265, 322 by Scott Cunningham/Merrill; p. 149 courtesy of the Library of Congress; p. 234 by Karen Mancinelli/Pearson Learning.

Pearson Education Ltd.
Pearson Education Singapore Pte. Ltd.
Pearson Education Canada, Ltd.
Pearson Education—Japan
Pearson Education Australia Pty. Limited
Pearson Education North Asia Ltd.
Pearson Educación de Mexico, S.A. de C.V.
Pearson Education Malaysia Pte. Ltd.

10 9 8 7 6 5 4 3 2 1
ISBN: 0-13-094314-2

To our first and best teachers—
Mary and Joseph Pierce
Kathryn and James O'Callaghan

Preface

How Do Early Childhood Teachers Ensure That "No Child Is Left Behind"?

Across the country, teachers and administrators are struggling to respond to the federal legislation mandate that every child receive a quality literacy education. One of the key components of the No Child Left Behind Act is research-based literacy instruction. The key to successful literacy instruction, however, is a reflective teacher with a rich knowledge base of child development and pedagogy.

Our purpose in writing this textbook is to help early childhood teachers acquire an understanding of *assessment for learning.* This process studies the child's literacy performance and bases instruction on the needs of the individual child. The teacher "follows the child," which is critical to early childhood instruction. We model how to implement scaffolded literacy instruction using developmental benchmarks in a clear, pragmatic style. It is now mandated in the No Child Left Behind Act that teachers gather evidence of student learning. This text provides performance-based literacy assessment to help teachers gather data on student progress. Throughout the text we illustrate how to scaffold literacy instruction for the child reading at the emergent, early, and fluent levels.

What Makes Portraits of Literacy Development *Different From Other Literacy Textbooks?*

- *Portraits of Literacy Development* illustrates the importance of oral language to literacy instruction and demonstrates how to improve academic discourse.
- Teachers are shown how to scaffold literacy instruction for emergent, early, and fluent readers throughout the entire literacy cycle.
- Assessment instruments are provided which are linked to instruction. The appendix contains master copies of key assessment instruments that teachers can reproduce and use with their students.
- The diverse classroom of today is addressed and teachers are shown how to differentiate instruction and assessment for the 21st-century classroom.

What Is the Purpose of This Textbook?

As we interact with preservice and professional teachers, we are constantly asked how to integrate literacy instruction and assessment. Early childhood teachers are aware that using assessment data to improve literacy performance is critical, yet very few have been shown *how to actually do it.*

We have used our decades of experience teaching literacy in early childhood to create a practitioner-friendly text. The real classroom with its many challenges is the springboard to present developmental benchmarks for literacy at the emergent, early, and fluent levels. The literacy benchmarks are based on national standards issued by the International Reading Association and the National Council of Teachers of English and are therefore applicable across all 50 states. Supporting our instructional and assessment strategies is a framework for developmentally appropriate learning as outlined by the National Association for the Education of Young Children.

Our goal is to illustrate how developmental benchmarks for literacy may be used to anchor instruction and assessment. As the teacher becomes immersed in the benchmarks, the instructional focus shifts to following the child while the teacher develops a well-trained "literacy lens." As the 21st-century classroom becomes more diverse and challenging, the early childhood teacher will need to draw on this knowledge to ensure that no child is left behind.

How Is This Textbook Organized?

This book is organized into four parts. Part I presents the foundations of literacy instruction and the research findings that support the instructional strategies presented in the text. It also explains the constructivist theory supporting the scaffolded literacy instruction that is presented throughout the text.

Part II explores the importance of oral language development to literacy development. The chapters describe how to support the development of academic discourse for emergent, early, and fluent readers. Teachers are also shown how to connect oral language with writing development across the literacy continuum. Instructional strategies as well as assessment instruments for oral language development are included in the chapters.

The third part focuses on literacy instruction for emergent, early, and fluent readers. Each chapter presents the developmental benchmarks for literacy at the emergent, early, and fluent levels. Chapter 6 demonstrates how to assess and develop phonemic awareness as well as the alphabetic principle. Chapter 7 describes the literacy needs of the child at the early literacy stage, and Chapter 8 focuses on the fluency level and building comprehension across the curriculum. Chapter 9 discusses the importance of phonics instruction across all three literacy levels and also provides assessment instruments for phonological processing.

Part IV describes how to "put it all together." Chapter 10 illustrates how to differentiate instruction and assessment for all children, especially the English language learner as well as the child with special learning needs. The section concludes with Chapter 11, which deals with pragmatic issues regarding portfolio assessment such as scheduling and preparing for parent conferences.

What Are the Special Features of This Textbook?

The special features of this textbook include the following:

- *Portraits of Literacy* scenarios drawn from the authors' own classroom experiences are integrated throughout the text.
- Each chapter has links to technology, meeting the needs of diversity and involving parents.
- Each chapter has additional professional and children's literature references.
- Assessment instruments linked to instructional strategies are included in every chapter to gather evidence of student learning.
- The appendix presents key assessment instruments for emergent, early, and fluent readers which can be reproduced to create a literacy portfolio.
- Developmental benchmarks for oral language as well as literacy are presented for emergent, early, and fluent readers.
- Chapter 9 presents a complete compendium of strategies and assessment instruments for phonological processing across literacy levels.
- Chapter 10 illustrates how to differentiate instruction and assessment to meet the challenges of today's diverse classroom.
- Every chapter presents instructional strategies and assessment tools for scaffolding oral language and literacy instruction across the literacy continuum.

Acknowledgments

As we write the final words of *Portraits of Literacy Development,* we are reminded that all language endeavors are accomplished in collaboration with others. Indeed, this is true of our book. We wish to begin by thanking our students in the early childhood classrooms where we taught and where we observed. We have learned so much from children who use language in so many creative ways, always in pursuit of meaning. We wish to thank our teacher candidates who continue to be so responsive, "trying out" our suggestions and giving us feedback. A special thank-you goes to all early childhood teachers across our nation, dedicating their professional lives to helping children on their pathways to literacy development. Our own teachers can never be forgotten! Thank you for sharing your craft and helping us to read and write. For our colleagues at Fordham University who mentored us and encouraged us to write about what we know and believe, especially Terry Cicchelli and Carolyn Hedley, we thank you and cherish your words. We thank our colleagues at Iona College who continue to maintain a community of learners.

We thank each of our reviewers who provided us with feedback and suggestions: Lola Davis, University of Central Oklahoma; Sara McCormick Davis, Portland State University; Adrienne L. Herrell, California State University, Fresno; Terry H. Higgins, The Ohio State University–Newark; Leanna Manna, Villa Marie College; Linda Medearis, Texas A&M International University; Edythe H. Schwartz, California State

University, Sacramento; Sally Smith, Hofstra University; and Thomas D. Yawkey, Pennsylvania State University.

A very special thanks to all of the kind people at Merrill/Prentice Hall: Dorothy Marrero, who introduced us as writers to Merrill/Prentice Hall; Christina Tawney, who worked with us diligently and gently when our road became bumpy; Autumn Crisp, who helped up get through the final stages; Kevin Davis, our editor; and Linda Bayma, our production editor.

M. M. Bakhtin, a Russian philosopher of language, emphasized that no text, written or spoken, is ever complete because each time that a text is read, new meanings are reconstructed. We send a very special thank-you to our readers. After you read *Portraits of Literacy Development,* we hope that you tell us how we have assisted you or how we can further support you in helping young children to acquire all forms of language. Please send any suggestions to Pantonacci@iona.edu or Cocallaghan@iona.edu

Patricia Antonacci
Catherine O'Callaghan

Discover the Companion Website Accompanying This Book

The Prentice Hall Companion Website: A Virtual Learning Environment

Technology is a constantly growing and changing aspect of our field that is creating a need for content and resources. To address this emerging need, Prentice Hall has developed an online learning environment for students and professors alike—Companion Websites—to support our textbooks.

In creating a Companion Website, our goal is to build on and enhance what the textbook already offers. For this reason, the content for each user-friendly website is organized by topic and provides the professor and student with a variety of meaningful resources. Common features of a Companion Website include:

For the Professor—

Every Companion Website integrates **Syllabus Manager™**, an online syllabus creation and management utility.

- **Syllabus Manager™** provides you, the instructor, with an easy, step-by-step process to create and revise syllabi, with direct links into Companion Website and other online content without having to learn HTML.
- Students may log on to your syllabus during any study session. All they need to know is the web address for the Companion Website and the password you've assigned to your syllabus.
- After you have created a syllabus using **Syllabus Manager™**, students may enter the syllabus for their course section from any point in the Companion Website.
- Clicking on a date, the student is shown the list of activities for the assignment. The activities for each assignment are linked directly to actual content, saving time for students.
- Adding assignments consists of clicking on the desired due date, then filling in the details of the assignment—name of the assignment, instructions, and whether it is a one-time or repeating assignment.
- In addition, links to other activities can be created easily. If the activity is online, a URL can be entered in the space provided, and it will be linked automatically in the final syllabus.
- Your completed syllabus is hosted on our servers, allowing convenient updates from any computer on the Internet. Changes you make to your syllabus are immediately available to your students at their next logon.

For the Student—

- **Introduction**—General information about the topic and how it will be covered in the website.
- **Web Links**—A variety of websites related to topic areas.
- **Timely Articles**—Links to online articles that enable you to become more aware of important issues in early childhood.
- **Learn by Doing**—Put concepts into action, participate in activities, examine strategies, and more.
- **Visit a School**—Visit a school's website to see concepts, theories, and strategies in action.
- **For Teachers/Practitioners**—Access information you will need to know as an educator, including information on materials, activities, and lessons.
- **Current Policies and Standards**—Find out the latest early childhood policies from the government and various organizations, and view state, federal, and curriculum standards.
- **Resources and Organizations**—Discover tools to help you plan your classroom or center and organizations to provide current information and standards for each topic.
- **Electronic Bluebook**—Paperless method of completing homework or essays assigned by a professor. Finished work can be sent to the professor via email.
- **Message Board**—Virtual bulletin board to post and respond to questions and comments from a national audience.

To take advantage of these and other resources, please visit the *Portraits of Literacy Development: Instruction and Assessment in a Well-Balanced Literacy Program, K–3* Companion Website at

www.prenhall.com/antonacci

Educator Learning Center: An Invaluable Online Resource

Merrill Education and the Association for Supervision and Curriculum Development (ASCD) invite you to take advantage of a new online resource, one that provides access to the top research and proven strategies associated with ASCD and Merrill—the Educator Learning Center. At **www.EducatorLearningCenter.com** you will find resources that will enhance your students' understanding of course topics and of current educational issues, in addition to being invaluable for further research.

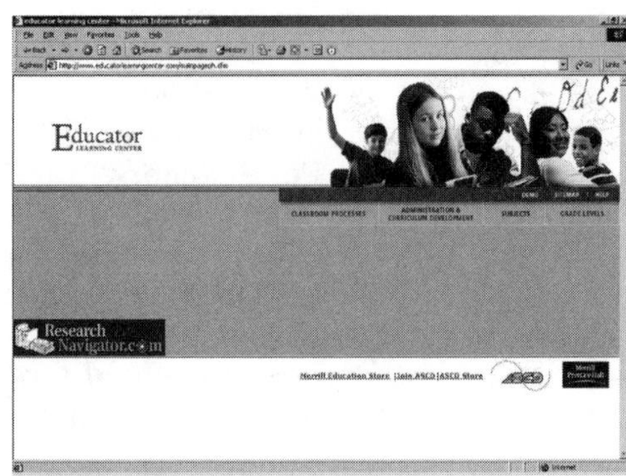

How the Educator Learning Center will help your students become better teachers

With the combined resources of Merrill Education and ASCD, you and your students will find a wealth of tools and materials to better prepare them for the classroom.

Research

- More than 600 articles from the ASCD journal *Educational Leadership* discuss everyday issues faced by practicing teachers.
- A direct link on the site to Research Navigator™ gives students access to many of the leading education journals, as well as extensive content detailing the research process.
- Excerpts from Merrill Education texts give your students insights on important topics of instructional methods, diverse populations, assessment, classroom management, technology, and refining classroom practice.

Classroom Practice

- Hundreds of lesson plans and teaching strategies are categorized by content area and age range.
- Case studies and classroom video footage provide virtual field experience for student reflection.
- Computer simulations and other electronic tools keep your students abreast of today's classrooms and current technologies.

Look into the value of Educator Learning Center yourself

Preview the value of this educational environment by visiting **www.EducatorLearningCenter.com** and clicking on "Demo." For a free 4-month subscription to the Educator Learning Center in conjunction with this text, simply contact your Merrill/Prentice Hall sales representative.

Brief Contents

Contents

Note: Every effort has been made to provide accurate and current Internet information in this book. However, the Internet and information posted on it are constantly changing, and it is inevitable that some of the Internet addresses listed in this textbook will change.

PART I

THE FOUNDATIONS OF LITERACY DEVELOPMENT IN YOUNG CHILDREN

CHAPTER 1

Building a Framework for Assessing Language and Literacy Development of Young Readers and Writers

Profile of an Early Childhood Classroom

One morning in March, Sharon's first graders were particularly loud. The children were filled with excitement about an author study in which they were engaged. One small group was gathered around two easels finishing their paintings of the animals in The Mitten. *Another group was at the writing center drafting pages for their new book,* The Lost Hat, *patterned after Brett's* The Mitten. *While Sharon was at the table with a third group of children immersed in a guided reading lesson, the door swung open. The principal stood in the doorway with a generous smile. Hiding behind the principal, afraid to show her face, a new child was being introduced to the teacher and the class. The children stopped, looked up, and three energetic children bounded across the classroom to greet Melissa, who drew away from her new classmates. For a brief 3 minutes, the principal took Sharon aside explaining that Melissa was new to the area, had no previous schooling, and was being placed in the first grade because of her age. Her other, more serious problems were that she was homeless and separated from her twin sister, both living with different foster parents. The class hovered around Melissa to help her get settled, while Sharon found her a place to put her belongings.*

During her first week of school, Melissa hardly spoke to the children but would quietly approach Sharon for assistance. Sharon worked with Melissa every day and began to assess her for concepts and skills related to early literacy and language development. Sharon soon found out that Melissa could not say the alphabet and was not able to recognize any of the letters, nor could she write her name. During shared reading, Melissa was very attentive and seemed to enjoy the stories but did not participate. She watched the other children carefully as they went to the big book and read the refrains from the story, picked out the words, and talked about their predictions.

As the weeks passed, Melissa picked up some concepts about print and was acquiring a sense of story. Early in April, she asked if she could retell the story. Much to her surprise, the children clapped when she finished. Melissa began to write her name, and she drew pictures and wrote single letters for words under each picture, reading the letters as her story. She learned a small bank of sight words, and was able to point to the, an, *and* on *during a follow-up lesson in shared reading. By the end of May, Melissa could recite the alphabet and identify all but five letters. Sharon documented Melissa's literacy growth, and she kept a portfolio of her work including Melissa's writing, story retellings, checklists of letter knowledge, and annotations of Sharon's observations of Melissa's oral language.*

May approached quickly, when all children in Grades 1–6 take reading achievement tests. Melissa had to take the test even though she had only 2 months of schooling. The test results were used to determine the children's achievement and the teachers' success.

Sharon knew how the test results were used in the school district. Melissa would be considered a child who made no progress and classified as "at risk for learning." Melissa's reading achievement test results showed she scored in the third percentile. Thus, 97% of all students in the first grade read better than Melissa. Comparing Melissa's test scores to all first-grade students would mean that Melissa failed to achieve.

Sharon did not compare Melissa to anyone! She gathered up Melissa's portfolio and set up a conference with her foster parents, the school psychologist, and the principal. The purpose was not to discuss Melissa's test score, but to show what Melissa had learned. It was apparent that Melissa had made a significant achievement in acquiring language and literacy skills and concepts within the 2 short months that she was immersed in a rich literacy environment. As the conference concluded, it was clear that everyone was optimistic about Melissa's literacy growth—especially her foster parents who had received specific ideas on how to help her.

Sharon continues to use assessment that is aligned to instruction to document children's ongoing growth in language and literacy. She knows that standardized tests do have a function in achieving accountability, but is reminded by Melissa that such tests do not provide the whole picture of a child's achievement and a teacher's success. She knows that an accomplished portrait of each child's language and literacy growth may be painted through using developmentally appropriate assessment with systematic methods for its documentation.

Making Instructional Decisions

Instructional Choices

When Melissa arrived in the first grade with no previous schooling, Sharon knew she had to make an instructional decision. Like some of the teachers within the district who were faced with similar dilemmas, Sharon could have placed Melissa with a small group of children who were at the emergent stage of literacy instruction. Such a choice would assume that Melissa had developed some concepts of print and skills already acquired by the children within that group. Further, such an instructional choice would mean that Melissa would receive formal reading and writing instruction when she did not know any words, letter names and sounds, or how to write her name. Instead, Sharon chose to follow Melissa's path of development. She carefully observed Melissa's language and literacy behaviors and assessed her phonemic awareness and letter knowledge, as well as many other benchmarks for the emergent stage of literacy development. After 1 week, Sharon was able to describe what Melissa knew and needed to learn. Using ongoing assessment, Sharon worked with Melissa to reach the benchmarks within her stage of development. Sharon carefully assessed each instructional sequence to monitor Melissa's growth and provided literacy instruction and activities to "nudge" her development further.

Consequences of Our Choices

Sharon's instructional choices bore consequences for Melissa, her family, and for Sharon herself. Because Sharon taught at Melissa's developmental level, Melissa learned without frustration and loss of confidence. Through Sharon's ongoing assessment, Melissa was learning all of the concepts and skills she needed. Her family worked closely with Sharon, who made suggestions for reading and writing practice that would benefit Melissa. Sharon benefited from her instructional decision as well. Each time she worked with Melissa and observed her literacy growth, her choice was validated. When Sharon received the children's standardized test results at the end of the school year, Melissa's test scores could have been devastating to Sharon if she had not tracked her literacy development. Melissa's literacy portfolio showed the enormous growth she had made in just 4 months!

Foundations of Instructional Decisions

Sharon's instructional decisions were not unfounded. To each choice, she brought knowledge of children's development in language and literacy and an understanding and use of **best practices.** Sharon used assessment strategies aligned with instruction. Consistently, she used Melissa's assessment results to determine the best instructional sequence for Melissa; that is, instruction that was developmentally appropriate for her student. Just as important, Sharon used Melissa's assessment results to inform her own teaching. She wanted to validate that the practices she used in teaching Melissa resulted in her learning.

Best practice refers to exemplary teaching strategies or approaches used in the classroom. Student learning is a litmus test determining the value of teachers' practices.

Like Sharon, teachers need to know the foundations of literacy and language and how they relate to best practices in instruction and assessment. The term *foundations of literacy and language* refers to theories and research on how children learn and develop oral language, reading and writing. Our personal beliefs are shaped by our knowledge of theories and research as well as our own teaching practices. Therefore, this chapter begins with a comparison of literacy practices in early childhood classrooms, with varying approaches tied to different beliefs about language and literacy acquisition and development. We take our readers through changing methods in teaching young children to the current views on language acquisition and development and its relationship to how young children learn to read and write. The intent is to lay the groundwork that has led to the development of the best practices used in promoting language and literacy in young children.

As you read Chapter 1, reflect on the following topics:

- How teaching reading and writing has changed over time by considering your own experiences in primary school and how you learned to read and write
- The definition of *literacy*
- The foundation of oral language in learning to read and write
- The development of oral language in children
- Ways to assist children in language growth

Some Changing Views on Literacy Learning

Over the past 40 years, enormous amounts of research have accumulated that provide rich descriptions of young children's language acquisition and literacy development. Teachers have made contributions to the best practices used in early childhood literacy settings. These ideas have made us think differently about how young children acquire language and become readers and writers. As a result, classroom practices have taken a different direction with respect to approaches used to teach and assess children's learning. In addition, the environments of early childhood classrooms that foster best practices in literacy development look dramatically different.

On any Saturday afternoon, observe the children's sections at the library or the local bookstores. They are occupied with children as young as 2 years of age. As parents and children examine the books, they carefully select their weekly measure for home reading. Indeed, at the beginning of the 21st century, we can only be amazed by the vast treasure of children's books that are available and the large number of parents and children who share in this wealth of story. The world of children's literature has indeed changed, and so has the market. The number of consumers of children's books has increased significantly. The colorful picture storybooks are eye catching and their topics and genres are full range. The stories—whose authors and illustrators cross social and cultural borders—captivate even adult readers. Parents, children, and the books themselves play a significant part in the literacy story. The more active role that parents play in their children's literacy development reflects new ways of thinking about language and literacy development. This section begins with a brief discussion about changing views of teaching literacy to young children and the early approaches to teaching reading and writing in the primary grades.

Early Views on Literacy Instruction

Saturday afternoon at the library looked quite different 40 years ago. First, such a wide variety of literature was not available to young children. Parents were not encouraged to take an active role in their children's literacy development. Now, more and more educators are advising parents to read to and with children at an early age, and politicians and a number of special-interest groups as well as the media are urging parents to read and to talk with their children.

This changing scene in our libraries and bookstores has been partially caused by the way literacy development in the young is currently viewed. To understand the dramatic differences, let us go back in time. Part of the differences result from how literacy development was viewed and how young children were taught to read and write.

As we turn back the clock to reflect on the time-honored approaches used in teaching young children how to read, we realize that traditional practices are becoming a part of our history. Let's consider the traditional views of literacy that were once the mainstay of early reading and writing instruction. Our reflections on the old will establish the need for the current approaches that are gaining prominence in early childhood classrooms today.

Perspectives on oral language. When children enter school, they can use language to communicate. Because young children learn to speak at home before entering school, oral language was thought of as coming first before reading and writing, or having primacy over print. Wells (1987) summarized the enormous strides in language acquisition that children make between birth and the early school years. By age 5, most children have mastered most of the basic language structures.

What approaches did teachers use to develop young children's oral language? The dramatic achievement in oral language acquisition by children at home was one factor that propelled educators to view language forms sequentially. That is, educators considered oral language learning coming first before print language and before children entered school. Therefore, the role of language acquisition and development was left primarily to the parents. Print forms of language, reading, and writing were the primary job of the teachers. Most children came to preschool and kindergarten knowing how to speak, and by that time they understood spoken language. Therefore, teachers felt that language could essentially be developed within the home and on its own.

The theoretical claims for taking a passive approach in developing oral language came from Chomsky (1965). He explained language learning through a biological-based predisposition for language called the language acquisition device (LAD). His essential claim was that all individuals have knowledge of the rules that underlie the indefinitely large numbers of grammatically well-formed sentences that can be spoken and understood. Chomsky's view was aligned with the prevailing view on children's learning. The young child was essentially passive and waiting to be molded intellectually, and linguistically, by the environment. Because of these ideas, there was little emphasis placed on formal or informal instruction and assessment of oral language development by early childhood teachers.

The reading readiness program. *Why were reading readiness programs thought to be crucial in learning how to read?* Readiness programs were an integral part of reading programs across the nation. Before children received formal instruction in reading in the first grade, they were placed in a **reading readiness program.** The readiness programs were aimed at getting children ready for formal instruction in reading through teaching a set of skills or competencies that were considered prerequisite to learning how to read (Morrow, 1997). The term *reading readiness* implied that children were not ready to learn to read, and therefore, they had to be prepared for formal instruction in reading. They had to learn about how letters looked and sounded before using them to read and write (Crawford, 1995). The reading readiness view suggested that as a result of age maturation, children will become readers. Therefore, it was not until a given period that children were viewed as readers and writers. In many cases, children needed to pass a formal reading readiness test before they were allowed to receive formal reading instruction.

Reading first, writing second. *What did sequencing instruction mean to the teaching of reading and writing?* The notion of sequenced instruction related to when children were taught to read and write. Further, the notion of connecting reading and writing during instruction was not viewed as a positive factor in children's literacy development. In kindergarten and first grade, the emphasis was on reading instruction. Writing was not defined as the composing process but as tracing or copying letters, words, and sentences; therefore, the emphasis on writing instruction in the early grades was on the formation of letters and words. As a result, children were not encouraged to compose stories until after they learned how to read.

Scope and sequence of skills instruction. *How did teachers follow a scope and sequence of skills in their instruction?* Sequencing instruction was based on the belief that all children learn certain skills before others. Therefore, within many traditional reading programs, skills were taught in a specific sequence. The teachers followed a specific scope (skills designated to a specific grade) and sequence (the order in which the skills were taught). The scope and sequence of skills to be taught were found in the teacher's guide for the basal readers, and the skills to be taught at each grade level were determined by the textbook publishers. It also meant that children's reading achievement was guided by a grade-level performance. The grade-level achievement concept is with us today, as we are reminded by the familiar characterization of children's performance in relation to their grade: "They read at, below, or above grade level."

For teachers using a specific basal reader this meant that they would introduce the name and the sound of a certain set of letters first, such as *r, n,* and *a.* Children would then read a very short story comprised of words using these three letters. For children learning how to read, decoding came first; comprehension skills came after children could sound out the words (Fries, 1962). The idea was that if children became automatic in letter and word recognition, comprehending the stories would follow. The notion was that before children can begin to comprehend text, their attention must be free to do so. That is, if beginning readers were busy thinking about the letters, letter sounds, and words, they could not attend to the meaning of the text. Therefore, this meant that readers need to be fully automatic in decoding words before they are trained to comprehend text (LaBerge & Samuels, 1985). Thus, traditional models of early reading instruction placed an emphasis on decoding first and comprehension instruction after children mastered the decoding skills.

Grouping patterns for reading instruction. *How did teachers group children for instruction?* The typical reading program in early childhood settings was designed around grouping children based on their ability. Oftentimes, classroom teachers had three reading groups—high, average, and low. During the course of the year, and for many children throughout their school life, they remained within the same instructional group.

For the most part, what distinguished the three groups was *the pacing of the instruction.* Children in the high-achieving group read more stories over the course of the school year, whereas children in the low-achieving group read fewer stories during the same time. The bulk of instructional time for low-ability children was spent on building skills (Allington & Cunningham, 1996).

Reading achievement evaluation. ***How was reading achievement measured and determined?*** In early literacy programs, measuring reading achievement in young children was accomplished through a formal standardized test in reading. Regardless of their literacy development, all children in the first grade took a first-grade standardized test in reading at the end of the school year. Just as the instruction in reading was sequenced and grade-leveled, so were the tests. The results, therefore, were related to a grade-level performance.

The standardized tests were used to rank the order of schools' performances and to rank the order of children's performance. Each child's achievement was compared to his standing within the group.

A summary of early views and practices. Although there were numerous early reading and writing practices, the following represent those considered most prevalent.

1. Oral language was viewed as developing within the home, and it received minimal attention in the classroom.
2. Young children were placed in reading readiness programs before given formal reading instruction.
3. In teaching children how to read, teachers followed a scope and sequence of skills to be taught.
4. In early reading programs, the emphasis was on decoding first. Instruction of reading comprehension followed.
5. The teaching of reading and writing were not connected.
6. Writing instruction in the early grades placed emphasis on letter formation and consisted of copying letters, words, and sentences rather than the composing process.
7. Young children were grouped for instruction; many children stayed in the same groups over the course of the year.
8. At the end of the year, children's reading achievement was assessed through the use of a standardized reading achievement test in terms of a grade-level in reading.

Recent Views and Practices in Language and Literacy Development

During the past three decades, due to a wave of research in early literacy, educators have begun to rethink children's language and literacy acquisition and development (Sulzby & Teale, 1991). The effects of the research led to dramatic changes in literacy practices used in early childhood classrooms. The once familiar terms like *reading readiness* were gradually replaced by terms like *emergent literacy.* The time-honored practices used in the primary grades are making room for approaches that relate to the newest thinking about early literacy and child development.

Views on oral language development. Teachers recognize that young children's oral language is quite remarkable. By the time they reach age 4, they have a substantial vocabulary of at least 1,000 words (Morrow, 1989) and they are capable of constructing simple sentences. Although there have been many studies conducted on the size of children's vocabulary, most recent research show a range of 2,500–5,000 words for 5- to 6-year-olds; for students with learning disabilities, the size is significantly less (Beck & McKeown, 1991). Teachers and educators are now aware that most children who enter school have acquired language; however, they realize that their language is not fully developed. Teachers also know about the link between language development and literacy learning. This means that children's continuous advancements in oral language development are necessary for literacy growth and development.

How do teachers in early childhood classrooms promote oral language development? For early childhood teachers, oral language development is viewed as the linchpin to becoming readers and writers. Additionally, spoken language is now viewed as affecting how and what children learn. Being aware that children's oral language is central to their school achievement, teachers do not leave its development to chance. Oral language opportunities are built into each facet of the literacy program. All aspects of the curriculum such as science, social studies, and mathematics provide further opportunities for language growth and development. The most effective teachers in early childhood classrooms promote language development within literacy and across the curriculum. These teachers know that oral language development is indeed a critical part of becoming literate.

Meeting Diverse Needs: Making text connections means helping children relate to the story. This is especially critical for children from diverse cultures in understanding a story that may not be relevant to their own.

Before reading a book, the teacher guides the discussion around the story as children share related experiences. The teacher is helping the children to make text connections through their language exchanges. After reading, children are encouraged to talk further about the story making deeper connections. Writing a story will be preceded by a discussion of the topics and elaboration on details. When they finish writing, children will share their stories. They listen attentively to the questions and comments from their friends who often give them fresh ideas to add to their stories.

Literacy events are not the only context where oral language develops. At centers, different purposes for language use are encouraged by the kinds of experiences that the teacher designs. Children are encouraged to express themselves during sharing time. Role playing and dress-up corners offer contexts that promote imaginative language use. Teachers build knowledge around other areas of learning such as science, math, social studies, and art concepts through the use of conversation and language exchanges.

In early childhood settings, oral language development is woven into the fabric of the literacy program as well as into each piece of the curriculum. Teachers not only actively develop children's oral language but they also monitor children's growth through informal assessment.

Views on early literacy development. The concept of reading readiness had been gradually replaced by emergent literacy. Supported by research on early literacy development, we now have new ways of thinking about how and when the young child begins to develop literacy concepts. These changes were brought about by literacy research in the early 1980s. One of the major contributors and pioneers who helped to change the course of thinking on early literacy is Marie Clay (1991). The use of the term *emergent literacy* to describe children's developing concepts of print first appeared in her research on children learning to read and write. Among others who are responsible for the foundations of more current approaches to literacy are Sulzby (1985, 1986, 1989), Teale (1984, 1986, 1987), Strickland and Morrow (1989), and a number of other researchers, educators, and practitioners.

How has the concept of emergent literacy affected literacy approaches in early childhood settings? From this research we know that children begin to develop concepts of print or literacy concepts at a very young age. Their concepts about print are developing or emerging as they become involved with literacy experiences that they encounter from infancy and on throughout their lives. This notion implies that children do not need a readiness program to begin to learn about print. Sulzby (1989) offers a definition of the term *emergent literacy* as "the reading and writing behaviors that precede and develop into conventional literacy." Unlike the reading readiness concept, emergent literacy does not deny the right of the young child to enter the process of becoming literate. Rather, the concept of emergent literacy promotes the idea that in a literate society, the young child, as early as 1 and 2 years old, is in the process of becoming literate. Children have an early initiation in the literacy process because of their membership in a culture that values print, where print is readily available, and where print has a number of functions that enter into the daily routines of everyone's lives. Because of the prolific uses of reading and writing, most children become aware of the basic print concepts before they enter kindergarten. What differs is the degree of development in each child.

In early childhood settings, teachers are aware that children have different print experiences at home and that they are at different stages of literacy development. Children are viewed as readers and writers even though their literacy concepts are not fully developed. Emergent literacy approaches changed the traditional grade-level curriculum to a child-centered one where teachers build upon the emerging concepts that children are developing.

Views on integrated language forms. Within a literacy program for young children, there is no separation of language forms. The development of reading, writing, speaking, listening, viewing, and illustrating do not occur sequentially nor do they stand alone, isolated from the other language forms. All of the elements of literacy develop together and interactively as well (Strickland, 1990).

How do teachers integrate the language forms in their literacy programs? Teachers now know that all language forms are intricately related, and that engagement and learning in one language form supports learning in others (Freeman & Hatch, 1989). Therefore, in their literacy lessons, teachers do not teach one component of literacy such as reading in isolation, excluding other language forms. Consider how oral language development may be integrated in reading instruction during the story walk or book introduction. After guided reading, for example, the teacher may ask the children to respond to the story either in writing or through drawing. Below are two examples of the strong connections across language forms that show that learning in one aspect of literacy supports other components.

> *After Maura listens to the teacher read Eric Carle's* The Very Hungry Caterpillar, *she goes to the art center where she attempts to draw the parts of the story. As she begins her artistic retelling, she thinks about the beginning, middle, and end of the story. Turning to an onlooker, Maura begins to describe what parts she will include. Juan negotiates with her to put in his favorite part, as Maura listens and then reluctantly agrees to make an addition to her retelling. In this literacy event, listening, speaking, and illustrating were essential aspects of the development of literacy for Maura as well as for Juan. The dialogue around the story encourages both children to think more deeply about the story elements. Juan's addition to Maura's retelling pushes her to think about the parts of the story from another's perspective.*
>
> *Moving to the writing table we can observe Jamal, a first grader, who is taking part in a guided writing lesson and figuring out how to spell the*

word home. *The teacher standing behind him asks him to say the word and to think about the first sound. Mr. Lewis guides Jamal through each phoneme of the word. Jamal writes the word carefully. He then proceeds to complete his story. It is clear that this guided writing lesson included a lesson in phonics. Jamal had to think about the letter that represented each phoneme or sound.*

Notice how all language forms are integrated. We saw how reading is supported by speaking and drawing as in Maura's retelling of the story. We also saw how writing supports phonics as in Jamal's lesson in guided writing. Unlike traditional models of literacy where each language form was separated and taught in isolation, we see early childhood teachers providing literacy instruction that integrates the language arts. They are building on the children's strengths and their literacy development—which may be the ability to talk about the parts of a story—to develop other aspects of literacy. Instruction that is part of a balanced literacy program is designed to incorporate multiple language forms.

Taking different pathways to literacy development. ***Is there a specific order in which children learn literacy skills?*** Reutzel and Cooter (2000) described the basal readers of the late 1970s to the mid-1980s as reflecting the basic skills approach to reading instruction. The assumption was that children learned to read and write by learning through the same sequence of skills.

More current research shows that children do take different pathways in learning how to read and write (Clay, 1998). That is, although certain children learn some skills before other skills, the reverse is true for other children. Much of children's literacy development is based upon family experiences with print prior to entering school. Therefore, there is no single grade curriculum that fits the needs of each child in the classroom. Teachers know that there are no predetermined skills that will match the literacy needs of their children. Therefore, today's teachers carefully design literacy instruction for the specific needs of their young readers and writers. They vigilantly select developmentally appropriate books for guided reading and organize highly specialized instruction around the strengths and weaknesses of the children. They monitor children's progress through ongoing assessment to determine the benchmarks that children have reached. Through ongoing assessment that is aligned with their instruction, teachers know the skills that children have developed and what skills need to be learned.

Grouping children for instruction. From the past, educators have learned about ability grouping and its negative effects on children. Indeed, it is a practice whose "time has passed" (George, 1988). Ability grouping is not the same as grouping for the same-skill instruction or grouping children with similar needs for minilessons. Rather, ability grouping was synonymous with intellectual capacity, so the lower group was considered the slower group. Research showed that with traditional ability groupings, the kinds of instruction across the groups differed significantly (Allington, 1983). For example, children in the higher groups were asked to read more and to write more. The pace of instruction for the low-ability group was slowed and the curriculum differed as well. Typically, children in the low-ability group spent most of their instructional time learning isolated skills rather than reading and writing. According to Allington and Cunningham (1996), this type of instruction had devastating effects on the children who needed a richer type of reading instruction.

How do teachers group children for instruction? Grouping children for literacy instruction is an important aspect of effective teaching. In today's classrooms there are several grouping patterns. Within one early childhood classroom, over the course of 2 hours, children are likely to experience a range of grouping patterns for different kinds of literacy activities and instruction. Grouping for instruction depends on the nature and purpose of the learning experience.

Whole-group instruction occurs with all of the children who have different instructional needs and print experiences. The teacher may be modeling literacy through reading aloud to the class, or she may be at a large chart paper composing the morning message thinking aloud the writing process. **Small-group instruction** may take place with six children who have the same skill needs and are participating in a guided reading lesson. This group of children is at the same stage of literacy with similar types of reading experiences, and they work together with a leveled book appropriate for direct instruction of concepts and skills that are needed by each member of the group. A teacher may also use small-group instruction for children who have the same interests but who are at different literacy levels. Because they share an interest in a topic, they will work together with the teacher on a joint writing project. The teacher may also use **individual instruction** with children who have a specialized need and would benefit from a one-on-one type of instruction with the teacher. In each case, the purpose and nature of the literacy activity or instruction determines the grouping patterns. Children who are grouped for guided reading because they have the same skill needs do not stay in the same group over the course of the school year, because the teacher knows their skills do not develop at the same rate. Grouping is dynamic in that it changes as children's literacy follows highs, lows, and plateaus. Using assessment to determine group membership for instruction is an important skill a teacher needs to develop.

Grouping is an important aspect of effective teaching and a significant factor in creating an effective learning environment. Further, children benefit from working together. It is, therefore, valuable to place children in different patterns of groupings throughout the day.

Changing views on literacy evaluation and assessment. Today's teachers are viewing assessment based on newer definitions of literacy derived from current research and theory. Traditional models of assessment were linked to a more linear view of literacy. With the emphasis on extracting meaning from the printed page, children were first taught to become fluent decoders and then they acquired the skills of vocabulary development and comprehension skills (Chall, 1983). The ways children were assessed in reading and writing reflected this traditional view of literacy.

More recently, **critical literacy** has brought us to define reading and writing in broader terms. Language, in its multiple forms, is used as a tool for thinking, problem solving, and communicating (Heath, 1983). Therefore, literacy is no longer viewed as the handmaiden to an intellectual activity; rather, it is the core of scholarly endeavors. Such definitions of literacy bring teachers beyond instructing students to extract the meaning from text, to making a critical analysis of the text they read and hear. Students who learn to approach literacy from a critical perspective learn to make personal, text, and world connections between what they know and their new text encounters. Comprehension is thus viewed as a constructive process. That is, the readers or the listeners construct meaning based on their analysis of the author's message as well as their own personal experiences. Teachers who assess children's responses to text are sensitive to their different backgrounds that yield multiple meanings. Both the National Council of Teachers of English (NCTE) and the International Reading Association (IRA) use a broader definition of literacy to include "the capacity to accomplish a wide range of reading, writing, speaking and other language tasks associated with everyday life" (NCTE & IRA, 1996, p. 73). Included in their contemporary definition are the multiple tasks related to listening as well as those depicting and viewing illustrations, graphics, and visuals.

Aligned with this thinking, the assessment practices used today should no longer be narrow or linear in their scope. Assessment approaches need to consider cultural and linguistic diversity as differences and not as deficits. The way teachers use assessment results is also an important issue that needs to be considered. Instead of using test results to sort and rank children for their achievements, it would be more productive to use them to inform teaching for student learning.

What assessment practices are used in early childhood settings? Current views on literacy are creating dramatic changes in assessment practices. Today's teachers are aware of the complexity of the literacy process, and they also know that continuous monitoring of children's language and literacy growth may lead to more effective teaching and secure rich opportunities for student progress. One major shift in classroom assessment has included the change from paper-and-pencil tests to teacher observations of children's language and literacy engagements. Additionally, there has been a decreased reliance on the results of standardized tests and a greater use of classroom assessment results to make decisions about instruction.

In primary classrooms where instruction and assessment are aligned, running records and retellings to monitor reading progress are used. Teachers are engaged in "kidwatching" children's language in a variety of contexts and annotating their observations. *Kidwatching* is a term that has been used by Goodman (1985) to describe a systematic use of observation as an alternative to testing.

Increased numbers of teachers are using portfolios with children. Their intent is to represent children's literacy growth in a wider range of language experiences. The literacy portfolio often provides rich descriptions of how a child uses language over the course of a year. It generally contains representative work samples of all language forms and offers a comprehensive description of a child's accomplishments over a specific period.

What is changing, too, is the role that assessment plays in instruction. Teachers who align assessment with their instruction are no longer waiting for the end-of-the-year standardized tests to determine the effectiveness of their approaches on student learning. Rather, they carefully monitor children's language and literacy growth on a daily basis and use the assessment results to adjust their teaching to children's development.

A summary of current views and practices in language and literacy. The current reading and writing practices considered most prevalent are as follows (see Figure 1.1):

1. Children come from homes with varying print experiences that are the beginning or emerging concepts of print.
2. Teachers regard very young children as "readers" and "writers."

NOW AND THEN

A Comparison of Early and Current Literacy Approaches

The Way We Were	The Way We Are
• Oral language was developed at home. The connection between oral language and literacy development or learning was not emphasized.	• Oral language is developed and assessed. Language is seen as the foundation of literacy and learning, and therefore it is a critical part of the curriculum.
• For children to become readers, they had to experience a rite of passage—the readiness program. Prior to formal reading instruction, children were placed in a reading readiness program.	• Very early in their lives, children begin to develop critical concepts of print. While literacy concepts are emerging, children see themselves and are seen by others as readers and writers. They are in the emergent stage of literacy.
• Children were taught reading and writing as a separate activity. After children learned how to read, usually after the first grade, they were taught how to write. For young children in nursery school and kindergarten, composing stories was not encouraged.	• Children are engaged in multiple types of literacy activities from the start. Therefore, reading and writing are taught together because both processes are connected—development in one process supports development in the other. When children show a desire to write stories, they are encouraged to do so; there are no grade-level boundaries.
• Instruction in reading followed a scope and sequence. This meant following a set of skills in a specific order, often designated by a particular grade level. Children's reading achievements were therefore linked to grade levels. Thus, their progress was characterized by a single grade level, which read as "reading at a 2.5 grade level."	• Learning how to read and write are complex processes that do not follow a specific sequence. In their journey to becoming literate, children take different paths. Their growth is described by literacy stages, which are indicated by benchmarks that they reach on their journey. Literacy instruction is determined by the specific needs of the child, not by a grade-level curriculum.
• Grouping children for instruction in traditional classrooms meant grouping by ability where children stayed in one reading group—low, average, or high—for the entire school year.	• In early childhood settings, teachers use multiple grouping patterns, which are determined by the purpose and nature of the literacy instruction. For guided reading, the teacher carefully groups students based on their literacy needs, but these groups are flexible and may change many times over the school year.
• Standardized achievement tests in reading were the traditional tools that teachers and administrators used to track children's literacy growth. These tests were often used to make important instructional decisions about young children.	• Teachers are beginning to develop more systematic approaches to monitor children's literacy progress in an ongoing way. They are aligning instruction and assessment, documenting children's progress and using assessment results to inform their own teaching. Standardized tests are used in grades 3 and 4, and these formal evaluation tools provide *one* source of information about a child's literacy growth.

Figure 1.1
A Comparison of Early and Current Views of Language and Literacy Practices for Young Children

3. Using a child-centered literacy program, the teacher recognizes the children's varying degrees of literacy development in designing a developmentally appropriate curriculum.
4. Oral language is recognized as a significant factor in a child's academic achievement, and it is developed through instruction and assessment.
5. The literacy programs in today's early childhood literacy classrooms use an integrated approach in teaching the language forms.
6. Children are grouped for instruction using different patterns dependent on the purpose and nature of the literacy learning.
7. Teachers do not rely on formal or standardized assessment to guide their instruction, nor do they wait for the end of the year to monitor achievement.
8. Assessment is ongoing, it is aligned with instruction, and it is used to monitor children's literacy growth and to improve teaching and student learning.

Creating a Foundation for the Framework for an Early Childhood Literacy Program

As we move from our discussion on comparing traditional with current models of literacy instruction, we begin to ask questions about the more recent changes in literacy instruction and how they will relate to our beliefs and practices related to teaching young children.

The literacy framework teachers build to guide the instruction and assessment of young children will directly affect their language and literacy growth not only in their early years but in the latter grades as well. How is such a framework for teaching and learning created? The architecture of an effective literacy framework is designed by the blueprints of each teacher's beliefs and understanding of how children learn to read and write. Knowledge of literacy acquisition and child development that influences the type of print environments designed for young children are critical to the framework. Current research related to literacy and how literacy develops in young children provide important supports to the building of a literacy framework, so important that it determines the literate potential of diverse children. Further, knowing how to design learning pitched at the development of the young child contributes a major piece. Finally, the foundation of the framework must include an understanding of oral language in young children and its connection to literacy. Let us begin our framework for literacy instruction and assessment first by defining literacy.

Defining Literacy as a Social Act

As we have discussed, the literacy practices within classrooms change over time. These changes in literacy practices are influenced by the way teachers think about literacy. Bloome (1991) promotes a more current view of literacy, one that paints a broader picture of literacy. He suggests that educators step back from defining literacy through typical reading and writing activities designed for classroom instruction. What is needed is a definition broader in scope—one that places the social aspects of literacy at its very core. Teachers must ask themselves how they actually read, write, speak, listen, view, and depict in their everyday lives. For young children, literacy is defined by the many ways print is used at home. Children see parents writing down telephone messages or "to-do lists." They also hear discussions about the messages and lists of things to do. Children come to know that print is used in a variety of ways and for many purposes. When they were read to and talked to about the story, literacy was being defined through a social context and literacy was given a social meaning.

Cochran-Smith (1984) and others emphasized that defining literacy is accomplished through the social relationships within the classroom between the teacher and students. These relationships define what is to be learned and how it is to be learned. Just as the social contexts occurring at home give rich meaning to print and the ways it is used, literacy develops within the classroom within social contexts as well. The teacher and the children have realistic expectations about the literacy tasks and how they will be accomplished. Because every classroom is different, the definition of literacy is indeed dynamic. Think of the changing dynamics of a group of children, across ages and grades, across literacy development, and in different regions of the country. For each group, literate action is indeed different because the literacy accomplishments are unique to the group.

If we take this social perspective in defining literacy, then all children are members of the group. Knowing their backgrounds will help to understand how they construct and reconstruct literacy as part of their everyday lives. In this sense, defining literacy means going beyond the classroom because children bring their family and community experiences with them to school. It also means going beyond the written text to include all aspects of the communicative process. Thinking and talking about stories are important aspects of literacy. Connecting story events to daily lives is also literate activity. These connections are different for groups and for the members within one group. Therefore, literacy is woven into the social and cultural aspects of children's lives.

Becoming Literate

As we continue to build a framework for literacy instruction for young children, we need to consider the cognitive processes involved in a child's lifelong journey in becoming literate. Two major theorists, Jean Piaget and Lev S. Vygotsky, provide insights in explaining language and literacy development. Although their theories are extensive, with research showing numerous applications, we will limit our discussion to the major themes related to language and literacy development. Because both theorists support the notion of constructivist learning, this view of literacy learning is the beginning and focus of our discussion.

How do young children comprehend stories? According to a **constructivist** view of literacy, young language users actively engage in meaning making. They construct meaning from the text by using all that they know from past experiences about the story that they are reading. In other words, the readers go beyond extracting the author's meaning to construct new meanings. Comprehending a story is not viewed as trying to understand what the author wrote. Rather, comprehension is an active process where children build new meanings. The meanings that they construct are connected to their lives in real ways.

Whereas Piaget referred to the use of schema or conceptual knowledge that the reader draws upon in building meaning around the text, Vygotsky (1986) emphasized the social nature in which new meanings are derived. He explained that young readers develop meanings from text that are culturally established as well as shared. Their meanings arise from discussion of the text, and they are shared with the group.

Stages of Literacy Development

Stages of literacy development refer to sets of behaviors that children acquire in a relatively predictable sequence. A Piagetian view of literacy development emphasizes the role of a child's developmental stage in learning to read and write. According to Piagetian theory, *predetermined stages of literacy behavior* act as a link to the development of novel concepts. As a *developmental constructivist,* Piaget saw development leading learning. This means that a child's literacy growth is determined more by the prior stage of literacy accomplishments than by teacher intervention. Piaget also viewed the role of *activity* as critical to learning. For children to learn, they must be actively engaged in the task. Let's take a look at Jamal's literacy stage of development as he is actively involved in reading his favorite bedtime story.

> *Jamal loves to hear stories, especially when they are read to him. Over and over, he listens to the story* Goodnight Moon. *Then, unsuspectingly Jamal opens the book and begins to read to the delight of his mother. She praises him, and then she asks him to point to the words* Goodnight *and* room. *Jamal points to the picture of the room, insisting that it is the word* room.

Jamal understands that books contain stories that can be read for enjoyment. His concept of word and reading words differs from an adult's concept, and he therefore will engage in unconventional reading that is determined by his stage of literacy development. To point out each word and urge him to read the words rather than the pictures would indeed frustrate Jamal who is not at this point in literacy development.

For Vygotsky, children do pass through stages of language and literacy development. Although each stage is critical in deciding appropriate instruction, a Vygotskian approach to children's development emphasizes **social interaction** and **mediation** as the keys to further development. Unlike Piaget, Vygotsky placed less emphasis on predetermined stages in the development of new literacy concepts and skills and more on mediating learning through social interaction. Like Piaget, Vygotsky viewed the role of activity as central to the child's learning.

Scaffolding Within a Child's Stage of Literacy Development

As young children see print in their environment, listen to stories that are read to them, and watch adults and older siblings write messages, they begin to acquire knowledge about print. Children, like Jamal, are at an early stage of literacy development, and they will acquire new concepts related to literacy through scaffolding.

Think how parents help their young children learn to speak. They simply adjust their own language so their children understand what they are saying. This process is referred to as **scaffolding,** a term used by Bruner (1983) in describing how adults will relinquish to the child more of the responsibility for learning with the child's increasing capabilities. Scaffolding is used by both parents and teachers in storybook-reading activities. A parent may introduce stories by reading the entire book to the child and talking about the pictures and the story. As the child becomes more familiar with the task, the task is shared. Now the parent encourages the child to turn the pages. This type of teaching is often seen in early childhood settings as well. Within the context of shared-book activity, the teacher shares a big book with the children. At first the teacher reads the entire book. In the rereading of the story, the children participate at their level. The teacher considers the children's development and suggests a level of participation, such as reading the refrain that they have heard and can remember. The level of responsibility given to the children will be increased, so that it matches their level of development.

Ideas for Scaffolding Literacy in Young Children

- Listen and observe children to understand what they can do by themselves and when they need assistance.
- Model lessons, such as writing a message, and encourage joint participation in a familiar part of the task.
- During shared-book activity, encourage one child to turn the pages or point to the words while you read the big book.

The Role of Language in Learning

From a Vygotskian perspective, language plays a critical role in learning. Indeed, language is considered a *mental tool* that is used for learning. Further, it is through language or social interaction that the adult *mediates* the child's literacy development. Language is the tool that makes it possible for an individual to internalize a social mechanism, such as storybook activities. Once a child acquires language, he has the capacity to regulate thought and activity. For example, in the case of Jamal, he can listen and talk about the story as well as think about it. This is possible because Jamal has acquired a certain competency with language. Later in this chapter, as you read the discussion on oral language development, you will begin to appreciate the complexity of language and its impact on schooling and living.

Mediating Within the Child's Zone of Proximal Development (ZPD)

Vygotsky emphasized the role of development in children's learning and theorized that children's learning leads their development. In other words, the child's development and the role that the teacher plays are critical to learning. According to Vygotsky (1978), effective instruction occurs within the child's **zone of proximal development (ZPD).** One may think of the ZPD as the distance between the child's actual development and the child's potential development. Actual development determines what a child can accomplish independently, whereas potential development is defined by levels of tasks that the child can perform with the assistance of a teacher or a more competent peer. It is within this potential area of development that children benefit most by instruction and mediation by the teacher. Let us look at Tania, a teacher in the first grade taking a small group of 6-year-olds for reading instruction.

> *Tania selects a book at the children's level that is appropriate to use for guided reading with this group. Before the children in the group read the book, Tania guides them through the book. She conducts a "book introduction." During this phase, the teacher develops the children's sense of story, familiarizing them with the characters, setting, and story events. She assists them in many ways. First, she begins by talking about the meanings*

they will encounter in the story as she and the children page through the story. She deliberately stops at words she anticipates will pose problems to this group and engages them in word-solving activities. Then Tania encourages the children to read the story by themselves. She listens in, providing the necessary assistance to any child who may have a problem.

Tania knew the children's level of development and selected appropriate materials, mediated their story understanding and word-solving strategies before they read, and assisted them while reading. Vygotsky would describe this teaching as assisting children within their zone of proximal development. Tania used social interaction throughout their path of learning. Knowing that the book was within their potential range, she mediated their attempts. When this level of book becomes easy enough for these children to read independently, it will be at their **actual development,** so Tania will select the next level, the level at their **potential development** for guided reading instruction. From a Vygotskian perspective, the children's literacy and the teacher as mediator are critical to learning or the transformation of thought—that is, the development of ideas. Therefore, teaching within the zone of proximal development requires that the teacher offer appropriate support to children. As learning proceeds, the children gain control over aspects of this level of text. The teacher is flexible, responding by adjusting the level of support given to the child, from very explicit help to vague prompts and cues.

Ideas for Teaching Literacy in the ZPD

- Know each child's development through the use of ongoing assessment results.
- Select appropriate developmental texts.
- Design the instruction to meet the child's needs by observing and listening to the child during instruction.
- Provide appropriate feedback to assist the child in knowing what to do.

The Development of Oral Language in Young Children

Only when we begin to teach young children how to read and write, and when we become a kidwatcher—looking closely at their accomplishments in listening and speaking—do we gain an appreciation of the process of language acquisition and language learning. It is true, however, that the role oral language plays in our visual interactive culture is taken for granted and often goes unnoticed. Once in a while we are reminded of its major impact in living a full life:

> Without *language* we would have no speech, history, culture, literature, art or technology, buildings or motor cars, schools or universities, and perhaps not contamination or atomic bombs, and no injustice or cruelty. All these things and more, depend on our capacity for abstract symbolic thought which is interdependent on *language* development. (Borgstein, 2001, p. 1, emphasis added)

If language is so pervasive in our lives, think of how important it is in a child's life. Early childhood teachers simply cannot take language for granted. Genishi emphasized how young children's lives are affected by language in school contexts: "Language gives our thoughts substance, as we talk to ourselves, language helps us plan, understand what happens to us, and form our ideas. Language is part of the individual's uniquely human ways of knowing, feeling, and being. . . . it shapes our identities" (1987, p. 78). In Britton's classic work *Language and Learning,* the author artfully describes "language as a means of organizing a representation of the world" (1993, p. 5), and he advises us that "we cannot afford to underestimate the value of language as a means of organizing and consolidating our accumulated experience, or its value as a means of interacting with people and objects to create experience; nor can we, on the other hand, afford to ignore the limits of its role in the total pattern of human behaviour" (p. 320).

When teachers and caregivers possess this disposition toward language, they will place it at the heart of their curriculum, creating one that is simply language based.

Building the foundation of our literacy framework would not be complete without an understanding of theory and research that is related to language acquisition and learning. Therefore, our discussion will include the following: (a) the characteristics of language, (b) the role of speech in the child's cognitive development, (c) the components of language, (d) the functions of language, (e) the theories on language acquisition, (f) the stages in children's oral language acquisition, (g) second language learning, and (h) adult assistance in children's language development.

The Characteristics of Language

At least once in our lives we have all reflected on the nature of language. Our ruminations have probably led us to a definition of language that includes, at least in part, the following basic features shared by human languages.

Language is social. Through and through, language is social. It is an invention of humans for the purpose of communicating. We learn our language from our experiences (Genishi, 1988). We connect with our friends daily through the use of language. We fulfill our basic needs through requests using our language. We plan our future, sharing our goals with others through the use of language. We describe our experiences through the use of language. It is no wonder then that Vygotsky emphasized the sociality of language: "The word's first function is the social function, and if we want to trace how the word functions in the behavior of the individual we must consider how it functioned formerly in social behavior" (quoted in Dixon-Krauss, 1996, p. 10). The words that we use are tied to our actions as we conduct ourselves with others as members of society. Therefore, when we think of language, we cannot exclude the society or community or person from which it is derived.

Language is dynamic. Language is an invention of humans and used by people within a community. These communities or cultures to which people belong are not static; they are constantly changing. Thus, the languages that are used within these dynamic cultures change as well. Consider the school as a culture and the changes that have taken place in schools over the past quarter century. The approaches that teachers use to instruct children have changed from a basal reader approach to a whole language approach to a balanced literacy program. The language changed to accommodate these changes in instruction. Therefore, language is a dynamic process.

Language is distinctively human. Language is uniquely human invention. This is not to say that other animals, such as cats, birds, dolphins, and chimps, do not have a way of communicating. However, there are deep-seated differences between human language and other forms of communication. Unlike communication systems used by animals, human language is semantic, it is productive, and it has the capacity of displacement (Piper, 1998). This means you can use words to represent objects

Conversations with children play a critical role in language development.

(semanticity); you can use language in a variety of different ways, creating new and different utterances (productive); and finally, you can create a message that is not connected (displaced) to the immediate environment. Can you think of an animal that uses a communication system defined by these elements?

Language is a system of signs. As a system of signs, language allows us to represent objects and actions without having them present. For example, we use the word *orange* to represent the fruit, so the actual object does not have to be present. A sign system enables us to have power over mental behavior. For example, we can use the written form of language as a reminder to do something, to be on time for an appointment, and so on. It is because of this feature that language is a **psychological tool** for learning. We can use language not only to communicate with one another but also to think through problems.

Language is indeed a mental tool that we can use for learning. When a young child has mastered language, then language can be used for symbolic thought. For example, young children progress from holding up their fingers to orally using numbers to tell how old they are. However, children in preschool and kindergarten do not have the same mental concepts of language as adults. They may use the word *small* to represent an object that is small, square, and yellow. To an adult, the word *small* may be used to signify one attribute of an object. As children's thought and language develop, they use it more precisely to represent ideas that have greater complexity.

Goodman argued that "we must see everything in language in relationship to meaning" (1996, p. 12). As a system of signs, language enables us to interact with others, to fulfill our basic needs through making requests.

Language is rule governed. Like other languages, the English language is governed by a system of rules. As children acquire language, they must learn and apply the rules of the language. These rules determine the order in which we place words in a sentence, the meaning created, and the formation of different words. We know children are learning the rules of the language, when someone utters a sentence that breaks the rules. The response invariably is, "It sounds funny!"

Portrait of a Young Child Appropriating Book Language

The first-grade children in Pat's classroom start out the day with a shared-book reading. They are comfortably sitting around the big book *The Bremen-Town Musicians.* As Pat reads the book and points to the illustrations, the children respond with giggles. Then Shayla asks, "How can animals sing?" "Like animals," Darren answers matter-of-factly. Pat turns the page and reads, "the animals peered through the window." Then immediately Shenika stops her to ask, "What does *peered* mean?" Pat points to the picture on the opposite side of the page and asks Shenika, "What are the animals doing?" "Looking through the window, staring at the robbers," answers Shenika. "That's right," Pat responds. "That is what *peer* means; it means to look carefully." When the story is over, Pat gets the children ready for center time. In a playful manner, Shenika goes outside the classroom door and puts her face close to the window waiting for Pat's attention. Pat gestures to her to join the group, and Shenika raises her voice saying, "I'm peering through the window; look at me, I'm peering at you!"

The Role of Speech in Children's Cognitive Development

The evidence is mounting on the connection between oral language and children's learning to read and write. "Oral language is the foundation on which reading is built, and it continues to serve this role as children develop as readers" (Hiebert, Pearson, Taylor, Richardson, & Paris, 1998). The link between the two is explicit, especially when we observe children who are beginning to learn to read. As they decode unknown words and make a mistake (miscue), it is the miscue or error that shows how they use language knowledge in figuring out unknown words. For example, the child may substitute "kitty" for "cat" in the text: *The cat ran out of the room.* The reader's miscue fit into the word order as well as the meaning of the sentence. This demonstrates that as we read, we use our knowledge of language in interacting with the text. Children have a better chance at breaking the code of the printed word when their language is substantial, because they have more resources to draw upon. Decoding is not the only facet of learning how to read; comprehending text is a major aspect in children's literacy development. Their oral language abilities are a determining factor in their understanding of what they read (Snow, Burns, & Griffin, 1998). Therefore, facilitating oral language development will yield benefits in children's literacy growth.

Exposure to print language benefits the child learning oral language skills as well. There are many ways of immersing children in print. One of the oldest teaching strategies shared by parents and teachers is reading aloud to children. When we read stories from literature to children, we are exposing them to the best models of language. Although children may not remember every new word that is introduced, their receptive vocabulary is more advanced than their expressive language. The context of the story and the expression of the reader along with the illustrations will facilitate comprehension of the story as well as individual words. Oftentimes, children are curious about a new word they have not heard, and will ask as in the case of Shenika.

Involving Families: Encourage parents to have children retell the story they read together.

The language philosopher M. M. Bakhtin writes that language is appropriated and not learned from dictionaries, rather from entering into the "stream of human communication" (Holquist, 1990). This theory suggests that language learners are active participants in meaningful dialogue. We learn new words when they are consequential to us, as in the case of Shenika who was curious about the word *peer.* She asked about it, and used it in a playful way; she "tried on her new word" as she acted it out.

The Components of Language

As we communicate with one another, we do not think of the components of language that we use. Indeed, it would be difficult to carry on a conversation and think of different aspects of our language at the same time. The chief components that are present in our spoken language are phonology, semantics, morphology, syntax, and pragmatics. According to Barron (1992), the most noticeable aspect of human language is its sound system, phonology. This is because when we listen to speakers, even though we may not see them, we can determine their gender, age, and, from their dialect, their place of birth. So, let us begin with phonology.

Phonology refers to the speech sounds in our language. Every language has its own set of sounds, and the English language has 35 different sounds. When children are first acquiring language, they must learn the combination of sounds to produce spoken words. They do this through listening to others, being part of a speech community, and by imitating the spoken words to communicate with others. This blending of sounds forms meaningful units called words. There are other features of phonology that affect meanings that children must learn. These are **pitch** or **intonation** (how high a speaker produces a sound), **stress** (how a speaker stresses one syllable over another), and **volume** (how loud or soft a person speaks). You no doubt remember the change in your parents' pitch and volume when you were being corrected for some negative behavior. These tonal qualities added meaning to the message they intended to communicate.

Semantics refers to the meaning of the language. Because the primary role of language is to convey meaning, teachers must be concerned about the development of this aspect of language. When children first begin to use language, the meaning that they attach to words is simple. As their language develops, the number of words that they know increases as well as the meanings for the words.

Morphology is that aspect of language that refers to how words are built from morphemes, the smallest meaningful units of sound. We enjoy observing children's language as they develop this aspect of the language system. For example, as Andrew struggles to put on his sneaker he says, "These foots of mine are too big for these sneakers." Andrew understands that adding an *s* to a noun signifies a slight change of meaning, from singular to plural. He needs to learn that there are exceptions to this rule, and *foot* is an exception. As the smallest unit of sound that carries meaning, sometimes single words are morphemes. The word *sneaker* is a type of footwear. Adding an *s* to *sneaker* would make it mean "more than one sneaker." Both *sneaker* and *s* are morphemes. However, the relationship of *foot* and *feet* is more complex, and learned later in a child's development of language.

Syntax refers to the combination of words into sentences following a set of rules. By the time children enter kindergarten, they have mastery over most syntactic structures. They may not produce the most complex sentences, but they understand them.

Pragmatics is the component of language that refers to the social context in which language is used. It is true that we use language differently depending on the context and the person(s) to whom we are speaking (Bloom & Lahey, 1978). Contrast your language use during a job interview and at a baseball game. Simple encouragements by the teacher of young children will alert them to consider the context in their language use. For example, a small group of children in the play corner become excited and the volume of their voices is raised. The teacher quietly reminds them to use "their inside voice."

The Functions of Language

In addition to looking at the elements of language, we can observe and study why children use language. Halliday (1975) developed a useful classification for language functions (see Table 1.1). He maintained that language has a "range of possible meanings, together with the means whereby these meanings are realized or expressed" (p. 8). In other words, just as we use language to express a variety of meanings, we also use it for multiple reasons. In encouraging language development, we must be aware of the different language functions. If teachers provide children with language experiences that favor the use of certain language functions, then children will become proficient in language use for these reasons. Therefore, language programs must be balanced, providing children with opportunities to use language for different purposes.

Sheila runs to the play corner where Tanya is sitting and tells her how her brother fell off the swing and had to go the doctor. She cries, "Let's play doctor!" Jena is on the playground and asks the teacher to use the bathroom. At the art center Kenjii orders, "Paul and Cedric, put (the) crayons in (the) box and (the) scissors on (the) shelf." This type of "child talk" is a familiar part of early childhood settings. Although the children's speech patterns may appear to be similar, the purposes for which each child used language differed. Their purposes for speaking are known as

Table 1.1
The Purposes for Using Language: Halliday's Functions of Language Use

Language Function	Description	Example
Instrumental	To satisfy basic needs; to get things done; to get what we want	"Another cookie, please?" "Can I go to the bathroom, now?"
Regulatory	To control the behavior of others; to get others to do what we want them to do	"Put your car next to mine." "Jamal is playing with us, right, Jamal."
Interactional	To establish social relationships with others	"Leah is my friend. I saw Leah in the market."
Personal	To express ourselves, often through an opinion or a strong feeling; to show our individuality	"My mommy took me to the market. I help Mommy watch Baby Freddie." "These are my pictures. My pictures are going in my book."
Imaginative	To create our own world; to express fantasies through role playing and dramatic play, poetry, and storytelling	"I am a fish out of my bowl!"
Heuristic	To inquire, to solve a problem, to investigate, to wonder	"Oh, the duck egg cracked! Does it mean it will open now? Let's watch now. Is it coming?"
Informative	To relate information and report facts—the language of school	"This is red, this is yellow." "Two more makes three in all."

the functions of language. Using Halliday's classification of language functions, can you categorize each child's purpose for using language?

Instrumental language is used when children speak to get what they want or to satisfy their needs or desires. Younger children use instrumental language in the form of a request. A teacher's role is to teach children appropriate ways of making requests. As children grow older, the form of instrumental language changes from simple requests to persuasion, negotiation, and argument.

When children use language to control the behavior of others, they use **regulatory language.** In the play corner or on the playground, this type of language is used frequently by children to ensure that the games are played correctly by telling everyone what to do. Forms of regulatory language include speaking to give orders, manipulate others, or control the behavior of another. Parents, caregivers, teachers, and administrators frequently use regulatory language. Indeed, positive use of regulatory language is part of every facet of our culture.

Listen to children as they greet each other in the morning after a break or a long weekend. They reestablish their relationships with their expression of friendships. This is called **interactional language.** Falling into this category of language use are expressions of encouragement or negotiation. An example is when children encourage each other during games or play, or when children negotiate with their friends as they bargain for a toy. The development of interactional language use is critical, because it is the language that promotes and establishes social relationships.

The type of language that has often been neglected, but is sorely needed, is **personal language** (Pinnell, 1985). Personal language is used for social identity—to express one's personal opinions or beliefs. Through its use, children can express

Imaginative language in children develops through participation in play activities.

their individuality. Early childhood teachers encourage personal language when they invite children to make personal connections to literature or tell about experiences related to concepts that are being taught.

Through play, children construct fantasy worlds, and through **imaginative language** they tell about their creative adventures. Imaginative language can be heard when children busy themselves in the play corners, when they begin to write their stories, and when they spontaneously tell or retell stories. It is unfortunate that imaginative language does not persist and develop beyond kindergarten, because unless it is encouraged, it disappears. Its value cannot be overemphasized, for it is the language from which creative writing, fresh new stories, and poems are made.

When children construct their own knowledge through inquiry-based problems or projects, when they inquire about a phenomenon, when they explore or seek a solution to a problem, the language that they use is **heuristic language.** Teachers who actively engage students in their own learning, who set up learning experiences that promote investigation, and who ask open-ended questions promote language that is heuristic in nature.

The final category for classifying language use is **informative language.** Informative language is the language of the classroom, and it is the language that is used more frequently by teachers. Although used primarily to communicate information, this type of language is not restricted to one form, for example, retelling facts. Informative language may be used for higher level forms of communication, such as when teachers request children to evaluate a character's behavior in a story or to compare one version of a Cinderella story with another.

So, what is the point of encouraging children to use a variety of language functions? Why assess the purposes for which children use language? If children use language for only one or two purposes, then those are the only language functions that will be developed. Therefore, it is important for teachers to monitor children's language growth with respect to the type of language that they use. It is equally important to assess children's language environments to determine what functions are encouraged through the selection of literacy activities.

Theories of Language Acquisition and Development

A theory of language acquisition tries to explain how language is learned. A number of theorists have tried to describe how children accomplish such tasks. Briefly, the theories of language acquisition fall into the following major categories: behaviorist, linguistic, cognitive, and social interaction theories. Within each category there are theories with different variations. For our purposes, we will briefly describe the major differences among the four theories.

The major proponent of the **behaviorist theory** was Skinner (1957). Using the principles of classical and operant conditioning, the behaviorists explain how the child learns language. For the behaviorist, language is acquired through conditioning that involves a stimulus, a response, and a reward. The parent or the caregiver models language through talk and through conversation with the child. The child responds by imitating the adult's language and is rewarded with an affectionate answer or reaction such as a smile or a clap. According to the behaviorist model of language learning, the social environment plays the major role in language learning, with stimulus, response, and rewards being critical to learning. However, the theory has left some unanswered questions: Are rewards always necessary for language growth and development? How can we account for the creative speech in young children's language?

One of the most widely known theories of language learning, classified as the **linguistic theory,** is attributed to Chomsky (1965, 1975). Also known as linguistic nativism, this theory explained the development of language through the language acquisition device (LAD) that we possess for the purpose of discovering the rules underlying the structure of the language. Accordingly, the LAD is an innate structure that the linguists use to explain how children learn to construct complex sentences over a very short period. One major criticism of the linguistic theory, although it has a vast number of proponents, is that it does not explain the impact of environment on language learning.

The **cognitive theory** of language acquisition is represented by many theorists, one being Piaget, who held that language development is an aspect of cognitive development but not considered as central to development in general, depending upon the maturation of the child's cognitive system. Further, language learning for a cognitive theorist is stage based—that is, children go through predictable stages of language growth and development. As referred to earlier, Bruner introduced the role of scaffolding a child's language in providing the assistance needed for language growth. To clarify the role of scaffolding in children's language development, Bruner (1978) states: "A study of detailed mother/child interactions . . . shows that successful communication on one level is always the launching platform for attempts at communication on a more adult level. The mother systematically changes her baby talk in order to 'raise the ante' or alter the conditions she imposes on the child's speech in different settings" (p. 251).

The **social interaction theory** views the social environment as playing a critical role in language development, where children are viewed as active participants

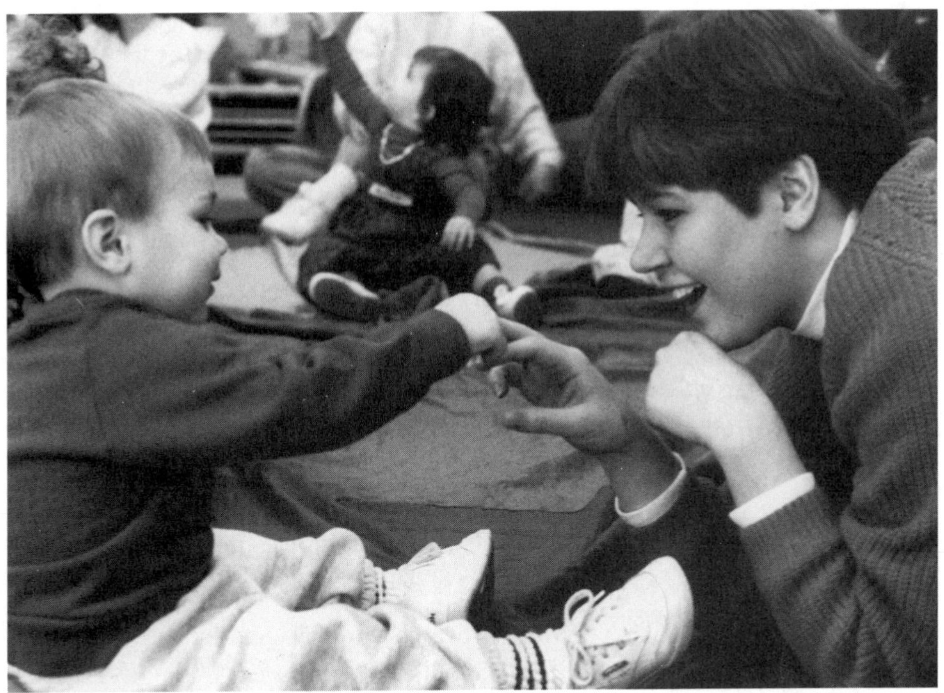

Parents and caregivers scaffold children's language by talking and responding to the child, always considering the child's language development.

in this process. Social interaction theorists view children as having a predisposition to language, but unlike the linguists who emphasize the LAD as the important innate structure that accounts for language learning, they view the use of language in social contexts as critical for its development. Vygotsky (1978) highlights the social origins of language and thought. He valued the role that play assumes in preschool not only on the development of thought but also on the development of language. Vygotsky stated, "In their play children project themselves into the adult activities of their culture and rehearse their future roles and values" (quoted in John-Steiner & Souberman, 1978, p. 129). Their play activity is accompanied by language that is consistent with the role they assume. Therefore, children's use of language is developed through play because, "in play a child is always above his average age, above himself" (Vygotsky, 1978, p. 98). In other words, the context of play provides children an opportunity to "try on" their language that is slightly beyond their language development.

Stages in Children's Oral Language Acquisition

Educators know from research that the first years of a child's life are the time of considerable growth for language development. Language growth just doesn't happen. It is critical for early childhood teachers to know the important stages of language development in children so that they will be able to scaffold their growth in language.

Children advance through predictable stages of language acquisition when parents and caregivers provide the necessary scaffolds for the language learning.

When does language begin to develop, and what can we expect from children as they are learning to speak? What are the first signs of language acquisition? While we listen to an infant crying, we may feel that this type of sound behavior is merely showing a sense of displeasure. Yet the first cry that a child makes is part of language development, for crying is a form of communication, with different types of crying communicating different needs. This type of communication that infants use to communicate is prelinguistic. The crying that infants make differs; we know from experience that some children may cry less and others more frequently, depending on many factors. The new area of brain research is revealing a depth of understanding related to language development in infants. "Infants under six months respond with equal interest to the sounds of all languages, but they soon develop perceptual maps that directs them toward the sound of the language they hear most frequently and away from the sounds of other languages" (Newberger, 1997, p. 6). These studies have clear implications of infants' development of the sound structure of their language.

Children 4 to 5 months old create many different types of sounds. These sounds are often accompanied by gestures that are part of their language growth and provide a way for them to communicate. For approximately the first year babies pass through the stages of crying, to babbling, to making sounds that are developed from combinations of consonants and vowels. Between the ages of 1 and 2, babies begin to use linguistic forms of communication. During this period, children develop a very small vocabulary bank of approximately three to four words but attach complex meanings to these words. Between the first and second year there is rapid vocabulary growth of up to 300 words. After another considerable growth period they begin to communicate in sentences that gradually grow in complexity. By the time the child enters the first grade at age 6 or 7, the simple sentence has grown in length and complexity, and includes adjectives and conditional clauses.

Using Technology: Share with parents Web sites that provide information on children's development. One such Web site is http://www.enfagrow.com/language008.htm.

The Enfamil site is for parents and offers topics on child development related to social, emotional, language, cognitive, and physical development as well as good nutrition.

The following paragraphs describe in more detail the periods in oral language development from birth through age 7.

The first period: Infancy through eleven months. During this period, children's language develops through crying, gestures accompanied by vocalizations, gurgling, babbling, and cooing. Their smiles are a form of communication. From 3 to 6 months, babbling is pervasive, including *ma, ma, da, da, nee, nee.* From 6 to 11 months, the child's language includes more sounds and the imitation of sounds.

The second period: First to second year. The child's language during the first and second years includes words. Within the first year, the child will say one word that communicates complex meanings, a speech behavior known as a **holophase.** Children begin the second period speaking three to six words that gradually develops into 50 or more words. Within the second year, the child's vocabulary continues to grow to about 100 words. At the same time, children within this period listen to and understand spoken messages, respond to a simple request, name pictures with words, engage in a conversation, begin to sustain a topic, and develop the use of intonation in communicating.

The third period: Third to fourth year. During their third year, children are speaking in words and experiencing rapid vocabulary growth—up to 300 words. They can be understood more easily. They respond to more complex requests, that include two or three directions. In their fourth year, they pronounce words more clearly and they speak in simple sentences. Their vocabulary growth is now up to 1,500 words. They engage in conversation and try to be understood. By age 4, a child can resolve conflict through dialogue.

The fourth period: Fifth to seventh year. During their fifth year, children's vocabularies have increased to 2,000 words and demonstrate an understanding of many more words. By age 5, they use complex sentences including pronouns and the past tense of verbs. By ages 6 and 7, children's sentence structures become increasingly more complex, and the length of their sentences increases to approximately eight words. Although there is general disagreement regarding vocabulary growth, children at the age of 6 know a minimum of 3,000—5,000 words with many estimates even higher. Children engaged in conversation within this period of language development can sustain a topic for increasingly longer periods.

There is value in following milestones in a child's development, and language is no different. However, whereas children follow predictable language growth periods, they should not be held to a rigid timetable. These periods of language growth should be used only as guidelines to provide parents, caregivers, and teachers with proposed expectations. "The way children learn language and the speed of that learning reflect an intertwining of biological givens, social dimensions, personality and belief structures, and perhaps intelligence" (Baron, 1992, p. 64). As with all benchmarks, teachers use language growth stages to help identify children with special needs while monitoring their growth.

Second Language Learning

One of the most dramatic changes within U.S. schools has been in the student population. Over the past two decades, there has been a significant increase in school enrollment of African American, Hispanic, and Asian students, many of whom are second language learners. In the largest cities, minority students have indeed become the majority: "In 1997, 44% of students statewide were minorities. . . . In New York City 84% of students . . . were minorities" (University of the State of NY, 1998, p. 11). Therefore, it is not unusual for teachers of young children to have many second language learners in their classrooms.

Many challenges face children who are learning to speak a second language. First, they are expected to reach the same academic standards in the same time frame as for children who are native English speakers. For a second language learner this is a major ordeal. Although the challenge to all teachers is to provide effective language and literacy development to all children, assisting second language learners to develop oral language and literacy skills in all areas of the curriculum demands consistent effort. Garcia (1997) described the teacher as a "key player" in creating effective linguistic environments for second language learners in early childhood classrooms. Knowledge of language and literacy development in second language learners may facilitate teachers in designing effective literacy programs that are pitched at the children's development.

Growth periods for second language learners. It is true that children in early childhood settings and classrooms may be at different stages of English fluency. As children develop proficiencies in their new language, literacy develops as well (Hurley & Tinajero, 2001). For second language learners there are predictable growth periods, just as there are for young children acquiring their first language. According to Tinajero and Schifini (1993), by knowing children's language competencies, teachers will be able to adjust their instruction to meet their literacy needs. Children who are learning a second language pass through fairly predictable language growth periods. In the first stage, the **preproduction period,** the child uses gestures and drawings to communicate. Simple sentences and the use of a few words and phrases mark the early production phase. As the children enter the stage of **speech emergence,** they begin to understand simple text accompanied by illustrations and comprehend spoken language that is meaningful to them. In the **intermediate growth period,** children use language with increased levels of accuracy and begin to express their thoughts. Children at the **advanced fluency growth period** use language with ease and produce a variety of complex sentences. It is in the advanced fluency growth period that children who are second language learners are on par with native English speakers.

As educators learn more about language acquisition and growth in young children and as they observe their language, they develop a set of expectations for children's language use. They will also learn more effective ways to assist children in their lifelong journey of language and literacy development.

Meeting Diverse Needs: The key to teaching second language learners is making language interesting and relevant. The uses of language in the classroom must be comprehensible and slightly beyond the student's present level of competence (Krashen, 1988).

As teachers assess children's language development, they need to know about cultural differences that may affect the way children communicate, both verbally and nonverbally. For example, Americans talk frequently and loudly. Children in many American homes are expected to express their attitudes and opinions freely, whereas children from other cultures may not participate in a conversation with such freedom; instead, they defer to authority. Eye contact is considered a sign of honesty and forthrightness to Americans, whereas to Latinos/Latinas it is considered disrespectful for a child to maintain eye contact while speaking to his teacher. Many of these factors need to be considered in assessing a child's language development. Without knowledge of these differences, teachers may incorrectly assess a child's language growth.

Assisting Language Growth in All Children

All children need to develop oral language competencies, and this is especially true for children with language learning disabilities. Research shows that children who are lagging behind their peers in oral language competencies develop serious reading and writing problems and are at risk in other academic areas. Their social behaviors and interactions often parallel their school achievements (Howard, Shaughnessy, Sanger, & Hux, 1998). Teachers need to pay attention to the developmental needs of children's language and may offer assistance to all children. Consider how teachers may use the following forms of scaffolding for language development in all young children:

Listen when a child talks to you. Be a good listener! Listen to each child, and do not interrupt the child. Part of language learning is listening; we come to know a great deal of the child's language growth through listening.

Model good language use. Demonstrations and modeling are powerful teaching strategies. Be conscious of the components of language you use so that they are developmentally appropriate for the children to whom you are speaking. Articulate so that children may be conscious of the correct sounds and pronunciations of the language. Expand the children's language by using new words and then explaining their meanings. To achieve vocabulary development, read children's literature and stop to clarify the meaning of new words. Demonstrate appropriate conversational style, emphasizing interactive rather than directive conversation. In conversing with children, your polite language, your noninterruptive behaviors, and your direct eye contact with the speaker during the conversation will be learned by the children in your care.

Promote vocabulary through "text talk." It is true that children come to school knowing so many words! At the age of 4 children's vocabulary is estimated to be about 3,000 words and reaches 6,000 by age 6 (Norton, 1993). Even though children experience rapid growth in vocabulary in their early years, they do not experience similar language development in their school years. One beneficial approach to systematically increasing word knowledge is "text talk." Beck and McKeown (2001) suggest using challenging books that are read aloud and discussed with children. Cochran-Smith (1984) emphasized that the key to learning oral language through read-alouds is not in only listening but also in talking about the ideas. The role of talk that focuses on books is critical in the process of becoming literate.

Design a rich language environment. Language activities that actively involve children in talk develop their language. To encourage children's wide use of language, create opportunities where they are required to use language for a variety of functions.

Scaffold children's attempts at language. Listen carefully to children when they are speaking, so that you can provide the appropriate assistance that they may need to continue. When you do not understand a child, ask for clarification and then offer the necessary help. As Wells (1986) suggests, adults need to "modify their speech when talking to young children in a number of ways: keeping their utterances short and grammatically simple, using exaggerated intonation to hold the child's attention and to emphasize key words, limiting the topics talked about to what is familiar to the child, and frequently repeating and paraphrasing what they say" (p. 45).

Engage in a one-to-one conversation. Engage *often* in conversation with children. When children come to you eager to tell you something that happened to them at home or on the way to school, take advantage of their enthusiasm to create a **dialogic moment.** Listen to them, and encourage their attempts to retell a story or express a feeling. Try to use time for one-to-one conversations with children on topics that are of specific interest to them.

Children's language acquisition and development are critical to literacy learning as well as learning in all content areas. Teachers of young children can no longer view language as developed because upon entrance to school, most children can speak and understand directions. Rather than taking a passive approach to language development, effective teachers promote literate thinking through active language response guided by the child's language development.

Discussion Questions and Activities

1. Observe a preschool center and a second-grade classroom. Describe the literacy practices in both contexts and note their similarities and differences.
2. Describe the basic theories of language acquisition. For each theory, choose a language activity that supports that theory.
3. Work together in groups to list your experiences with language use during the past week. For each language context, determine its purpose. Then, using Halliday's system of classifying language functions, categorize each language use. Which function of language did you use most?
4. Become a kidwatcher in an early childhood setting. At the play corner, listen to children use language for 5 minutes and decide on the function of the children's language use. Continue to observe and classify children's language functions in different settings.
5. Listen to a 3-year-old speak and a 5-year-old in conversation with others. Describe what they know about language use and compare their language skills.
6. Choose a piece of children's literature that is appropriate for reading to a group of young children. Select three words from the book that may extend beyond the children's range of understanding and use. Tell how you would explain the words as you read aloud to the group.
7. Select a group of children in preschool, kindergarten, or the primary grades. Tell three different ways you would promote language growth for their approximate level of development.

Additional Web Sites

Child Development Institute
http://www.childdevelopmentinfo.com/development/language_development.shtml
This site provides information on the stages of language development.

ERIC Clearinghouse on Languages and Linguistics Digest
http://www.cal.org/ericcll/digest/ncrcds.04html
This site offers resources on fostering second language development in young children.

ERIC.EECE Clearinghouse on Elementary and Early Childhood Education
http://www.ericeece.org
The site provides information and resources related to elementary and early childhood development.

National Clearinghouse for Bilingual Education
http://www.ncela.gwu.edu/ncbepubs/pigs/pig22.htm
The site contains an article on assessing language development in bilingual preschool children.

Additional Readings

Bowman, B. T., Donavan, M. S., & Bums, M. S. (Eds.). (2001). *Eager to learn: Educating our preschoolers.* Washington, DC: National Academy Press.

Hadaway, N. L., Vardell, S. M., & Young, T. (2001). Scaffolding oral language development through poetry for students learning English. *The Reading Teacher, 54*(8), 796–809.

Klein, H. A. (2001). The world of words. *Childhood Education, 77*(4), 234.

Perez, B. (2002). *Learning in two worlds: An integrated Spanish/English biliteracy approach* (3rd ed.). Boston: Allyn & Bacon.

Roskos, K., & Christie, J. (Eds.). (2000). *Play and literacy in early childhood: Research from multiple perspectives.* Mahwah, NJ: Erlbaum.

Additional Children's Literature

Adler, D. A. (1992). *A picture book of Florence Nightingale.* New York: Holiday House.

Freeman, D. (1978). *A pocket for Corduroy.* New York: Puffin.

Garza, C. L. (1990). *Family pictures: Cuadros de familia.* San Francisco: Children's Book Press.

Kasza, K. (1987). *The wolf's chicken stew.* New York: Putnam & Grosset.

Pinkney, A. D. (1994). *Dear Benjamin Banneker.* San Diego, CA: Harcourt Brace.

Steig, W. (1986). *Brave Irene.* New York: Farrar, Strauss & Giroux.

Children's Literature References

Brett, J. (1989). *The mitten.* New York: Scholastic.

Brown, M. W. (1947). *Goodnight moon.* New York: Harper & Row.

Carle, E. (1994). *The very hungry caterpillar.* New York: Philomel.

Grimm, Brothers. (1980). *The Bremen-Town musicians.* New York: Doubleday.

CHAPTER 2

The Beginnings of Young Children's Literacy Development

The Framework for a Well-Balanced Literacy Program

Portrait of a Young Child Developing Literacy Concepts

"Charlie," calls his mother. "Charlie, it is time for bed!" Charlie peeks out from behind the chair where he is hiding. "Me go, me go." Charlie makes his way toward his mother, then runs back to the small table and reaches for two books. As his mother picks him up and takes him to the bedroom, Charlie is holding his two books and looking at their covers. Suddenly, he lets out a cry, "This one, this one!" His mother understands that Charlie has selected his favorite again for tonight, Goodnight Moon. *After Charlie is put in bed, their story routine begins. "So, Charlie, what book is it tonight?" Charlie holds up his favorite, and his mother takes it from him. She reads the cover, and they look at the picture together. Page after page, they read together. At times, Charlie takes the page to turn it. After the story is over, Charlie responds, "Good night, bear! Good night, truck! Good night, Mom!" As Charlie's mother kisses him good night, he continues to chant his "Good nights."*

As you read Chapter 2, reflect on the following topics:

- The variety of concepts of print that children learn at home before they enter school
- How literacy is acquired through social interactions with others
- The meaning of developmentally appropriate practices and how they affect what children learn
- The stages of literacy development
- Why a balanced literacy program that is comprehensive in nature is critical to further children's literacy development

Literacy Development Begins at Home

Although research has shown that children enter the classroom with rich and varied language and literacy experiences (Strickland & Morrow, 1989), it is clear that learning language and becoming literate do not begin and end in the classroom. As with Charlie, in many cases, literacy begins at home with family routines such as storytime. Case histories of early readers provide documentation that young children have learned to read before they go to school (Clark, 1976; Doake, 1986; Durkin, 1966). If there is one study that clearly speaks to literacy as an early developmental process, it is Doake's (1981) observational case study of one child, Raja. For 1 year, Doake observed Raja as an infant whose parents read to him daily. During the first weeks, the infant was a passive listener who occasionally glanced at the book during the readings. After the first 2 months, he was more active and showed a developing interest through his visual inspection of the book that became careful and more comprehensive. His listening attention developed over time, as did his interest in stories. By 5 months, Raja's attention span for familiar stories grew to 40 minutes and by 9 months to 75 minutes. The message is clear: Literacy develops over time, and the child's disposition to become a reader and writer may begin long before a child comes to school. *Becoming literate is a developmental process*—that is, children develop literacy concepts gradually and through authentic experiences such as those that occur at home. However, literacy development does not occur solely by maturation or development. Rather, children become literate within the context of a literate society as they are supported by parents, caregivers, and siblings engaged in literacy events. The focus of this chapter is on how young children develop print concepts long before they come to school, and how they continue in their development during their first years in school.

Literacy as a Social Act

As discussed in Chapter 1, becoming literate is a social act. The everyday occurrences within the family involve literacy, and children play a major role in these acts. The contexts in which literacy is acquired are social; that is, the roots of literacy are anchored within the social network of the family. What this means is that literacy is attached to the everyday tasks of life, and children who are integral members of the family grow in their understanding of literacy as they use all forms of language in meaningful ways. For example, the child who watches her father make out a grocery list for his weekly trip to the market insists on knowing what her father is writing. The young child learns that you can write down things to be remembered later, an important function of print. In the market, the child and her father use the grocery list to buy those items written down, and as they move through the aisles, they search the shelves reading the grocery items to find what is on the list. Within this social context, the child is developing fundamental literacy concepts through an authentic literacy act.

Another example of literacy learning occurs during family dinnertime. The child listens and is a part of the stories that are being exchanged. The young child has a story to tell and each family member eagerly awaits, carefully listens, asks questions, and offers responses. The child tells the story and responds to the questions. From this authentic literacy act, the child's story sense is emerging and developing, as she also learns about questions and responses within the context of storytelling.

Meek (1992) indicates that children learn to read when they are encouraged to act like readers and praised for their efforts because "learning to read in the early stages, like everything else a child has come to know, is an approximation of adult behavior with a genuine, meaningful function" (p. 24). Therefore, when children turn the pages of the book and when they tell the story as if they are reading, we can think of such approximations as children taking their first steps toward reading.

Holdaway (1979) terms this reading-like behavior as *reading-like play.* He further elaborates on the child's emerging literacy concept as "almost unintelligible at first, this reading-like play rapidly becomes picture-stimulated, page-matched, and story-complete" (p. 40) as children develop another fundamental literacy concept. This type of literacy growth can be accomplished in a child's early years by parents encouraging reading-like behaviors as well as creating print-rich experiences that are accompanied by the guidance of the adult who interprets the meaning that the print represents.

A number of studies show that children come to school knowing many concepts about print. Through a variety of informal literacy experiences at home, young children bring to preschool and school a wide background with varying degrees of concepts and skills related to reading and writing (Bissex, 1980; Doake, 1981). Only a few children who enter kindergarten may know how to read, but this does not mean that those who cannot decode print have failed to acquire important fundamental concepts of print.

Parents, older siblings, and caregivers enthusiastically share the world of print communication with young children. Indeed, we live in a society that is dependent upon access to information in its many varied forms, much of which contains the written word. Because children are a significant part of the family, they are immersed in multiple forms of information and their delivery systems eagerly shared by parents and siblings. Being a part of the print world, children begin to acquire the fundamental concepts of literacy or concepts about print before they come to school. Research confirms the kinds of print concepts that many children have learned in the context of family and home life.

Children are well on the way in the development of cognitive and linguistic concepts and skills (Sticht & McDonald, 1989) at a young age. Through rich family interactions with language and print, they are developing concepts of print, and the same is true for children from diverse cultures (Taylor & Dorsey-Gaines, 1988). For second language learners, literacy concepts develop within family routines as well.

The benefits of parents reading to their children are innumerable. Among the rewards are developing children's language and their interests in reading.

Hartle-Schutte (1993) studied Navajo children to find that "children who grow up in literate environments, where reading and writing are used for functional purposes, will grow up literate" (p. 652). Many children experience story routines at bedtime, like Charlie. There are many other varied literacy practices that occur throughout the day involving children as observers or participants. Before children learn to talk, they see adults read books, newspapers, and magazines, they observe them as they write down messages or use grocery lists as reminders during their weekly trips to the market. They watch their older brothers and sisters read and do homework and search the Internet for questions to homework answers. At the age of 3, Jill watched her 10-year-old brother Sean as he chatted online with his friends. "I talk with Niles; I talk now," Jill declared. She knew that Sean was talking to his friends with words typed on the computer. Through this experience, Jill was developing the functions of written language before she entered kindergarten. This very example also highlights the social nature of learning and language development, for it was through Jill's interactions with her brother Sean, within their social contexts, that Jill is becoming literate.

Literacy Concepts Developed at Home

Before Jill goes to sleep each evening, she and her mother share a routine that is very special. Jill selects a book from the shelf for them to read. They snuggle together reading the book and talking about the characters and events. Sometimes Jill reads; that is, she pretends to read as she turns each page. Even though an onlooker may declare that Jill has not learned to read, she does possess reading-like behaviors, and indeed, she is developing concepts of print (Clay, 1991) that are fundamental in learning how to read. Below are some of the important print concepts that Jill, and others like her, have acquired within the context of the family before entering school.

- **Book-handling skills and book concepts:** There is a certain way that a skilled reader picks up a book, holding the book right-side-up, opening it to begin to read, and turning the pages. Skilled readers also know about specific books. Jill observed as her parents read to her each night. Through these nightly story routines with her family, Jill gradually acquired book-handling skills necessary for reading (Snow & Ninio, 1986). Jill learned concepts about
  - The front of the book
  - The back of the book
  - The book has an author and an illustrator
  - Where the story begins and ends
  - Directionality of print, from left to right
  - The boundaries or spaces between words
  - The first word on the page
  - The last word on the page

  The stories that were read to Jill and that she retold led her to develop a concept that stories that can be shared.

Involving Families: Children have learned about books from book routines their parents established with them at an early age. Those children who participated in daily routines benefited more. For the classroom, establish literacy routines that become a part of classroom life. Set aside a time daily for storytelling, read-alouds, and independent reading. Keep the routines alive by introducing creative contexts. For example, one day you may wish to retell a story with puppets or through the use of a flannel board.

- **Book-sharing routines:** Book-sharing routines are established when parents read to and with their children. Such routines begin very simply, by parents reading to children and talking about the book, asking questions, and encouraging participation. Slowly, as children acquire the routine and as they begin to understand their roles within the routine, they increase their participation in the book-sharing activity (Taylor & Dorsey-Gaines, 1988).
- **Story concepts:** Story concepts or **story schema,** an understanding of the parts of a story and how stories proceed, develop over time. Story understanding emerges as a concept when children hear others tell or read stories to them. Gradually, they learn that stories have a setting that includes characters, a time, and place. They learn to expect a set of story events as an important part of the story that leads to the solution of the problem. Although children cannot articulate the parts of the story, they begin to develop the abstract idea of the parts of a story when parents and caregivers read books that contain well-developed stories. By the time children enter kindergarten, at approximately 5 years of age, they know that a story has a beginning, middle, and an ending. Even though their retellings of stories are short, they mention each of the major parts without details.
- **Signs and symbols contained in books:** In Chapter 1, we characterized language as a system of signs. Words are signs that represent objects or actions that

do not have to be present when speaking about them. This becomes another fundamental understanding that children acquire about books, that is, children learn that books contain illustrations and stories that *represent* objects, people, and actions (Snow & Ninio, 1986).

- **Pleasure derived from reading books:** When adults read to children and convey pleasure during their book-sharing routine, children attach positive emotions to the act of reading (Doake, 1986). Why do some children come to school with a disposition that endears them to storytime? Some love reading and writing, whereas other children have not developed an interest for literacy activities. Katz (1995) has emphasized that developing effective dispositions toward reading and writing are critical in creating lifelong learners.
- **Conventions of writing:** Jill begins to write because she has observed family members engaging in writing activities. She knows that the squiggly lines on the paper stand for words that convey meaning. She also understands that long words are represented by many letters or lines and short words are conveyed with fewer letters. Gradually, children pass from the scribbling stage when they begin to acquire **alphabet knowledge,** that is, they learn letter names and how to form the letters.

Reaching Milestones by Young Readers and Writers

Developmentally Appropriate Practices

In designing an early childhood literacy program, as in all learning for young children, teachers need to be concerned about **developmentally appropriate practices.** A developmental approach to instruction and assessment is informed by "what we know of the learner's developmental status and our understanding of the relationship between early experience and subsequent development" (Katz, 1995, p. 109). In other words, teachers' instruction and assessment for children need to be guided by where the child's development is and how it relates to the child's next stage of development. Bredekamp and Copple (1997, pp. 8–9) suggest that in making important instructional decisions that are developmentally appropriate, teachers need to consider three dimensions of knowledge:

- Knowledge of children's development and the nature of the learning processes that guide which activities and interactions will foster safe, healthy, interesting, achievable, and challenging learning environments
- Knowledge of children's individual characteristics including their personal interests, experiences, and their strengths
- Knowledge of the children's social and cultural backgrounds that will lead to responsive and adaptive instruction and assessment

The National Association for the Education of Young Children (NAEYC) has broadened its former position to include creating learning environments for the education of *all* young children. The NAEYC's current position addresses the complexity of teaching in diverse classrooms and mandates the need for responsive instruction and assessment. Although the following principles may not be exhaustive, they provide a way of thinking about instruction for the young—in other words, they offer a blueprint for developmentally appropriate practice (Bredekamp & Copple, 1997, p. 23):

- Children construct their own understanding of concepts *and* they benefit from instruction by more competent peers and adults.
- Children benefit from opportunities to see connections across disciplines through integration of curriculum *and* from opportunities to engage in in-depth study within a content area.
- Children benefit from predictable structure and orderly routine in the learning environment *and* from the teacher's flexibility and spontaneity in responding to their emerging ideas, needs, and interests.
- Children benefit from opportunities to make meaningful choices about what they will do and learn *and* from having a clear understanding of the boundaries within which choices are permissible.
- Children benefit from situations that challenge them to work at the edge of their developing capacities *and* from ample opportunities to practice newly acquired skills and to acquire the disposition to persist.
- Children benefit from the opportunity to collaborate with their peers and acquire a sense of being part of a community *and* from being treated as individuals with their own strengths, interests, and needs.
- Children need to develop a positive sense of their own self-identity *and* respect for other people whose perspectives and experiences may be different from their own.
- Children have enormous capacities to learn and almost boundless curiosity about the world, *and* they have recognized, age-related limits on their cognitive and linguistic capacities.
- Children benefit from engaging in self-initiated, spontaneous play *and* from teacher-planned and teacher-structured activities, projects, and experiences.

The position on using developmentally appropriate approaches in teaching young children is supported by researchers and educators in the field of early childhood.

Teachers of young children who are guided by the position statements related to developmentally appropriate practice are cautious of the differences in the literacy development within children who may be at the same age level or grade level. That is, children within the same grade or at the same age level do experience differences in literacy development. Educators' understanding of the effects of developmental differences on learning has led them to replace the traditional grade-level curriculum with a child-centered one. Such a curriculum is developmentally appropriate because it ensures that instruction for each child and the materials selected for instruction in reading will be aligned to the child's level of literacy development. In keeping literacy instruction aligned with developmentally appropriate practice, Bredekamp and Copple (1997) suggest three dimensions of knowledge need to be considered. Therefore, the teacher poses these related questions: What literacy concept or skill has the child developed at the level of independent performance? What concepts and skills are emerging and need specific kinds of instruction to bring them to development? What kinds of practice would strengthen and reinforce the concepts, strategies, and skills that have been taught to the child? What materials for reading and writing would be interesting and stimulating? What kind of instruction will be responsive to the child's cultural background or special needs? In using these questions to guide and plan instruction, the teacher also needs to know the developmental milestones or stages of literacy development as discussed in Chapter 1. These are the predictable stages reached by most children. The stages are marked by **benchmarks** or **performance indicators,** which can be used to determine the child's stage of literacy.

Establishing Literacy Benchmarks

Children's growth in reading and writing may be tracked through developmental stages. It is important to understand that learning or development in children is not always clearly defined, and therefore, teachers should not place children in stages or categories of development. More specifically, a child's development in one skill may place her in one stage, and her development on another skill may mark her at a different stage. The stages of literacy development are meant as a guide to track children's literacy development through the performance indicators or benchmarks. Within each stage are benchmarks that children need to reach; these are the performances that define literacy development. Teachers need to be aware of and accountable for the performance outcomes that children need to develop.

Three Stages of Development: Emergent, Early, and Fluent

The emergent stage. When children set out on their literacy pathway, reading and writing concepts are beginning to emerge or become apparent. The first stage is called the **emergent stage** because many of the skills are just starting to develop. Children begin to develop concepts related to books such as page turning and holding the book right-side-up. We read about Charlie, who knows that books contain stories and that certain books are favorite ones to be read over and over. Many 5-year-olds at this stage can recognize a word or two on the page, know where to begin and end a story, can find the title of the book on its cover, and understand many more concepts related to books.

The early stage. As children move into the **early stage** of literacy development, they show a greater sense of story than they demonstrated in the previous stage. Indeed, they can retell a story adding more details. They can recognize more words on a page, they can write words, their written stories are much longer, and they know the letters of the alphabet as well as most of their sounds. However, the hallmark of the early stage is the acquisition of the **alphabetic principle.** Children demonstrate that they understand the relationship between letters and sounds by their achievement of decoding unknown words. By the end of first grade, most children have reached the early stage.

The fluent stage. At the **fluent stage** of literacy development, children are on the road to independent reading and writing. Teachers observe children reading for longer periods. Children read larger books, they use a wide variety of strategies for understanding text, they develop interests in genres and for reading books by certain authors, and they are writing longer stories as well as informational text. The mission of schools is that all children will be at the fluent stage by the end of the third grade.

Monitoring Children's Literacy Development Through Benchmarks

One way to monitor children's performances in reading and writing development is to think about major areas of literacy achievement and their related benchmarks. Therefore, we have separated the benchmarks for literacy development into the following three major categories: **book sense, story sense,** and **literacy behaviors.** Attached to each of the literacy categories are performance behaviors. The outcomes of children's learning are further classified at the three stages as benchmarks for literacy development. In Figure 2.1, the performance outcomes at three stages of literacy growth are organized into three major areas of reading and writing development.

BENCHMARKS FOR LITERACY DEVELOPMENT IN YOUNG CHILDREN
BOOK SENSE

Emergent Literacy Stage	Early Literacy Stage	Fluent Literacy Stage
• Demonstrates that books contain stories	• Knows the book parts and can talk about them	• Requests a wider variety of authors, genres, and chapter books • Uses different parts of the book (e.g., table of contents and index) to find information
• Finds the front and back of the book and places the book in the correct position for reading	• Distinguishes between the authors and illustrators and comments on their contributions	• Makes own books that are longer with more complex parts • Identifies unique styles of authors and illustrators
• Points to the title and the author of the book	• Uses the table of contents when directed to do so	• Integrates authors' and illustrators' styles into own books
• Knows where the story begins • Knows the direction of print • Points to a word, an illustration, the end and beginning of a sentence, and the period at the end of a sentence	• Finds the index of the book	• Possesses a disposition of respect for books

Figure 2.1
Benchmarks at the Emergent, Early, and Fluent Stages of Literacy Development

BENCHMARKS FOR LITERACY DEVELOPMENT IN YOUNG CHILDREN
STORY SENSE

Emergent Literacy Stage	Early Literacy Stage	Fluent Literacy Stage
• Listens to a story for an extended period	• Engages in independent reading for a longer period	• Chooses to engage in independent reading for longer periods
• Responds to a story by telling how it made him or her feel	• Asks for specific books to be read aloud or to be shared	• Selects and reads a variety of genres • Writes a wide variety of genres
• Retells and writes a story to include the beginning, middle, and end	• Retells a story that includes the (a) setting, (b) theme, (c) story problem, (d) most story events, and (e) resolution	• Maps the sequence of story to show the relationships among the story elements
• Talks about the characters in the story	• Responds to stories read and heard and makes connections to personal experiences	• Discusses the different parts of the story
• Requests a favorite book to be read	• Appropriates and uses the "book language" in story discussions	• Begins to make connections between books from the same genres by
• Repeats the story refrain during a shared reading	• Writes more complete stories and reads them back	• Comparing and contrasting stories
• Recognizes a familiar story that was read	• Composes written stories using familiar stories as models	• Comparing stories for style

• Responds to stories with personal experiences	• Writes nonfiction books	• Comparing informational books for content
		  • Critiquing stories for personal response
		  • Understanding stories that may not relate to personal experiences
		  • Connecting different texts
		  • Connecting story events with world events
		  • Comparing stories for content and style
		• Demonstrates within narrative and expository writing different connections: personal, text, and world

Figure 2.1
Continued

BENCHMARKS FOR LITERACY DEVELOPMENT IN YOUNG CHILDREN
LITERACY BEHAVIORS

Emergent Literacy Stage	Early Literacy Stage	Fluent Literacy Stage
• Sees self as reader and writer	• Participates during guided book introductions and begins to initiate questions and responses to story	• Demonstrates an increased desire to read and write independently
		• Uses revising strategies
• Recognizes a small number of high-frequency words	• Participates in book discussions	• Selects appropriate books for reading independently
• Participates during the book introduction or picture walk	• Reads left to right with a fast sweeping return to the next line	• Continues to increase rates of reading
• Begins to make predictions based on picture clues	• Increases rates of reading and writing	• Adjusts reading rates for different purposes and difficulty levels of text
• Points to words when reading	• Engages in visible word-to-word matching while reading	• Reads with expression
• Names and recognizes uppercase and lowercase letters; writes uppercase letters and most lowercase letters	• Begins to use multiple sources of information—semantic, syntactic, visual cues as well as pictures—to decode unknown words	• Uses the three cues—semantic, syntactic, and visual—with ease for decoding unfamiliar words
		• Continues to increase reading and writing vocabulary
• Knows initial consonant letter sounds in words	• Reads and writes words using most letter–sound relationships	• Challenges the story content
	• Spells more sight words correctly	• Questions the author's assumptions
• Participates during story discussions	• Begins to use punctuation marks in writing	• Knows when he or she understands and does not understand text
• Reads to the end of the story	• Begins to use comprehension strategies	• Possesses and uses a variety of strategies when confronted by text he or she does not understand
		• Conducts book discussions independently
		WORD-SOLVING STRATEGIES
		• Uses varied strategies (usually unobservable) to read and write unknown words
		• Reads and writes a large bank of sight words automatically
		• Writes many words using standard spelling
		• Uses base words, inflections, plurals, and affixes in reading and writing
		• Uses base words to make new words
		• Uses base words to derive meaning from unknown words

Figure 2.1
Continued

What Teachers Need to Know About Literacy

For each young child, learning to read and write is a complex achievement. Teachers acquire the complex knowledge and skills required for effective teaching over years of focused study and reflective practice. Our goal in this section is not to supply a shopping list of what teachers need to know, but rather to offer a starting point for teachers to begin thinking about the outcomes, the content, and the routines for designing effective lessons, remembering that the key to successful instruction is pitching the lesson to each child's literacy development. What follows are components of literacy instruction for young children.

The Development and Role of Phonemic Awareness in Reading

The debate is over! There is no longer doubt among educators about the significant role that phonemic awareness plays in a child's learning to read a language that has an alphabetic orthography such as English (Yopp, 1992; Yopp & Yopp, 1995). A weakness in children's phonological awareness often hinders their efforts in learning how to read, a finding that applies for students with and without disabilities (Bruck, 1992; Byrne & Fielding-Barnsley, 1995). Further, there is evidence that direct instruction of phonemic awareness in children who lack the concept and skills will indeed benefit their reading achievement (Cunningham, 1990).

Phonemic awareness: Children possess phonemic awareness when they recognize that words are made up of a discrete set of sounds that they can manipulate.

What is phonemic awareness? According to Stanovich (1986), **phonemic awareness** is the "conscious access to the phonemic level of the speech stream" as well as the ability to "manipulate representations at this level" (p. 36). Children must know that words are made up of individual speech sounds, and they must be able to change the sounds in words to manipulate them. In order for young readers to be able to decode printed words, they first must be able to hear the separate sounds in the spoken words.

It cannot be assumed that children who enter kindergarten or first grade are aware that spoken language is composed of words (Adams, 1990). For many adults, this may seem an easy skill to learn, but there are children who lack this essential skill when they enter school. A teacher, therefore, must know that phonological development, of which phonemic awareness is a part, is a concept that develops over time. Children entering preschool and kindergarten possess phonemic awareness to varying degrees. This is why teachers in preschool, kindergarten, and the primary grades should know how to assess young children for their stages of growth in phonemic awareness as well as training techniques they can use with children for phonological development. Fundamental to knowing how to assess phonemic awareness is knowledge of its related skills.

The stages of phonemic awareness that children develop are as follows:

- **Rhyming words:** An awareness that some words have similar endings that rhyme
- **Beginning sounds:** An awareness that some words begin with the same sound
- **Ending sounds:** An awareness that some words end with the same sound
- **Medial sounds:** An awareness that some words have the same sounds in the middle of the word

- **Syllables in a word:** An awareness that words have syllables and the ability to count the syllables in a word
- **Onsets and rhymes in words:** An awareness that words have an onset and a rhyme and an ability to divide a word into these parts (The first sound *k* in the word *cat* is the onset. The ending sound *at* in the word *cat* is the rhyme.)
- **Phoneme segmentation:** An awareness and an ability to segment a word into its phonemes, its smallest sounds
- **Phoneme deletion:** An awareness and an ability to delete a single sound or phoneme from a word
- **Phoneme blending:** An awareness and an ability to blend sounds or phonemes into words

Whereas phonemic awareness relates to the consciousness of sounds in spoken words, **phonics** is the study of the relationship between the phoneme (smallest speech sound) and grapheme (the letter or group of letters that represent the sound). When children are learning how to sound out or decode a word, they are engaged in a phonics lesson. Therefore, **phonics refers to the relationship between the written and the spoken elements of words.**

Before children can understand the connection between the spoken and written word, they must have a fundamental understanding of phenemes or **phonemic awareness.** Children in the first grade learning how to decode words, for example, must have an awareness of the sounds within spoken words. Phonemic awareness also consists of concepts that are further developed with instruction in reading and writing. Children initially have varying degrees of phonemic awareness. As they work to decode unfamiliar words to write stories with words they do not know how to spell, and as they receive instruction in word-solving strategies and spelling strategies, children's phonemic awareness is further developed. Consider a child who is writing a story and comes to a word that she has not written before. What does she do? First, she might say the word out loud. Then she may think about the sounds that she hears in the words. She writes down the letter or letters that she thinks stand for each sound in the word she hears. This act promotes her phonemic awareness. When the teacher is available to guide the child through this process, her ability in phonemic awareness is further developed.

Becoming phonologically aware is a complex process bound to many different language experiences and activities that prepares children for later reading instruction, including instruction in phonics, word analysis, and spelling (Blackman, 1999). Therefore, a well-balanced literacy program incorporates phonemic awareness instruction and assessment as a precursor to effortless decoding skills.

Alphabet Knowledge

Letter knowledge and its relationship to decoding. What is meant by alphabet knowledge? Knowing letters goes far beyond singing the alphabet (which is one of the many starting points for most children) to include naming and recognizing letters, both uppercase and lowercase, and knowing the names of the sounds that a letter makes. Letter knowledge grows beyond these skills that young children need to learn to read to become independent readers. Throughout the years, researchers have studied the relationship between children's alphabet knowledge and learning how to read. In one of Chall's (1989) more recent studies, she maintained alphabet knowledge as being a dominant indicator of reading success in the child's future life. Although phonemic awareness is fundamental in learning how to read and its related tasks involve auditory processing skills, letter knowledge is equally important in recognizing and decoding words; however, its related tasks rely on visual processing. Phonemic awareness and letter knowledge are linked as the foundation in producing strong decoding skills. Even though the tasks surrounding learning letters and sounds are often perceived as simple, early childhood teachers do appreciate the complexity of learning letters and the **alphabetic code**—the corresponding sound of the letters—that is needed to read a text.

From the time children enter the world, they use visual information to solve problems (Bryant, 1974). Young children can recognize objects that they have seen, thereby demonstrating visual processing, and they use visual memory to recall objects. To recognize and recall letters, visual information is used. The recognition of letters and words for children is not achieved with the same ease as the recognition of environmental stimuli due to the abstract nature of print. However, letter recognition does improve with practice (Clay, 1991).

What is it about letters that a child must know, and how do we begin to teach the letters and their sounds to children? According to Adams (1990), a child must know the **letter names** and be able to recognize the uppercase and the lowercase letters. Because it is easier to discriminate the uppercase letters, children usually learn these first, and preschool teachers may wish to work on these letters before the lowercase letters. Children must be able to name the letters before formal instruction in reading. Letter names are typically learned while children are being taught to discriminate one letter from the other.

Another important aspect of letter knowledge is the sounds that are associated with each letter or group of letters. Children need to know that sounds map onto the printed letters. Another way of referring to this concept is the alphabetic principle, which is a feature of the English language. This means that each speech sound of the language is represented by a graphic symbol. In the word *cat,* there are three phonemes and three graphemes. Whereas the phonemes relate to the smallest sounds in a word, the graphemes relate to the letter symbols that represent each phoneme or spoken sound. Look at the example below:

Graphemes

Cat

Phonemes

/c/ /a/ /t/

In the example of the word *cat,* there are three graphemes that correspond to the three phonemes. For children learning to read, they must learn the relationship between the spoken sounds and the written word, known as letter–sound relationships. As previously mentioned, this study is known as phonics, the relationship between phonemes and graphemes that is needed for decoding unknown words. Many educators refer to mastery of the alphabetic principle as *breaking the code.* Thus, one of the major concepts and set of skills that is developed at the early stage of literacy development is the alphabetic principle, a prerequisite for becoming a fluent reader and writer.

Different approaches to teaching about letters. In some classrooms, children acquire alphabet knowledge in a specific sequence and in a very direct way: First they learn the names of the letters, followed by letter recognition, and finally they learn the letter sounds. Oftentimes, the teacher places more of an emphasis on

explicit teaching of each letter, showing them how it is shaped and telling them, step-by-step, how to write the letter.

In classrooms with a balanced literacy program, children are also encouraged to learn about letters **implicitly** or **indirectly** on their own as they use them in their reading and writing. With this approach they learn about letters through sharing books with adults and peers, and as they begin to write stories and notes, they may not know all of the letters. They may play letter games and engage in letter activities during center time. Using the indirect or implicit method, children construct their own knowledge of letters within various literacy experiences.

Children benefit from both approaches to learning letters. Although they need direct or explicit instruction of letter knowledge and how the code works (Adams, 1990), children also benefit from learning about letters through multiple contexts that engage them in independent letter activities where they learn implicitly about alphabet knowledge. In essence they need a *balanced and comprehensive literacy program,* which is discussed at length later in this chapter.

The Role of Writing in Learning to Read

We now know that there is a strong connection between becoming a reader and learning how to write. Research on emergent writers (Bissex, 1980; Clay, 1991; Holdaway, 1979; Taylor, 1980; Teale & Sulzby, 1986) has revealed that

- Children come to school highly motivated to use the print forms of their language, including writing.
- Both processes—reading and writing—develop simultaneously; learning one process supports learning the other process.
- Direct instruction in writing develops young writers.
- A rich literacy environment that includes demonstrations and collaboration promotes engaged writers.

When literacy concepts and skills are learned during reading contexts, young authors will try to use what they have learned in their own attempts at writing. For example, during shared reading, the children see the teacher move the pointer in the direction of the print; he may also use the shared-reading session to build a bank of sight words and take the opportunity for a spelling lesson. Finally, he may return to that same book to teach some punctuation marks such as the period or quotation marks. In their writing, children will try to integrate and use the print concepts they have learned by continuing to use the directionality of Standard English texts. Some children may try to spell the sight word that was introduced that day, whereas another may work on a piece of writing, attempting to use that familiar punctuation mark, the period. Clearly, written texts provide the conventional print forms and the spelling of words that young children need in their first attempts at writing (Bean & Bouffler, 1997). In addition, young readers and writers imitate the ideas and the illustrations from the stories they heard by appropriating them for their own stories. Therefore, writing needs to be encouraged, taught, and monitored in the younger grades (Teale & Sulzby, 1986) as well as celebrated to demonstrate children's accomplishments.

Promoting early writing instruction. To encourage and develop writing in young children, Hiebert (1986) suggests a literacy-rich environment. Such an environment includes effective writing instruction as well as the planned activities that

Engaging young children in writing activities promotes all forms of language skills.

support children's attempts in writing. The physical environment has an effect on writers and writing. Consider a primary classroom that, in the words of Andrea Butler, is "dripping in print." The room contains displays of children's written work, word walls that are actively used for instruction as well as a resource by children. There are attractive posters, objects are labeled, group stories are hanging at eye level for reading, group books are displayed on the open bookshelf. In a classroom corner is the writing center, to which all children have easy access. Children go to the writing center that stores paper of all sizes and styles, with and without lines; pencils and pens, crayons, and markers that are thick and thin; scissors; construction paper; used birthday and holiday cards; pictures cut from magazines; copies of magazines and newspapers; and so forth. In such a classroom where children's work is displayed, they know that an author's writing is respected. Children will use other writing for developing their own ideas. With access to words all around, children will scan the walls for the word they need, as they try to put together ideas or spell out the sounds in the word. Such an environment encourages and celebrates the attempts of young writers.

Children learn writing concepts from observing others write as well as through their own writing experiences. Just as their experiences to develop and shape their reading concepts begin at home, children's first experiences with writing emerge and are mediated by their parents, caregivers, and older siblings (Purcell-Gates, 1996). When they come to preschools and elementary schools they know about writing, and they enjoy engaging in written forms of expression, both drawing and writing. Teachers need to encourage and nurture their dispositions and skills for writing.

The Role of Strategy Development in Learning to Read

All proficient readers and writers have **strategies** that they use in understanding text while reading or in composing text while writing. The word *strategy* is a term that is frequently used in education that has multiple meanings. Let us begin by clarifying what is meant by the development of strategies for proficient reading and writing. Within the context of a child developing a strategy that leads to proficient meaning, the term has been defined as "a practiced but flexible way of responding to recognizable contexts, situations or demands" (National Council of Teachers of English [NCTE] & International Reading Association [IRA], 1996, p. 75). Within this definition are two key words, *practiced* and *flexible.* Strategic readers and writers have a set of plans that are practiced, or they are learned to such a degree that they can be summoned on demand and employed effortlessly. However, employing strategies for decoding words effortlessly takes both knowledge and practice. Strategies also need to be flexible because the demands placed on a child when reading and writing texts differ in many ways. All texts are not written the same way; for example, they differ in sentence structure, in vocabulary, concept density, sentence length, and so forth. Therefore, reading various types of texts demands using different reading strategies. The same is true for writing because the task demands for composing a text differ. Further, when one reads for different purposes, the demands change; therefore, the strategies used will change as well. Consider the demands placed on a reader in the three following contexts: (1) reading a letter or e-mail from a friend, (2) reading a book for pleasure, and (3) reading the questions on a standardized test. They all differ in purpose, complexity, and disposition of the reader. Thus, reading strategies must be flexible. To ensure that flexibility, teachers must provide children with a variety of strategies from which to select the appropriate one to use on demand. Teachers who offer children the opportunity to use strategies in a wide range of literacy contexts and activities, teachers who offer direct instruction in several types of literacy strategies, and teachers who provide children with practice in strategy use will guarantee to young readers and writers flexibility in the use of literacy strategies.

- Can you think of one approach or strategy you would use for reading a book for pleasure?
- A different approach for reading directions to fill out your tax forms?
- Can you think of one different way you approach writing an e-mail to a friend?
- A different approach for writing a research paper for school?

Strategy Development and the Use of Cueing Systems

Children come to school with different kinds of experiences and conceptual knowledge. They also come to school knowing about the language and how it works. As they begin to learn to read, they draw upon what they know to develop a set of strategies to read and write. They also develop strategies that eventually become effortless, or implicit, that guide the strategic reader in decoding new words and constructing meaning from text. Clay (1993a) has categorized the sources of information that children draw from in executing reading strategies as semantic, syntactic or structural, and visual. Because readers use these sources of information in understanding what they are reading, they are also referred to as *cues.* Each type of cue is described below.

Semantic cues: This type of information comes to readers from their life experiences, from discussions and conversations, from books that were read to them and stories they heard, even from television. Any type of information that provides meaning or background knowledge from which the reader draws upon may be classified as a **semantic** or a **meaning cue.**

Syntactic or structure cues: *Syntax* refers to the structure of the language, the rules that provide order to the spoken and written language. By the time they enter school, children know about language and how language works. They may not be able to articulate the rule that governs the correct order of the words in a sentence, but their response—"That sounds funny"—demonstrates their implicit knowledge of the structure of the language. They know when the order of words within a sentence is incorrect. For children, to say "The dog barking is" sounds funny. **Syntactic** or **structural cues** are sources of information on how our language is put together that readers use to aid them in decoding words or constructing meaning from text.

Visual cues: Visual cues come from a reader's knowledge of letter–sound relationships and how words look in print. Therefore, they are often referred to as grapho-phonological cues. As young children engage in all types of literacy activities, they acquire letter knowledge that includes the sounds that a letter or sequence of letters make when they are reading. They know sight words. They also know that long words need more letters. They build knowledge about the relationship of the printed words and the spoken words. Their knowledge of the alphabetic code enables them to use **visual cues** within print to decode unknown words.

How readers use the cueing system. Semantic, syntactic or structural, and visual cues comprise what is known as the **cueing system.** Strategic readers use all three aspects of the cueing system simultaneously and effortlessly while reading. It is indeed a complex process, but oftentimes, the reading strategies used are not apparent. This is especially true when reading easy material that poses no challenge. This changes when a reader is confronted with a problem within the text. For example, when coming to a word that is unfamiliar, the reader may scan the text around the unknown word looking for clues, analyze the word for meaningful parts, or think of a word that might be related. In any case, the reader is using multiple strategies and drawing upon current knowledge: world knowledge, language knowledge, and knowledge of words. The purpose is to make sense of the text.

What beginner readers know and need to learn. From the time children enter the world, they begin to acquire knowledge through their numerous interactions with adults and with environmental stimuli. They learn about the language (syntactic knowledge), they acquire conceptual knowledge (semantics), and they learn about many aspects of the printed word (grapho-phonological knowledge). Thus, when children come to school, they bring many concepts and skills that may be used for formal instruction in reading. To prepare them to use the three areas of knowledge or their cueing system efficiently, teachers work to develop specific strategies.

Using the cueing system. When children enter kindergarten and first grade, teachers work with them to further refine their language, their conceptual knowledge, and concepts of print. They learn specific letter–sound relationships that they can use to decode words. In other words, children must learn phonics, *the code,* and strategies to use their knowledge with efficiency. As previously discussed, using their knowledge of phonics effectively means that children must use the three aspects of the cueing system together. Clay (1993b) describes how teachers may assist children in their goal of becoming fluent or strategic readers. Using the cueing system to decode and construct meaning suggests that children will learn to do the following: (1) They will monitor their reading for meaning and accuracy as they use the cueing system. (2) The children will search for the semantic, syntactic, and visual cues within the print so that they may engage in word solving of the new and unfamiliar words they encounter. (3) When engaged in word solving, they will cross-check the multiple cues. For example, if the word is *puppy* and the child reads *dog,* because it is a good meaning fit, she will learn to cross-check by using visual cues visual and discover it is not the word because of the way *dog* looks and how it sounds. (4) The children will uncover new ideas about text from reading. (5) They will self-correct miscues or errors because of accurate use of the cueing system and cross-checking. Each time a child reads and uses these strategies, she becomes a better reader and is on the road to fluency. By using the cueing system and its strategies, children construct meaning about these rules or strategies, how they operate and when to use them, and what to do when they get to a word that is unfamiliar. Clay (1993a) asserts that the goal of teaching strategies is "reached when children have a **self-extending system**—a set of operations just adequate for reading slightly more difficult text" (p. 39, emphasis added). Children are trained to use strategies until they become proficient in their use. It is also important that teachers consider the children's literacy development to guide their selection of books. Books must be slightly

While you read A *Portrait of a Young Reader Using the Cueing System,* think about the three sources of knowledge that Sema may use when she comes to a word she does not know. Then think about what Sema does when she comes to an unfamiliar word in the story.

A Portrait of a Young Reader Using the Cueing System

Sema is reading a book during guided reading. The book is at her appropriate level for instruction; therefore, it poses a few challenges in decoding new vocabulary words. This will give her practice in using word-solving strategies, and if she needs assistance. Valerie, her teacher, is at her side to guide her through. Sema comes to two new words, *wobbly tooth.* She stops at the word *wobbly* because she does not know it. Next, Sema applies some of the strategies that her teacher taught her before reading this book. Sema examines the first part of the word and tries to say it—"Wahb," she utters. Her eyes go to the end of the word to *-ly* and she says, "le." Then Sema examines the large illustration and goes back to the beginning of the sentence. She blurts out, "Wobbly, wobbly tooth," and continues to read. Valerie observes her and encourages her in her word-solving strategies with an approving look. After Sema finishes her story, the teacher calls her over and asks her if she remembered what she did when she didn't know the word. Sema thinks about it and recalls how she looked at the way the word begins and ends and thought about what would make sense there. The teacher reminds her that she might have gotten help from the illustration. "Very good!" Valerie adds. That is what good readers do when they do not know a word.

Guided reading provides each child direct instruction on learning how to use reading strategies.

challenging—within the children's zone of proximal development—for them to benefit from using strategies on challenging words.

What strategies did Sema use to solve for the unknown word? During guided reading, children read books that provide a slight challenge to them to engage them in strategy use. Sema was reading and came to a word she did not know, so she used three different types of strategies that Valerie taught her for identifying unknown words while reading, or word solving. What did Sema do when she came to the word she did not know? She looked at the beginning of the word for initial sound, and then she looked at the ending of the word. She was using *visual cues.* At the same time, her eyes went to the illustration, another source of information to get meaning. Thus, she used a *semantic cue.* Finally, Sema reread the sentence that provided her with a source of structural information, a *syntactic cue;* that is, she checked to see if *wobbly* fit the correct word order within the sentence. Sema searched for cues, used the cues to solve an unknown word, and cross-checked to see if she was accurate. When she blurted out the word, Sema demonstrated that she solved her problem because the word was a good fit. What did Valerie do while Sema was word solving? Valerie allowed Sema time to work through the problem. She listened in and observed Sema's attempts and was ready to offer assistance if needed. Notice how Valerie reinforced Sema's use of the strategies for decoding unknown words. She asked her to reflect on how she went about solving the unknown word *wobbly.* The kind of assistance that Valerie offered Sema was effective teaching.

What Sema learned is part of what young readers need to learn to reach fluency. Although reading is effortless for adults, for a young child, learning to read is challenging, an appreciation that early childhood teachers acquire very quickly. By the time children reach fluency, by the end of the third grade, readers should be able to recognize 80,000 words (Juel & Minden-Cupp, 2000). This is no small feat. To reach this stage of proficiency, children must receive hours of effective direct instruction in phonics and in the strategies needed to decode unknown words, as well as practice in reading independently. Snow (1999) emphasized that such focused instruction is especially important for children who come from impoverished homes, for children who are classified with special needs, as well as for students who are linguistically diverse. For them, the challenge is even greater.

Making Connections to Further Comprehension

When we read, our goal is to understand what we have read. Deriving **meaning** is therefore the purpose of reading. This should be a fairly simple starting point, yet as we begin to explore what readers comprehend, we find that the meanings readers derive from text oftentimes differ from one reader to the next. In our discussion of comprehension, we will define it as using a definition that explains the factors that affect meaning or account for meaning. We know that reading for meaning is a complex process. What contributes to the complexity of the process are the factors that affect the meaning that is constructed by the reader. Consider the following set of factors that account for what the reader constructs as meaning from text:

- **Reading is an interactive process** (Anderson & Pearson, 1984). The reader interacts with the text to construct meaning. What the reader brings to the text matters. That is, readers need to have knowledge about the concepts within the book they are reading or have some personal experiences related to the events of the story. **Prior knowledge** determines how the readers interact with the text and the meanings they construct from the text.
- Reading is a **transactive process** (Rosenblatt, 1938, 1978, 1991). Readers transact with text and their transactions affect the meanings that they will construct. Readers transact differently, because they are different. Rosenblatt discusses the multiple factors that a reader brings to a book or a poem, at any given time, that directly affect comprehension: How does the reader feel—what kind of mood is the reader experiencing? What is the purpose for reading? What are the values of the reader—social, political, religious, and so on—that may affect the meanings derived from the book? What is happening now—what are the current events, the mood of the day, the weather, immediate personal experiences, and so forth—that relate to the text? All factors that come into play while reading determine the meaning that is constructed.
- Reading is a **strategic process** (Anderson, Hiebert, Scott, & Wilkinson, 1985). Strategic readers use a variety of strategies for comprehending what they read. They have well-developed strategies that they can draw upon when they need to do so. They know when they need to activate prior knowledge, when they need to slow down and when they can read faster, because these readers have self-monitoring strategies. Strategic readers have expectations for reading that relate to the purpose, and they bring them to the foreground during their reading. The kinds of strategies that are acquired affect what will be understood and remembered.

Developing Strategies for Meaning

The goal is to provide the foundation for young children to become successful readers. Therefore, educators need to know what strategic readers do when they construct meaning from text. In other words, what are the strategies that efficient readers use to successfully comprehend text? Teachers also need to keep in mind the factors that affect what young children will comprehend while reading.

Let us begin with the assumption that comprehension is a constructive, interactive, and transactive process that involves the reader and the author as well as the present, past, and future contexts in which the reading occurs. For the purposes of our discussion, we will focus on the most useful strategies for beginner readers that will provide them with a start to independent reading. In developing strategies for comprehending text, it is helpful to think of what teachers can do before, during, and after reading with children. Therefore, we can classify strategy instruction into three categories: **before-reading strategies, during-reading strategies,** and **after-reading strategies.**

Before-reading strategies. As teachers work with children they learn so much from them. One day during an independent reading period, one of the authors approached a boy named Alex who was staring at his book. As she observed him, he continued, looking at the front and back covers, flipping through the pages. She could not help but nudge him on to read. He taught her a lesson that she'll never forget when he quipped, "I gotta get ready, I'm warming up!" Alex knew a great deal about himself and learning. Yes, we all get ready or prepare for our next task. Reading is no different, especially for young children. They need adult guidance through a structured preparation period that they will use when they are reading independently.

Before reading, there are many strategies that will help children while they are reading to comprehend the text. First, children need a *purpose for reading.* This may be as simple as a *story walk,* looking at the pictures of the book and asking the children to predict what they will be reading. Second, children need to be able to use their knowledge so that while they are reading, they can understand the concepts. Before reading, the teacher *activates their prior knowledge.* Many children have experiences and conceptual knowledge that relates to the text, but it takes instruction for them to use it consistently while reading. When children demonstrate that they may lack the experience necessary to comprehend the text, it is critical for the teacher to *build knowledge* before reading the book so that the children will understand what they are reading. These guided discussions during the prereading phase, called a **picture** or **story walk** or **book introduction** when it occurs during guided reading, help children not only to establish a purpose for reading but also to develop routines that they can use to build strategies for approaching a new book.

Teachers expect young readers to begin to try out their cueing strategies. For the prereading session, the teacher will select some possible words that may present a challenge to the readers. In the prereading session the children will also receive direct instruction in word work, both in phonic knowledge and strategy use, to help them solve an unfamiliar word they read in the text.

During-reading strategies. While they are reading, the children will have the opportunity to use their cueing systems. It is the goal of the teacher to bring children to fluency by leading them to predict, confirm, and correct as they read. While they are reading, the teacher carefully observes them, listening in while they are reading, ready to assist them in their efforts. By using strategy language, the teacher offers them a clue in selecting the correct strategy for the problem. For a reader who reads a word that does not fit, the teacher may say, "Does that make sense?" or "Read the sentence before that one, and see if the word fits." In any case, for the young reader, the development of strategies and strategy use leads to fluency and greater independence in reading. Therefore, the teacher monitors their strategy development and slowly increases the complexity of strategy use to align with their development.

While children are reading, asking them specific questions related to the story will provide assistance to them in constructing meaning from what they are reading. To do this, the young readers need to make connections to the story. Three powerful types of connections that strategic readers use are (1) text-to-self connections, (2) text-to-text connections, and (3) text-to-world connections (Harvey & Goudvis, 2000). Before, during, and after reading the story, the teacher may begin to develop these strategies through questioning. In a **text-to-self connection,** the question type will elicit a personal response that connects the reader and the text. For example, when reading Tomie dePaola's *Charlie Needs a Cloak,* the teacher may point out to the children a sweater that is made from wool and ask, "Do you have a sweater, gloves, or scarf that is made from wool?" This will help them to relate on a personal level. In a **text-to-text connection,** the question asked should help children think of connections in the book they are reading or between two books. "Yesterday, we read a story just like this one. Do you remember its name? How were the stories alike?" Or, for connections within a story, "Where else in the story did the author say that?" Stories relate in some way to our world experiences that daily unfold around us. Jenny, a second-grade teacher, was talking to the children about the apartment building around the corner from school that was damaged by fire over the weekend. She announced that there would be a collection to help those people who had lost their personal belongings in the fire. In her read-aloud for the morning, Jenny selected Vera B. Williams's book, *A Chair for My Mother.* She used this book to make **text-to-world connections** by asking, "How can we help the people in the apartment building who lost their belongings the way the neighbors in the story helped?" Encouraging children to develop these strategies helps them to think more deeply about the text and thereby derive more meaning from what they are reading.

After-reading strategies. Another major goal of the teacher is to revisit the story that was just read and to encourage children to integrate meanings that they gain from reading into their conceptual knowledge. For most young children, this essential strategy is acquired through instruction, assistance, and practice. They soon understand that in literature they can discover new ideas and experiences, have different feelings, and meet new friends. Many after-reading strategies involve children thinking about text in different ways or making deeper connections to the stories they read through discussion, writing, dramatic, play and oral language activities.

Comprehending Narrative and Expository Text

Narrative Text

It is true that stories are central in children's lives. For many, stories have become a routine. To varying degrees and depending on their home experiences, children see stories as a source of enjoyment and as a form of entertainment. It is no wonder that children learn how to read through stories or narrative text.

Although we propose that early childhood classrooms be warehouses for reading materials so that children have easy access to different types of literature, teachers need to be aware of the differences in the structure of text—that is, the way books are written. The structure of text differs across literature, and there is an effect of the text type on children's comprehension. Because children listen to stories very early in life—when they are read to, when they watch videos of stories, and when they hear stories being told around the dinner table—they develop a certain sense for story. As mentioned, this is called story schema.

Used in this context, the word *schema* refers to an abstract concept or a set of related knowledge. Rumelhart (1980) explains that we have many different schemas. For example, if we frequent different restaurants, over a certain period, we would likely develop a schema for restaurants that would assist us with all the routines and procedures needed for dining in restaurants. Once we have had numerous experiences in attending a restaurant, our experiences are transformed into conceptual knowledge about dining at a restaurant. Thus, when we enter the restaurant, we know to wait to be seated. With our well-developed restaurant schema, we would then use the restaurant knowledge in understanding how to dine out and make the best of this restaurant experience. The same is true for reading books. There are differences in the way books are written. Stories are one type, and they are written using a narrative style. Most stories have a fairly similar structure, and most children come to school with a basic story sense or a story schema. They will use their story schema for comprehending stories, remembering certain parts, comparing one story to another, and for writing stories. They will make the best of storytime by using their story schema!

Story Grammars and Elements of a Story

One way of understanding a story schema is to identify the elements that are common to stories. Many researchers such as van Dijk and Kintsch (1977), Mandler and Johnson (1977), and Thorndyke (1977) have developed a set of rules known as **story grammars** that describe the elements of a story and the relationship among the story parts. Story grammar is quite similar to the grammar related to the structure of language. Children have knowledge of language structure and know when the word order of a sentence is not grammatically correct. They demonstrate their understanding by saying, "It sounds funny!" They may not be able to articulate the rule that the word order fails to follow, but they know implicitly when it is incorrect. The same is true for stories. After listening to stories, children get a sense of story as they begin to develop story schema. They may not be able to tell you the parts of a story, but they do have expectations while listening to the story.

Although there are variations among researchers in their descriptions, most include the following elements in a story grammar:

1. **Setting:** Every story has a setting which includes the main characters, the time the story occurs, and the place. Authors may emphasize one part of the setting over the others.
2. **Problem:** The main character has a major problem that helps to define the goal of the story.
3. **Goal:** The goal of the story is what the main character(s) must do to solve the problem.

4. **Initiating event:** The story event sets the story in motion.
5. **Story events:** The events in the story consist of what the character must do to reach a solution—all the attempts carried out to solve the problem.
6. **Resolution or conclusion:** The solution or nonsolution (in the event that the problem is not solved) is the resolution or the conclusion of the story. The conclusion also includes the main character's reaction to the events and the resolution.

Children develop a story schema by listening to and, later on, by reading stories. As children listen to more complex stories, their story schemas develop. Having a story schema will help a child understand a story and organize her own stories for telling or writing stories. Listening to children's stories provides us with insight on how well developed their story schemas are; for example, at the emergent level, a child's schema for story enables her to tell the beginning, middle, and end to include the main character, the story problem, and the ending. Having children retell a story is another way to determine how developed their story concept or story schema is. McConaughy (1980) used the written retellings to determine the differences between very young children, older children, and adults in their story schemas. She found that schemas differ in the way the information is organized and what is remembered. Summaries of retellings by young children were simple and descriptive. One sample retelling of a child in kindergarten showed a beginning, middle, and an ending.

Some children do possess well-developed story schemas, because of their frequent exposure to stories. Other children may have difficulty organizing, retelling, and remembering elements. This is especially true for some students with special needs who may have understood the story and demonstrated personal response to the story. Yet, they struggle in their retellings, both written and oral, not knowing where to put different elements. In other words, they lack organization in their ability to retell a story. Many teachers use graphic organizers that contain generic questions that may be applied to most stories to help children organize their ideas so that they can participate in story retellings. Encouraging children to write stories, to reenact stories through creative dramatics, and to use puppets in telling and retelling stories will further develop their story schema and their ability to use story schema to retell stories.

In summary, the meaning that is constructed by young children is dependent upon their schemas that guide them in their interpretations of the story. Equally fluent readers will construct a variety of interpretations from the story because of their different backgrounds and story schemas. Among other factors that affect how children construct meanings from stories are their conceptual knowledge related to the ideas within the story, their familiarity with stories that are similar, and their dispositions or interest toward reading stories.

Expository Text

Teachers are finding more children selecting information books or nonfiction types of literature. These books contain expository text structures and are quite different from narrative style of writing. Expository texts include informational books, textbooks, essays, and any writing that is intended to inform or convey knowledge. Researchers such as Meyer (1975) and others have identified text structures in expository texts. The patterns or structures most frequently used in information books are as follows:

- **Compare-contrast structure**—the author points to likenesses and differences.
- **Cause-effect structure**—the author describes how an event occurs as a result of a certain set of factors.
- **Time-order structure**—the author puts occurrences into certain time sequences.
- **Problem-solution structure**—the author presents a problem or a question followed by a solution.
- **Descriptive structure**—the author imparts a set of facts, events, and ideas. (McNeil, 1992, p. 167)

These structures form a schema that readers use in facilitating their recall of information and organization of ideas needed for comprehension. Readers who develop a schema for expository text structures are more likely to recall more of what they read than poor readers without such schemas (Meyer, Brandt, & Bluth, 1980).

Some aids in the development of schema for expository reading include introducing young children to informational books very early. Listening to and reading informational books also help to develop schemas used by authors. Children can engage in oral and written retellings of informational books as the teacher assists and guides their retelling with the necessary prompts. Graphic organizers that use the same pattern guides that the author uses to write the book will serve as a frame for children to organize their information in written retellings. Teachers use before- and after-reading strategies to prepare children for reading informational books by developing their knowledge needed for understanding and using strategies to help extend what they have learned from reading. Specific strategies will be discussed in Chapter 7 in this text.

Responding to Text

Reader-response theory is aligned with the constructivist perspective of reading and meaning making. Using a constructivist approach to explain comprehension, as children read they construct their own set of meanings, with each set depending on the reader's experiences and prior knowledge. Rosenblatt (1938, 1978) provided some of the earliest works on reader-response theory, which many researchers and educators have applied to reading instruction (Beach, 1993; Galda & Guice, 1997; Rosenblatt, 1991).

You may recall that earlier approaches in teaching young children how to read placed an emphasis on the reader being able to determine what the author intended. In other words, comprehension meant to extract the meaning from the text. How did the reader's meaning of the text match the author's? There was indeed "one right answer" when a comprehension question was posed to students. That notion of meaning has changed with a constructivist approach and with reader-response theory. As children read, they use all of their experiences and prior knowledge as well as their purposes for reading to interpret the text from a particular point of view; they construct meaning by transacting with the text. Reader-response theory posits that a text may be open to multiple interpretations. Further, certain pieces of literature are more apt to evoke a wide range of meanings than other types, and the purpose for reading affects the degree to which interpretations of a text are made. The reader takes a certain **stance** toward reading a story, or sets a particular purpose for reading.

According to Rosenblatt (1978), readers will take either an aesthetic stance or an efferent stance while reading. As stated, stance is determined by the purpose the reader engages and the type of text that is read. Usually, a reader will take an **aesthetic stance** when reading for enjoyment, and the focus is on images, feelings, thoughts, and emotions that are evoked. Every reader has a different personality, comes to the text with different experiences, and as a result, will interpret a story differently. Rosenblatt calls every reading of a story or a poem a "singular event" and a "lived through experience." In this type of reading, one takes an aesthetic stance toward the text.

A reader who is looking for information, trying to determine what the author's intended meaning is, reads with an **efferent stance.** Compare a poem and a cookbook. The nature of each text differs, and the purposes for reading each text differ as well. While reading the poem, it is likely that the reader will take an aesthetic stance, and its reading will evoke images and feelings, emotions and attitudes. While reading a cookbook, the purpose most likely will be to follow the directions as closely as possible to the intended meaning of the author. Thus, the reader will take an efferent stance while reading this type of text.

It is important to make two points: First, a teacher's goal is to help children become flexible as independent readers. Flexibility means that children independently set a purpose for reading related to the type of book they select. A well-balanced reading program offers opportunities to take both an aesthetic stance in reading as well as an efferent stance.

The second point is that most reading includes both stances—it is not an "either–or" situation (Rosenblatt, 1991). Consider your own reading habits and the stances that you take while reading a novel. When you come to a part that you just don't understand, images, feelings, and emotions will not be evoked. What you must do is to stop and think about what the author means. You therefore switch from an aesthetic stance to an efferent stance and then back to the aesthetic stance. Therefore, teachers who provide different kinds of books—informational, which can be used to place children in an efferent stance as they read for meaning that is closely aligned to the authors', and stories and poems, which can be used to place children in a aesthetic stance as they read for enjoyment—will be working toward developing readers who are flexible in setting purposes. Additionally, the way we set the purpose for reading also influences children's ability to be flexible while reading. If we ask children to read only to determine what the author meant, or to read for a personal response, then we are putting them in one stance, providing them with one purpose to read. This may limit their development of flexible use of strategies during reading.

A Framework for a Well-Balanced Literacy Program

In designing an effective literacy program for young children, teachers need a set of guideposts to allow for balance and integration of all of its parts. More than a decade ago, Cambourne (1988) introduced such a model that has been applied to language and literacy learning called **the conditions of learning.** Paralleling the theories of constructivism, the conditions of learning create the framework for implementing a literacy program that seeks to maintain balance and at the same time is comprehensive in scope.

The following principles of language learning comprise the conditions of learning that we have applied to a well-balanced literacy program for young children:

- **Immersion:** Within the classroom children are immersed in print. All types of text are available including a wide range of literature, leveled books for guided reading, book boxes containing books for independent reading from which to select, word walls, labels on materials, magazines and newspapers, children's published books, group stories displayed on the wall, greeting cards, and menus in the restaurant corner.
- **Demonstrations:** Learners need many demonstrations of how language is used and how print works. Therefore, in a balanced literacy program, teachers provide models of how to read and write. Demonstrations may be in the form of a read-aloud, think-aloud, modeled writing, and shared reading. The demonstrations often occur in a variety of contexts, at times to the whole group, to the small group, and often to individuals who need skill work. Young children need to *see* what is being taught. Demonstrations and modeling may be in the form of explicit or direct instruction, or they may take on implicit or indirect approaches to showing how language and print work.
- **Engagement:** Learning through engagement is what Dewey (1990) meant when he argued against passivity, pleading that "the school itself shall be made of active community life" (p. 14). Bringing the principle of active learning to a literacy program means that the children need to internalize literacy through their own performances of the reading and writing demonstrations they observe. Such literate demonstrations will further children's reading and writing lives. They know that such engagements involve risks, but they attempt their new challenge, knowing there will be no harsh consequences. In all aspects of a balanced literacy program, the nature of the tasks encourages active and engaged learners. Think of guided writing. The teacher assists the child only when the child needs assistance. The teacher carefully guides the writer to perform at the more challenging level. He is there with the guidance to help the child gain control if she loses it, to encourage her to move forward, and to offer instruction. Guided writing is designed on the principle of facilitating learners' engagement, as is each component of a balanced literacy program.
- **Expectations:** In his model of language and literacy learning, Cambourne argues that high expectations of learners are "powerful coercers of behavior." Because learning is pitched at each child's literacy level, it is expected that all learners will do well, and they will achieve what they expect to achieve. Children with special needs can and do perform when the expectations are high, but within their boundaries of current performance. The teacher knows that all learning is developmental, and therefore, teaching is developmentally appropriate pitched at each child's development.
- **Responsibility:** Encouraging young children to take responsibility for their own learning is an important aspect of effective teaching as well as learning. For the very young child, the responsibility for learning is a partnership between the

teacher and the child. Gradually, the teacher releases the responsibility for learning to the child, but is always there—at times in the foreground and other times in the background—as the coach who encourages, as the observer who monitors and documents growth, and as the teacher who plans developmentally appropriate instruction and activities for each child's success. Within a balanced literacy program, responsibility is attached to each literacy context. It is always the child who is at center stage.

> There are numerous ways early childhood teachers may provide time for children to use the strategies they have learned. One way is through **paired reading** where children read together. "Pairing readers with similar ability levels is a useful scaffolding technique" (Griffin, 2002, p. 766).

- **Use:** Learners need time to practice what they have learned. For example, they are offered demonstrations of how the reading process works through read-alouds, and they receive direct and systematic instruction in phonics and in word-solving strategies during guided reading. It is independent reading that provides an opportunity to practice the strategies they have learned. The same is true for writing, listening, viewing, and speaking. Children need time to employ strategies while engaging in literacy activities; they need time to reflect on their work, examining and assessing what went well and what needs to be fixed.
- **Approximations:** Everyone makes approximations when they learn. As we attempt something new, the first try, or even the second, may not always reach our expectation. Consider learning how to drive a car. Do you remember your first attempt at parallel parking? After inspection of the placement of the car, was it pulled perfectly next to the curb? In the process of becoming literate, as children attempt to use new skills or concepts, their learning occurs over time; it is not instant. Goodman (1986) explains that "errors, miscues, or misconceptions usually indicate ways in which a child is organizing the world at the moment. As children develop conceptually and linguistically, their errors shift from those that represent unsophisticated conclusions to ones that show greater sophistication" (p. 13). The early childhood teacher who is sensitive to the development of young children sees errors, miscues, and misconceptions as development. Teachers use children's approximations to respond appropriately in ways that will benefit the children's learning, to plan for their instruction, and to select materials that are aligned to their development.
- **Response:** According to Cambourne's (1988) model of learning, children need feedback. When teachers are more attuned to the children's development, response from the teacher would be more beneficial to children's learning. They know where the child is at her desired goal, and the response may be what the child needs to nudge her development. The optimal type of response is one that is relevant, appropriate, timely, readily available, nonthreatening, and that has no strings attached.

Jarrod is writing a story about the zoo that the class had visited the day before. Because he has three birds, he was especially interested in the Bird House.

Our class went to the zoo.

We went into the birdhouse.

Jarrod stopped and thought. He noticed his teacher Lillia standing behind him and turned to her, not saying a word. Lillia knew he wanted help. She asked him to read his story, and after reading it, he declared, "I have nothing more to say." Lillia and Jarrod talked with a great deal of enthusiasm about what they both saw at the zoo in the Bird House. After their lively discussion, Jarrod went back to his paper and finished his story.

Jarrod and Lillia's discussion was the interaction that this young writer needed to finish his story. Lillia knew that the response essential for Jarrod at this point was a discussion that would provide him with ideas to finish his story. Their talk led to the development of a new idea. Lillia knew that Jarrod had plenty to write about, and she also knew he needed to talk about it before he could get it down on paper, so she responded to his need. There is no formula for a response, but teachers' responses do need to follow the development and the needs of the child. Responses need to be direct and stimulate development and learning.

Elements of a Well-Balanced Literacy Program

Life in the 21st century is filled with changes. Some of the most rapid changes that occur relate to technology development and the access to information. Children are already a part of this rapidly changing world, and the goal of educators is to help them participate more fully with equal access to the abounding information. As we discussed in Chapter 1, the newer definitions of literacy are broad and more comprehensive than the traditional ones. These definitions evolve from cultural activities that place increasing demands on fluency in language and literacy.

We now know that teaching children to read and write is only the beginning. Literacy and literate thinking involve more complex ways of using language. Children need to learn to use the spoken and print forms of language in a variety of ways. To embrace this challenge, teachers need to integrate current theory and research on literacy acquisition and development with best practices. Teachers are responding with a comprehensive and a balanced literacy program. The components of a balanced literacy program are derived from best teaching practices with young children that are propelled by current theories and research on language and literacy acquisition and development. Strickland (2000) reminds us that what is crucial within a balanced literacy program is the nature of the teaching. Balancing the ways teachers instruct young children throughout the day is one hallmark of the program. Cambourne's (1988) model of learning provides the framework for organizing instruction around effective learning. What do young children need in order to become literate? Early literacy learners need direct and systematic instruction, demonstrations of how print works, immersions in language and literacy, engagement and use of language and print, and responsiveness and feedback to each child's performance. The balanced literacy program includes these effective principles of literacy learning, and it is therefore organized around the kinds of instruction, activities, and assessment that young children will derive the most benefit from. Figure 2.2 shows the elements of a well-balanced literacy program.

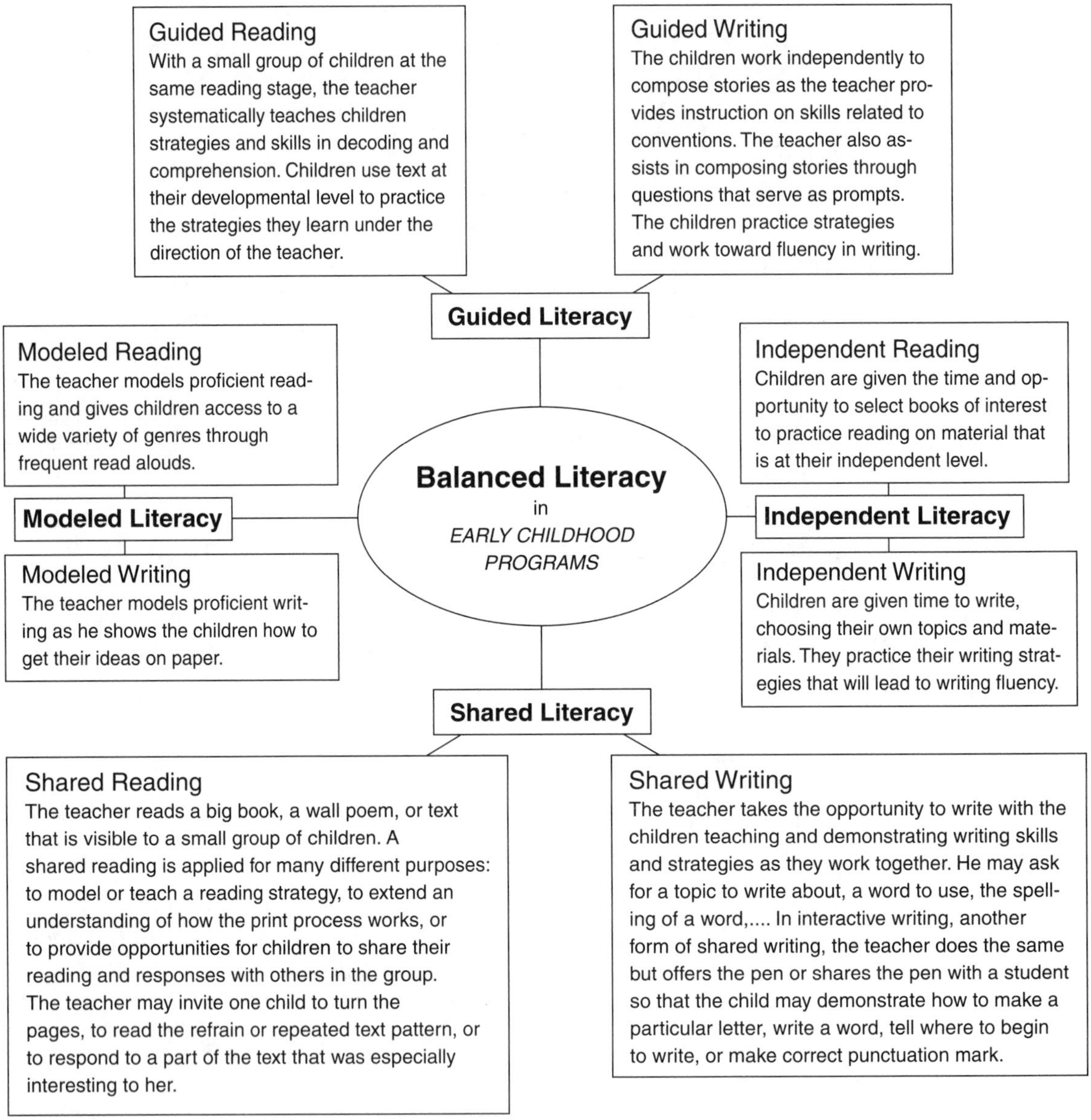

Guided Reading
With a small group of children at the same reading stage, the teacher systematically teaches children strategies and skills in decoding and comprehension. Children use text at their developmental level to practice the strategies they learn under the direction of the teacher.

Guided Writing
The children work independently to compose stories as the teacher provides instruction on skills related to conventions. The teacher also assists in composing stories through questions that serve as prompts. The children practice strategies and work toward fluency in writing.

Guided Literacy

Modeled Reading
The teacher models proficient reading and gives children access to a wide variety of genres through frequent read alouds.

Modeled Literacy

Modeled Writing
The teacher models proficient writing as he shows the children how to get their ideas on paper.

Balanced Literacy in *EARLY CHILDHOOD PROGRAMS*

Independent Reading
Children are given the time and opportunity to select books of interest to practice reading on material that is at their independent level.

Independent Literacy

Independent Writing
Children are given time to write, choosing their own topics and materials. They practice their writing strategies that will lead to writing fluency.

Shared Literacy

Shared Reading
The teacher reads a big book, a wall poem, or text that is visible to a small group of children. A shared reading is applied for many different purposes: to model or teach a reading strategy, to extend an understanding of how the print process works, or to provide opportunities for children to share their reading and responses with others in the group. The teacher may invite one child to turn the pages, to read the refrain or repeated text pattern, or to respond to a part of the text that was especially interesting to her.

Shared Writing
The teacher takes the opportunity to write with the children teaching and demonstrating writing skills and strategies as they work together. He may ask for a topic to write about, a word to use, the spelling of a word,.... In interactive writing, another form of shared writing, the teacher does the same but offers the pen or shares the pen with a student so that the child may demonstrate how to make a particular letter, write a word, tell where to begin to write, or make correct punctuation mark.

Figure 2.2
The Elements of a Well-Balanced Literacy Program

Guided Literacy

Guided literacy is one component of a balanced program that ensures that children learn concepts and skills related to language use and literacy through systematic and direct or explicit instruction in strategies at their development level. Because both guided reading and writing are directed at the specific literacy development of the children, they are placed in small groups with instruction, materials, and feedback that are developmentally appropriate to their specific levels or literacy processes. Grouping children for instruction is a critical aspect of explicit or direct instruction, because the teacher may focus on the children's specific needs (Neumann & Bredekamp, 2000).

Iversen and Reeder (1998) describe the successful **guided reading session** as one that provides children with opportunities to

- Deepen and widen their understanding of text
- Learn the skills and strategies required to independently read increasingly more text
- Learn how to use aspects of language such as structure, rhyme, rhythm, and alliteration to decode and comprehend text
- Engage in reading strategies such as predicting, locating, checking, confirming, and self-correcting
- Learn about book language and concepts about print; for example, author, illustrator, and title
- Extend sight vocabulary (p. 59)

Within the guided writing session, the teacher assists the children in their efforts to compose their messages. A rich guided writing session is one that provides children with opportunities to

- Compose their own text by integrating their ideas and thoughts in a coherent and cohesive message
- Discover new ways to express ideas
- Build a writing vocabulary
- Compose a wide variety of texts—stories, informational text, letters, directions, and so on
- Learn the letters and their sounds as they write meaningful messages
- Learn spelling strategies for writing new words
- Learn the spelling of frequently used words
- Learn a variety of punctuation marks

Shared Literacy

Shared literacy is another format for teaching children about language and print. The context that the teacher sets up for shared reading and writing is different than that used for guided literacy. The teacher may use a large or small group, and the children do not have to be grouped by skill or need. In shared reading, the teacher uses a big book, as he and the group interact about the print and concepts, constructing meaning or talking about the conventions of print. In the big book *Mrs. Wishy-Washy,* the teacher may take the opportunity to teach sight words, such as *look,* because this word is dominant in the text and appears several times. In any case, the teacher takes this pleasurable opportunity for interactive instruction.

In a shared writing lesson, the teacher may be working with a group of children around a large paper as they are dictating the story to her. The teacher may invite individual children to come up and "share the pen" to show the group how to write a letter, to begin a sentence or a word, or even to finish a sentence. In a shared literacy context, the pen or the book is shared with the group to learn with one another or to demonstrate to the group what one knows.

Modeled Literacy

In this literacy context, children receive demonstrations of the language processes. For example, in a read-aloud, the teacher carefully selects a piece of literature that he reads with enthusiasm and expression, clearly articulating each word, turning the pages, and showing each picture to the children to help them construct meaning. He is modeling not only fluent reading but also page turning and the use of illustrations to build meaning. At the same time, the teacher is sharing his pleasure for reading with the children, an extremely important literacy disposition held by lifelong readers. The book that the teacher uses for the read-aloud should be carefully selected and considered an excellent piece of children's literature, because the book becomes a model of language to the children who are listening.

Modeled literacy is also important in developing the writing process in young children. The morning message is one context the teacher may use to model how to write. As the teacher writes down the message, he may engage in a think-aloud. A think-aloud helps children connect to what the teacher is doing. For example, as the teacher begins the message "Today is Wednesday . . ." he may say, "*Today* is the first word of the sentence, so I must begin it with an uppercase letter." In this short message, he is demonstrating how accomplished writers get their message down on paper. Cambourne's (1988) model of learning includes demonstrations of what is being learned as a necessary condition in learning. Demonstrations may and should occur within all of the elements of a balanced literacy program, but they are explicit and intentional within modeled literacy.

Independent Literacy

Children need time to practice literacy strategies and skills. Teachers provide time for children to select books that are easy enough for them to read independently. This important aspect of the program promotes fluency in reading and provides children the practice they need in using the strategies they have learned. In addition to the structured independent reading time, teachers need to encourage self-initiated periods of independent reading. Children's writing development is also supported by time to engage in independent writing. Journal writing and story writing are very popular writing activities to promote writing fluency. When one of the authors taught first grade, the message board was introduced. The initial goal was to promote balance in the purposes for which one writes. As children started the procedure, they could not get enough time or paper to write all the messages to their classmates. Indeed, it was a successful vehicle for independent writing to promote fluency.

Using Technology: Morrow, Barnhart, and Rooyakkers (2002) found that the most frequently used Web sites by students in an early childhood literacy course for lesson plans were http://www.lessonplans.com and http://www.lessonplanspage.com.

The literacy program needs to be balanced for all children. For some time, the approach to teaching children with disabilities was to provide them with increased skill practice. Strickland (2000) explains that children who are at risk in learning to read and write especially need the time for independent literacy. Although struggling readers may have a difficult time in selecting appropriate reading material, the teacher may assist them and suggest those books that are within their independent reading levels. Strickland also suggests that rereading familiar books "helps build confidence and fluency, a skill that requires special attention for less capable readers," critical elements within the well-balanced literacy program (p. 106). Seeking balance within the literacy program means achieving a well-rounded program for all children through the wide range of literacy activities and instruction that young children need to reach fluency.

The Potentials and Possibilities of Using Standards

Standards are statements related to student learning and student outcomes. A standard defines what is valued within a discipline and provides descriptions of what is considered quality work. Performance standards outline a set of knowledge that children need to know and that is meaningful in today's world (National Education Goals Panel, 1996). These standards have become guideposts for many school communities including parents, students, administrators, and teachers by providing all stakeholders with a framework for designing a comprehensive curriculum and for achieving accountability.

English/Language Arts Standards

Each discipline that is taught in schools has a professional organization that serves teachers and educators throughout the world in keeping abreast with the current theory, research, policies, and practices related to that discipline. The professional organizations disseminate this information to members through international, regional, and local conferences as well as journals and newsletters. For reading instruction the professional organization is the International Reading Association (IRA), and for language arts instruction, the National Council of Teachers of English (NCTE). The NCTE and the IRA jointly defined the set of content standards for English and language arts. **Content standards** refer to "what students should know and be able to do in the English/language arts" (NCTE & IRA, 1996, p. 2). In many states, the Standards for the English Language Arts developed by IRA and NCTE were adopted as the standards used to monitor student learning in language and literacy in kindergarten through Grade 12 (K–12). In other states, these standards were modified to reflect what the states or school districts considered important. Consult the appendix at the back of this textbook for the IRA/NCTE version of the English/language arts standards.

What is the relationship between standards and assessment? Standards for student learning have their origin and purpose in national school reform, with the goal to ensure a quality education for all students propelled by high, rigorous standards. The aim is that all children, regardless of their socioeconomic level or cultural background, are ensured a rich curriculum. Assessment is the process by which these standards may be measured to determine whether the goal for all children has been reached. The standard is not a measure of assessment, but may be related through performance outcomes that are observable and measurable. In other words, to achieve quality assurance in a literacy program, educators need to document student learning through a program of assessment that is related to a standard-based curriculum. The discussion that follows will help to develop a set of criteria in designing an assessment program for the early childhood literacy classroom.

Guidelines for Assessing Young Children

At the beginning of each school year, teachers are presented with a major goal that they take very seriously. Their goal involves bringing each child in their care to substantial growth in learning. For the young child, language and literacy are central aspects of the early childhood curriculum. Therefore, the importance of continuously monitoring young children's language and literacy is critical to their learning and development as well as the teachers' planning for instruction.

Any early childhood program of assessment must follow the guidelines that ensure the evaluation of quality learning in language and literacy as well as meeting standards that account for the intellectual, social, physical, emotional, and cultural development of the young child. To guarantee that teachers are assessing all aspects of language and literacy that are necessary for quality learning, they use the standards set by the IRA and NCTE, which are responsible for literacy education. Because early childhood teachers are sensitive especially to the development of young children, early childhood educators use the standards developed by the NAEYC.

The **Standards for the Assessment of Reading and Writing** were created by the IRA/NCTE Joint Task Force on Assessment. The standards for assessment are used as a guide in constructing an assessment program to monitor literacy development for all children, including children with special learning needs and children who are second language learners. The standards suggest that when teachers are assessing children's language and literacy achievement the following factors must be considered: the interests of the students, the purpose for assessing children (i.e., to improve teaching and learning), the complex nature of literacy processes along with the culture of home and school, the fairness of each assessment tool, the teacher as the agent of the assessment program, and the role that parents take in the assessment of their children.

As we reflect on each of the standards for assessment, it is clear that what is called for is an assessment program that is child centered, taking into account each child's development, interests, and background. Another critical aspect of the standards is that they call for a system of assessment that is ongoing, linked to instruction, and based on multiple perspectives and sources of data. Finally, parents need to play an active role in the assessment plan.

In a joint position statement, the IRA and NAEYC (1998) stated that assessment of literacy in young children is essential: "Throughout these critical years **accurate assessment** of children's knowledge, skills, and dispositions in reading and writing will help teachers better match instruction with how and what children are learning" (p. 206, emphasis added). A program of assessment for young children must not only be aligned to their development but also must include broader measures of reading and writing.

Using the standards presented by the NAEYC for assessing children aged 3 through 8 will further refine the framework for assessment. Following is a summary of NAEYC's (Bredekamp & Copple, 1997) position on the assessment of young children. For NAEYC's complete position statement on the assessment of young children, consult its Web site at http://www.naeyc.org.

Applying the Standards for Assessing Young Children

Application to a balanced literacy program. Teachers of young children are highly concerned about their students. Their concern is focused on the whole child's growth. Reflecting on the Standards for Assessment of Reading and Writing (IRA/NCTE, 1994) and the **Position Statement of NAEYC for Standardized Testing of Young Children 3 Through 8 Years of Age,** we believe that the following assessment criteria define how children's language and literacy growth should be monitored within a well-balanced and comprehensive literacy program.

- Assessment is an ongoing process. It begins from the time the teacher and children enter the classroom until they leave at the end of the grade or period.
- Children are central to the assessment program; that is, teachers need to take into account their development as well as their cultural and linguistic backgrounds.
- Assessment is purposeful. Teachers need to *use* assessment results to monitor each child's progress toward the developmental stages or benchmarks, to design a program of instruction for their specific needs, and to inform parents, children, administrators, and other stakeholders of the progress and needs based on reliable and valid assessment results.
- Assessment needs to be integrated and aligned with instruction and used to inform teaching to make appropriate instructional decisions. It is difficult to learn the impact instruction has on student learning if assessment is not a part of the instructional plans. An example of using assessment to inform instruction is selecting developmentally appropriate books for children based on their performances during guided reading.
- Assessment needs to inform instruction. When teachers align assessment and instruction, they begin to look at their own teaching habits in light of what children are learning. Their decisions become informed because they are grounded in systematic use of assessment results.
- A well-balanced assessment program is designed with multiple literacy instructional contexts and activities. Because instruction is aligned to assessment, the literacy program defines the assessment program. Therefore, each aspect or context of learning will be aligned to assessment providing multiple sources of data and multiple perspectives on student performances.
- Assessment needs systematic documentation. Good teachers have always observed and assessed children. What they did not always do was to document children's learning. In order to use assessment results effectively, teachers need a systematic approach to document observations and other forms of assessing children's literacy development.
- Effective assessment programs need resources. Time is considered an important resource in assessing, documenting, and using the data for effective learning. For a teacher who has two assistants for 15 preschool children, the assessment program will be rich with data and instructional planning. In many urban classrooms, the resources are quite different. A classroom teacher may have 25 to 30 children and an assistant for 2 to 3 hours per day. These two assessment programs will differ radically.

Types of Assessment

Although there are many different ways to classify the methods used to measure the performance of children, the two broad categories into which all evaluation measures, assessment strategies, or testing instruments fall are **formal** and **informal** assessment techniques. Because the purpose of this book is to provide practical and useful ways to align assessment with instruction, the discussion that follows looks briefly at formal and informal assessment to emphasize their differences. Because we believe that the more valuable plan to monitor children's language and literacy is through the use of informal assessment aligned to instruction, our emphasis will turn toward informal or classroom assessment.

Formal Assessment in Early Childhood Education

Formal tests are often referred to as **standardized tests.** In contrast to the informal tests devised by teachers, and sometimes by publishers, standardized measurements are developed by publishers and are used by the administrator of the test in a standard way. One of the reasons these measures are referred to as *standardized tests* is that when teachers administer the tests, they follow set procedures. Such uniform procedures may include following similar directions given to the student, similar testing conditions, and similar time allowed to complete the test to ensure that there is uniformity. The purpose for imposing standard conditions during test administration is to allow school districts to use the results to compare performances across groups of students.

Reporting Results

Through statistical analysis, the results of children's performances on standardized tests provide a way of comparing group performances. The local newspaper may compare performance of schools and school districts by publishing the results of the standardized achievement tests administered to groups of children at the same grade level. There are different ways that test results may be reported for an individual child and for a group of children. The two most common types of scores are percentile rank and grade-equivalent scores.

Percentile rank scores. A percentile rank and a percent received on a test paper are not the same. **Percentile rank scores** show the position of an individual student within a group of similar students who took the same test. Another way of expressing percentile rank is comparing the student's performance to a comparable group of students. For example, if the test Jesse took was normed for second-grade students, and he had a percentile rank of 98, it means that Jesse's performance was higher or equal to 98% of the comparison group or the group for which the test was normed. It does not indicate a raw score; that is, it does not show that Jesse had a 98% or had 98 test items out of 100 correct.

Grade-equivalent score. Another way of reporting a student's performance on a standardized achievement test is through the use of a **grade-equivalent score.** If Jesse received a grade-equivalent score of 7.5 on a reading test, most people would interpret that Jesse is reading at the seventh-grade, fifth-month level. Misinterpretations of the grade-equivalent scores result from not realizing that these scores are very rough approximations, resulting from statistical estimates. The score does not mean that Jesse, a second-grade student, reads like a seventh grader or with the same strategies used by most seventh graders. To know whether Jesse reads like a seventh grader, one would need to observe Jesse's responses to typical seventh-grade text. How does he talk and write about what he reads? Because grade-equivalent scores have led to much confusion and misinterpretations, some publishers no longer use this type of test result.

Types of Standardized Tests

In the United States, standardized testing is approximately one century old. Over the years, the types of standardized tests have changed as a result of changing educational objectives. Most children in schools experience these tests as early as the first and second grades and some even in kindergarten. For many children, the majority of standardized tests taken in Grades 4 and higher are achievement tests. **Achievement tests** are **norm-referenced tests,** and they can be used to compare the performances. How did the child perform with reference to the group of children in the same grade that the test was normed? For reading achievement tests, norm-referenced instruments are broad, not providing information on a child's specific strengths and weaknesses. Another type of standardized test that is administered by some schools is the **criterion-referenced test.** The purpose of criterion-referenced tests is to determine how well students do in certain skill areas that are aligned to test objectives. Restricted to measuring skill areas, the test reveals a child's mastery of specific skills, usually associated with the grade level for which the test was designed. A third type of standardized test is the **diagnostic test** that is meant to target specific areas of weaknesses. In many cases, diagnostic tests are administered individually and to children who are experiencing reading problems.

Involving Families: When effective teachers share standardized tests with parents, they present them as one piece of information that reveals a child's development and achievement. Along with standardized test results, the teacher demonstrates to parents what the child has learned in relation to the benchmarks set by the school or district. When teachers keep portfolios on children's progress throughout the year, parents acquire a better understanding of the work that was accomplished throughout the year.

Problems With Standardized Tests

Standardized tests are used widely in schools across the nation as a means of demonstrating accountability, of monitoring, and for placement. They provide accountability to the public by showing how schools are performing and how programs are working. Indeed, parents and society have the right to know how well their children and schools are performing. Although formal measures of evaluation are necessary, administrators, teachers, parents, students, politicians, and the community need to be vigilant about attaching too much weight to standardized scores, or using these scores as the sole measure of accountability. Test results are a part of the big picture, and all stakeholders who are truly concerned about the welfare of their children and the efficacy of the school need to look at the other pieces of information supplied by a variety of informal assessment measures.

Problems with standardized tests for young children. Whereas there are many problems associated with formal assessment instruments, one major concern that all early childhood teachers need to consider is that they are grade-level measurements. When a test evaluates children's performance on grade-level content or skills, it does not consider the development of each child. That is, all children at the first-grade level must take the standardized reading test that was developed and normed specifically for that grade. However, there are some children who may not be able to read first-grade material designated for the test. The use of grade-level tests is a concept tied to a grade-level curriculum—a one-size-fits-all curriculum. Its use does not take into account the wide range of literacy stages within the grade.

There are other criticisms aimed at relying on standardized tests solely to monitor children's language and literacy development:

- If the standardized test becomes the only measure of accountability, teachers teach to the test, bypassing the language and literacy needs of children. Rather than a child-centered curriculum, the curriculum becomes test centered.
- The reliance on standard measures administered once a year offers little if any useful information in tracking the language and literacy growth of children.
- For second language learners, traditional assessment techniques are inconsistent with classroom practices that promote language learning (Moya & O'Malley, 1994), and such tests rarely follow the natural growth of children who are learning a new language (Bartolome, 1998).
- Another group of children who are tested with standardized literacy achievement tests are young children with special needs. As the nation's classrooms become more inclusive, accommodating special populations, we find that children with special needs are included in the same assessment programs as regular education students. Young children with special needs do not have the same learning needs, yet frequently, at the end of the school year, they are assessed with the same standardized achievement test that their regular peers take. Cooper and Kiger (2001) warn that there are many assessment practices currently used do not accommodate the needs of special learners. Because of the variety of needs of special learners, teachers must be aware that there is no one test that fits all learning needs.

It is true that in time there may be increased use of standardized tests for accountability measures. As with all instruction and assessment, educators need to be knowledgeable about the types of tests that are being used. This note of caution applies especially with the *way* the assessment results may be used. Jalongo (2000) warns teachers and administrators not to put too much stock into one test. "The important thing to remember about assessment is this: never make a major decision using one small bit of information. One test score may tell us something, but it doesn't tell very much" (p. 316).

Informal Assessment in Early Childhood Education

Recently, many terms have been used to describe informal assessment. Each of the terms on the following list has been used under the guise of informal assessment: *authentic assessment, naturalistic assessment, classroom assessment, performance-based assessment,* and *portfolio assessment.*

Authentic assessment is the term we will use to describe what teachers do in the classroom on a daily basis as they gather and collect multiple forms of data to describe and document children's literacy growth and development. The evidence that is collected is inclusive and appears in multiple forms because it represents children's varied ways of using language, written and spoken. Because there are many different ways in which children can use language and the language arts, teachers adapt their assessment programs to the ways children learn. An authentic assessment program goes beyond collecting data about children's language learning. (1) Assessment becomes a systematic method for documenting and monitoring children's progress. (2) Teachers use the assessment results to inform their own teaching. For example, a teacher may reflect: "What made Jaime so frustrated? How can I help him tomorrow in guided reading? Tony and Marya need more word-solving strategies. Which ones can be of benefit to them?" (3) Observing language learners, or kidwatching, as Goodman (1985) refers to it, leads teachers to a deeper understanding of how children acquire language and use language effectively. Although they have read about the theoretical foundations of language, kidwatching makes the theories come alive. (4) Assessment of children in authentic contexts provides a concrete way of talking about their progress to the children and their parents. (5) Authentic assessment permits teachers to be responsive to the developmental differences among children, to their special needs and learning styles, and to language and cultural differences. With authentic assessment there is no one-size-fits-all approach to assessing children, because teachers select the assessment based on the child's development.

Techniques used in informal assessment. Within the design of an efficient assessment program, organization is built in, because time is a commodity that is rare within all classrooms. As teachers begin to think about conducting ongoing assessment of all the children, there are three questions they need to raise: How do I acquire the data about children's progress so that it is as authentic or as natural as possible without being intrusive? How do I record the data efficiently to provide documentation of children's growth and learning? How do I organize the data so that is easily accessible for use? These three questions lead the teacher to identify the following tasks as part of a well-balanced assessment program: (1) gathering data on children's language and literacy behaviors and performances; (2) documenting children's language and literacy growth and development; and (3) organizing the data for accurately describing children's literacy growth and for informing instruction.

How do teachers acquire the data about children's progress in authentic and natural ways? Teachers of young children learn very soon that assessment in early childhood settings is a critical role in which they need to engage to promote optimum learning in all children. Although this task may seem overwhelming at first, a successful way to begin is to think of assessment as having three processes: the process of **gathering data,** the process of **documenting learning,** and the process of **organizing data for use.**

One of the most effective ways that teachers in early childhood settings gather data about the children's language and literacy development and learning is through **observation.** Jaggar (1985) posits that it is only with a thorough knowledge of children and of language and how it develops within a child that we can create rich language environments. Such language environments that are child centered and target their development need to be designed for the specific needs and interests of the students. Therefore, careful observation that is focused on children's oral language as well as their literacy—reading and writing—is how teachers monitor children's progress.

Being a kidwatcher or observing children speak and listen in a variety of settings, formal and informal, will allow educators to determine how children use language. While children are in the playground or at the learning centers, gathered around for a shared reading or sitting enjoying a snack, the teacher can obtain rich data to understand how a child is reaching the oral language benchmarks.

The process of observing children for monitoring literacy growth is also a valuable tool. During a story retelling by a child, the teacher not only listens to what the child is saying but also observes the child's gestures and other aspects of language to assess the child's growth. Within the context of guided reading, the teacher uses observation skills as he gathers data on the child's literacy behaviors such as tracking print during reading, turning pages, or simply knowing where a story begins. Observation is indeed the most important tool needed to gather the data to monitor children's progress that will lead to important decisions about the child and her teaching.

How do teachers record the data efficiently to provide documentation of children's growth and learning? This second process related to assessment—documentation—demands an efficient system for recording observations of language and literacy behaviors and analysis of the child's work. Good teachers have always observed children as they used language; what they failed to do was to systematically document students' language and literacy behaviors. For the busy teacher who is monitoring 20 or more students' growth in language and literacy, the system for documentation must be one that will fit into the busy classroom routines. Without a quick and efficient way to record observations or to analyze children's work, the teacher will not embark on this critical aspect of instruction. Ways to record observations of children's oral language growth and literacy progress will be demonstrated in Parts II and III of this textbook, within the context of instruction.

Observations of language and literacy occur within the context of the classroom, the playground, cafeteria, and so on. For example, as children play, the teacher may be focusing on the language exchanges that are taking place to determine the functions of language that are being used. The teacher may use an **annotated checklist** that provides a focus for his observation as well as an opportunity to write additional contextual information that he may use later when interpreting and understanding the child's use of language.

There are many different ways to use annotated checklists to document observations. In addition to observing children's oral language, the teacher may use the annotated checklist to record written or oral retellings of a story by children. Another way to document children's literacy development with an annotated checklist is during guided reading. Here the teacher observes the children's oral reading behaviors and records their developing strategy use. The checklist guides the teacher in looking for specific strategies to observe while the children are reading. Annotations to the checklist provide for a richer description of how the child uses a specific strategy. In Part II and Part III of the text we will demonstrate the use of annotated checklists to document children's language and literacy growth.

Oftentimes children's performances in reading and writing need to be analyzed. In addition to the observation of children during the reading process or while they are writing, teachers will have work samples of children's performances. For example, during guided writing or writers' workshop children may write stories or informational pieces. Their works are artifacts that may provide rich data to show children's literacy writing achievements. One way to document their growth is to use

writing rubrics that are specifically designed for the development of the writer and for the type of writing that is being analyzed. Rubrics allow for a clear understanding of the expectations for students' performances on specific literacy tasks and may be used in guiding assessment for a greater understanding of children's development.

How do teachers organize the data so that is easily accessible for use? When documenting the literacy growth of each child within a class of 20 or more children, teachers may become overwhelmed by the amount of paperwork. Having a system to collect the data will allow them to store the data safely in an organized way, to reflect on the assessment results, to discuss children's progress with parents and other professionals, and to interpret the results so they may be used in refining the literacy program. Using a system of **portfolio assessment** will lead to a systematic approach to documenting each child's literacy growth over time.

Many teachers confuse portfolios with work folders used to store children's work samples or artifacts. Using literacy portfolios is a process that implies an approach to assessment that is dynamic and developmental. As a method of assessment, teachers use the literacy portfolio as more than just a container or a warehouse to store children's work. Whereas the literacy portfolio will hold multiple sources of evidence that can be used to track language and literacy development, it becomes a tool that enables the teacher to systematically create a **portrait** of each child's literacy development over a period. Further, the portfolio will be useful for the teacher's reflective practice. That is, the teacher's reflections on children's attempts at language and literacy may lead to a greater understanding of the language and literacy processes that children use and may provide insights into the practices they use with young children. Finally, using the portfolio to collaborate with parents about their children's growth is a wonderful tool to make explicit the children's progress. In short, the conversation around the portfolio allows teachers to talk in concrete terms that parents are more apt to understand.

The last chapter of this book will review a model of a child's portfolio. Although each portfolio reflects individual differences—that is, the child's specific needs and development as well as the resources available to the teacher—the sample portfolio is a model intended to help readers design authentic portfolios for use in different contexts.

Discussion Questions and Activities

1. As a teacher of young children, you will observe that children come to school knowing some of the basic concepts of print. Observe 3- and 4-year-olds in a preschool or an elementary school setting during literacy time. Focus on the concepts of print they have acquired and the concepts they are developing through the literacy experience.
2. In this chapter, we have discussed some of the fundamental concepts about teaching young children to read that teachers need to know. Observe a first-grade classroom teacher during a guided reading session. Report to the class how the teacher demonstrated knowledge of these concepts, according to your observations.
3. Observe a small group of children using language. Describe their interactions. Why were they using language?
4. Why is it important to have an ongoing assessment program in early childhood classrooms?

Additional Web Sites

ERIC Clearinghouse on Reading, English, & Communication
http://www.indiana.edu/~eric_rec/
This site has links to assessment sites.

ERIC/EECE Clearinghouse on Elementary and Early Childhood Education
http://ericeece.org/pubs/digests/1999/katzle99.html
This site provides a full article to read by Lillian Katz titled "Another Look at What Young Children Should Be Learning."

NCTE/IRA Standards for the English Language Arts
http://www.ncte.org/standards/
The site offers the English/language arts standards developed jointly by IRA and NCTE.

Understanding Authentic Classroom-Based Literacy Assessment
http://www.eduplace.com/rdg/res/litass/
Read about authentic assessment at this site.

Additional Readings

Campbell, R. (2001). *Read-alouds with young children.* Newark, DE: International Reading Association.

Clay, M. M. (2000). *Concepts about print: What have children learned about the way we print?* Portsmouth, NH: Heinemann.

Cochran-Smith, M. (1984). *The making of a reader.* Norwood, NJ: Ablex.

Iversen, S., & Reeder, T. (1998). *Organizing for a literacy hour: Quality learning and teaching time.* Bothell, WA: The Wright Group.

Peregoy, S. (2001). *Reading, writing and learning in ESL: A resource book for K–12 teachers* (3rd ed.). Boston: Allyn & Bacon.

Stanovich, K. E., & Beck, I. (2000). *Progress in understanding reading.* New York: Guilford Press.

Taberski, S. (2000). *On solid ground: Strategies for teaching reading K–3.* Portsmouth, NH: Heinemann.

Additional Children's Literature

Ackerman, K. (1988). *Song and dance man.* New York: Knopf.

Baylor, B. (1976). *Hawk, I'm your brother.* New York: Scribner's.

Havill, J. (1989). *Jamaica tag along.* Boston: Houghton Mifflin.

McCloskey, R. (1948). *Blueberries for Sal.* New York: Viking Press.

Yep, L. (1989). *The rainbow people.* New York: Harper & Row.

Children's Literature References

Brett, J. (1989). *The mitten.* New York: Scholastic.

Cowley, J. (1999). *Mrs. Wishy-Washy.* New York: Philomel.

dePaola, T. (1973). *Charlie needs a cloak.* New York: Scholastic.

PART II

Oral Language Development in Young Children

CHAPTER 3

Linking Oral Language, Literacy Instruction, and Assessment for the Emergent Literacy Stage

Portrait of an Early Childhood Literacy Program

It's early morning in Ana Garcia's kindergarten room. Luis, Tommy, Carl, and Lucia are in the drama corner sitting around the kitchen table. Ms. Garcia has placed takeout menus from local restaurants in the play area and the children are using the props to order their supper. Luis asks his playmates, "So what are you gonna order today . . . hurry up!" Tommy responds, "I'll have some wonton soup and tortillas." Lucia quickly speaks up, "Tommy, you can't do that. Wonton soup doesn't come with tortillas." "Yes it does," says Tommy. "You can get it at the Spanish and Chinese restaurant on North Avenue." Carl, playing the server, scribbles on a pad as if to write down the order and the children proceed with their multicultural supper.

Early childhood classrooms are ripe with such exchanges every day and at every moment. In this chapter, we will explore how to build upon the foundation of oral language to facilitate growth in literacy. A discussion of the continuum from oracy to literacy will be presented as the rationale for a program centered in oral language. Instructional strategies and assessment tools to implement this oracy-to-literacy program for the emergent reader will follow. The chapter will conclude with another portrait from Ana Garcia's kindergarten classroom to illustrate how the instructional strategies and assessment tools are used.

As you read Chapter 3, reflect on the following topics:

- How you can develop oral language for the child at the emergent stage of literacy
- How benchmarks within the emergent stage of oral language development help you to think about how oracy and oral language skills develop in children
- How instruction and assessment are aligned for oral language at the emergent stage
- How the teacher may connect oral language activities and writing

From Oracy to Literacy: The Emergent Literacy Stage of Development

Oracy is the ability to speak and listen fluently.

The literacy process begins at birth with the child's immersion in the language of the home (Clay, 1972; Teale & Sulzby, 1986). As infants and toddlers engage in word play with their caretakers, they are learning the symbolic nature of language (Berk, 1995). Gradually, as they become more aware of their environment, young children begin to recognize that print also has meaning. Their conceptions of the world around them are constructed through oral language. **Oracy,** which is fluency in listening and speaking, is developed through immersion in a rich oral language environment (Harris & Hodges, 1995). It is through oral language that a young child builds conceptual frameworks in order to explore the world through the use of language (Wilkinson, 1984). Early childhood classrooms that offer a rich, diverse oral language environment facilitate the construction of conceptual knowledge. The language worlds of young children are diverse, with some children exposed to daily storytelling routines whereas other children are bereft of books. Some children are given direct guidance in literacy activities whereas others receive informal assistance. This diversity of language environments is illustrated in the students of early childhood classrooms and their range of ability levels.

The early childhood teacher recognizes that the child brings prior knowledge of language and literacy into the literacy program. For example, children who have gone grocery shopping with their parents are able to recognize environmental print signs such as *Kraft Macaroni & Cheese* and to understand the function of grocery lists. It is through daily conversations with their caretakers that children broaden their conceptual knowledge base and are exposed to new vocabulary (Clay, 1998).

Halliday (1982) described how this developmental process occurs, stating that there are three interrelated aspects:

- **Learning language.** Children interact with adults and other children to construct their own language system using the symbols and functions of oral language.
- **Learning through language.** Children use language in their school and community to learn about the world and deepen their knowledge base.
- **Learning about language.** As children use language they learn the nature and forms language can assume such as jokes, puns, and riddles.

The early childhood teacher builds upon this process through daily literacy activities. As the child enters the early childhood classroom, finger plays, nursery

The daily read aloud helps children to internalize language.

rhymes, and class discussions aid children in furthering their knowledge of language systems (Halliday, 1982). Learning the rules and structures of oral language is necessary to the development of emergent literacy. A developmentally appropriate early childhood classroom integrates reading, writing, listening, and speaking (Snow, Burns, & Griffin, 1999).

Scaffolding Oral Language in an Early Childhood Literacy Program

Oral language is the cornerstone of literacy learning. As children interact with their peers and teachers, they are using language to construct knowledge of the world around them (Vygotsky, 1986). Instructional strategies that integrate speaking, listening, reading, and writing help to strengthen skills in all the language arts (Loban, 1963). In Loban's classic study, he discovered a strong relationship between oral language abilities and literacy. For example, Loban's research indicated that children with weak oral language abilities had difficulties developing their literacy skills.

Emergent literacy is the developmental period when children begin to link oral language and printed text (Fountas & Pinnell, 1996). As children engage in meaningful literacy activities guided by their parents and teachers, they learn how language functions (Rogoff, 1990; Wells, 1990). Interactive literacy events such as the daily read-aloud have been found to be the single most important activity to build literacy in emergent readers (Bus, van Iizendoorn & Pellegrini, 1995). It is through the daily read-aloud that children begin to internalize literary language and story genres.

Choral readings of patterned books can also be used to develop phonemic awareness. Why is this simple instructional activity so powerful? Literacy is modeled for the children as they begin to internalize the behaviors of engaged readers.

Daily songs, choral readings, or nursery rhymes facilitate linguistic awareness. **Linguistic awareness** is the ability to use one's knowledge of sounds and syntax while reading (Harris & Hodges, 1995). Recitation of nursery rhymes or playing with sounds enables the young child to hear differences in phonemes, which is the precursor of phonemic awareness, or knowledge of sounds. Research has shown phonemic awareness to be an early indicator of reading achievement (Maclean, Bryant, & Bradley, 1987).

Phonemic awareness demonstrates that the child can segment the sounds he hears. Research has shown that differences in phonological sensitivity are related to the rate of acquisition of reading skills (National Research Council, 2001). An interesting new finding is that children with a large vocabulary are better able to segment sounds (Burgess & Lonigan, 1998; Lonigan, Burgess, & Anthony, 2000).

Involving Parents: If parents are not able to read in English, encourage them to read in their native language to their child or to tell family stories using photographs.

One instructional method for increasing children's oral vocabulary is dialogic reading.

Dialogic reading shifts control to the child (Whitehurst & Lonigan, 1998). During storytime, the parent or teacher becomes an active listener, giving prompts or asking questions. The child acts as storyteller responding to prompts about the pictures (National Research Council, 2001). Dialogic reading has been found to produce larger effects on reading and to create positive changes for language development in children across socioeconomic groups (Lonigan, Anthony, Bloomfield, Dyer, & Samwel, 1999; Whitehurst & Lonigan, 1998).

The discourse patterns of question and response that characterize dialogic reading help the child to function in school activities (Watson, 2001). Other discourse activities such as show and tell require young children to describe their object, provide definitions, and interpret responses. The ability to define and interpret

Dialogic reading prepares children for school discourse.

as well as to discuss prepare the child for the cognitive and literacy skills of elementary school (Watson, 2001).

Early childhood classrooms reflect the diverse language worlds of its students. Approximately 50% of school-aged children are English language learners (Cooper & Kiger, 2001). Research has demonstrated that second language learners succeed when they have a strong foundation in their first language (Cummins, 1979). Therefore, early childhood classrooms should attempt to supply materials in the child's first language to facilitate proficiency (Krashen & Biber, 1988). Research has also shown that respect and maintenance of the child's native culture will further aid second language learning (Ching, 1976).

In addition to second language learners, early childhood classrooms also have children with special needs such as hearing impairments or attention-deficit disorder (ADD). Research has shown that children with special needs also benefit from a language-rich environment that integrates the language arts (D'Alessandro, 1990). However, children with special needs will also need special accommodations to facilitate their language learning.

In summary, a strong early childhood literacy program builds upon a foundation in oral language. Literacy activities that integrate oral language, listening, reading, and writing strengthen the child's growing awareness of language and its uses.

Developmental Benchmarks for Oral Language at the Emergent Literacy Stage

This chapter demonstrates how early childhood teachers can use simple daily literacy activities to help facilitate students' development of emergent literacy benchmarks. Assessment tools to document students' growth and to inform practice are also included. Table 3.1 shows the developmental benchmarks for oral language learning at the emergent literacy level.

Table 3.1
Oral Language Developmental Benchmarks at the Emergent Literacy Level

Language Habits	Enjoyment of Language	Use of Literary Language
Can be understood by peers and adults	Enjoys tongue twisters	Uses book language heard from storybooks
Asks questions	Repeats and uses new words	Can retell a story in sequence
Identifies sentences that do not sound correct	Asks what new words mean	Enjoys making a play from a story
Follows rules for conversation	Adds words to knowledge domain	Can tell a story to go with a picture (one or two events)
Participates during sharing time and can state what others have said	Enjoys word play and idioms	Identifies a favorite book and tells why he likes it
Retains simple oral directions	Identifies rhymes	Orients listener to narrative by providing setting, characters
		Can talk about favorite storybook character

Using Technology: Learn about standards for literacy and language by using the Web sites for the International Reading Association (http://www.ira.org) and the National Association for the Education of Young Children (http://www.naeyc.org).

It is during the period of emergent literacy that both the adult and the child take active roles in the construction of literacy (Soderman, Gregory, & O'Neill, 1999). Through the process of modeling, shared literacy experiences, and guided practice, emergent readers and writers move toward independent practice. The following section describes the emergent literacy behaviors that are scaffolded by more capable language users during this period (Cooper & Kiger, 2001; Fountas & Pinnell, 1996; New Standards Speaking and Listening Committee, 2001).

Language Habits

Amy and Alston are intently looking at the shells Amy has brought in to class. "Do you like my shells, Alston?" Amy asks. "Yeah, they're okay," Alston replies. "I went to the beach this weekend," Amy says. "I hope I get to share them during circle time." "No, I think we're gonna look at our caterpillars," replies Alston.

Children at the emergent literacy level have internalized conversational rules such as turn taking. However, they are still developing the acquired skill of responding and building upon their conversational partner's remarks. For example, both Alston and Amy were more intent on their own thoughts than each other's comments. Children at the emergent literacy level are also still making grammatical errors, as evidenced in Alston's speech.

Enjoyment of Language

It is Wednesday morning in Ms. Garcia's kindergarten room. She is gathering the children together for one of their favorite games, Silly Rhyme Time. The children are gathered in a circle and they throw a ball of yarn to each other. When they release the ball, they say a word and the catcher must reply with a matching rhyme. "Okay, Jenny starts us off," says Ms. Garcia. "I know a good one—tub," Jennifer says as she throws the ball to Sammy. "Flub," responds Sammy. "Just like Flubber!" yells out Jose. All the children begin to laugh.

Young children enjoy playing with rhymes and especially like to create their own words. This simple game, Silly Rhyme Time, helps the children to construct their knowledge of patterns and sounds. As they develop their knowledge of new words, children begin to understand idioms such as "It's raining cats and dogs."

Use of Literary Language

Ana Garcia has just finished reading one of the children's favorite stories, *Make Way for Ducklings.* In the library corner, Ms. Garcia has placed props for the children such as a police officer's cap and a stop sign. James and Evan decide to get construction paper to make hats. "You can be the mother duck," says James. "I don't want to be the mother," snaps Evan. "I want to be the cop! Let's get Kelly to be the mom." The children create their hats and decide something is missing. "Wait—we forgot the sign for the park. What was it called again?" asks James. "Boston Common," replies Kelly. The children are ready to begin their skit and James narrates, "Once there was a family of ducklings . . . "

The children's impromptu skit of *Make Way for Ducklings* (1941) demonstrates their retention of its plot and main characters. As they created their props for the skit, the children demonstrated their knowledge of the setting for the story which was Boston Common. The interconnectedness of daily read-alouds and oral language is evidenced by the children's use of literary phrasing. The pupils in Ms. Garcia's kindergarten class have internalized literary language such as "Once there was . . . " which is so often the beginning phrase of picture books for children.

Modeling Oral Language for the Emergent Literacy Stage

As children at the emergent literacy level are immersed in a language-rich environment, they begin to engage in literacy behaviors. Children learn first to approximate these behaviors through engaging in literacy activities guided by a more competent language user (Rogoff, 1990; Wells, 1990). As literacy behaviors are modeled, children feel more confident to attempt them under the coaching or scaffolding of the teacher.

This section presents literacy activities for modeling strategies for the emergent reader. The instructional strategies focus on two categories of developmental benchmarks, **enjoyment of language** and **literary language.** The purpose of the activities is to help young children enjoy word play and create rhymes as well as increase oral vocabulary (see Table 3.1). Developmental benchmarks for use of literary language such as using book language and discussing favorite storybook characters are also targeted in the instructional strategies presented in the following section.

Instructional Strategies

Finger plays. Finger plays and nursery rhymes are wonderful ways to improve children's listening skills and phonemic awareness (Miller, 2000). Another purpose for incorporating these activities is to improve oral language skills due to the ease of mimicking the word patterns or repeated refrains (Miller).

Meeting Diverse Needs: Ask the English language learners what finger plays or songs they learned at home or in their previous country. Encourage them to share them with the class.

Teachers may choose to use the more familiar finger plays such as "The Itsy Bitsy Spider" or "Here's the Church, Here's the Steeple" (Sawyer & Sawyer, 1993). As teachers become more experienced with finger plays, they can easily change the lyrics to reflect any theme or holiday the children are studying. Young children enjoy playing with sounds by creating nonsense words and their own versions of songs or poems. The ability to manipulate sounds is the hallmark of phonemic awareness.

Rain

Rain on the green grass,
And rain on the tree,
And rain on the housetop,
But not upon me!

(Anonymous)

Acting out stories helps children to internalize literary language.

Way Down South

Way down South where bananas grow,
A grasshopper stepped on an elephant's toe.
The elephant said, with tears in his eyes,
"Pick on somebody your own size."

(Anonymous)
(Prelutsky, 1986)

Before modeling the finger play, the teacher should first read the words to the children and point to each one on a chart. If possible, icons such as an elephant trunk for *elephant* would help to develop sight word recognition. Another extension activity for finger plays is underlining the rhyming word patterns and then having the children create their own rhymes.

Nursery rhymes. It is important to begin with more familiar nursery rhymes such as "Hickory Dickory Dock" to increase the children's self-confidence and to encourage them to create their own rhyming substitutions. The rhymes can also be clapped out to facilitate the emergent reader's ability to segment sounds, which facilitates phonemic awareness. The ability to segment sounds is an important component of early phonics instruction.

Hickory Dickory Dock

Hickory Dickory Dock
The mouse ran up the clock
The clock struck one, the mouse ran down
Hickory Dickory Dock

Chalk talk. A chalk talk is a wonderful way to model storytelling through the use of pictures (Morrow, 1997). The story is told orally by the teacher through pictures that are drawn on a chalkboard or an easel (see Figure 3.1). Stories such as *The Very Hungry Caterpillar* (Carle, 1969) or *The Giving Tree* (Silverstein, 1986) are

1. Choose a book and decide which scenes to include in your chalk talk.
2. Write out your script and draw pictures for scenes.
3. Practice telling the story while you draw on the board or easel.

Figure 3.1
How to Do a Chalk Talk

excellent choices for a chalk talk. As the children become more acquainted with chalk talks, they can also construct their own if materials are available in the library corner.

Assessment Strategies for Modeling Oral Language

The instructional strategies previously discussed can be used to document children's literacy progress. This section will describe how observational checklists and anecdotal records can be used to identify children's progress toward the developmental benchmarks.

Assessment of Oral Language Behaviors During Finger Plays and Chalk Talks

In early childhood education, it is imperative that the teacher responds to each child's instructional needs (Bowman, Donovan, & Burns, 2000). One way for a teacher to develop a curriculum focused on the child is to assess the child in a naturalistic context (Bowman et al., 2000). As the children complete finger plays or pocket charts, a teacher can choose one child a day to observe closely and to collect data on his performance. Tables 3.2 and 3.3 show examples of observational checklists that may be used based on the developmental benchmarks.

Knowledge of developmental benchmarks helps early childhood teachers to record their students' journey along the literacy continuum. A balanced literacy program integrates both formal and informal assessment methods (Cooper, 2000). One informal technique is an anecdotal record. Anecdotal records describe what the student did and interpret the literacy action. Anecdotal records can be used to document improvements in reading and writing behaviors throughout the year (Tombari & Borich, 1999). A simple technique is to keep index cards at the ready to jot down important literacy events. Here is an example of an anecdotal record:

Name: Edwin Jones *Class: Kindergarten*

Date: October 20

Event: During the recitation of "The Duke of York" *nursery rhyme, Edwin volunteered to lead the class. He pointed to each word, left to right progression as he read the words from memory. His recitation was slightly ahead of the text.*

Interpretation: Edwin is on the brink of taking off! He is excited about reading and is approximating literacy behaviors. Edwin is relying solely on sight word knowledge and needs to use more decoding strategies to attend to print.

Kidwatching (Goodman, 1986) occurs when teachers record literacy behaviors as the children engage in authentic literacy tasks. Because finger plays, nursery rhymes, and morning roster routines are daily literacy formats, as the child enters the emergent literacy phase, anecdotal records are necessary to record their continual growth. Due to time constraints, teachers may choose to focus on only one child a day and collect observations in a systematic fashion.

Table 3.2
Assessment of Oral Language Behaviors During Finger Plays

Directions: Use the following rubrics while observing students during finger play activities.

Rating Scale for Finger Plays

Benchmarks for Oral Language	Target	Acceptable	Needs Improvement
Enjoys tongue twisters	Engages in and enjoys tongue twisters	Enjoys tongue twisters but does not participate	Does not participate or enjoy this activity
Repeats and uses new words	Is able to identify new words and use them orally in a sentence	Is able to identify new words but only sometimes uses them in a sentence	Cannot identify new words and does not use them in oral language
Identifies rhymes	Is able to identify rhymes	Sometimes is able to identify rhymes	Is still unable to identify rhyming words

Table 3.3
Assessment of Oral Language Behaviors During Chalk Talks

Rating Scale for Chalk Talks

Benchmarks for Oral Language	Level 3	Level 2	Level 1
Uses book language heard from storybooks	Participates in discussions and uses storybook language	Enjoys discussions but only sometimes uses book language	Does not participate or enjoy this activity
Retells a story in sequence	Is able to tell a story in complete sequence	Is able to partially retell a story but it may be missing some events	Cannot retell the story in sequence
Enjoys making a play from a story	Is able to create his own play to perform	Creates an incomplete play from a story	Is still unable to create a play from a story
Talks about favorite characters	Enjoys discussing favorite characters	Sometimes participates and describes favorite characters	Cannot describe favorite characters

Comments:

Shared Oral Language Experiences for the Emergent Literacy Stage

As discussed in Chapter 1, Vygotsky's theory of scaffolded instruction focused on a learning continuum. The teacher is careful to select activities that are in the child's zone of proximal development. The zone of proximal development is the problem-solving ability of the child under the assistance of a more capable peer or teacher

1. Choose a book the students have heard before.
2. Start the children by reading the first page. Then give the prompt "What's this?" on the next page.
3. Expand on the children's responses by providing new vocabulary words.
4. As the story proceeds, the teacher lets the children take over the storytelling.

Figure 3.2
How to Do Storytelling

(Vygotsky, 1978, 1986). Scaffolded instruction provides a model for the child and then challenges the child to perform the task under the guidance of his teacher, parent, or more capable peer. The following instructional strategies help the young child to develop his blossoming oral language abilities and to facilitate the development of all three benchmark categories.

Developmental benchmarks for **language habits** such as asking and responding to questions, participating during sharing time, and following rules for discussions will be targeted in the proceeding instructional strategies. Oral language behaviors such as using new vocabulary words and creating stories from illustrations, from the enjoyment of language and use of literary language developmental benchmarks checklist (review Table 3.1) will also be emphasized.

Instructional Strategies

Dialogic storytelling. Dialogic storytelling can be done with picture books or transparencies of illustrations from storybooks. During dialogic storytelling, the teacher acts as coach, prompting students with questions or hints. The children provide the narrative to accompany the pictures. Early childhood teachers often take Polaroid pictures or use a digital camera to record class events or trips (see Figure 3.2). These pictures can also be used for dialogic storytelling or wordless picture books. It is best to choose a storybook that the children have heard before so that a literary conversation can take place (National Research Council, 2001).

Rhyme time. Engaging in word play is an important activity for the young child. Constant exposure to different vocabulary words will facilitate development of **phonological sensitivity** which is the ability to segment sounds (Neumann & Dickinson, 2001). Rhyme time is a simple routine that can become a daily activity.

Teachers recite a song or poem which the students can use to clap out the sounds (Heilman, 2002). For example, the perennial playground chant "Miss Mary Mack" can be used:

Miss Mary Mack, Mack, Mack,
All dressed in black, black, black,
With silver buttons, buttons, buttons,
All down her back, back, back

After the clapping activity, the teacher can ask the following questions: Which words had the same sounds? Can you make your own words to rhyme with these? Gradually, the students begin to recognize word patterns and enjoy playing with sounds. This will facilitate the development of phonological sensitivity, or the ability to hear sounds in oral language.

Assessment Strategies for Shared Oral Language Experiences

It is important to document the young child's progress in developing the benchmarks for oral language at the emergent literacy level. As activities become increasingly challenging, the teacher needs data to determine the boundaries of the child's zone of proximal development. The checklists shown in Figures 3.3 and 3.4 can be used to assess the child's progress for shared oral language activities such as dialogic storytelling and rhyme time.

Guided Oral Language Activities for the Emergent Literacy Stage

It is during the guided phase of scaffolded instruction that the teacher acts as coach. The role of the teacher in the following activity is to facilitate the child's oral language skills. Therefore, the teacher follows the child's lead and offers prompts or elaborates on the child's language attempts.

This section discusses instructional strategies that target developmental benchmarks from the language habits and enjoyment of language categories (Table 3.1). These activities emphasize word play and creating a rich oral language vocabulary. Another instructional goal is to improve the students' conversational skills so they can be understood by their peers and other adults.

Instructional Strategies

Guided conversations. Guided conversations provide children with a model for oral language skills as well as turn taking. Adults also guide the young child's burgeoning skills by elaborating on the child's comments, extending his language, and by providing new vocabulary (Miller, 2000). The early childhood classroom is ripe

Directions: Place check mark next to observed behavior.

CHECKLIST FOR DIALOGIC STORYTELLING

Benchmark Behaviors	John	Marcy	Angela	Juan	Marta
Can be understood by peers when talking					
Asks questions					
Follows rules for conversations					
Participates during discussions					
Uses book language heard from storybooks					
Tells a story to go with pictures					
Talks about favorite picture					
Can restate what others have said in discussion					

Figure 3.3
Assessment of Oral Language Behaviors During Dialogic Storytelling

for adult–child conversations. These can occur during snack time, center activities, recess, or any other time of the day. When conversing with the child, the teacher should remember the following:

1. **Focus on the child's agenda.**
2. **Speak in simple sentences so the child can understand.**
3. **Watch the child for nonverbal reactions.**
4. **If you do not understand what the child is saying, repeat it back in a nonthreatening way.**
5. **Correct errors in syntax or overgeneralization by using the correct grammatical form when you respond to the child.**

Directions: Place check mark below observed behavior. Add comments if necessary.

CHECKLIST FOR RHYME TIME ACTIVITIES

Name of Child: ***Date:***

Word Families for Activity	Rhyming Pairs—Mastered	Rhymes—Not Mastered	Comments
hat			
sit			

Figure 3.4
Assessment of Oral Language Behaviors During Rhyme Time Activities

6. Use concrete objects or the child's interests to draw out the nonverbal child.

It is important that teachers not force the children to engage in conversation. As the young child becomes more comfortable and secure in his surroundings, he will want to engage with the teacher. An exciting class event or activity is often the catalyst to draw out the shy or nonverbal child. Elaborating on the responses of the child is another excellent way to increase the child's vocabulary. For example, if the child is talking about a trip to the supermarket and remarks, "I went grocery shopping with my mom," the early childhood teacher might respond, "I love to go grocery shopping and went this weekend as well. I bought some delicious cherries. Did you buy anything special?" This provides additional vocabulary words for the child to learn and a prompt to continue the conversation.

Assessment Strategies for Guided Oral Language Activities

Observing the child during the conversation and then recording observations is one way to document the progress of the child in mastering the oral language benchmarks. Anecdotal records help the teacher to describe milestones the child accomplishes over the school year. In addition to anecdotal records, the teacher can use checklists (see Figure 3.5) to collect data on the child's progress at the emergent literacy level.

CHECKLIST FOR GUIDED CONVERSATIONS

Name of Child: ***Date:***

Benchmark Behavior	Always	Many Times	Sometimes	Rarely	Never
Can be understood by peers					
Asks questions					
Uses correct sentence structure					
Follows rules for conversations					
Participates during discussion and restates what others have said					

Comments:

Figure 3.5
Assessment of Oral Language Behaviors During Guided Conversations

Independent Oral Language Activities in Oral Language for the Emergent Literacy Stage

The final phase of scaffolded literacy instruction is independent practice. Up to this point, students have had literacy strategies modeled for them and have practiced through guided oral activities. Now, emergent readers and writers are ready to demonstrate their skills. The following strategies allow for students to demonstrate their mastery of developmental benchmarks at the emergent level.

As the young child gains confidence in his own abilities, his use of new vocabulary words and literary language begins to blossom. The strategies described in this section focus on developing oral language behaviors through independent activities. By the independent stage of the instructional cycle, the young child should be demonstrating many of the oral language behaviors presented in the developmental benchmarks checklist. Therefore, instructional goals for the following strategies will be to assess oral language behaviors such as the child's use of vocabulary, conversational skills, and engagement in word play. The following instructional strategies will target all three developmental benchmark categories: language habits, enjoyment of language, and use of literary language.

Instructional Strategies

Flannel board stories. Flannel board stories are wonderful opportunities for children to retell their favorite stories. Picture books such as *Blueberries for Sal* (McCloskey, 1948) can be used for this instructional activity. The teacher photocopies the main characters and glues the pictures to felt material. The materials are placed in the library or drama corner for the children to retell the story with their favorite characters.

Telephone. Every early childhood classroom has a plastic phone in its drama corner. A discarded cell phone can also be used as a prop for make-believe telephone conversations. This traditional early childhood activity helps the young child to practice turn taking and social discourse patterns (Miller, 2000; Watson, 2001).

Assessment Strategies for Independent Oral Language Activities

The assessment instruments shown in Table 3.4 and Figure 3.6 may be used to collect evidence of student development in oral language benchmarks. Teachers should use the data to determine if students have progressed to the next level of oral language development.

Table 3.4
Assessment of Oral Language Behaviors During Flannel Board Activities

Rating Scale for Flannel Board Activities			
Benchmarks for Oral Language	**Level 3**	**Level 2**	**Level 1**
Can be understood by peers and adults	Can be clearly understood by peers and adults	Can be understood most of the time by peers and adults	Oral language is not able to be understood
Asks questions	Is able to ask questions in class	Sometimes asks questions in class	Rarely asks questions in class
Follows rules for conversation	Is able to participate in a conversation	Sometimes follows rules for conversations	Is still unable to fully participate in a conversation
Talks about favorite characters	Enjoys discussing favorite characters	Sometimes participates and describes favorite characters	Cannot describe favorite characters

Comments:

Directions: Using your observations, record oral language behaviors demonstrated during telephone conversations.

ANECDOTAL RECORD FOR TELEPHONE CONVERSATIONS

Observation Date	Student's Name	Oral Language Benchmark Behavior	Comment

Figure 3.6
Anecdotal Record Form for Telephone Conversations

Connecting Oral Language and Emergent Writing

Classrooms that facilitate oral language are also equipping the young child with the necessary skills and conceptual knowledge for emergent literacy. A young child that is immersed in a rich oral language environment will absorb the vocabulary and sentence structure that is being used every day (Snow, Burns, & Griffin, 1998). Conversely, research has also shown that children with poor language abilities are at risk for literacy problems (Shiel, 2002).

Immersing the child in a rich oral language model will also help to scaffold the child's emergent writing. Connecting oral language with emergent writing is a natural follow-up to any instructional activity in the early childhood classroom. The young child learns through play, so linking drama corner or block activities with oral language and writing helps the emergent reader and writer to gradually understand literacy processes.

Language-oriented play activities help the young child to focus on four key areas of literacy development (Shiel, 2002):

- **Linguistic awareness**—the child gradually becomes aware of his language abilities.
- **Decontextualized language**—the child gradually understands that oral text does not have to only be dialogue.
- **Writing**—the child begins to understand that communication is possible through the written word.
- **Reading**—the child begins to "pretend" to read, which demonstrates that the child is trying to gain meaning from text.

Every day in early childhood classrooms, children and teachers are conversing about their activities or stories. This immersion in oral language is a natural connection to emergent writing. Recent research has found that the interaction between oral language and the conceptualization of writing occurs at a much younger age than previously thought (Silva & Alves-Martin, 2002).The young child begins to understand that oral language is linked to the written word even before he knows the graphophonic system.

Ferreiro (1988) studied preschool children's evolving conceptualization of writing and determined that there were three levels of understanding.

- **First level:** The child begins to differentiate between drawings and written letters. Gradually, the child begins to understand that a sequence of letters is needed to form a word.
- **Second level:** The child begins to expand his knowledge of words by exposure. This exposure may be from environmental print or daily read-alouds.
- **Third level:** Finally, the child realizes that oral language can be written down. The child begins to use inventive spelling which gradually becomes alphabetic writing. However, the child is still misspelling words.

The early childhood teacher helps children to understand the connection between oral language and the written word by recording conversations or activities. The following section describes instructional activities that help the emergent reader and writer to use oral language to improve literacy skills.

Instructional Strategies

Early childhood classrooms generally contain a block corner that is in daily use. As children construct buildings, towns, or other structures, their conversations about what they are building can be used to facilitate emergent writing. Figure 3.7 shows how to do block corner writing.

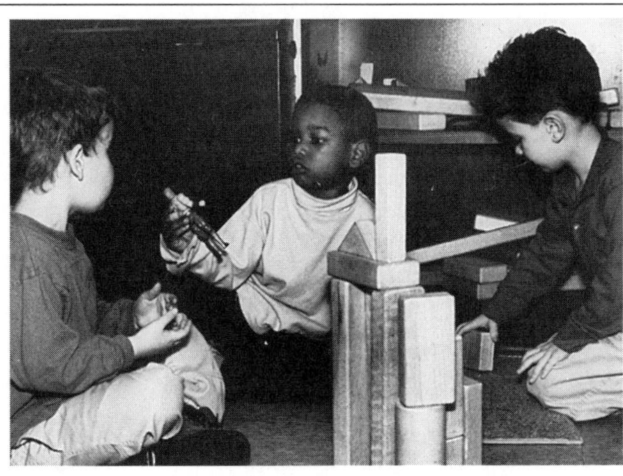

- As the children build their structures, engage them in conversation. Use open-ended questions to urge the children to elaborate.
- After the children have finished building their structures, ask what they want to say about the building and write it down. If the children do not want to verbally describe their work, they might write in a *Block Corner Journal* about the structure. The children also may choose to draw instead of write.

Figure 3.7
How to Do Block Corner Writing

Table 3.5
Assessment of Oral Language Behaviors During Block Corner Writing

Checklist for Block Corner Writing

Conceptualization of Writing	Target	Acceptable	Needs Support
First level: *The child understands that words are made from letters*			
Second level: *The child understands that words are spelled differently*			
Third level: *The child begins to use inventive spelling to record speech*			

It is important that the teacher picks up the students' cues and follows their lead in the conversation. Table 3.5 illustrates an assessment instrument that may be used for the block activity (Ferreiro, 1988).

The assessment instrument shown in Table 3.5 can easily be adapted to include oral language assessment by including the benchmarks for oral language development.

In addition to the block corner, most early childhood classrooms have daily story sessions as well as dramatic play activities. The strategies presented in Figure 3.8 describe how to integrate these early childhood routines with writing.

Another activity that uses conversation as a springboard for emergent writing is the dramatic play corner (see Figure 3.9).

The assessment instrument shown in Table 3.6 may be used to record the performance of your students in either the story discussions or dramatic play scripts activities (Shiel, 2002).

These language-oriented play activities help the young child to develop a foundation for literacy. By recording oral language activities, the emergent reader and writer begins to recognize letters and sounds, which eventually leads to the segmentation of words. This evolving conceptualization of reading and writing begins with daily play activities and conversations. It is often the simplest routines of daily classroom life that yield the most evidence of student development.

Summary of the Instructional Cycle

The instructional cycle for oral language development at the emergent literacy level is now complete. This chapter has presented oral language instructional strategies that can be used for modeled, shared, guided, and independent activities. The

- Before, during, and after the story, engage the children in a conversation about the story. Ask about their favorite part of the story or favorite characters.
- After the conversation, ask the children to summarize their opinion of the story and then record their comments on chart paper.

Figure 3.8
How to Facilitate Story Discussions

- Join the children in the dramatic play corner as they engage in a skit.
- As you observe the children, record their dialogue on paper.
- After the skit, read aloud the children's dialogue and discuss it.

* Title the skit and put it in the classroom library for independent reading.

Figure 3.9
How to Write Dramatic Play Scripts

Table 3.6
Assessment of Oral Language Behaviors During Recorded Conversations

Rating Scale for Recorded Conversations			
Outcomes	**Target**	**Acceptable**	**Needs Improvement**
Linguistic awareness	Is able to talk or write about own language use	Is partially able to talk or write about own language use	Is not yet ready to reflect on own language use
Decontextualized language	Is able to construct oral text without the support of dialogue	Can sometimes construct oral text without dialogue support	Is not able to construct oral text
Writing	Communicates meaning through drawing or writing	Communicates meaning through drawing and some writing	Communicates meaning through drawing only
Reading	Pretends to read or decodes print	Sometimes decodes print but mainly uses pictures	Uses only pictures and does not decode

Comments:

teacher decides which strategies to use based upon the assessment data. A pattern should emerge concerning each student as well as trends across the class profile. These important data are then used to shape future oral language instruction. In Figure 3.10, a master assessment checklist is shown that may be used at the end of the instructional cycle to identify class patterns of behavior.

Master Assessment

Directions: Based on your observations, place check marks next to the benchmarks demonstrated by 90% of the students in the class.

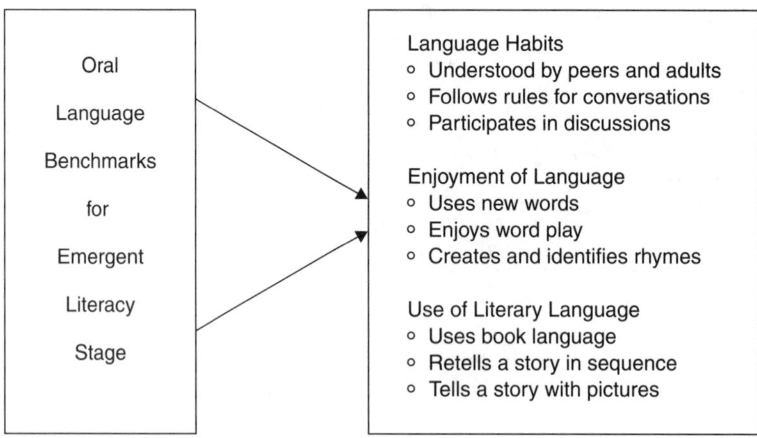

Figure 3.10
Master Assessment for Oral Language Development at the Emergent Literacy Stage

Portrait of the Instructional Cycle for Oral Language Experiences at the Emergent Literacy Level

Edwin is an inquisitive 5 year old in Ms. Garcia's kindergarten class. His energy is boundless as he moves from the block corner to the computer. Ana Garcia is focusing on Edwin's progress toward developing concepts about print. During storytime, Edwin's responses are unfocused and his attention appears to wander.

Ms. Garcia begins by using the finger play "Way Down South" to observe Edwin. He joins in on the verse and also repeats the gestures. Because it is an active lesson, Edwin's attention remains centered on the finger play. As the children leave the rug to move to the centers, Ms. Garcia notes Edwin's behavior on an index card she keeps in her pocket. She will record the entry in her assessment notebook during her free period.

On Wednesday, Edwin joins the class for a dialogic reading of *I Went Walking* (Williams, 1989). Ms. Garcia deliberately stops at the picture of the basket with a cat's tail peeking out and asks, "What do you think this is?" Edwin responds, "I don't know." "Are there any clues to help you?" Ms. Garcia prompts. "No," Edwin answers. The other students chime in that it is a cat and they can guess the answer by the cat's protruding tail. After the dialogic reading, Ms. Garcia notes on the Checklist for Dialogic Storytelling that Edwin was unable to make predictions or to use pictures to tell a story.

The following day, Ms. Garcia calls together a guided reading group, which includes Edwin, to work on making predictions. To scaffold this process, Ana uses the title, cover, and picture clues to demonstrate how to make predictions. After a discussion of the picture walk, she calls on Edwin to share his predictions for the next few pages. He is able to use the picture clues to make educated guesses, but needs more support in generating a focus question before reading.

The instructional cycle ends in the following weeks as the students finish reading *I Went Walking.* Edwin has practiced making predictions for the past 2 weeks and is ready to complete the flannel board activity in the literature center. His boundless energy is apparent as he presents his flannel board story to his peers with sound effects and prompts. Ms.Garcia records his progress on the Checklist for Flannel Board Activities after the performance and notes that Edwin has finally mastered making predictions from picture clues and is beginning to construct meaning from text.

Discussion Questions and Activities

1. Observe an emergent reader conversing in the classroom. How does the child's language sample reflect storybook language?
2. Engage in a rhyming activity with a young reader. Based upon your observations, describe how the child is developing phonemic awareness.
3. Implement the guided conversations instructional strategy. Reflect on how you followed the child's lead and extended his language.
4. Design and implement your own oral language activity and assessment for a child at the emergent literacy stage. What information did you learn about the child's language and literacy development?

Additional Web Sites

Between the Lions
http:www.pbskids.org/lions
This is a wonderful resource for teachers and parents as it provides activities to accompany the books presented in the television show.

Carol Hurst's Children Literature Site
http://www.carolhurst.com
This site provides teachers with descriptions and activities for thousands of children's books across K-8.

International Reading Association
http://www.ira.org
This site provides teachers with current news on reading methods and resources to links for further information about literacy.

National Association for the Education of Young Children
http://www.naeyc.org
This organization is the premier association for teachers of early childhood and offers wonderful resources and support.

Wallach and Wallach's Tongue Twisters
http:www.auburn.edu/~murraba/twisters.html
This site provides teachers with great tongue twisters to develop phonemic awareness.

Additional Readings

Beales, D., de Temple, J., & Dickinson, D. (1994). Talking and listening that support early literacy development of children from low-income families. In D. Dickinson (Ed.), *Bridges to literacy: Children, families and schools.* Cambridge, England: University of Cambridge Press.

Cazden, C. (1992). Play with language and metalinguistic awareness: One dimension of language experience. In *Whole language plus: Essays on literacy in the United States and New Zealand.* New York: Teachers College Press.

Snow, C. (1983). Literacy and language: Relationships during the preschool years. *Harvard Educational Review, 53*(2), 165–189.

Additional Children's Literature

Angelou, M. (1994). *My painted house, my friendly chicken and me.* New York: Clarkson N. Potter.

Canon, J. (1993). *Stellaluna.* San Diego, CA: Harcourt.

Carle, E. (1984). *The very busy spider.* New York: Philomel.

Carle, E. (1990). *The very quiet cricket.* New York: Philomel.

Dorros, A. (1991). *Abuela.* New York: Dutton.

Eastman, P. (1960). *Are you my mother?* New York: Random House.

Gag, W. (1956). *Millions of cats.* New York: Coward-McCann.

Greenfield, E. (1978, 1995). *Honey I love.* New York: HarperCollins.

Maitland, B. (2000). *Moo in the morning.* New York: Farrar Straus and Giroux.

Sturges, P. (1999). *The little red hen makes a pizza.* New York: Philomel.

Children's Literature References

Carle, E. (1969). *The very hungry caterpillar.* New York: Philomel.

McCloskey, R. (1941). Make way for ducklings. New York: Viking.

McCloskey, R. (1948). *Blueberries for Sal.* New York: Viking.

Prelutsky, J. (1986). *Read-aloud rhymes for the very young.* New York: Knopf.

Silverstein, S. (1986). *The giving tree.* New York: HarperCollins.

Williams, S. (1989). *I went walking.* New York: Harcourt.

CHAPTER 4

Linking Oral Language, Literacy Instruction, and Assessment for the Early Literacy Stage

Portrait of a Talk-Rich Classroom at the Early Literacy Stage

In Kathryn Harron's first-grade class, the students are engaged in literacy tasks during their language arts block period. One small group is meeting with Ms. Harron while other children are working on the computer. Gloria and Marianne are sitting in the library corner illustrating a storyboard for Madeline *(Bemelmans, 1939). As they draw, the girls are saying aloud, "In an old house in Paris that was covered with vines, lived twelve little girls and the youngest one was Madeline." "I know," says Gloria, "let's put Miss Clavel here by that tower Ms. Harron told us about." "Oh, you mean the Eiffel Tower," responds Marianne.*

The girls' literary conversation exhibits the vocabulary and concepts they had internalized during class discussions about books. It is during the early stage of literacy development that young children build upon their knowledge of language and the printed word. As they gain mastery of the literacy process, the early childhood teacher provides the necessary framework to increase their strategies. This chapter will discuss how to facilitate the early reader and writer's attempts to shift toward print-governed decoding of text. We will discuss how to use oral language activities to further develop the emergent literacy concepts that were begun in kindergarten and preschool. Assessment instruments to gauge students' progress will be provided as well. The chapter will conclude with another portrait from Kathryn Harron's first-grade class to illustrate the implementation of the activities and assessment tools presented in this chapter.

As you read Chapter 4, reflect on the following topics:

- How you can develop oral language for the child at the early stage of literacy
- How benchmarks within the early stage of oral language development help you to think about how oracy and oral language skills develop in children
- How instruction and assessment are aligned for oral language at the early stage
- How the teacher may connect oral language activities and writing

The Early Literacy Stage of Development

The early stage of literacy development builds upon the prior knowledge and concepts about print that the child acquired during the emergent years (Kuhn & Stahl, 2000). One way teachers recognize the transition from emergent reading to print-governed attempts is the child's reluctance to read with phrases such as, "I don't know the words" (Kaderavek & Sulzby, 1999). It is during print-governed storybook reading that early readers use their knowledge of word patterns and decoding to interact with text (Kaderavek & Sulzby). The early readers' shift toward decoding of text signals their readiness for systematic phonics instruction (Erikson, 1963). Through systematic phonics instruction students begin to group letters and to recognize phonemic patterns, thereby providing them with the tools to move toward fluency (Soderman, Gregory, & O'Neill, 1999). Children in the early stage of literacy development are becoming more skilled at cross-checking and using pictures to confirm their decoding. The early reader, through daily instruction in strategic reading, gradually gains confidence and begins to take pride in reading achievement (Taberski, 2000).

Immersion in a Talk-Rich Classroom

Besides systematic phonics instruction, the early reader also needs daily doses of **"languaging"** (Soderman et al., 1999) which is the infusion of enriched informal communication as well as instructional language. Just as the early literacy classroom must be marinated in print, it should also be immersed in rich oral language modeling.

Young children use the oral language models of their teachers to copy the teacher's use of stress, pitch, and dialect. From daily interactions with their teacher, early readers and writers begin to understand complex sentence structure and the multiple meanings of words (Soderman et al., 1999). Their use of pitch, stress, and dialect will become apparent as they shift toward fluent reading of text. Children moving toward fluency begin to use the natural phrasing of oral language to interact with the text (Kaderavek & Sulzby, 1999; Kuhn & Stahl, 2000).

A talk-rich classroom immerses the child in rich vocabulary and engages the child in conversations about various concepts.

Immersion in a talk-rich classroom helps children at the early literacy stage to acquire the necessary skills for literacy. It is important that children at this stage be exposed to a variety of talk in the classroom just as they are provided with multiple genres of

It is important to provide a talk-rich classroom and multiple genres of literature.

literature (Raban, 2001). Through classroom discourse, teachers and students construct meaning and build conceptual frameworks (Smith, 2001).

Language as a Tool for Thinking

As the young child moves toward competency in literacy, language increasingly becomes a tool for thinking (Vygotsky, 1978; Wells, 1981). Engaging in classroom conversations, role plays, or interviews empowers the student to respond to text in a novel way (Bell, 1999). As children talk about texts or experiences with their teacher or peers, new vocabulary words are used and concepts are internalized (Wells & Chang-Wells, 1993).

Peer talk about texts or experiences has been shown to increase the desire to read and to improve comprehension (Griffin, 2001). As early readers engage in exploratory talk, they begin to sequence stories and to critique the literary elements of a story (Calkins, 2001). Oral interpretation of a story, either through collaborative conversations or role playing, provides the students with a link between oral language and reading. Through oral interpretations of texts, children at the early stage of literacy begin to communicate their ideas about literature with growing confidence and ability (Galda, Cullinan, & Strickland, 1997).

Engaging in classroom conversation empowers the student to respond to text.

Another way to respond to text is through choral reading of poetry. Poetry is a wonderful method to engage children of varying abilities in the enjoyment of oral language (Hadaway, Vardell, & Young, 2001). The rhythm, cadence, and phrasing of poetry help the beginning reader to gain meaning and fluency (Christison & Bassano, 1995; Gasparro & Falletta, 1994). The brevity of poetry also helps struggling readers attempt to read text they normally would avoid (Cullinan, Scala, & Schroeder, 1995). As children engage in choral poetry readings, they hear the poem first modeled by their teacher. This especially helps second language learners understand the rhythm and pacing of the English language (Hadaway et al., 2001).

In summary, a talk-rich classroom provides children from varying language backgrounds the opportunities to hear and use a variety of language discourses. Children from homes with plentiful opportunities for oral language development enter school with a firm foundation for literacy (Wells, 1986). Therefore, early childhood teachers who provide a talk-rich classroom are leveling the playing field for all children.

Developmental Benchmarks for Oral Language at the Early Literacy Stage

It is during the early stage of literacy that young children begin to develop confidence in their abilities to read and write. As their literacy improves, the child at the early

Table 4.1
Oral Language Benchmarks for the Early Literacy Stage

Language Habits	Enjoyment of Language	Use of Literary Language
Participates in discussions and asks questions Asks focus questions for purposes of learning Initiates and sustains a conversation Talks to self to correct or problem solve Self-corrects grammatical errors during conversations Can respond to the idea or question of conversational partner If second language learner, begins to switch between the two languages Is able to summarize information from a nonfictional text or presentation	Enjoys riddles and jokes Plays with alliteration or tongue twisters Continues to add words to knowledge domains Continues to learn and use new vocabulary words Participates in silly rhymes or poetry readings Begins to use persuasive techniques	Continues to use language heard in storybooks Marks end of oral narrative with coda and includes quotations in story Continues to sequence stories and can provide more details Can describe settings and characters Begins to enjoy metaphors and symbolic language Defends claims in book talks by referring explicitly to parts of text

literacy stage is also gaining skills in oral language ability. Table 4.1 lists the developmental benchmarks for oral language at the early literacy stage, and the following section describes them in detail (Cooper & Kiger, 2001; New Standards Speaking and Listening Committee, 2001).

Language Habits

> Ms. Harron is sitting with Ricky during snack time. "How is your father doing, Ricky?" Ms. Harron asks. "He's home," says Ricky. "I'm glad for you, Ricky," Ms. Harron responds. "Did you have a celebration?" "Yeah, we had a party," Ricky answers. "I love parties, especially all the great food. Did they have any of your favorite foods?" asks Ms. Harron. "We had cake and potato chips. I really like chips, especially Ruffles," answers Ricky.

Ms. Harron begins the conversation by prompting Ricky about his father. This is a topic that she knows Ricky wants to discuss. At this stage of development, children desire to share their emotions with the adults in their lives but may need this process facilitated. Gradually, through response and elaboration, Ms. Harron entices Ricky to build upon her conversation and provide more language in his responses.

Enjoyment of Language

> It is Wednesday afternoon and the first graders are getting reading for their choral poetry session. "Let's go sailing on a sailing ship," laughs Carlos. "When the wind blows," responds Matt. "I know a rhyme for blows—there it goes!" quips Josey. The boys quickly stop their banter as Ms. Harron calls the class to meet her for the poetry session.

Children at the early literacy stage are continuing to develop their knowledge of rhymes and word patterns. They also enjoy participating in poetry sessions and sharing their nonsense words with peers. This language play is essential for children to develop the ability to segment sounds and to read strategically.

Use of Literary Language

> On Friday morning, Ms. Harron gathered the students together to role play their favorite character. "I'm gonna be the Cat in the Hat," says Evan. He has prepared a tall, red and white striped paper hat for his performance. "How do you want to begin, Evan?" asks Ms. Harron. "I'll begin, 'I'm the Cat in the Hat who sat on the mat,'" says Evan. "That does sound like Dr. Seuss," laughs his friend Jeffrey, and everyone joins in the fun.

Evan is role-playing the Cat in the Hat by using the literary language he has internalized from his favorite Dr. Seuss books (Dr. Seuss, 1957). During the early literacy stage, children's schemas of literary language are expanding. Their oral language is beginning to reflect the vocabulary and concepts gleaned from daily exposure to the rich model of children's literature. Children at the early literacy stage are also now able to describe characters, plot, and setting in more detail than they were doing at the emergent level.

Modeling Oral Language for the Early Literacy Stage

An important phase of scaffolded instruction is the modeling of expected skills or abilities. During the early stage of literacy development, the early childhood teacher challenges young readers and writers to improve their beginning reading skills by providing more difficult texts. Similarly, in order to increase the early reader and writer's oral language skills, the teacher models strategies or skills that are increasingly difficult. This section provides activities for modeling oral language for the early stage of literacy development.

Instructional Strategies

Family storytelling sessions. Children of all ages love to hear stories about their teachers and families. Teachers can bring in pictures from their photo albums of childhood family vacations and tell a story about it. Other topics of interest for a family storytelling session include

- Their first pet
- A time when they got into trouble
- A deceased member of the family that they never met but heard stories about
- Their first day of school
- How they learned to read

Content area presentations. It is important that the teacher use a concrete prop such as a picture, postcard, or other item to illustrate the tale. Stories should have a beginning, middle, and end as well as dialogue. The teacher can audiotape these stories so the children can listen repeatedly to their favorites. Once the children have seen the teacher model family stories, they can present their own tales to their peers.

Involving Parents: Encourage parents to tell family stories or to talk about the family member they most admired as a child.

Many early childhood teachers integrate literacy learning with the content areas. Young children who are exposed to vocabulary

Content area learning helps children with academic discourse.

from the content areas will gradually internalize words into conceptual frameworks. In order for young children to know how to do an oral report, for instance, teachers must begin to model nonfiction presentations. During an integrated literacy and content area unit, such as one on insects, the teacher can bring in a cocoon and present information on how a caterpillar is transformed into a butterfly. The teacher should have key ideas written on chart paper so the children can observe how to use notes to construct an oral presentation. If concrete objects or props are not available for the presentation, videos or pictures about science or social studies may be used.

Assessment Strategies for Modeling Oral Language

Observations and anecdotal records, which were previously discussed in Chapter 3, can also be used for assessing oral language modeling. During modeling activities, the teacher is assessing the responses often during the lesson. Table 4.2 presents a checklist for oral language development during the early literacy stage.

Shared Oral Language Experiences for the Early Literacy Stage

During the next phase of scaffolded instruction, shared oral language strategies, the teacher and student jointly engage in oral language activities. The purpose of this phase of scaffolded instruction is to help the young child gain confidence in her own abilities and begin to master the necessary oral language developmental benchmarks. This section describes several instructional strategies for oral language at the early literacy level that may be used as joint, shared activities.

Table 4.2
Assessment of Oral Language Behaviors During Modeling Activities

	Rating Scale for Modeling Activities		
Benchmarks for Oral Language	**Target**	**Acceptable**	**Needs Improvement**
Conversational skills	Participates in discussions and asks questions; can also summarize information from books	Sometimes participates in discussions and partially summarizes information	Is not able to participate in discussions or to summarize text
Enjoyment of language	Continues to learn new vocabulary words and enjoys riddles	Sometimes uses new vocabulary words and enjoys jokes	Does not use new vocabulary words and does not enjoy riddles or jokes

Instructional Strategies

Choral poetry. Choral poetry is a wonderful way to engage children and to facilitate their enjoyment of its word play. During choral poetry recitals, the teacher places the words to the poem on a chart or easel. The children can use this as a reference point while they are learning to memorize their lines. With choral poetry readings, teachers may choose to supply the refrain and the children recite the verse. The poem can also be acted out with props or pictures. It is best to begin with a brief, simple poem and when the children have mastered the style of choral poetry readings, more challenging poems may be used.

Let's Go Sailing

Let's go sailing on a sailing ship (refrain)
When the wind blows
Let's go sailing on a sailing ship
What the captain says goes

(Hennings, 2001)

Letter bag game. Young children need concrete objects to encourage oral expression and language development. One way to facilitate this process is to use a shopping bag of letters as a prop. The teacher pulls out a letter and says, "I am going to send Maryann a pretend letter because she saved my puppy. Dear Maryann, One day I was coming home from school and . . . Who would like to finish my letter?" As the children become proficient in completing these oral story starters, teachers can modify this activity by having the children begin the letter as well. Content area literacy may also be incorporated into this lesson by using postcards from different states or foreign countries. This allows the children to use their knowledge about each state or country and to use new vocabulary words (Miller, 2000).

Meeting Diverse Needs: Children from different cultures might want to bring in postcards or items from their native country to use with this strategy.

Assessment Strategies for Shared Oral Language Experiences

The assessment instruments shown in Figure 4.1 and Table 4.3 may be used to gather evidence of student learning during the shared instructional strategies described earlier.

Guided Oral Language Activities for the Early Literacy Stage

Guided instruction for oral language development involves a shift in control from the teacher to the student. During this phase of scaffolded instruction, the student is ac-

Directions: Place indicator in the proper column based on your observations.

CHECKLIST FOR CHORAL POETRY READING

Oral Language Behaviors	Behavior Present +	Somewhat Present /	Not Observed —
Indicates confidence through posture			
Uses gestures and facial expressions appropriately			
Uses voice and delivery appropriately			
Participates with peers and joins in on cue			
Is able to recite poem from memory			

Figure 4.1
Assessment of Oral Language Behaviors During Choral Poetry Reading

Table 4.3
Assessment of Oral Language Behaviors During the Letter Bag Game

Rating Scale for the Letter Bag Game

Benchmarks for Oral Language	Target	Acceptable	Needs Improvement
Continues to use language heard from stories	Uses storybook language in discussions	Sometimes uses storybook language in discussions	Never demonstrates knowledge of storybook language
Arranges ideas in logical order	Can sequence ideas for letter	Can sequence ideas somewhat logically for letter	Cannot sequence ideas for letter; ideas are random
Brings own "voice" to story	Has a distinct style	Is beginning to develop a style of storytelling	Has yet to develop her own "voice"

tively engaged in the literacy process and the teacher acts as coach or facilitator. While students gradually gain fluency of their oral language skills, the teacher records their performance to determine mastery of oral language benchmarks. This section illustrates how to guide children's oral language development at the early literacy stage.

Instructional Strategies

Talk back to books time. As children begin to develop their reading skills, they enjoy sharing their newly discovered love of reading. One method for encouraging this passion to read is to provide talk back to books time (Calkins, 2001). Calkins argues that this activity creates a curriculum of talk that helps young readers to refine their literary understandings. For this activity, teachers can provide a chart of phrases that students can use in their discussions.

Conversation Starters
I noticed that . . .
I liked the part when . . .
It reminded me of the story where . . .

After the daily read-aloud or individual reading time, teachers can ask the children to meet with their book talk partner. Children may need to draw their favorite scene or jot down notes about the story before they begin to converse. Gradually, as the students begin to gain confidence, the teacher can encourage them to begin to support their responses with quotes from the text. During talk back to books time, the teacher circulates around the room jotting down anecdotal records or marking checklists. Some teachers tape record students' discussions which then become models for others to follow in elaborating and responding to peers' ideas.

Using Technology: You can keep abreast of the latest children's books by logging on to http://www.carolhurst.com and signing up for the free monthly newsletter.

Conducting interviews. Most children at the early literacy stage of development are immersed in the fictional world of storybooks. However, it is equally important for them to be exposed to expository text. Expository text or nonfictional work exposes the early reader and writer to the vocabulary and concepts of science, social studies, and math. As children experience the content areas, they gradually develop the necessary conceptual framework for reading and writing expository text. A fun way to engage young children in expository text is to ask them to interview a grandparent, neighbor, or guest speaker on a certain topic. Topics for the interview could include the following:

- Coming to America as an immigrant
- Workers in the community
- Veterans of American wars
- Family heroes

Children will have to be given sample questions to ask the person being interviewed. If the interviewee gives permission, it is best to tape record the interview so that the students can record their responses. When the child has completed her note taking, she gives a formal oral presentation to the class on the information gleaned from the interview.

Assessment Strategies for Guided Oral Language Activities

The assessment instruments shown in Figure 4.2 and Table 4.4 may be used to collect data for the guided oral language activities that were presented in the previous section.

Directions: Place indicator in the column based on your observations.

CHECKLIST FOR TALK BACK TO BOOKS TIME

Oral Language Benchmark	Behavior Present +	Somewhat Present /	Not Observed —
Participates in discussions and asks questions			
Self-corrects grammatical errors during conversations			
Can respond and elaborate on idea of conversational partner			
If second language learner, begins to switch between two languages			
Continues to use language from storybooks			
Continues to sequence stories and provide more details			
Describes characters and setting			

Comments:

Figure 4.2
Assessment of Oral Language Behaviors During Talk Back to Books Time

Independent Oral Language Activities for the Early Literacy Stage

The final phase of scaffolded instruction is the independent component where the student assumes full responsibility for the language task. The role of the teacher during this phase is informed observer, noting the child's progress as she tackles language activities unassisted. During the tasks, the teacher records the student's performance to determine whether the child has mastered the oral language benchmarks for the early literacy stage. This section describes several ways to provide

Table 4.4
Assessment of Oral Language Behaviors During Oral Presentation of Interviews

Rating Scale for Oral Presentation of Interviews

Benchmarks for Oral Language	Level 3	Level 2	Level 1
Participates in discussions and self-corrects grammar	Participates in discussions and self-corrects grammar	Sometimes participates in discussions and is beginning to self-correct grammar	Does not participate in discussions or self-correct grammar
Can respond to conversational partner	Builds upon partner's ideas	Sometimes builds upon partner's ideas	Does not respond to partner
Has volume and pitch	Has proper volume and pitch	Is beginning to develop volume and pitch	Has inappropriate volume and pitch

strategies for oral language development that may be done independently at the early literacy level.

Instructional Strategies

Storyboard stories. Engaging in talk back to books time will help to provide children with the necessary literary concepts for storyboard stories. Storyboard stories is an activity that uses illustrations as a concrete prompt for the children to construct their own stories. Teachers can provide early readers with wordless picture books such as *Tuesday* by David Wiesner (1997) as a model. The children are then divided into groups and given chart paper that has been divided into story frames. The group plot out their story and then create the illustrations. The children may decide to write out the script of the story for their presentation. After the illustrations are completed, the children narrate the story for their peers. If the children have access to PowerPoint software, they may choose to create a slide presentation using photos or scanned illustrations instead of the storyboard. This activity will probably take early readers approximately 1 week to complete.

Character for a day role playing. Children at the early literacy stage of development are continuing to construct their schemas or knowledge base of literary genres and language. A fun activity for children at this stage is to role play their favorite storybook characters. This activity works especially well after the children have been immersed in author study or have read several books about the same character such as the *Curious George* series.

During the character for a day activity, the children choose which storybook character they would like to impersonate. The children can create their own props and costumes as well. For example, if a child chooses to be the Cat in the Hat, she might create a tall, red and white striped hat. The children may use notes for their presentation as they talk to their peers in character. This role-playing activity allows early readers and writers to use the literary language from their favorite storybooks as well as new vocabulary words they have internalized.

Figure 4.3
Storyboard Stories

"Once upon a time, there was a cowboy in the desert searching for lost gold. He brought with him lots of tools to find the gold. One day . . . "

Assessment Strategies for Independent Oral Language Activities

The assessment instruments presented in Figure 4.4 and Table 4.5 may be used to ascertain students' progress in developing the oral language benchmarks for the early literacy stage.

Connecting Oral Language and Early Writing

This chapter has discussed myriad ways to integrate oral language in the early childhood classroom. Oral language is also a natural springboard for writing during the early stage of literacy. Oral language is the foundation for both reading and writing (Snow, 1983). It is through daily conversations and stimulating class discussions that young children develop the conceptual knowledge necessary for reading and writing.

Engagement in reading and writing is a dynamic process of combining motivation and the necessary strategies to comprehend and compose (Swan, 2003). As children talk, read, and write about a topic, their knowledge base expands (Gunning, 2003; Swan, 2003). It is imperative that young children begin to talk, read, and write about topics from science, social studies, and math (Snow, 1983). When young children discuss dinosaurs, plants, or triangles, they are developing the conceptual framework that will help them to comprehend or compose content material.

During the early stage of literacy, young children write the way they speak. They write as if they are telling a story orally or giving an explanation (Bereiter & Scardamalia, 1982). They often do not plan their writing, but spontaneously add sentences as they compose (Dahl & Farnan, 1988). As children mature as writers, their thinking begins to change as they write (Gunning, 2003). When this change occurs, children begin to conclude, evaluate, and critique as they write (Calkins, 1983). Writing then becomes the springboard for critical thinking. Therefore, the recursive processes of speaking, listening, reading, and writing will evolve into critical thinking as the child's conceptual framework is developed. This section describes how to use

Directions: Place indicator in the proper column based on your observations.

CHECKLIST FOR STORYBOARD STORIES			
Oral Language Benchmark	**Behavior Present** +	**Somewhat Present** /	**Not Observed** —
Participates in discussions and asks questions			
Self-corrects grammatical errors during conversations			
Can respond and elaborate on idea of conversational partner			
If second language learner, begins to switch between two languages			
Continues to use language from storybooks			
Continues to sequence stories and provide more details			
Describes characters and setting			

Figure 4.4
Assessment of Oral Language Behaviors During Storyboard Stories

Table 4.5
Assessment of Oral Language Behaviors During Character for a Day Role Playing

Rating Scale for Character for a Day Role Playing			
Benchmarks for Oral Language	**Target**	**Acceptable**	**Needs Improvement**
Participates in discussions and self-corrects grammar	Participates and self-corrects grammar	Sometimes participates in discussions and is beginning to self-correct grammar	Does not participate in discussions or self-correct grammar
Keeps interest of audience	Keeps audience's attention	Is beginning to develop techniques to gain attention	Does not keep audience's attention
Has volume and pitch	Has proper volume and pitch	Is beginning to develop volume and pitch	Has inappropriate volume and pitch

- After the students have shared their family pictures, ask the following focus question: Who is your family hero?
- Ask the children to pair up and discuss why they chose a certain relative as their hero. They must explain what the relative did to be heroic to them.
- After they have discussed it with their partner, each child creates a book called *My Family Hero* and illustrates it.
- After the children have finished their books, the class may share their heroes with their parents at a special celebration.

Figure 4.5
My Family Hero Instructional Strategy

some of the previously mentioned oral language activities and integrate writing for the early literacy stage of development.

Instructional Strategies

Earlier in the chapter, we discussed how family stories may be used to construct conceptual knowledge and vocabulary. These activities also stimulate writing, as illustrated in Figure 4.5.

This writing extension is a wonderful way to celebrate the diverse cultures of students and their families. It also helps children to see that heroes are present in their own families and not just in comic books or cartoons. This activity is also a natural springboard for talking about famous heroes and their contributions to the nation or to the world. As recent research has shown, it is important to introduce content area vocabulary during early childhood and this writing extension activity introduces the child to myriad vocabulary words from around the world.

If a child has only recently arrived in the United States, she may be reluctant to share with her peers or unable to do so because of language difficulties. It is important to remember that children should not be forced to share family stories if they are uncomfortable doing so. Teachers may offer the choice of writing about a national hero they admire or someone they have read about as an alternative to a family hero story. Table 4.6 lists assessment criteria for the activity.

Interviewing a character. Earlier in the chapter, we discussed how children love to role play their favorite storybook characters. Another suggested activity was interviewing a family member about their experiences. One way to extend these two activities and integrate them with writing is to have a collaborative interview activity (see Figure 4.6).

The assessment instrument presented in Figure 4.7 may be used to record students' performances on this collaborative activity.

Table 4.6
Assessment of Oral Language Behaviors During the My Family Hero Writing Activity

Rating Scale for My Family Hero Writing Activity			
Benchmarks for Oral Language and Writing	**Target**	**Acceptable**	**Needs Improvement**
Sustains conversations and responds to questions	Converses with partner and responds to questions	Converses with partner and partially responds to questions	Student is unable to talk about their hero and does not answer questions.
Sequences a story and provides details	Sequences family hero story and provides several details about hero	Sequences story and provides some details about hero	Is unable to sequence hero story and does not provide details about hero
Understands that oral language can be written down and uses inventive spelling	Is able to write down story and uses inventive spelling	Is able to communicate story through writing and uses some inventive spelling	Is still communicating only through pictures and not through the printed word

- After finishing a storybook, have students choose a partner for the project.
- Each partner chooses her favorite character in the story.
- One student role plays the character while the other partner conducts the interview. Then students reverse roles.
- After the interview, each partner records her summary of the interview.

Figure 4.6
Collaborative Interview Activity

This activity can be modified in several ways. Instead of recording their interviews, students may want to write a newspaper report about their favorite storybook character. In addition, students may choose to interview a favorite president or other historical figure. This activity would integrate literacy, oral language, and the content areas. The next activity will describe how to use choral poetry to facilitate children's writing.

Integrating choral poetry and writing. Young children love books that rhyme and the language of poetry. Choral readings of poetry, as discussed earlier in this chapter, are wonderful ways to build fluency and encourage reluctant speakers to

CHECKLIST FOR THE COLLABORATIVE INTERVIEW ACTIVITY

Performance Indicators for Collaborative Interview Activity	**Rating Scale** **4 (Mastery); 3 (Target); 2 (Acceptable); 1 (Needs Support)**
• Students discuss characters and use literary language	
• Students respond to questions and conduct conversations	
• Students are able to record summary of character interview	
Total Score	

Figure 4.7
Assessment of Oral Language Behaviors During the Collaborative Interview Activity

join in classroom activities. Choral poetry can also be excellent springboards for developing fluency in writing.

As students delight in the language of choral poetry, they are increasing their oral vocabulary and developing their knowledge of sentence structure. For example, the poem referred to earlier, "Let's Go Sailing," gives the child the opportunity to delight in the repeated refrain and join in the fun. An extension of a choral reading is to create a class verse to continue the poem or to create a new poem based upon the model that the class recited.

Let's Go Sailing

Let's go sailing on a sailing ship (refrain)
When the wind blows
Let's go sailing on a sailing ship
What the captain says goes

(Hennings, 2001)

The class might create the following verse:

Let's go sailing on a sailing ship
And see where we go
Let's go sailing on a sailing ship
And watch as the wind blows
Let's go sailing on a sailing ship
Far away and home again!

Once the students feel comfortable writing the extended verses as a class, the teacher might start them off by asking the students to add one more line on their own. As they become more confident, this can be increased to two lines until they are writing a verse independently.

The following checklist can be attached to a clipboard for quick observational assessment as the early childhood teacher walks around the room. It may also be used as small writing groups conference with the teacher.

Checklist Instrument for Writing Choral Poetry

Performance Indicators Choral Poetry ✓ Enjoys poetic language ✓ Feels comfortable using poetic language ✓ Is able to record one line of verse ✓ Is able to record two lines of verse ✓ Records one complete verse of poem	Mary	Evan	Liz	Tomas

Summary of the Instructional Cycle

The instructional cycle for oral language development at the early literacy level is now complete. This chapter has presented oral language instructional strategies that can be used for modeled, shared, guided, and independent activities. The teacher must be aware of the developmental continuum for oral literacy so children can be gently pushed toward the next level. As children master the benchmarks for oral language at the early literacy level, they can be introduced to strategies for the fluency stage. The master assessment checklist shown in Figure 4.8 may be used at the end of the instructional cycle to identify class patterns of behavior.

Master Assessment

Directions: Based on your observations, place check marks next to the benchmarks demonstrated by 90% of the students in the class.

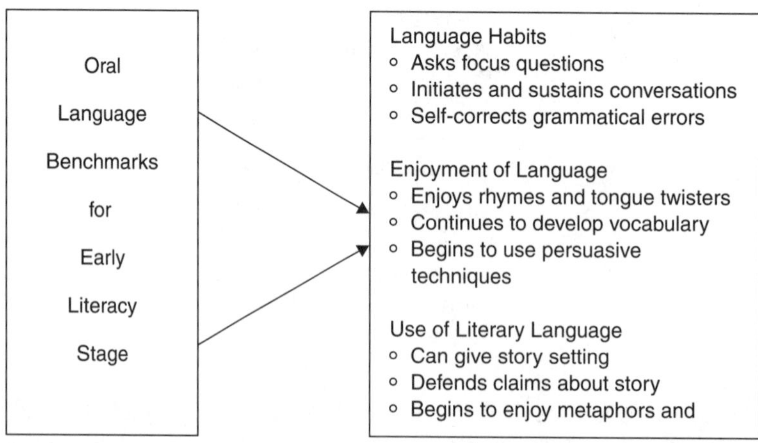

Figure 4.8
Master Assessment Cycle for Oral Language Development at the Early Literacy Stage

Portrait of the Instructional Cycle for Oral Language Experiences at the Early Literacy Level

It is Monday morning in Ms. Harron's first-grade class. Grace is busy in the library corner listening to the tape of Ms. Harron's stories. Grace's favorite story is when Ms. Harron talks about how she got into trouble as a little girl for cutting her sister's hair with her new school scissors. "It cuts!" Grace says aloud with Ms. Harron's taped voice. Ms. Harron is focusing on Grace this week due to her reluctance to join in class discussions or activities. Ms. Harron jots down an observation that Grace obviously enjoys these taped family stories and that they should be sent home with her for one night to share with her mother.

Later in the week, Grace is sitting with her friend Marianne as the class plays the letter bag game. Grace chuckles with delight as her friend Marianne is the first to be called on to continue the letter. Marianne picks Grace to continue the letter story and Grace hesitates. Just as Ms. Harron gets ready to prompt her, Grace begins, "then the puppy ran into the attic and Ms. Harron called 911. She was afraid the puppy was hurt." After the game activity, Ms. Harron completes the Rating Scale for the Letter Bag Game and notes that Grace was able to speak without prompting for the first time. Ms. Harron notes that this is a major improvement for Grace.

Several weeks later, Grace is working on her character for a day role-playing project. She has chosen to impersonate Pippi Longstocking (Lindgren, 1950) because she always gets into trouble. Grace has braided her hair and painted freckles on her face to look like Pippi. She seems shy and anxious before beginning. Grace looks down at her note cards and begins, "No more plutifaction . . . I'm not going back to school" and all her friends start to laugh. Ms. Harron reacts in delight because Grace is starting to overcome her fear of speaking in front of the class. After her performance, Ms. Harron notes on the Rating Scale for Character for a Day Role Playing that Grace used gestures and facial expressions and showed confidence. She also notes that Grace still pauses and hesitates during an oral presentation, yet is definitely overcoming her shyness.

Discussion Questions and Activities

1. Engage a young child in a family story. Record the child's use of vocabulary, sentence structure, and story sequence.
2. Implement the letter bag game instructional strategy. Assess how the children are developing literacy skills through oral language.
3. Observe an early childhood classroom and record how the teacher is implementing a curriculum of talk. How would you change the instructional strategies?
4. After implementing some of the strategies and assessment tools in this chapter, design your own oral language activity and assessment for the early literacy stage. Reflect in your journal on the data you collected about the students' oral language development.

Additional Readings

Berko, G. (2001). *The development of language* (5th ed.). Boston: Allyn & Bacon.

McCabe, A. (1996). *Chameleon readers: Teaching children to appreciate all kinds of good stories.* New York: McGraw-Hill.

Snow, C., Burns, M., & Griffin, P. (1998). *Preventing reading difficulties in young children.* Washington, DC: National Academy Press.

Additional Web Sites

New Zealand Ministry of Education
http://www.minedu.govt.nz/
New Zealand is at the forefront of literacy education and this site offers teachers terrific strategies and assessment tools for grades K-8.

Speaking and Listening Skills to Preschool through Grade 3 Students
http://www.ncee.org
This site offers wonderful instructional strategies for teachers.

United States Department of Education
http://www.ed.gov
This is a website that every parent and teacher should visit regularly to keep informed on federal legislation as well as recent reports.

Wiggleworks by Scholastic
http://teacher.scholastic.com/wiggleworks/index.htm
This site is to accompany the Wiggleworks software produced by Scholastic and offers wonderful ideas for teachers.

Additional Children's Literature

Aliki. (1974). *Go tell Aunt Rhody.* New York: Macmillan.

Brett, J. (1989). *The mitten.* New York: Putnam.

Brown, M. (Ed.). (1977). *Hand rhymes.* New York: Dutton.

Fox, M. (1986). *Hattie and the fox.* New York: Bradbury.

Gershator, D., & Gershator, P. (1995). *Bread is for eating.* New York: Holt.

Giesel, T. (1957). *The cat in the hat.* New York: Random House.

Hong, L. (1993). *Two of everything.* New York: Whitman.

Martin, B., Jr. (1981). *Brown bear, brown bear, what do you see?* New York: Holt.

Numeroff, L. (1991). *If you give a moose a muffin.* New York: HarperCollins.

Trelease, J. (1995). *The read-aloud handbook.* New York: Penguin Books.

Children's Literature References

Bemelmans, L. (1939). *Madeline.* New York: Penguin Books.

Lindgren, A. (1950). *Pippi Longstocking.* New York: Puffin Books.

Seuss, Dr. (1957). *The cat in the hat.* New York: Random House.

Wiesner, D. (1997). *Tuesday.* Clarion Books.

CHAPTER 5

Linking Oral Language, Literacy Instruction, and Assessment for the Fluency Stage

Portrait of Students Using Academic Discourse

Omar, a third grader in James McElroy's class, is sitting in the Literacy Center reading Happy Birthday, Dr. King! *(Jones, 1994). His friend Raphael stops to ask, "Why are you reading that baby book?" "It's not a baby book and I'm preparing my speech about Dr. King. I want to put lots of new stuff in it," explains Omar. "Like what?" asks Raphael. "I'm going to talk about Rosa Parks." "Who was she?" asks Raphael. "She wouldn't give up her seat on a bus. She was like Dr. King," replies Omar.*

The Fluency Stage of Literacy Development

As children enter the fluency stage of literacy, their ability to read and write independently soars. However, this does not mean that they have mastered critical thinking or oracy, which is the ability to use communication skills to generate ideas. As discussed in Chapter 2, the foundation of critical thinking and oracy is an adequate knowledge base or one's schemata.

As you read this chapter, reflect on the following topics:

- How you can develop critical thinking through oral language for the child at the fluency stage
- How benchmarks within the fluency stage of oral language development help you to think about how oracy and oral language skills develop in children
- How instruction and assessment are aligned for oral language at the fluency stage
- How the teacher may use assessment results to plan for student learning

How Does Critical Thinking Develop Through Oral Language?

Schemas represent one's knowledge base about concepts, objects, and the relationships between objects, situations, or events (Gipe, 1998). This knowledge base is constructed through experiences and discussion about those experiences (Piaget, 1948; Vygotsky, 1978).

As students tackle new tasks or discuss texts, they draw upon their schemas to assimilate the new information (Piaget, 1948). The child with more elaborate and varied schemas will be equipped to comprehend new text and to converse on different topics.

What Is Academic Discourse?

Vygotsky (1978) stated that children use language as a mental tool to comprehend their world. Their reliance on oral language to explore new forms of discourse is especially apparent during the fluency stage. It is during the fluency stage that students are expected to explore a variety of genres. The more elaborate text structure, such as expository text, presents sophisticated ideas in complex language or **academic discourse** (Fountas & Pinnell, 2001). The discussions that accompany these experiences help the children to internalize the new language structures. The assimilation of these complex language structures into their schemas enables students to use language to argue a point, discuss literary elements, and generate ideas (Bakhtin, 1981; Piaget, 1948).

Academic discourse is a more complex language structure where children use language to argue a point, discuss literature, and generate ideas.

Using Language to Communicate Ideas

As students exchange ideas through classroom discourse, they are using language to summarize, clarify, compare and contrast, and classify (Raban, 2001). Varied experiences with language such as presenting arguments or famous speeches energize children's thinking and literacy (Farris, 2001). As students engage in "instructional conversations" (Tharp & Gallimore, 1988), they weave together understandings from difficult text and expand their ability to interpret it. Participating in this purposeful talk is a vital link to internalization and utilization of literate models of thinking and communicating ideas (Wells & Charg-Wells, 1993).

Instructional conversations such as interpretations of famous speeches have been found to help children achieve fluency in reading and writing (New Standards Speaking and Listening Committee, 2001). As children first try out academic discourse or content vocabulary, they elaborate on their schemas and can tackle more difficult text. Instructional conversations help children practice the academic talk that they will need to master as they advance in school. In order to achieve fluency in academic discourse, students must master the following oral communication skills:

- Stating their point to others
- Backing up their point with text
- Interpreting text
- Collaborating with others to build understanding
- Discovering new themes or meanings (New Standards Committee, 2001)

Teachers who provide varied language activities that integrate academic disciplines empower their students to master academic discourse (Farris, 2001). Instructional strategies such as literature discussions or book talks are types of activities that encourage children to use oral language to generate ideas.

Literature Discussions

Literature discussions or **book talks** enable children to critique a story's literary elements such as plot, characterization, or setting. As children engage in book talks, they are required to defend their opinions about books by using citations from the text. This is an important academic skill that will be required as the child advances through the grades.

Involving Parents: Send a class newsletter once a month to the parents informing them of the books the children are reading. Invite them to talk to their child and read together.

Participation in literature discussions also helps children become competent critical readers because [they build upon the individual participant's prior knowledge] (Galda, Cullinan, & Strickland, 1997). Listening to their peers' literary response also elaborates their own conceptual understanding of text that is assimilated into their schemas (Bakhtin, 1981; Piaget, 1948). Besides critical thinking, book talks also serve to instruct students in the pragmatics of language. From talking about books, children can learn how to listen to others and communicate their own opinions (Galda et al., 1997). Learning to engage in rich conversations and to listen to diverse opinions is a vital social skill for success in both school and the workplace (New Standards Committee, 2001). Last, participation in literature discussions has been found to increase motivation for reading and to create lasting engagements with text (Kasten, 1997).

Developmental Benchmarks for Oral Language at the Fluent Literacy Stage

The development of oral language during the fluency stage of literacy is critical to further cognitive growth. As the second or third grader begins to cognitively problem solve and to see another's perspective, oral language is used as a tool for thinking (Vygotsky, 1978). Table 5.1 shows the developmental benchmarks for oral language learning at the fluent literacy level. The following section describes the developmental benchmarks further by providing a classroom scenario for each category.

Table 5.1
Oral Language Developmental Benchmarks at the Fluent Literacy Level

Language Habits	Enjoyment of Language	Use of Literary Language
Participates in discussions and asks questions Asks or answers specific questions Initiates and sustains conversations Explains or speaks from another's perspective Expresses and solicits opinions Shifts from formal to informal usage	Continues to develop persuasive techniques Uses double meanings or multiple meanings of words to create riddles and jokes Continues to learn and use new vocabulary words Uses and explains metaphoric language Provides definitions of words he knows	Continues to use language heard in storybooks Gives increasingly elaborate descriptions of story elements Defends opinion of text with examples Gives an author performance by reading from his own work Critiques text by citing evidence in story

Language Habits

In James McElroy's third-grade class, the students are engaged in book talk, discussing their favorite story, *Charlotte's Web* (White, 1952). Charlie is arguing that *Charlotte's Web* is like Winnie the Pooh books because the animals can talk. "No," replies Rachel. "In *Winnie the Pooh* there weren't any sad parts, but in *Charlotte's Web,* I cried."

The children are engaged in **accountable talk** about literature. Unlike their younger siblings, children in second and third grade are beginning to use specific details in the literature to defend their opinions. This gradual shift toward logical reasoning is facilitated by conversations about books with their peers.

Enjoyment of Language

Tasha and Sabrina are sitting in the library corner during their language arts block period. Sabrina is reading a book on volcanoes for her science project and quickly comes to a word she doesn't know. "What is lava?" asks Sabrina. "I know what that is because I saw it on the Discovery Channel," replies Tasha. "Lava is the hot stuff that comes pouring out of the volcano when it erupts." "I get it now," states Sabrina, and she goes back to reading her book.

Tasha is scaffolding Sabrina's expanding knowledge base regarding volcanoes. Children at the fluency stage of literacy have internalized thousands of words in their lexicon that can be orally defined. Second and third graders, when encouraged to use their oral vocabulary, expand their lexicon by sharing definitions, as seen with Tasha and Sabrina.

Use of Literary Language

It's Friday afternoon in Mr. McElroy's third-grade classroom, which means it's storytelling hour. The children are sitting in a circle listening to Ottar as he tells his story, "The Cold-Hearted Man." The children listen attentively and jot down comments and questions to ask Ottar when he is finished. "Why did you call your story 'The Cold-Hearted Man'?" asks Raphael. "I wanted to show how uncaring and nasty he was and how love changed him," replies Ottar.

Ottar used the metaphor "cold-hearted" to introduce the theme of his story. This literary technique is gradually acquired during the fluency stage as the child becomes more proficient in literature. Second and third graders are capable of internalizing the literary language they have heard and gradually using it in their oral language. As with any concept or skill, multiple experiences with literature and opportunities to draw upon those experiences increase the use of literary language.

Modeling Oral Language for the Fluency Stage of Development

During the fluency stage of literacy, children are using their speaking and listening skills to negotiate, interpret, and problem solve (New Standards Committee, 2001). It is the role of the teacher during the modeling phase to illustrate how to use oral language to express ideas and to argue a point. The following section provides instructional strategies and assessment tools for modeling oral language for the fluent student.

Instructional Strategies

Famous speeches. During the fluency stage of literacy, it is especially important to integrate oral language with other content areas such as social studies. This integration can occur as children are exposed to the many famous speeches of history. For example, students can listen to Dr. King's "I Have a Dream" speech and critique it by answering the following questions:

- What is the purpose of the speech?
- How does Dr. King use pauses, pitch, and tone to get his message across?
- How did Dr. King build his argument?

Teacher think-aloud. It is during the second and third grade that children are increasingly immersed in expository text such as their science textbooks. The different structure often poses major comprehension problems. The think-aloud technique is an example of how oral language can scaffold critical thinking.

The first step in this technique is the teacher modeling how to do a think-aloud with a social studies or science textbook. Figure 5.1 illustrates the teaching steps in this mini-lesson.

Story impressions. Once students reach the fluency stage of literacy, the teacher shifts instruction toward increasing comprehension skills. One way to aid students in this process is to model for students how to use picture clues or story titles to create a first impression of the story. The students can then be paired to discover their first impressions of a book.

- The first thing I do is look at the chapter headings and summary at the end. This gives me an idea about the chapter.
- Then as I read, if there is a word or question I have about the text, I write it on a sticky note and put it on the page.
- As I read each section, I summarize it in my head or write it down.
- After reading the whole chapter, I write down my summary of the chapter using the chapter headings.

Figure 5.1
Think-Aloud

Assessment Strategies for Modeling Oral Language

During the fluency stage, the primary assessment tool for oral language modeling is observation. The teacher has the option of writing anecdotal records of the children's responses during the modeling stage or using a guided checklist. The checklist shown in Figure 5.2 can be used to assess the instructional strategies, or the teacher can create her own guided checklist.

Shared Oral Language Experiences for the Fluent Literacy Stage

As the child sees oral language being used to express ideas, opinions, or solutions to problems, he becomes more confident in using speech. As the child becomes more at ease with using language the instructor can gradually begin to shift control of language to the child. The following instructional strategies for shared oral language activities will illustrate this process.

Instructional Strategies

Book talk. Responding to literature is the external evidence of what happens in the mind of the reader as he interprets text (Galda et al., 1997). According to Rosenblatt (1978), the reader can engage the text for pleasure which is aesthetic response or for information which is an efferent stance. (See Chapter 2 for a more complete discussion of aesthetic and efferent reading.)

During the fluency stage of literacy, students can engage in literature discussions from both an aesthetic or efferent stance by exploring literature through discussions. Talking about books by citing their favorite parts or by arguing the merit of a work helps the students to construct meaning (Purves, Rogers, & Soter, 1995). This explanatory talk helps students to wonder about the world around them.

One activity that integrates oracy and critical thinking is a book talk (see Figure 5.3). During this activity, the teacher assigns a common reading of quality children's literature for the class. After reading the book, the teacher leads the book talk by listing open-ended focus questions on chart paper to stimulate responses. The teacher should also ask the students to contribute a few open-ended questions of their own to the preparation chart. After jotting down the questions, the teacher can open the discussion by modeling a response to the first question.

The discussion should then shift to the students, with the teacher keeping the students on task if the talk veers away from the focus on literature. As students become more skilled and comfortable with book talk, they can participate in small-group sessions with the teacher as facilitator among the groups. A tape recorder can be used at each table so that the teacher can assess each group's progress (Cooper & Kiger, 2001). Figure 5.4 presents a sample schedule for a book talk.

Arguing a point. Oracy, the ability to speak and listen fluently, is the building block for critical thinking. As students use oral language to reason and problem solve,

CHECKLIST OF MODELING ACTIVITIES			
Developmental Benchmarks	**Developed**	**Developing**	**Not Observed**
Language habits: Participates in discussions and asks questions Asks or answers specific questions Initiates and sustains conversations Explains or speaks from another's perspective Expresses and solicits opinions Shifts from formal to informal language			
Enjoyment of language: Continues to develop persuasive techniques Uses double meanings or multiple meanings of words to create riddles and jokes Continues to learn and use new vocabulary words Uses and explains metaphoric language Provides definitions of words he knows			
Use of literary language: Continues to use language heard in storybooks Gives increasingly elaborate descriptions of story elements Defends an opinion with text Critiques books by referring to citations from text			

Figure 5.2
Assessment of Oral Language Behaviors During Modeling Activities

- Did you have strong feelings as you read this story? If so, during which part?
- How did the author build suspense?
- Did the characters remind you of any other characters you may have read about?

Figure 5.3
Book Talk

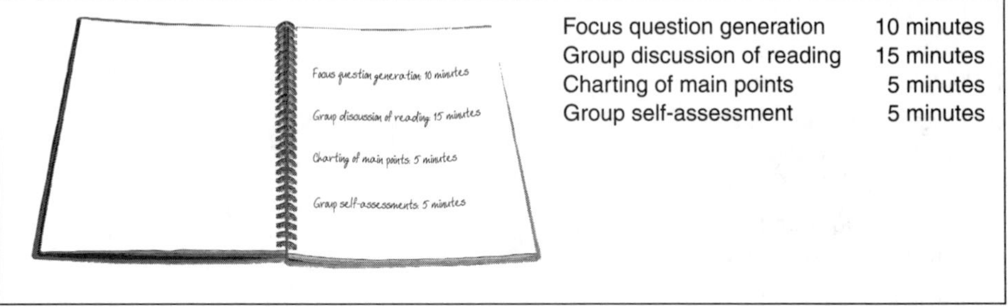

Figure 5.4
Sample Schedule for Book Talk

their cognitive development is enhanced (Lyle, 1993). One instructional strategy for using oracy to strengthen cognitive development is arguing a point.

In this strategy, children learn to present an argument or persuasive speech which they can defend in a discussion. Here is how to implement this strategy:

- The class reviews the persuasive speech of Dr. King, "I Have a Dream," which the students studied in a previous lesson.
- The class brainstorms some successful techniques to use when arguing a point and which to avoid. The teacher charts their responses.
- The teacher sets the context for the class argument by telling the children they are to be sent to a desert island. They are allowed to bring only 10 items and 2 people. The class is then divided into groups, and each group must come to a consensus about their survival plan. The teacher begins the list by stating that she would bring a doctor so that any illnesses or wounds could be healed. This provides the children with a model to follow and they respond with their choices.

1. The teacher helps to prepare the students by brainstorming possible open-ended questions about topics.

2. After practicing their interviews with peers, students conduct the interviews in pairs or individually. They ask participants for permission to tape record or simply take notes. When the interviews are concluded, students thank the participants.

3. After the interviews, students review their notes and organize a presentation.

4. The students share their information with the class through oral presentations.

Figure 5.5
Student Interview

Interviews. Interviews are wonderful techniques for strengthening students' oral language and critical thinking skills. They are also excellent tools to integrate literature, as well as the content areas. For example, after reading about the Civil Rights movement, students could interview their parents or grandparents for personal recollections. The procedure for conducting an interview is listed in Figure 5.5.

Assessment Strategies for Shared Oral Language Experiences

The assessment instrument shown in Table 5.2 and Figure 5.6 may be used to gather evidence of student learning during the shared oral language activities.

Guided Oral Language Activities for the Fluent Literacy Stage

During this phase of scaffolded literacy instruction, the teacher releases control to the student and takes on the role of coach or facilitator. The following instructional strategies may be used to facilitate children's use of oral language to develop critical thinking.

Instructional Strategies

Reciprocal teaching. Reciprocal teaching (Palinscar & Brown, 1986) is an excellent strategy for making essential comprehension skills explicit. The teacher

Table 5.2
Assessment of Oral Language Behaviors During Book Talk

Checklist for Book Talk			
Benchmarks for Oral Language	**Target**	**Acceptable**	**Needs Improvement**
Language habits	Asks questions and sustains conversations	Sometimes questions and converses; does not begin conversations	Does not ask questions or start conversations
Use of literary language	Elaborates on story elements and critiques text with evidence	Is beginning to elaborate on story elements and to critique text	Does not elaborate on story or critique it

CHECKLIST FOR ARGUING A POINT AND INTERVIEW ACTIVITIES

Developmental Benchmarks	Developed	Developing	Needs Improvement
Language habits:			
Participates in discussions and asks questions			
Asks or answers specific questions			
Initiates and sustains conversations			
Explains or speaks from another perspective			
Expresses and solicits opinions			
Shifts from formal to informal language			

Figure 5.6
Assessment of Oral Language Behaviors During Arguing a Point and Interview Activities

scaffolds modeling how to predict, question, summarize, and self-monitor while reading text. After the students grasp the technique, they can implement the strategy themselves (see Figure 5.7). After the students have seen the technique modeled by their teacher a few times, they can begin to write down their responses instead of providing them orally.

1. Predicting—The students make predictions based upon the title and pictures.
2. Questioning—The students construct questions to guide their reading after they have reviewed the text.
3. Summarizing—After reading the selection, the students construct a summary of key points in the text.
4. Clarifying—Students and teachers reflect on any comprehension problems during reading of the text and possible repair strategies.

Figure 5.7
Reciprocal Teaching

Poetry. As children become more fluent, it is important to expose them to many different genres, especially poetry. Exposure to poetry allows fluent readers to play with language devices in their own poems.

Language devices are techniques used by poets to produce special effects. Some examples of language devices are as follows (Sawyer & Sawyer, 1993):

- **Onomatopoeia** —use of words whose sounds suggest the meaning of the word such as "snap, crackle, pop"
- **Personification** —when an inanimate object is given human qualities
- **Metaphor** —a figure of speech in which one thing is spoken or written about as if it were another
- **Alliteration** —the repetition of an initial consonant in a line such as "bouncing baby boy"

Meeting Diverse Needs: Choral reading of poetry and poetry interpretation are effective ways to engage students struggling with reading.

As discussed in Chapter 4, choral reading of poetry is one instructional strategy for guided oral language instruction. Another is **poetry interpretation,** in which poems are dramatically performed. The teacher scaffolds the process by providing the poem to the children and discusses possible ways to act out the poem. The children may choose to interpret the poem through dance, illustration, sound effects, or gestures.

One excellent poem to use to introduce poetry interpretation is "Five Little Chickens":

Said the first little chicken with a queer little squirm,
"I wish I could find a fat, little worm"
Said the second little chicken with a queer little squirm,
"I wish I could find a little bug"

After the children have become more adept at poetry interpretation, they can tackle poems that are focused on imagery and couplets. An excellent poem for this transition is "Wind" by Christina Rossetti (1986).

Functions of language. Halliday (1973, 1975) identified seven categories for functions of language that children use to express themselves at home and at school. As children become fluent, it is important to demonstrate how to use oral language to communicate their needs. The seven categories of the functions of language (Jaggar & Smith-Burke, 1985) are:

Functions of Language

Instrumental	Used to satisfy needs (e.g., "I need a tissue")
Regulatory	Using words to control the behavior of others (e.g., "I want you to sit down")
Interactional	Used to establish relationships (e.g., "Will you help me with this project?")
Personal	Used to express personality and uniqueness (e.g., "I like to build model ships")
Imaginative	Used to express creativity or imagination (e.g., in poems or writing)
Heuristic	Used to explore the world and build knowledge (e.g., "I wonder why . . .")
Informative	Used to communicate information (e.g., the morning message as the class gathers)

Using Technology: The Internet is a vast resource to help children with heuristic language. The BBC Web site at http://www.bbc.co.uk offers multiple worlds to explore.

It is especially important during the fluency stage that students use the heuristic function of language to explore the world around them. Heuristic language is critical for the construction of knowledge and is one of the most important functions of language. Students use heuristic language when they problem solve or explore topics. It is only through active engagement in research or inquiry that students develop heuristic language.

Instructional Strategies for Functions of Language

Instrumental language	Children can analyze commercials on television for propaganda and discuss their findings.
Regulatory language	Students can create their own classroom rules and consequences. They can implement their rules through conflict mediation when classroom problems occur.
Interactional language	Using cooperative groups or paired activities will increase the use of interactional language.
Personal language	Students can bring in a symbol for themselves and explain to the class what it means.
Imaginative language	Poetry sessions where children share the poems they created will help to increase imaginative language.
Heuristic language	Give students "brain teasers" to solve and prompt more discussion by using the phrase "I wonder why . . ."
Informative language	Create a weekly news broadcast where students write the script about local, national, and world news and perform it for their peers.

Questioning the character. Questioning the character is a good follow-up to interviewing, which was discussed in an earlier section of this chapter. Once the students have mastered the art of questioning, they can explore responding as a character in literature. Here is how it works: The readers stop at a critical point in a story. One student takes the role of a central character, whereas another student role-plays an interviewer. The event is explored through the multiple perspectives of the characters involved. Figure 5.8 outlines the procedure for the questioning the character activity.

1. The teacher shows the class a tape of an interview so they understand the style of reporting. The class discusses the types of questions that were asked by the reporter.
2. At a critical point in the book or story, the class divides into groups of four: one student is the reporter, two others take character roles, and the fourth is the recorder. The recorder may choose to tape record the sessions or make notes.
3. After the session, each group reports on the characters' responses and the varied perspectives of a single event. The teacher may choose to chart the responses for comparison and contrast.

Figure 5.8
Questioning the Character

1. The teacher chooses a specific focus for the content area discussion. The students read their textbook to acquire background knowledge or view an Internet site. This construction of schemas about the topic is fundamental to the success of the strategy.
2. Students are placed in groups of four to respond to the focus question. The group records their responses for class discussion.
3. After an allotted time, the teacher records each group response on a chart and the class creates one response to the focus question.

Figure 5.9
Focused Talk

Focused talk. In order to achieve oracy—the ability to generate critical thinking through communication skills—students must practice **focused talk.** Focused talk is guided conversations on informational topics. The informal setting allows students to explore ideas and generate new themes or connections through dialogue. Focused talk can also be used with narrative text with the same procedures (see Figure 5.9 for instructions).

Assessment Strategies for Guided Oral Language Activities

The assessment tools shown in Figure 5.10 and Table 5.3 may be used to ascertain how students are progressing during the guided oral language activities. Data gathered from the instruments are used to plan future lessons.

Functions of Language

This matrix can be used to record observations of students' use of the functions of language. If the students are observed using a specific function of language, the teacher marks the grid (+); if students are not observed using a function, she marks the grid (−). The teacher may want to create a master list of all functions of language as a final observation.

	Instrumental	Regulatory	Interactional	Personal	Heuristic
John					
Omar					

Directions: Place indicator in the column based on your observations.

CHECKLIST FOR GUIDED ORAL LANGUAGE ACTIVITIES			
Developmental Benchmarks	**Most of the Time**	**Some of the Time**	**Almost Never**
Language habits: Participates in discussions and asks questions Asks or answers specific questions Initiates and sustains conversations Expresses and solicits opinions			
Enjoyment of language: Continues to develop persuasive techniques Continues to learn and use new vocabulary Provides definitions of words he knows			
Use of literary language: Continues to use language heard in storybooks Defends opinions of text with examples Critiques text by citing evidence from story			

Figure 5.10
Assessment of Oral Language Behaviors During Guided Activities

Table 5.3
Assessment of Oral Language Behaviors During Poetry Interpretation

Checklist for Poetry Interpretation			
Benchmarks for Oral Language	**Level 3**	**Level 2**	**Level 1**
Enjoyment of language	Continues to use and learn new words; uses and explains metaphors	Sometimes uses new words; partially understands metaphors	Does not use new words or metaphors
Use of literary language	Gives a performance; critiques poem by citing evidence	Is beginning to give a performance and sometimes critiques poetry	Does not give performance or critique text

Independent Oral Language Activities for the Fluent Literacy Stage

At the fluent stage, students can use their speaking and listening skills to strengthen critical thinking. The instructional strategies for independent practice that are presented in this section are reader's theater, famous speech presentations, group think-share, paired retellings, and painted stories.

Instructional Strategies

Reader's theater. Reader's theater is an excellent way for students to respond to the literature they have been reading. Students present their interpretation of a reading by writing and performing their version of the story. Additionally, reader's theater is beneficial for second language learners. Because the script is rehearsed before it is performed, children with special needs are given the chance to excel. Figure 5.11 outlines how to facilitate reader's theater.

Famous speech presentation. During the modeling stage of scaffolded instruction in this chapter, students were exposed to a famous speech by Dr. Martin Luther King, Jr. During the independent stage, students can perform their interpretations of famous speeches (see Figure 5.12). These presentations should occur after the students have studied the historical speech and the context of the events surrounding it.

Group think-share. The purpose of the group think-share (Kagan, 1994) is to brainstorm responses to critical thinking questions. The group sharing of responses allows all members of the class to participate in class discussions. When teachers are

1. Students select the piece of literature they want to dramatize.
2. Groups read and discuss story elements—plot, characters, setting, and theme.
3. Students write their script.
4. Students select props and settings and rehearse the play.
5. Children perform the play for peers, parents, or guests.

Figure 5.11
Reader's Theater

attempting to stimulate a discussion, it is often the same extroverted students who answer questions. This technique allows all students to feel confident in their work and creates a willingness to share in group discussions (see Figure 5.13).

Paired retellings. Retelling is the ability to summarize text in one's own words. Paired retelling is two students reading to each other and then summarizing the text.

1. The teacher selects a historic speech by Winston Churchill, Franklin Delano Roosevelt, Abraham Lincoln, George Washington, or any other historical figure.
2. Students discuss speaker's theme, persuasive style, and organization of argument.
3. Students rehearse speech.
4. Students perform speech for peers or parents.

Figure 5.12
Famous Speech Presentation

1. The teacher assigns students to groups of four.
2. The teacher poses a critical thinking question and allows time for students to jot down their answers.
3. In groups, students share their responses and jot down a group answer.
4. Groups share with the class and note how their thinking changed.

Figure 5.13
Group Think-Share

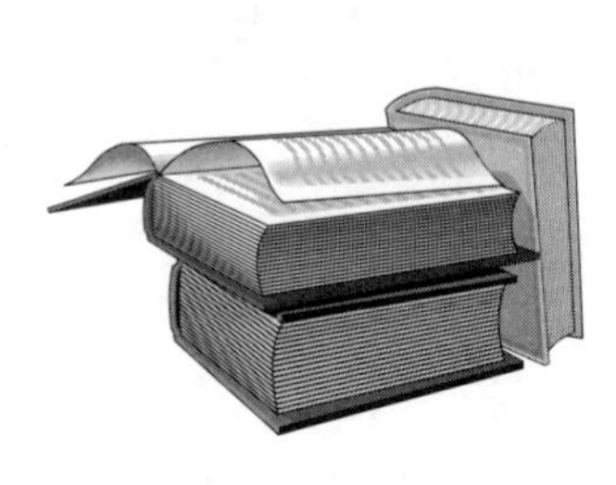

1. The teacher selects a passage for retelling.
2. In pairs, students read to each other and then summarize the passage.
3. Partners expand on each other's summaries with questions and embellishments.
4. Partners jot down their joint retellings of the passage to share with the class.

Figure 5.14
Paired Retellings

1. Students select a painting to interpret for the class. The teacher should have at least four selections for the students to choose from.
2. After the students have selected a painting, they are given time to study it and to jot down the central plot of the story. If necessary, the students may have to write out their complete story to accompany the painting.
3. Once they are ready, students present their paintings and accompanying story. Afterward, the teacher records similarities and differences among the painted stories.

Figure 5.15
Painted Stories

It is also a principal strategy to evaluate comprehension. This strategy (see Figure 5.14) can be used for both narrative and expository text (Wood, 2001).

Painted stories. Art is a powerful medium for communicating ideas. Paintings or illustrations can be creative tools for generating storytelling. One strategy, **painted stories,** uses well-known paintings by artists such as Norman Rockwell. Students are asked to tell their own story to interpret the painting. Painted stories are wonderful ways to explore multiple viewpoints. Steps for creating painted stories are shown in Figure 5.15.

Table 5.4
Assessment of Oral Language Behaviors During Independent Activities

Checklist for Independent Activities			
Benchmarks for Oral Language	**Level 3**	**Level 2**	**Level 1**
Language habits	Shifts from informal to formal language and solicits opinions	Sometimes shifts from informal to formal language	Never shifts language mode or solicits opinions
Enjoyment of language	Continues to use and learn new words; uses and explains metaphors	Sometimes uses new words; partially understands metaphors	Does not use new words or metaphors
Use of literary language	Gives a performance; critiques text by citing evidence	Is beginning to give a performance and sometimes critiques text	Does not give performance or critique text

Assessment Strategies for Independent Oral Language Activities

The assessment instrument shown in Table 5.4 may be used to reflect on students' performance of the independent oral language activities. Teachers may use the evidence to decide students' level of oral language proficiency.

Group Assessment for Group Think-Share

This assessment tool is to be used by the group for self-evaluation. Through this tool, teachers are provided with vital information concerning the group's metacognition.

Developmental Benchmarks	I can do this behavior	I need some help with it
Participates in discussions and asks questions		
Asks or answers specific questions		
Initiates and sustains conversations		
Expresses and solicits opinions		
Continues to learn and use new vocabulary		

Famous Speech Presentations

This assessment tool is designed for teachers to quickly evaluate students' presentations. If developmental benchmarks are observed, the teacher marks (+); if they are not observed, she marks (−).

	Continues persuasive language	Uses and explains metaphoric language	Continues to learn and use new vocabulary	Shifts from formal to informal language
Ottar				
Raphael				

Connecting Oral Language and Fluent Writing

During the fluency stage of literacy development, the young child is beginning to read, write, listen, and speak for critical thinking and understanding. Integrating oral language and writing helps to facilitate this process. When children speak about historical personalities and then write about them, the knowledge learned through one domain is transferred to another (Morrow, Pressley, Smith, & Smith, 1997). Additionally, teachers who use an integrated approach are helping their students to elaborate and expand their conceptual knowledge base (Walmsley & Walp, 1990).

As children expand their knowledge base and improve their oral language abilities, they are expected to be able to research and write reports in the content areas. This can be extremely difficult for children with special needs or for students struggling with literacy. The activities presented in this chapter such as the famous speech presentation help all children to acquire and expand their schemas through discussion and collaboration. Integrating these oral language activities with expository writing is a natural extension for the students. Many students struggle with writing research reports, yet there are instructional strategies to develop self-regulated writers. When students are given opportunities to engage in expository writing activities where they are able to select their level of challenge and to collaborate with peers, their chances for success rise considerably (Perry & Drummond, 2002).

Biographical writing is an expository writing activity that is collaborative and self-evaluative. As students prepare their famous speech presentation, they may also engage in a biographical study of their historical figure. Biographical studies integrate oral language as well as reading and writing. They are also a powerful tool for young children to learn about different cultures and ideas while their language skills are refined (Taylor, 2002). As students read, write, and speak about their historical figure, they are elaborating their conceptual knowledge base and beginning to understand world culture.

In addition to expository text writing, oral language at the fluency level can also be easily connected to composing poetry. As children perform their oral poetry pre-

- The teacher provides the students with biographies of famous people as models for writing one.
- The teacher guides the students as they use books, newspapers, and the Internet to gather information on their subject.
- The teacher provides the students with a graphic organizer such as a timeline to help draft the biography.
- After students have illustrated their biographies, they can share them with peers and place them in the class library.

Figure 5.16
Biographical Study

sentations, an extension activity might be to write their own poetic verse. Children use their knowledge of poetry as well as their misconceptions about it when they attempt to compose verse (Tompkins, 2002). Children are often adamant that poetry must rhyme, and therefore have to be coaxed to experiment with verse. It is important to vary the types of poems students practice for their presentations in order to expand their definition of poetry. A collaborative class poem composition is a wonderful way to start children on the journey of poetic writing which is such a creative, joyous process.

The following section describes how to connect oral language activities at the fluency stage of literacy and writing. Assessment instruments will also be presented to accompany the instructional strategies.

Instructional Strategies

The first instructional strategy describes how to use the famous speech presentation instructional strategy presented earlier in the chapter as a springboard for expository writing. Figure 5.16 describes how to facilitate a biographical study in the classroom.

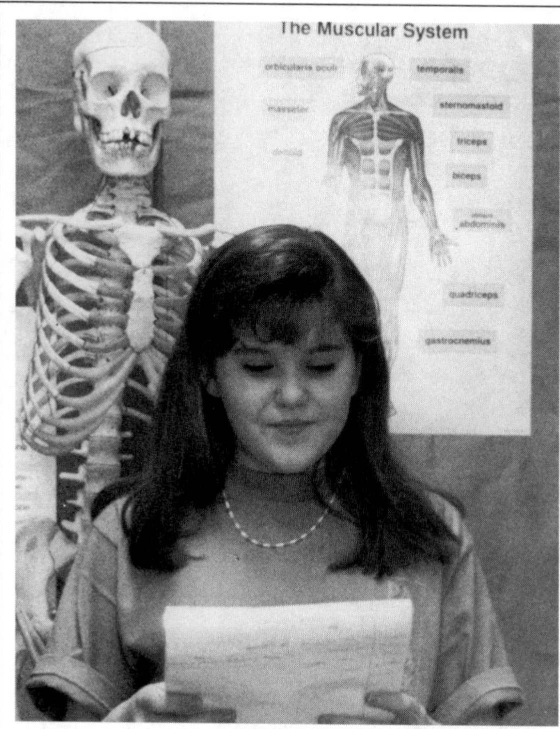

- The teacher asks the children to go home and think about an issue or topic that they care about.
- The students research their topic on the Internet and in the library.
- The teacher provides the children with a descriptive web graphic organizer to help them outline their argument.
- The students write their persuasive speech and share it with a peer for feedback. The student and teacher review and edit the speech before it is presented to the class.
- An option is to have the students vote on the issue they changed their mind about due to the speech.

Figure 5.17
Persuasive Speech

Another extension of the biographical study is "link-up" (Taylor, 2002), where students list the essential characteristics and traits of their subject and then try to find someone who shares a majority of those traits. This activity helps the children to see the connections among people and cultures and to see patterns across disciplines.

After the students have completed their famous speech presentations and biographical studies, a wonderful cumulative activity is to compose a persuasive speech. Figure 5.17 describes how to facilitate this activity.

Summary of the Instructional Cycle

The instructional cycle for oral language development at the fluency level is now complete. This chapter has presented oral language instructional strategies that can be used for modeled, shared, guided, and independent activities. The teacher decides which strategies to use based upon the assessment data. A pattern should emerge concerning each student as well as trends across the class profile. This im-

Table 5.5
Assessment of Oral Language Behaviors During Writing Activities

Checklist for Writing Activities			
Outcomes	**Target**	**Acceptable**	**Needs Improvement**
Biographical study	Integrates content into biographical study and shares it with class in clear, organized style	Partially uses content and presentation is somewhat clear	Does not use research content in biographical study
Persuasive speech	Uses volume and pitch to deliver speech using persuasive techniques	Uses some persuasive techniques	Does not use persuasive techniques

portant data is then used to shape future oral language instruction. The master assessment checklist shown in Figure 5.18 may be used at the end of the instructional cycle to identify class patterns of behavior.

Master Assessment

Directions: Based on your observations, place check marks next to the benchmarks demonstrated by 90% of the students in your class.

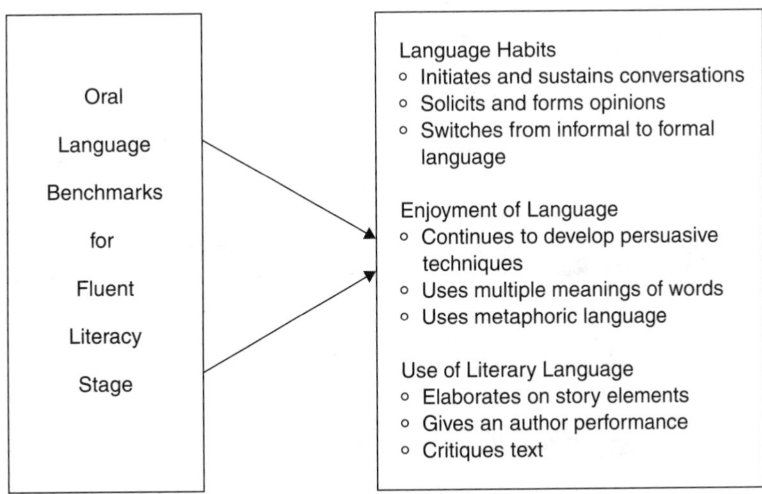

Figure 5.18
Master Assessment for Oral Language Development at the Fluent Literacy Stage

Portrait of the Instructional Cycle for Oral Language Experiences at the Fluent Literacy Level

It is October in James McElroy's third-grade classroom. James has a new addition to his class—Wendy Wu, who arrived from China 2 years ago. Wendy can communicate in English, but is still not fluent yet in writing. She is able to read on a third-grade level but remains very shy in front of her peers.

James has begun to implement his unit on human rights to correspond with the class's visit to the United Nations building. The children went to the famous site last week and enjoyed their visit. The students were eager to talk about what they saw and James used their responses to connect to his theme of human rights. James began, "We saw how the United Nations is trying to help people all over the world. In America, a famous African American leader named Dr. King fought and died to give all people equal rights." James knows that Wendy does not know much about Dr. King and he wants to supplement her knowledge base. He shows pictures of Dr. King leading marches and in jail cells. The day after the field trip, the children watched a video of Dr. King's speech "I Have a Dream."

In order to help Wendy, James has the class break up into pairs to jot down their impressions of the speech. As James moves from group to group, he overhears Wendy say to her partner, "Write that Dr. King wanted all people to be free." After jotting down their responses, the class completes their interpretation chart of the speech.

At the end of October, peers from the other third-grade class have come to listen to their friends perform their favorite speech about human rights. One of the first students to perform is Wendy Wu. Wendy begins by saying, "I chose Dr. King because he wanted all people to be free. That is why my family came from China. We wanted to be free." James smiles as he jots down on Wendy's checklist that she has internalized the persuasive argument of Dr. King.

Discussion Questions and Activities

1. During the fluency stage, the child learns academic discourse which prepares him for future work. Observe children at the fluency stage conversing in class. Record any academic discourse and reflect on the concepts illustrated in their conversations.
2. Children's literature provides an excellent vehicle for instructional conversations.

Select a book from the recommended list and engage fluent readers in book talk. Record your observations as anecdotal records.

3. It is difficult for students to shift from informal to formal discourse. How would you help your students to achieve this transition in discourse?

Additional Web Sites

Four-Blocks Literacy Model
http://www.wfu.edu/~cunningh/fourblocks/
The site offers help in planning the language arts curriculum, especially for primary teachers.

International Reading Association
http://www.reading.org
This site contains links to READING Online, IRA's new electronic professional journal.

Kathy Schrock's Guide for Educators
http://kathyschrock.net/
Links are provided to such resources as book talks, lesson plans, writing guides, and more.

Literacy.org
http://www.literacy.org

National Council of Teachers of English
http://www.ncte.org
This website provides teachers with myriad ideas for integrating the language arts.

Scholastic, Inc.
http://www.scholastic.com
This Web site cannot be missed by anyone who teaches elementary school students.

Teachers Helping Teachers
http://www.pacificnet.net/~mandel/
Resource links are provided for teachers from all fields.

The Teacher's Toolbox
http://www.trc.org/toolbox.html
The Web site gives useful information for teachers from all fields and includes links to many sites for K–12 teachers.

The Kids.com
http://www.thekids.com
The site has links to illustrated stories from around the world.

Additional Readings

Bowman, B., Donovan, M. S., Burns, M. S. (2000). *Eager to learn: Educating our preschoolers.* Washington, DC: National Academy Press.

Bruner, J. (1983). *Child's talk: Learning to use language.* Oxford, England: Oxford University Press.

Cecil, N. L. (1999). *Striking a balance: Positive practices for early literacy.* Scottsdale, AZ: Holcomb Hathaway.

Morrow, L. M. (1997). *The literacy center.* York, ME: Stenhouse.

New Standards Speaking and Listening Committee. (2001). *Speaking and listening for preschool through grade three.* Pittsburgh: National Center on Education and the Economy and the University of Pittsburgh.

Additional Children's Literature

Dyer, G. (2001). *40 Poems for "T": The fun of writing poetry.* Catskill, NY: Press Tige.

Greenfield, E. (1991). *Night on neighborhood street.* New York: Dial Books.

Griego, Y., Maestas, J., & Auaya, R. A. (1980). *Cuentas: Tales from the Hispanic Southwest.* Santa Fe: The Museum of New Mexico.

Hamilton, V. (1985). *The people could fly.* New York: Knopf.

Hopkins, L. (Ed.). (2001). *My America: A poetry atlas of the United States.* New York: Harper.

Hudson, W. (1993). *Pass it on: African-American poetry for children.* New York: Scholastic.

Knudson, R. & Swenson, M. (1999). *American sports poems.* New York: Orchard.

Mendez, P. (1989). *The black snowman.* New York: Scholastic.

Mollel, T. (1997). *Ananse's feast.* New York: Clarion Books.

Young, E. (1989). *Lon Po Po.* New York: Philomel.

Children's Literature References

Jones, K. D. (1994). *Happy birthday, Dr. King.* New York: Modern Curriculum Press.

White, E. B. (1952). *Charlotte's web.* New York: HarperCollins.

PART III

LITERACY DEVELOPMENT IN YOUNG CHILDREN

CHAPTER 6

Literacy Instruction and Assessment for Emergent Readers and Writers

Portrait of an Emergent Reader

Tamika is busy in the library corner, sitting on the rug, curled up with her favorite book. During the read-aloud, the teacher, Ms. Garcia, asked Tamika for her book request because it was her birthday. "I want 'Honey, I Love'" *(Greenfield, 1978, 1995), responded Tamika. The class joined in the refrain and talked about sounds they enjoy hearing. Now, Tamika is revisiting the text and can be heard saying, "but honey I love the way my mother talks." She looks at the pictures and recites her favorite story from memory. "You sound just like Ms. Garcia," says Damien to Tamika. Tamika responds with a proud smile.*

Scaffolding Emergent Literacy in an Early Childhood Classroom

It is during the emergent literacy years that children play with language. Their approximations of reading and writing are vital links in the literacy continuum toward fluency. The child begins these approximations after years of immersion in oral language. As you read in the previous chapters, as children hear and engage in rich oral language models, they absorb vocabulary concepts, syntax, and story structures. This foundational knowledge about language will be tapped during the emergent literacy years. Early childhood classrooms that integrate emergent reading and writing reflect the developmental process of literacy acquisition.

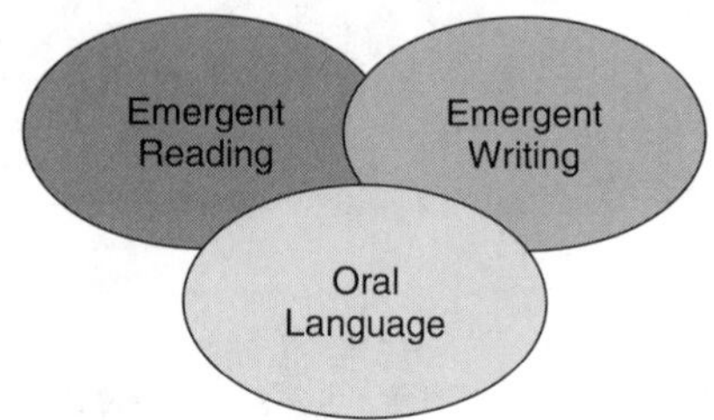

Reading Chapter 6

As you read this chapter, reflect on the following topics:

- What children at the emergent stage of literacy development already know about reading and writing
- How benchmarks within the emergent stage of literacy development help us to think about what literacy concepts and skills children need to learn
- How instruction and assessment are aligned for the emergent reader and writer
- How the teacher may use assessment results to plan for student learning

What Is Emergent Literacy?

Emergent literacy is a relatively new concept in the development of reading and writing. Previously, teachers and reading theorists espoused reading readiness which held that children could not begin formal reading instruction until they had acquired prerequisite skills (Gessell, 1925).

In the 1980s Clay introduced the term *emergent literacy,* which promoted the idea that literacy occurs along a continuum and that children acquire concepts about print long before they enter formal schooling. These concepts about print are learned from formal storytelling sessions or from watching adults engage in literacy. Clay's (1982) concepts of print include

- Words have meaning and pictures accompany the words to convey meaning.
- Reading on a page is in a left to right direction.
- Written words represent spoken words.
- We read from top to bottom and then continue onto the next page.
- Words consist of letters.
- Sentences begin with capital letters and end in periods.

Building Blocks of Emergent Literacy: Phonological Processing and the Alphabetic Principle

One predictor of children's literacy development is their phonological processing skills (Whitehurst & Lonigan, 2001). Phonological processing skills include the following:

- **Sensitivity to sounds.** Young children are able to hear the sounds in words.
- **Manipulation of sounds.** This skill involves being able to play with the onset and rime of words. Children mastering this phonological skill are able to hear the word *mat* and, when asked to change the beginning sound, can create *cat.*
- **Use of sounds in words.** This final phonological processing skill involves using the knowledge of sounds to decode and encode words.

Phonological sensitivity, defined in Chapter 3 as the ability to detect and manipulate the sound structure of oral language, does not need exposure to written language to develop. However, phonological sensitivity is the precursor to identification of phonemes and decoding. Research shows that prereaders with a large oral vocabulary are better able to segment sounds (Burgess & Lonigan, 1998; Lonigan, Burgess, & Anthony, 2000). Children who do not enter early childhood classrooms with phonological sensitivity are shown to benefit from phonological training in their reading and spelling skills (Bus & van Ijzendoorn, 1999).

Phonemic awareness, a phonological processing skill, is the ability to segment sounds or phonemes (Snow, Burns, & Griffin, 1998). Phonemic awareness is a necessary skill used in associating letters with sounds. Research has shown that training in phonemic awareness as well as instruction in letter–sound correlations promotes literacy acquisition (Byrne & Fielding-Barnsley, 1991). According to Adams (1990), there are five ability levels of phonemic awareness:

Phonemic awareness and the alphabetic principle are the building blocks of literacy.

- To hear rhymes and alliterations as measured by knowledge of nursery rhymes
- To compare and contrast the sounds of words for rhymes and alliterations
- To blend and split syllables
- To perform phonemic segmentation by counting out the number of phonemes in a word
- To manipulate phonemes by adding or deleting a particular phoneme

The alphabetic principle, which is the realization that each letter represents a sound or phoneme, develops alongside phonemic awareness. Children who cannot identify individual letters will have difficulty recognizing the sounds letters represent (Bond & Dykstra, 1967). An early childhood classroom that facilitates both phonemic awareness and the alphabetic principle works on the following skills:

- Rhyming words
- Counting words in sentences
- Counting syllables in words
- Segmenting and blending syllables
- Segmenting and blending phonemes
- Substituting sounds

Emergent Reading—Acting Like Readers

Young children's knowledge of vocabulary and development of phonological sensitivity is aided through daily storytelling by caretakers and teachers. Storybook reading

Using Technology: You can learn more about emergent literacy by checking out the Center for the Improvement of Early Reading Achievement at http://www.ciera.org.

facilitates literacy acquisition as it helps young children to learn vocabulary (Snow & Goldfield, 1983), syntactical construction, and use of decontextualized language (Sulzby, 1985). When children repeatedly hear favorite storybooks, they internalize the written language features and begin to ask questions about the content of the story rather than its pictures (Kaderavek & Sulzby, 1999).

It is through these daily read-alouds that children learn to associate storybook reading as a pleasurable activity. Because the child has no control over the process, she is placed in a state of disequilibrium and gains mastery by asking her caretaker or parent to "read it again." As children listen to repeated readings in a safe environment, they are encouraged to take risks and approximate words as the caretaker asks, "What do you think it says?" It is through these daily language lessons that young children begin to engage in emergent reading behaviors (Doake, 1985).

At first, children will use the pictures to guess at the words until gradually they begin to use their phonological processing skills to decode words. This transition from approximating reading to beginning to tackle the printed word occurs after years of immersion in oral language.

What Is Emergent Writing?

According to Graves (1983), when children come to school about 90% believe they can write. The job of early childhood educators is to build upon that confidence and facilitate the development of emergent writing (Sedgwick, 1999).

As with emergent reading, young children begin to write long before they enter school. Their early scribbling and drawings are approximations of the writing process (Dyson, 1989). As they draw and scribble, children are internalizing concepts about letters and sounds and are learning from their mistakes (Ferreiro, 1986). Through writing, young children learn not only about phonemes and the alphabetic principle but also about how to reconstruct their experiences and concepts about the world around them (Birnbaum & Emig, 1983). It is through daily approximations of writing and reading that young children begin to master the literacy process.

Stages of Emergent Writing

Similar to emergent reading, young children begin writing by using pictures to convey meaning. At first they draw large pictures, and gradually letters begin to appear with the pictures, but they do not correspond with phonemes. An important shift occurs when children begin to phonetically write the words they wish to accompany their picture. As they learn more words, their pictures decrease in size because they are no longer necessary to convey the child's meaning. Sulzby (1989) categorized this process as consisting of seven stages, shown in Figure 6.1.

Spelling Development

As children shift into invented spelling, their writing activities also facilitate their knowledge of phonics. A visitor to an early childhood classroom will often find an

STAGES OF EMERGENT WRITING	DESCRIPTION	SAMPLE
Drawing	The child's illustration is the story.	
Scribbling	The child may write a series of letters or squiggly lines.	
Letterlike forms	This is similar to the previous stage; however, the child separates the letters.	PZ
Prephonemic spelling	These are conventional letters but no phonemes are attached.	PBT WZF QM
Copying	The child copies from environmental print or signs around her, like *exit.*	EXIT.
Invented spelling	The child is spelling phonetically but may be missing a few letters (e.g., *dg* for *dog*).	DG
Conventional spelling	The child uses conventional spellings. There may be a few errors.	I Lik Milk.

Figure 6.1
Stages of Emergent Writing
Source: Morrow (1989).

emergent writer diligently sounding out as she writes, "THE GRL SAT DWN" (Read, 1971). As children develop and are instructed in word patterns, their spelling skills occur in five stages (Gentry, 1982). Figure 6.2 breaks down the five stages of spelling development.

Activities for Emergent Literacy

Emergent literacy is the developmental period when children begin to link their oral language and printed text (Fountas & Pinnell, 1996). As children engage in meaningful literacy activities guided by their parents and teachers, they learn how language functions (Rogoff, 1990; Wells, 1990). Interactive literacy events such as the daily read-aloud have been found to be the single most important activity to build literacy in emergent readers (Bus, van Ijzendoorn, & Pellegrini, 1995). It is through the daily read-aloud that children begin to internalize literary language and story genres. Choral readings of patterned books can also be used to develop phonemic awareness. Why is this simple instructional activity so powerful? Literacy is modeled for the children as they begin to internalize the behaviors of engaged readers.

PREPHONETIC STAGE OF SPELLING DEVELOPMENT—RANDOM LETTERS		
Characteristics of Writing • Scribbles and draws shapes that look like letters • Makes random letters and shapes • Uses no spaces between words • Draws pictures to express meaning	Knowledge of Spelling • Lacks letter–sound relationship • Begins to copy small words	Writing Sample NBWSDG
EARLY PHONETIC STAGE OF SPELLING DEVELOPMENT—CONSONANTS		
Characteristics of Writing • Begins to show letter–sound relationships • Uses invented spelling • Uses initial consonants • Spells words with consonants • Uses spaces between words	Knowledge of Spelling • Knows longer words have longer spellings • Matches some consonants with correct sounds • Begins to decode words when reading	Writing Sample CT DG FSH
ADVANCED PHONETIC STAGE OF SPELLING DEVELOPMENT—VOWELS		
Characteristics of Writing • Spells words using letter–sound relationships • Spells words based on how they look • Begins to use long vowels in spelling words	Knowledge of Spelling • Knows how to spell some sight words • Knows most consonant sounds • Sees distinctive features in words (i.e., the extenders in *yellow*)	Writing Sample The cat sat on the mat.
TRANSITIONAL STAGE OF SPELLING DEVELOPMENT—VOWEL AND CONSONANT COMBINATIONS IN WORDS		
Characteristics of Writing • Spells words using more standard forms of spelling • Relies more on visual memory, how words look, to spell words • Spells more sight words correctly • Spells words using familiar letter patterns • Spells words by representing all syllables	Knowledge of Spelling • Knows and applies basic spelling rules • Knows and spells some words with their endings (e.g., *-s, -ing, -ly*) • Knows short and long vowels and begins to use them correctly in spelling • Knows correct spelling of more sight words	Writing Sample I can swim along the riverbank.

Figure 6.2
Stages of Spelling Development

STANDARD STAGE OF SPELLING DEVELOPMENT—CORRECT SPELLING		
Characteristics of Writing	Knowledge of Spelling	Writing Sample
• Spells most words using standard or correct spelling • Begins to spell words that have multiple spellings (e.g., *their, there, they're*) correctly • Relies on meaning and syntax as well as phonics to spell words	• Knows compound words, root words, affixes • Knows more rules and applies them to spelling • Knows compound words and contractions	The boy can't read his book.

Figure 6.2
Continued

Daily songs, choral readings, or nursery rhymes facilitate linguistic awareness. As discussed previously, linguistic awareness is the ability to use one's knowledge of sounds and syntax while reading (Harris & Hodges, 1995). Recitation of nursery rhymes enables the young child to hear differences in sounds (which is the precursor of phonemic awareness, or knowledge of sounds), which research has shown to be an early indicator of reading achievement (Maclean, Bryant, & Bradley, 1987).

In addition to nursery rhymes and songs, early childhood classrooms spend precious time daily reading aloud favorite storybooks. This language format (Bruner, 1983) mimics the familiar bedtime storytelling routine in many families, which research has shown to be the single most important activity for facilitating literacy success (Bus et al., 1995). Discussions during and after reading the storybook broaden children's schemas and enrich their vocabulary (Snow, 1994). Daily read-alouds also expose children to a variety of genres and literary language, enabling them to begin recognizing familiar plotlines (Anderson, Hiebert, Scott, & Wilkinson, 1985). Daily read-aloud activities also facilitate children's concepts about print (Clay, 1982) such as left to right directionality. Extensions of the storytelling session may also include word study of new vocabulary, thereby promoting phonemic awareness (Fountas & Pinnell, 1996).

Building upon children's budding knowledge of the alphabetic system is one of the core responsibilities of the early childhood teacher. Knowledge of the letters and sounds as well as phonemic patterns gradually unfolds through the teacher's guidance (Clay, 1982; Fountas & Pinnell, 1996). Phonemic awareness is facilitated through language play in reading and writing (Yopp, 1988). Children's approximations of spellings are strong indicators of their alphabetic knowledge (Read, 1971). Furthermore, engaging in emergent writing facilitates emergent reading as children practice spelling patterns and begin to build a sight word vocabulary (Chomsky, 1979; Sulzby, 1985).

The **language experience approach,** which is described in more detail later in this chapter, has long been a successful activity for all language learners. In the language experience approach (Stauffer, 1980), the teacher acts as scribe and writes down the learner's words verbatim. The child's writing becomes the text for the reading lesson.

The power of this strategy is that language learners see their oral language translated into printed matter. The text becomes the base for word play, vocabulary, and comprehension activities. This approach can be used with adult students as well as second language learners.

A strong early childhood literacy program builds upon a foundation in oral language. Literacy activities that integrate oral language, listening, reading, and writing strengthen the child's growing awareness of language and its uses. This chapter will demonstrate how early childhood teachers can use simple daily literacy activities to help facilitate students' development of emergent literacy benchmarks. Assessment tools to document students' growth and to inform practice are also included.

Developmental Benchmarks for the Emergent Literacy Stage

It is during the period of emergent literacy that both the adult and the child take active roles in the construction of literacy (Soderman, Gregory, & O'Neill, 1999). Through the processes of modeled, shared literacy experiences, and guided practice, emergent readers and writers move toward independent practice. Table 6.1 lists the developmental benchmarks for the emergent literacy stage. The following section describes the emergent literacy behaviors, which are scaffolded by more capable language users during this period (Fountas & Pinnell, 1996).

Developing Emergent Literacy Benchmarks

Emergent readers are beginning to retell stories by relying on picture clues and can often recognize their own names on classroom charts or signs. Viewing themselves as readers and writers provides the impetus to further their knowledge of the world of literacy.

Table 6.1
Developmental Benchmarks for the Emergent Literacy Stage

Letter Knowledge	Story Sense	Book Sense	Word-Solving Strategies
Points to the letters in name Writes name in uppercase and lowercase letters Can match letters Says the letters of the alphabet Knows some letter sounds in isolation Can write some letters in uppercase and lowercase	Listens to a story for an extended time Responds to a story by telling how it made her feel Retells a story and includes beginning, middle, and end Talks about characters in a story Responds to stories with personal experiences Repeats the story refrain during shared reading	Shows an interest in books Finds the front and back of book Points to the title of book and author's name Turns pages and knows where to begin Points to word on page Knows the direction of print	Reads emergent-level text through memorization and language patterns Reads and writes some sight words Uses pictures in story to recall words Begins to identify sounds in print

Portrait of Readerlike Behaviors

Damien and Carl are sitting in the book nook of their kindergarten room. Today they are perusing *It Looked Like Spilt Milk* (Shaw, 1993) which Ms. Garcia had read aloud to the class yesterday. Together they recite their approximations of the text for each page by using the colorful illustrations as prompts. "They said it looked like a squirrel but it wasn't. They said it looked like an angel . . . but it wasn't," Damien and Carl recite together.

Letter knowledge. Ewelina's exposure to an environment marinated in print has helped to facilitate her interest in letters and words. Gradually Ewelina will learn that letters represent sounds.

Portrait of an Emergent Writer

Ewelina is busy at the writing center of Ana Garcia's kindergarten classroom, concentrating on a task. Ewelina's friend Jennifer comes over to ask, "Do you want to play at the computer with me?" "No, I have to finish my mail," responds Ewelina. Typical for her age, Ewelina is focused on writing to her friend.

Ewelina writes to her friend,

DR BL HLO EWELINA
(Dear Bill, Hello Ewelina)

Ewelina's emergent writing illustrates her ability to write her name and knowledge of uppercase letters. She is also beginning to attempt to phonetically decode words.

Story sense. Ana Garcia's kindergarten class is illustrating their sense of story. They can determine the beginning, middle, and end of the story and describe their favorite characters. Emergent readers are also beginning to describe their responses to various stories and how they made them feel. It is clear that the stories read during daily storytime model critical emergent literacy behaviors as children begin to internalize them (Soderman et al., 1999).

Portrait of a Child's Sense of Story

It is Monday afternoon, and Ms. Garcia begins the afternoon with a read aloud. Today she has chosen *I Went Walking* because the children requested it as it is one of their favorites. As Ana reads this patterned book, the children join in with the repeated refrain, "I went walking and what did I see?" They remain attentive throughout the story and the discussion that follows.

Book sense. Damien and Carl's pretend reading of *It Looked Like Spilt Milk* also demonstrated their book sense because they began their retelling by reading the title page and then naming the author and illustrator. Both boys were able to approximate reading from a left to right progression and to derive meaning cues from pictures in the story. Clay (1975) referred to these behaviors as concepts about print and argued that children were demonstrating their emergence as readers. Damien and Carl's approximation of reading behaviors illustrates the beginning of the literacy continuum as children move toward fluency.

Word-solving strategies. Ewelina's friend Jennifer loves to draw and spends most of her time in the arts and crafts center. Today she is creating a drawing of two cats, spurred on by Ms. Garcia's reading of *Millions of Cats* (Gag, 1956). Her drawing has lots of details, such as earrings for cats, and takes up the whole page. After finishing the drawing, Jennifer decides to title her picture with two words she selects from the class word chart—*cats* and *dogs.* Jennifer recognized the words *cats* and *dogs* from her multiple exposures through the daily read-aloud and word chart. Her recognition of simple sight words and use of pictures to recall words documents typical word-solving skills of the emergent reader. As Jennifer begins to associate letters and sounds, she will begin to recognize familiar phonemic patterns.

Developing Literacy in Emergent Readers and Writers Through Modeled Activities

As children at the emergent literacy level are immersed in a language-rich environment, they begin to engage in literacy behaviors. Children learn first to approximate these behaviors through engaging in literacy activities guided by a more competent language user (Rogoff, 1990; Wells, 1990). As literacy behaviors are modeled, children feel more confident to attempt them under the coaching or scaffolding of the teacher.

Teaching Through Modeling

Children's first exposures in learning to read and write occur within interactive and constructive contexts. In Chapters 1 and 2 we discussed how children first learn about reading and writing through real and natural experiences. They carefully observe

Types of Modeled Literacy Instruction	Examples of Modeled Literacy Instruction
• Implicit modeling involves a literacy experience that is not directly identified as a teaching event	• Reading aloud • Writing aloud • Shared reading
• Explicit modeling involves showing children how to do something	• Showing children where to put the author's name in writing a story • Demonstrating how to change your voice when reading dialogue
• Talk-aloud involves presenting a series of steps for completing a literacy task	• Modeling the steps in writing an informational paragraph
• Think-aloud involves thinking out loud the steps that a strategic reader or writer uses to accomplish a task	• Thinking out loud about how to edit a story for punctuation and capital letters; during shared reading, thinking out loud aloud about how to use multiple cueing strategies in word solving when reading unknown words

Figure 6.3
Types of Modeled Literacy Instruction

adults reading and writing and begin to construct the concepts about print. Scaffolding or modeling the literacy process is an important type of instruction that is especially required by beginning readers and writers (Dole, Duffy, Roehler, & Pearson, 1991). Providing effective literacy instruction includes **demonstrations** to children on how reading and writing work, an aspect of the balanced literacy program called modeled literacy. There are different ways to demonstrate or model the literacy processes (see Figure 6.3). In this section, you will read about several ways to model literacy instruction at the emergent stage of development. After each instructional strategy, an on-the-spot assessment tool is described for determining student learning and documenting literacy growth within the context of instruction. This section presents literacy activities for modeling strategies for the emergent reader and writer. Each activity uses oral language as the foundation for integrating the language arts throughout the activity.

Phonemic Awareness Activities

Copy that sound. As stated, research has shown that children benefit from phonological awareness training (Lonigan et al., 2000). Early childhood classrooms that focus on rhymes and phonemic segmentation are also facilitating the alphabetic principle. The alphabetic principle is the concept that letters represent phonemes. The activity Copy That Sound (Figure 6.4) may be used to introduce the children to the concept of identical sounds and recognizing them.

Sound stretch. The sound stretch activity can be used to model phonemic segmentation. It may take students a few practice sessions before they are able to master counting sounds in words. Figure 6.5 describes how to do the sound stretch activity in the classroom.

- The teacher shows children small cymbals, toy telephone with ringer, crying baby doll, and bike horn and demonstrates the sounds they make. The children copy the sounds with their voices.
- The teacher blindfolds one child and has another child make a noise with one of the items. The blindfolded child must guess which object made the sound.

Figure 6.4
Copy That Sound

- The teacher models with a large rubber band how to stretch out a word as he says the word. For example: *MMMM/AAA/NNN.*
- The teacher models with a stretched-out band how to bring the rubber band back to its original length as he says the word quickly. For example, *man.*
- Children practice on their own stretching out words.

Figure 6.5
Sound Stretch

- The teacher explains that he will say the sounds in a word slowly. The children take turns saying it quickly. For example, the teacher says "k-a-t" and the children say, "cat". The teacher says "cow-boy" and the children say "cowboy."

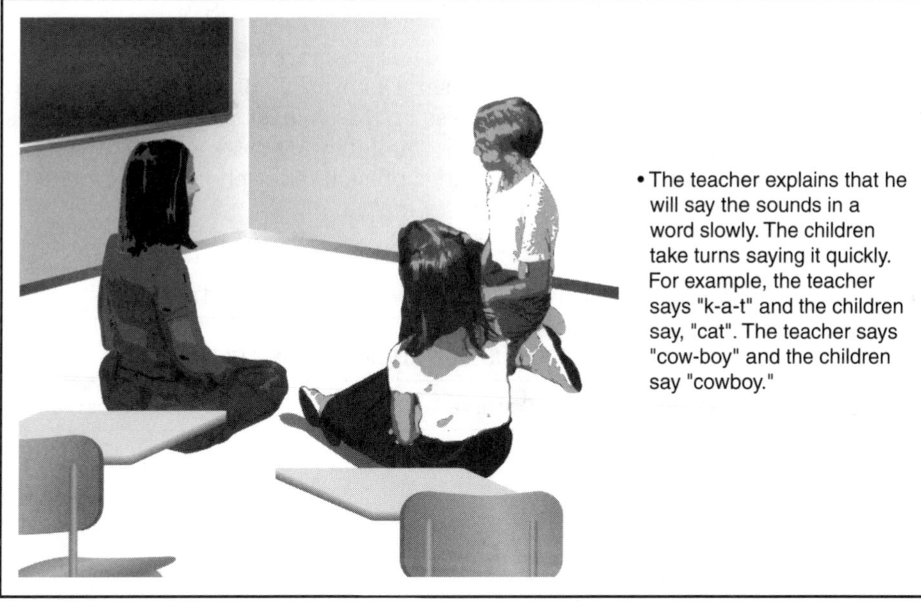

Figure 6.6
Follow-Me Game

- The teacher chooses a nursery rhyme to focus on such as "Hey Diddle Diddle," and writes it on chart paper for the children to see.
- The children say, chant, and clap the rhyme or they may act out the rhyme with props.
- After the children are familiar with the rhyme, the teacher reads the first two lines and asks, "Did you hear anything funny there?" He points out the words that are alike and says, "We call these rhyming words." The children are asked to find other rhyming words.
- As the children become familiar with this routine, names of other nursery rhymes are placed in a nursery rhyme box and the children select a new text to focus on for that day.

Figure 6.7
Nursery Rhyme Box

Follow-me game. Once the children are comfortable with phonemic segmentation, the teacher can begin to model blending of phonemes with this easy game (see Figure 6.6).

Involving Parents: On Parent Night, share these strategies with parents to use as they drive their children around town or to school.

Nursery rhyme box. Preschools are traditionally the place where children hear and sing nursery rhymes. However, due to the recent research on phonemic awareness, elementary-grade teachers are also incorporating nursery rhymes into their literacy lessons. The nursery rhyme box activity (Figure 6.7) may be used with any nursery rhyme (Soderman et al., 1999).

Assessment of Phonemic Awareness

In early childhood education, it is imperative that the teacher responds to the child's instructional needs (Bowman, Donovan, & Burns, 2000). One way for a teacher to develop a curriculum focused on the child is to assess the child in a naturalistic context (Bowman et al., 2000). The following assessment of phonemic awareness may be used for all of the activities presented for phonemic awareness: copy that sound, sound stretch, and the follow-me game.

Directions: Use your observations to identify behaviors demonstrated by students.

CHECKLIST OF PHONEMIC AWARENESS

Developmental Benchmarks	Observed—Date	Not Observed—Date
• Identifies words with same sounds • Identifies same-sound patterns • Identifies rhyming words • Separates sounds in short-vowel words (e.g., *man, cat, dog*) • Blends phonemes into words • Identifies syllables in two-syllable words through clapping • Identifies syllables in three-syllable words through clapping • Identifies rhyming words		

Modeling the Alphabetic Principle

Name call. The calling of names for the morning roster is a daily ritual in early childhood classrooms. The name call activity also can be used to develop letter and sound identification in order to promote word-solving strategies. Teachers may begin with a name pocket chart containing children's first names. As each child puts away her things, she moves her name to the *Present* column. Some teachers use digital cameras to take students' photos and attach them to the names to initially help children to recognize their names.

Child's Name	**Present**
Ana	
Bill	
Jennifer	

The name pocket chart can be used to find names that begin with the same letter or sound of the week as well as to focus on alphabetizing. For students entering

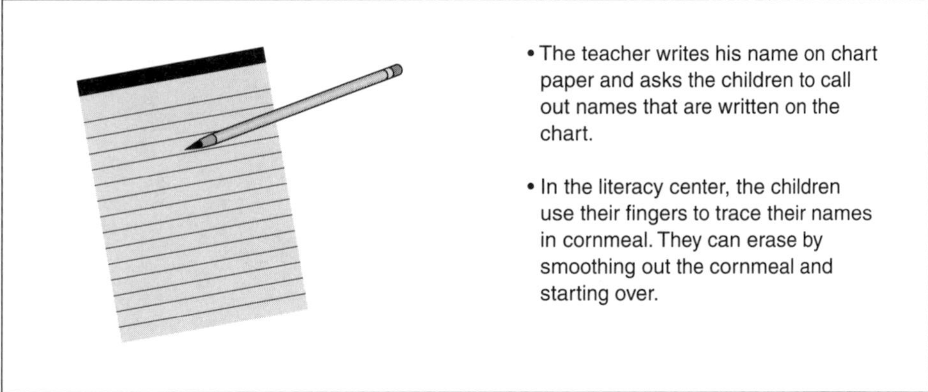

Figure 6.8
Cornmeal Writing

the emergent literacy stage, it can be used to identify uppercase and lowercase letters. As they develop fluency, children can write their names themselves and place them in the pocket chart (Fountas & Pinnell, 1996).

Cornmeal writing. Emergent readers and writers gradually develop the concept that words convey meaning and that letters represent sounds. The cornmeal writing activity, shown in Figure 6.8, can be used to help young children recognize that they can write what they say.

Assessment of Alphabetic Principle Activities

The following Assessment of Letter Knowledge can be used for a variety of purposes. The teacher may circle letters that the child can identify and recognize during the name call and cornmeal writing activities. A variation of the assessment tool is to place the letters on individual letter cards and ask the students to identify each letter. As the child responds, the letter is circled. Children are first asked for only uppercase letters, and then later on they are asked for lowercase letters. A third variation of the assessment is to ask the students for the sounds for each letter.

Spelling Activities

As children study phonemes and segmenting sounds, they are also developing their knowledge about words (Cunningham, 2000). The following activities are designed to facilitate the emergent reader's awareness of spelling patterns.

Word wall. A visitor to today's early childhood or elementary classrooms is often shown the classroom's word wall. There are several different versions of this activity; however, the word wall discussed in this section (Figure 6.9) emphasizes word patterns. It is important that teachers "do the word wall" (Cunningham, 2000) rather than just post new words in the classroom. Doing the word wall means introducing the word pattern to the children and internalizing its features.

Assessment of Letter Knowledge

Names Uppercase Letters	**Names Lowercase Letters**	**Knows Letter Sounds**
A	a	A
B	b	B
C	c	C
D	d	D
E	e	E
F	f	F
G	g	G
H	h	H
I	i	I
J	j	J
K	k	K
L	l	L
M	m	M
N	n	N
O	o	O
P	p	P
Q	q	Q
R	r	R
S	s	S
T	t	T
U	u	U
V	v	V
W	w	W
X	x	X
Y	y	Y
Z	z	Z

- The teacher selects a simple word pattern such as "the **at** family." After introducing this simple word pattern, he selects high-frequency words the children need in order to read or write such as "the."
- The teacher cuts around the configuration of the word or color codes it to give the children visual clues to discern the word pattern.
- Before placing the new words on the wall, the teacher dictates the new words in sentences. The students write the words on their papers.
- The students clap out the sounds in the word and discuss its features.
- The drill is repeated the next day. The remainder of the week, the teacher dictates any five words from the word wall as a review for the children.

Figure 6.9
Doing the Word Wall

- After the children have enjoyed the nursery rhyme, the teacher shows two of the rhyming words on index cards.
- The two cards are placed one on top of the other in a pocket chart. The teacher then asks the children to name the other rhyming words in the text. He selects only those words with the same spelling pattern to write on the index cards.
- After the pairs have been placed in the pocket chart, the teacher asks the children to name the spelling pattern for each word.
- The teacher models for the children how to transfer a known spelling pattern to write a new word. For example, he says, "Now that we know *fiddle, diddle,* I can write *middle* by using the same spelling pattern and adding an *m.*" He repeats with a few more words to illustrate this spelling strategy.
- The class completes the activity by adding new spelling words to the remaining rhyming word pairs in the pocket chart.

Figure 6.10
Rounding Up the Rhymes

The children may be given "portable" word walls (Cunningham, 2000) that consist of file folders with the words printed inside. These easy reference guides are used during guided reading sessions or when the students are writing independently.

Rounding up the rhymes. In the preceding section on phonemic awareness and the alphabetic principle, nursery rhymes were used to teach rhyming. After the children have learned the nursery rhymes, the same text may be used for the rounding up the rhymes activity described in Figure 6.10 (Cunningham, 2000).

Assessment of Spelling Activities

The student profile of spelling development (Figure 6.11) is designed to follow the child throughout the year. As the child moves from prephonetic to conventional spelling (review Figure 6.2), the teacher records the student's progress in the assessment tool.

Modeling Emergent Writing

Meeting Diverse Needs: Second language learners may be able to label only one or two items in a picture drawing. Gradually, they will learn more vocabulary. Write down the few words they do know.

The language experience approach. An early childhood classroom integrates emergent reading and writing in its daily activities. The language experience approach (Stauffer, 1980) is a traditional early childhood activity that continues to be used due to its integration of oral language, reading, and writing. In this activity, the teacher acts as scribe and writes down the children's responses. Usually the text is written after a common experience such as a field trip

Student's Name ______________________________

PREPHONETIC STAGE OF SPELLING DEVELOPMENT—RANDOM LETTERS

Date:

_____Scribbles and draws shapes that look like letters

_____Makes random letters and shapes

_____Uses no spaces between words

_____Draws pictures to express meaning

Grade_____/4

EARLY PHONETIC STAGE OF SPELLING DEVELOPMENT—CONSONANTS

Date:

_____Begins to show letter–sound relationships

_____Uses invented spelling

_____Uses initial consonants

_____Spells words with consonants

_____Uses spaces between words

Grade_____/5

ADVANCED PHONETIC STAGE OF SPELLING DEVELOPMENT

Date:

_____Spells words using letter–sound relationships

_____Spells words based on how they look

_____Begins to use long vowels in spelling words

Grade_____/3

TRANSITIONAL STAGE OF SPELLING DEVELOPMENT—VOWEL AND CONSONANT COMBINATIONS IN WORDS

_____Spells words using more standard forms of spelling

_____Relies more on visual memory, how words look, to spell words

_____Spells more sight words correctly

_____Spells words using familiar letter patterns

_____Spells words by representing all syllables by the end of this step

Grade_____/5

STANDARD STAGE OF SPELLING DEVELOPMENT—CORRECT SPELLING

_____Spells most words using standard or correct spelling

_____Begins to spell words that have multiple spellings (e.g., *their, there, they're*) correctly

_____Relies on meaning and syntax as well as phonics to spell words

Grade_____/3

Figure 6.11
Student Profile of Spelling Development

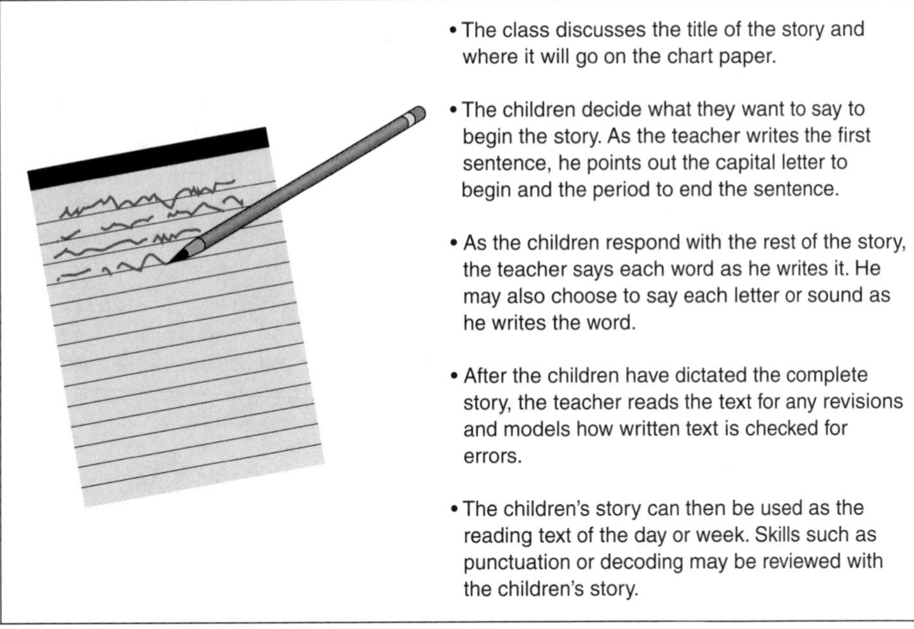

Figure 6.12
Language Experience Approach

or in response to a book or event (Soderman et al., 1999). Figure 6.12 outlines the language experience approach.

Daily news. The daily news activity is another traditional early childhood instructional strategy (Soderman et al., 1999). Similar to the language experience activity, the teacher acts as a scribe and records the children's news or school happenings. During the activity, the teacher models sentence construction and phonological processing (see Figure 6.13).

Assessment of Emergent Writing Activities

Emergent writing rubrics. The first assessment tool, the emergent writing rubric, presented in Table 6.2, is to be used as children transition from the scribbling or drawing stage of writing toward the prephonemic stage. Similarly, the profile of writing development shown in Figure 6.14 can be used to trace the child's transition through the stages of writing during the emergent literacy period.

Anecdotal records. Knowledge of developmental benchmarks helps the early childhood teacher to record the students' journey along the literacy continuum. A balanced literacy program integrates both formal and informal assessment methods (Cooper, 2000). One informal technique is an anecdotal record. Anecdotal records describe what the student does and interpret the literacy action. Anecdotal records can be used to describe improvements in reading and writing behaviors throughout

- The teacher begins the activity by writing on chart paper *TODAY IS MONDAY* with the accompanying date.
- The teacher models reading the text to the class and asks them to repeat it.
- The teacher asks the class if anyone has news he or she would like to share. The teacher writes the news by inserting the student's name. For example, "Shawonda said that her aunt is having a baby." After four or five students have shared news the teacher guides the class in reading the text. Some teachers only ask the leaders of the day to share their news.
- The daily news text may be used as the reading text of the day for review of skills and strategies. Some teachers collect the charts for monthly books that are bound and kept in the classroom library. At the end of the year, it becomes an excellent review of class happenings for the students.

Figure 6.13
Daily News

the year (Tombari & Borich, 1999). A simple technique is to keep index cards at the ready to jot down important literacy events. The following is an example of an anecdotal record:

Name: Tamika Amos Class: Kindergarten
Date: November 9

Event: In the Library corner, Tamika retold the story *Honey, I Love* from memory. She pointed to each word and read with expression. When Tamika was unsure of a word, she used picture clues to try and remember the storyline.

Interpretation: Tamika is still relying on picture clues to read text. She has not yet made the transition to decoding. Tamika can recognize some sight words and does have concepts about print such as left to right reading and the return sweep.

Table 6.2
Emergent Writing Rubric

Emergent Writing Behaviors	Target	Acceptable	Needs Improvement
Writes uppercase and lowercase letters	Uses both uppercase and lowercase letters	Sometimes uses uppercase and lowercase letters	Uses only uppercase letters
Writes consonants and vowel sounds in words	Writes both consonants and vowel sounds	Writes some vowel and consonant sounds	Writes only consonant sounds
Begins to write sentences and use punctuation	Writes sentences with punctuation	Sometimes writes sentences and uses punctuation	Does not write sentences or use punctuation

STAGES OF EMERGENT WRITING	DESCRIPTION AND NOTES ON WRITING SAMPLE	DATE OBSERVED
Drawing	The child's illustration is the story.	
Scribbling	The child may write a series of letters or squiggly lines.	
Letterlike forms	This is similar to the previous stage; however, the child separates the letters.	
Prephonemic spelling	These are conventional letters but no phonemes are attached.	
Copying	The child copies from environmental print or signs around her, like *exit.*	
Invented spelling	The child is spelling phonetically but may be missing a few letters (e.g., *dg* for *dog*).	
Conventional spelling	The child uses conventional spellings. There may be a few errors.	

Figure 6.14
Profile of Writing Development

Kidwatching (Goodman, 1986) occurs when teachers record literacy behaviors as the children engage in authentic literacy tasks. Since finger plays, nursery rhymes and morning roster routines are daily literacy formats, as the child enters the emergent literacy phase, anecdotal records are necessary to record their continual growth. Due to time constraints, teachers may choose to focus on only one child a day and collect observations in a systematic fashion.

Developing Literacy in Emergent Readers and Writers Through Shared Activities

Shared reading is a daily activity to scaffold emergent readers' use of strategies. During shared reading, teachers use a big book to read with the children, replicating the storytime experiences children engage in with their parents (Taberski, 2000). The purpose of shared reading is to explicitly demonstrate strategies such as making predictions or using picture cues to identify letters or words. Fluent readers use these strategies automatically; however, emergent readers require explicit demonstrations (Gunning, 1999; Taberski, 2000). Shared reading provides the emergent readers with a model of strategic reading that they can later attempt on their own during guided reading sessions or independent reading.

Shared Reading Activity

The text for shared reading may be on the students' independent reading level or slightly more challenging. A classic text is *I Went Walking* (Williams, 1989). This story can be incorporated into a science lesson on animals or be it can used for second language learners. The patterned text aids emergent readers engage in shared reading. For example, as the teachers and students read, "I went walking and what did I see? I saw a pig looking at me!" the teacher can stop at *pig* and demonstrate a word-solving strategy. "I wonder what word this is. . . . It begins with a *p* and I can look at the picture of the pink animal. I know a pig is pink, so this must be pig. Let me read it again to see if this makes sense."

I Went Walking is also an excellent text for demonstrating predictions. For example, as the students look at the picture of a basket in the text, the teacher states: "I wonder what that is under the basket? From the tail, I will guess it is a dog. Let's read on and see if I am right."

Shared reading also scaffolds the emergent readers' mastery of sight words. Sight words are high-frequency core words that appear regularly in print or in their environment (Gunning, 2000). *I Went Walking* can be used to introduce color words as sight words. For example, during the first reading, the teacher can model predicting the color word by cross-checking with the illustration. During the second reading, the color words can be read by the children.

Shared reading, created by Holdaway (1986), recreates a much-loved storytime routine for emergent readers. Within this comfort zone, children gain the confidence to approximate the strategies their teacher demonstrates.

Assessment of Shared Reading Activity

During shared reading or shared word study, the teacher has the option to record samples of the students' emergent reading behaviors, which is process-oriented assessment (Cecil, 1999). Process-oriented assessment records the strategy or behavior in a naturalistic context.

Directions: During shared reading time, indicate the book used and the literacy behaviors demonstrated by students.

EMERGENT LITERACY BEHAVIORS ASSESSMENT

	Mary	Jose
Title of book		
Known/unknown text		
Overall impression		
Strategies used		
Progress shown		
Further development		

The emergent literacy behaviors assessment can be used to document individual student responses during shared reading or shared word study. The following instrument, the assessment for phonological awareness, can also be used to collect data on the students during shared word study activities.

Directions: During instructional activities, observe students' literacy performance.

ASSESSMENT FOR PHONOLOGICAL AWARENESS

Developmental Benchmark	Observation	Interpretation
Identifies sounds and elements		
Recognizes rhymes and word patterns		
Can sort word patterns		
Orally blends onset and rimes, syllables		
Manipulates phoneme substitutes and deletes phonemes		

Word Study for Emergent Readers and Writers

Shared word study sessions are informal gatherings for emergent readers to engage in conversations about their word-solving strategies (Fountas & Pinnell, 1996; Taberski, 2000). It is important to first introduce the word patterns or core words during a class lesson. For emergent readers, beginning with six words will provide ample opportunities to develop their word-solving strategies.

Emergent readers on similar reading levels should be paired. Once the words have been demonstrated, each word study partner chooses about four or five words she wishes to study. They write their chosen words on a card and use magnetic letters to spell the words. It is important that the children trace the magnetic letters and spell them aloud at the same time to aid in the processing of the word patterns. After the partners study their chosen words, they flip the cards over and attempt to spell each word without help. Partners then correct each other's work.

During the week, partners meet again to create new words by changing the initial letter or lists of rhyming words, word ladders, or word sorts. The partners can record the words they've learned in their word study notebook at the end of the week (Fountas & Pinnell, 1996; Taberski, 2000).

Shared Phonemic Awareness and Alphabetic Principle Activities

Name that sound. During the emergent literacy years, children start to identify the beginning, middle, and ending sounds in words. A song that facilitates this process can be sung to the tune of "Old McDonald Had a Farm." In the song, children

- The teacher begins to the tune of "Old McDonald Had a Farm" by saying: "What's the sound that starts these words—*pig, potato, pot?"* (Waits for children to respond, *p.*)
- The children respond that /p/ is the sound that starts these words—*pig, potato, pot:* "with a /p/, /p/, here and a /p/, /p/ there, Here a /p/, there a /p/, everywhere a /p/, /p/..."

Figure 6.15
Name That Sound

- The teacher and children clap and say a verse for each child in the class. For example:

"Stephen, Stephen, how do you do? Who's that friend right next to you?"

- The teacher and children say the next child's name very slowly, stretching palms far apart as the word is stretched: "RRR, EEE, BB, EEE, CKCKCK, AAA."
- They clap once quickly and say the name fast: "Rebecca."

Figure 6.16
Clap Your Name

are asked to identify the beginning, middle, and ending sound. The teacher may decide which sound the song will target for that particular session. Figure 6.15 lists some suggestions for playing Name that sound in the classroom.

Clap your name. The Clap your name strategy, described in Figure 6.16, may be used to scaffold the emergent reader's ability to segment phonemes. The children

The teacher begins by singing:
"Listen, listen to my word,
then tell me all the sound you heard:
/r/ is one sound,
/a/ is two,
/s/ is the last in *race* it's true.
Thanks for listening to my word
and telling all the sounds you heard!"

Figure 6.17
Hearing Sounds

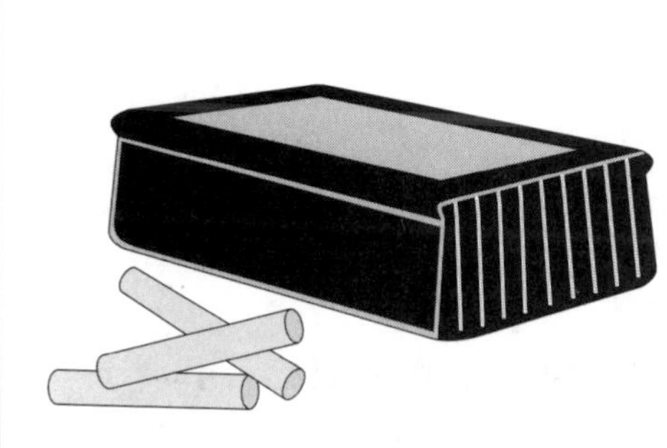

- Students and teacher sit in a circle and the teacher dictates a one-syllable word.
- Everyone writes the word on the slate board, including the teacher.
- The children then correct their work based on the teacher's board.
- Misspelled words and strategies to decode are discussed.

Figure 6.18
The Slate Game

learn to count the sounds in a word in the sound stretch activity from the previous section. Clap your name is the follow-up activity once students have mastered the concept of counting sounds.

Hearing sounds. Hearing sounds (Figure 6.17) is a follow-up activity to clap your name. The teacher may substitute words depending upon the phoneme that the students are studying at that particular time.

Information from the emergent literacy behaviors assessment can be used to highlight students' instructional needs. Several administrations over the course of a semester provide the teacher with a record of emergent readers' developmental progress along the literacy continuum.

Shared Spelling Activities

The slate game. This activity is used to facilitate children's awareness of the spelling features of blends, digraphs, and short vowels (Strickland, Ganske, & Monroe, 2002). Using slates makes the activity fun for children of all ages. Figure 6.18 describes the slate game activity.

- In small groups, the children bring words they are having difficulty spelling, based upon their writing folders.
- The children repeat the *first word* several times and think of any other words they know that are similar.
- The children try to spell the word, using the word wall, word patterns they already know, or posters and charts around the room.
- The teacher lists all the spellings on chart paper and asks the class to decide which spellings look "correct."
- One of the students looks up the word in a dictionary.
- The teacher congratulates the children for meeting the spelling challenge and giving it a try (even if it was incorrect).

Figure 6.19
Challenge Words

Challenge words. The challenge words activity can be used as a review of spelling strategies (see Figure 6.19). It also helps all children learn what spelling strategies their peers are using to tackle difficult words (Soderman et al., 1999).

Assessment of Shared Spelling Activities

Table 6.3, which contains spelling behavior rubrics, can be used to observe the strategies students are using to tackle unfamiliar words. Both the slate game and challenge words are activities designed to provide the teacher with observational data. Teachers may decide to use the profile of spelling development continuously throughout the emergent literacy period to compare data from other assessment tools.

Table 6.3
Spelling Behavior Rubric

Spelling Behavior	Level 3	Level 2	Level 1
Uses knowledge of phonics to encode word	Spells based upon knowledge of phonics	Sometimes uses phonics to spell words	Does not use phonics to spell words
Compares unknown words with familiar words	Uses knowledge of words to spell unknown words	Sometimes uses word knowledge to spell	Does not use knowledge of known words to spell
Uses word wall as a reference	Uses word wall as a reference	Sometimes uses word wall as a reference	Never uses word wall as a reference
Spells words based upon knowledge of syllabication	Uses knowledge of syllabication to spell	Sometimes uses syllabication to spell	Does not use syllabication to spell

- Children are grouped based upon their learning goals.
- The teacher and children discuss the purpose of their written text and the topic.
- The teacher uses conversation to support the process by asking the children how they would like to begin the text.
- The teacher decides when to "share the pen" with the students based upon their instructional needs. They might write one letter, one word, or a whole sentence.
- As the children write, the teacher comments on the features of the word without focusing on too many points, as the children will lose interest.
- After the text is written, the whole group reads the completed work.

Figure 6.20
Interactive Writing

Shared Emergent Writing Activity

Interactive writing. **Interactive writing** or **shared pen** is similar to shared reading in that the teacher and the students take turns in the literacy event. In interactive writing, the teacher decides when to "share the pen" with the students based upon the strategies or skills that are being focused on. This activity (Figure 6.20) can be used with narrative or expository text such as lists or content summary charts (McCarrier, Pinnell, & Fountas, 2000).

Assessment of Shared Emergent Writing Activity

The interactive writing observation sheet can be used alongside the emergent writing checklist which was discussed in the previous section. The literacy behaviors displayed during interactive writing are the same as the ones in the language experience approach and therefore these assessment tools may be used interchangeably.

INTERACTIVE WRITING OBSERVATION SHEET

Interactive Writing Behaviors	Observed—Date	Not Observed—Date
Participates in group discussion about experience		
Retells or summarizes story or news		
Verbalizes thoughts and feelings about an experience		
Writes letter, word, or sentence when called upon		

Developing Emergent Readers and Writers Through Guided Activities

Guided literacy instruction occurs when the teacher gathers a small reading group for additional support in acquiring emergent literacy (Cecil, 1999; Fountas & Pinnell, 1996). The small group might need support in making predictions, responding to text, or in applying word-solving strategies. The teacher decides on the literacy strategy or behavior to emphasize in each group based upon assessment records.

Picture walks and word ladders are two strategies for mediated instruction on story concept and word-solving strategies. Both strategies should be anchored in literature-based units that enable the emergent reader to draw upon background knowledge constructed during the unit.

Picture Walk

A picture walk before reading an unknown text provides the emergent reader with the prior knowledge and vocabulary necessary to successfully read the text (Cooper, 2000). A picture walk is a versatile strategy that can be used for narrative or expository text as well as for older, more advanced readers. The teacher begins the picture walk by following the procedures shown in Figure 6.21, which can be adapted for individual needs.

After the picture walk, the emergent reader has the background knowledge necessary to construct meaning and successfully read the text.

Assessment of Guided Picture Walk

Table 6.4 presents the Concepts about books rubric, a versatile assessment tool that may be used for guided picture walks or language experience stories. Teachers may also choose to use it as a developmental checklist.

Guided Activities for Phonemic Awareness and Phonological Processing

Marking sounds. The previous sections presented several activities for segmenting sounds. The marking sounds activity (Figure 6.22) may be used as a follow-up to the songs that were presented as shared literacy activities to help the children count phonemes under the guidance of the teacher.

- The teacher shows the students the cover of the book, highlighting the title, author, and illustrator. Their predictions are charted based on the cover.
- The teacher shows the illustrations and asks if the students have changed their predictions based on the illustrations. He uses vocabulary from the book whenever possible.
- The group may restate their predictions for reading. The students might also generate a focus question for reading.

Figure 6.21
Picture Walk

Table 6.4
Concepts About Books Rubric

Concepts About Books	Target	Acceptable	Needs Improvement
Makes predictions based upon cover and title	Uses cover and title to make predictions	Sometimes uses cover and title to make predictions	Never uses cover and title to make predictions
Shares background knowledge related to text	Shares prior knowledge in story discussions	Sometimes uses prior knowledge about text	Never uses prior knowledge about text
Gives responses to text that show comprehension	Responds to text with comprehension	Sometimes demonstrates comprehension through story response	Never or seldom demonstrates comprehension

- After children have mastered previous activities, the teacher shows students how to make sound boxes on their papers or on the chalkboard.
- The teacher says a word and demonstrates how to stretch it out by placing a marker into each box as the phoneme is heard.
- The children then say a new word, stretch it out, and slide a marker into each box as they hear the sound or phoneme.

Figure 6.22
Marking Sounds

Rhyming riddles. One of the phonological processing skills is to identify the beginning, middle, and ending sounds in words. The rhyming riddles activity (Figure 6.23) uses riddles to enable emergent readers to manipulate the onsets and rimes in words.

Rhyming game. A follow-up activity to rhyming riddles is the rhyming game (Figure 6.24). During the rhyming game, children must decide whether pairs of words rhyme. The teacher may choose word pairs based upon the word patterns that the students are studying.

Word ladders. Similar to picture walks, word ladders can be used with students at all reading levels (see Figure 6.25). After assessing students' mastery of shared word

- The teacher asks children riddles that require them to manipulate sounds in their heads. The easiest ones ask for endings. The next easiest are the ones that ask for a single consonant substitution at the beginning. The most difficult ones ask for a consonant blend or digraph at the beginning.

For example:

- What rhymes with *pig* and starts with /d/? *dig*
- What rhymes with *book* and starts with /c/? *cook*
- What rhymes with *sing* and starts with /r/? *ring*
- What rhymes with *dog* and starts with /fr/? *frog*

Figure 6.23
Rhyming Riddles

- The children walk around in a big circle taking one step each time a rhyming word is said by the teacher.
- When the teacher says a word that doesn't rhyme, the children sit down.

For example: *she, tree, flea, spree, key, bee, went.*

Figure 6.24
Rhyming Game

Figure 6.25
Word Ladder

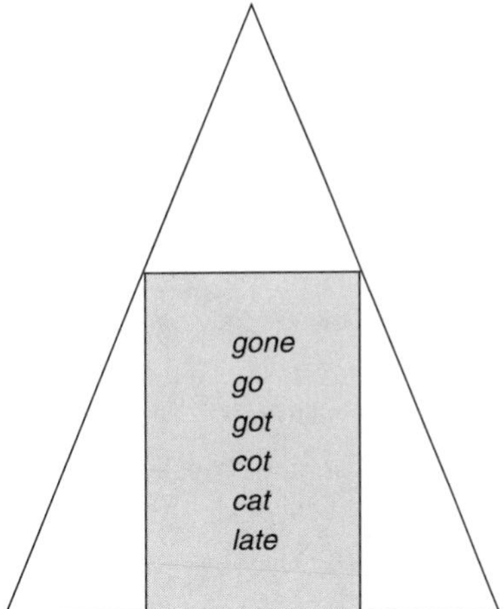

study activity, teachers may take a small group aside for coaching in word study solving strategies.

Word ladders are charts that demonstrate to emergent readers how to create new words by changing a few letters (Fountas & Pinnell, 1996). Manipulation of letters and sounds is a critical behavior for phonological awareness (Strickland, 1998). This activity can be a follow-up to reading a story, and draws upon words to which students have already been introduced through the read-aloud.

After scaffolding students' use of word ladders, teachers can also use word ladders for independent word-solving center activities.

Assessment of Guided Activities for Phonemic Awareness and Phonological Processing

The guided activities presented in this section mediate emergent readers' manipulation of letters and sounds. The phonological awareness checklist may be used for several instructional strategies to record students' mastery of developmental benchmarks.

PHONOLOGICAL AWARENESS CHECKLIST

Word-solving Behavior	Demonstrates	Needs Improvement	Not Observed
Has core frequency words			
Manipulates onsets and rhymes			
Sorts words according to pattern			
Is able to chunk words			
Uses structural analysis (of prefixes and suffixes, for example) to identify words			

- The teacher decides upon a "secret word" that can be made with all the letters. A list is made of other words that can be made from the one core word.
- The students receive file folders with pockets for letters and letters on cards.
- The teacher calls out the first word and then asks the children to change the word. For example, if *CAT* is the core word, the children make it *SAT* by changing the first letter. It helps the children to color code the pocket chart: blue for the initial sound of the word, yellow for the medial sound, and red for the final sound.
- The children make other words they know that are similar to the core word from the letters that are remaining.
- The teacher may choose to write the words that were created on chart paper for the children to review.

Figure 6.26
Making Words

- On chart paper, the teacher shows the children how to divide their papers to look this way: *C/AT,* with a line after the initial letter.
- The children are asked to write *FAT* underneath *CAT* and to tell what they notice about the words (that they end the same way).
- Then they write *SAT* underneath *FAT* and tell what they notice. After they respond, the teacher comments, "This is how we make word families."
- The teacher asks if they know any other words that would complete the chart. As they respond, he writes them on the chart paper. The students also copy the word *family* onto their charts.
- After the list is exhausted, the children chant the words in the word family. The teacher may call on individual students to identify select words or to read the entire list.

Figure 6.27
Onsets and Rimes

Guided Spelling Activities

Making words. This lesson is a wonderful follow-up activity to the slate game which was discussed in the previous section. In this activity, children use letter cards to make words they don't know from words they have already internalized (Cunningham, 2000). This instructional strategy can be done as part of a guided reading session. Figure 6.26 outlines the procedure for the making words activity.

Onsets and rimes. This activity makes a wonderful follow-up to making words because it also focuses on word patterns. The purpose of the onsets and rimes instructional strategy (Figure 6.27) is to facilitate the children's phonological awareness and knowledge of word features (Soderman et al., 1999).

Table 6.5
Spelling Behaviors Rubric

Spelling Behavior	Level 3	Level 2	Level 1
Uses knowledge of phonics to encode word	Spells based upon knowledge of phonics	Sometimes uses phonics to spell words	Does not use phonics to spell words
Compares unknown words with familiar words	Uses knowledge of words to spell unknown words	Sometimes uses word knowledge to spell	Does not use knowledge of known words to spell
Uses word wall as a reference	Uses word wall as a reference	Sometimes uses word wall as a reference	Never uses word wall as a reference
Spells words based upon knowledge of syllabication	Uses knowledge of syllabication to spell	Sometimes uses syllabication to spell	Does not use syllabication to spell

Assessment of Guided Spelling Activities

The spelling behaviors rubrics, which were presented in the previous section, may also be used to record students' developmental progress during guided spelling instruction (see Table 6.5).

Guided Emergent Writing Activity

Scaffolded writing. In early childhood classrooms, children are very comfortable dictating their stories to the teacher to be written down. However, they sometimes are reluctant to take the next step and begin to write down their own thoughts. The scaffolded writing activity (shown in Figure 6.28) was designed to gently push the emergent writer to the next level (Soderman et al., 1999).

Assessment of Guided Emergent Writing Activity

It is during this activity that the emergent writer is gently pushed toward independence. Therefore, the emergent writing rubric (Table 6.6) is a suitable tool for recording the child's first efforts toward emergent writing behavior.

Developing Emergent Readers and Writers Through Independent Activities

The final phase of scaffolded literacy instruction is independent practice. After the students have had literacy strategies modeled and practiced, emergent readers and writers are ready to demonstrate them. The following strategies allow for the student to demonstrate mastery of developmental benchmarks for the emergent reader and writer.

Independent Activities for Phonemic Awareness and the Alphabetic Principle

Buddy word solvers. This activity allows emergent readers and writers to practice their decoding skills and phonological processing with their peers. Buddy word solvers allow children to review word patterns or word features that the class has

- Ask the child to dictate the story. Instead of writing words, she puts blanks for each word. For example, if the child says "A cat sat," the teacher would write:

  ____ ____ ____.

- Read the lines pointing to the corresponding sentence as he "reads the sentence."
- Then ask the student to help you write the story. For example, 'the first word in your sentence was A, so I'll write 'A' there.
- After each line is written, read it together.
- If the child is ready, ask him to write one letter or put in the punctuation marks.

Figure 6.28
Scaffolded Writing

Table 6.6
Emergent Writing Rubric

Emergent Writing Behaviors	Target	Acceptable	Needs Improvement
Writes uppercase and lowercase letters	Uses both uppercase and lowercase letters	Sometimes uses uppercase and lowercase letters	Uses only uppercase letters
Writes consonants and vowel sounds in words	Writes both consonants and vowel sounds	Writes some vowel and consonant sounds	Writes only consonant sounds
Begins to write sentences and use punctuation	Writes sentences with punctuation	Sometimes writes sentences and uses punctuation	Does not write sentences or use punctuation

been studying (Pinnell & Fountas, 1998). Figure 6.29 details the buddy word solvers activity for the classroom.

Storyboards. Storyboards are wonderful activities for independent responses to literacy. After reading a story, emergent readers can retell the story through illustrations and sentences about their selected scenes. Once they have finished their

- After the class has had a mini-lesson on a particular word pattern or feature, word sort activities are placed in the literacy center.
- The buddy word solvers attempt to sort the words into the proper category based upon their rime.
- The final step is to write their categories of words on a worksheet for the teacher's assessment.

Figure 6.29
Buddy Word Solvers

- The teacher compiles a word sheet and distributes it to the class.
- Together with a partner, the children follow the spelling word study routine:

Look, Say, Cover, Write, and Check.

  - Look—the children study the features of the word.
  - Say—one child spells the word out loud.
  - Cover—the child tries to spell the word aloud while covering it.
  - Write—the child tries to write the word.
  - Check—the child and her partner correct the work.
- The children take turns spelling and checking each other's work.
- The final step is to leave the spelling study sheet in the literacy center for the teacher to assess it.

Figure 6.30
Buddy Spellers

storyboards, emergent readers can perform their storyboards with accompanying music and costumes if they so choose.

Independent Spelling Activities

Buddy spellers. Similar to the buddy word solvers, the buddy spellers activity allows emergent readers to practice their spelling skills with a partner (Pinnell & Fountas, 1998). In this activity, the children practice spelling words that have been chosen by their teacher for instructional review. For example, if the teacher notices from their writing samples that the children are still having problems with the CVCe (like) pattern, words with that pattern would be the subject for review (see Figure 6.30).

- The teacher shows the children his journal for writing and explains its purpose.
- On chart paper, the teacher demonstrates how they may use pictures, letters, and sounds to communicate their thoughts.

Figure 6.31
Journal Writing

Independent Emergent Writing Activity

Journal writing. Journal writing is a wonderful way to encourage young children to join the literacy club (Soderman et al., 1999). Journal writing (Figure 6.31) can be done at any stage of emergent writing. Emergent writers who are still relying solely on pictures may use their illustrations to tell their story. As they become more comfortable and phonologically aware, letters and sounds will gradually enter their journal writing to accompany their illustrations.

Assessment of independent emergent literacy activities. To complete the instructional cycle, teachers readminister the phonological awareness checklist and the concepts about books assessment. As students begin to demonstrate mastery of the developmental benchmarks, teachers may begin to move students to activities for the early reader.

Portrait of the Emergent Literacy Instructional Cycle

Tamika is an active five year old in Ms. Garcia's kindergarten class. She loves to organize her friends for retelling activities in the Library Corner and roleplaying in the Dramatic Play Center. Ms. Garcia has decided to focus on Tamika since she has yet to make the transition to decoding.

As Tamika was retelling the story **Honey, I Love** in the Library Corner, Ms. Garcia noted on her anecdotal record that she was reciting the story from memory. Since it was already November, Ms. Garcia was concerned about Tamika's lack of decoding skills. In order to alleviate this problem Ms. Garcia included Tamika in the focused phonemic awareness activities such as **Rhyming Riddles.**

Ms. Garcia used the following weeks to emphasize phonemic awareness and to encourage the students to spell unknown words through decoding. Tamika participated in **Journal Writing** in the Writing Center. Ms. Garcia noted that as December ended, Tamika used more inventive spelling in her journal writing. This shift towards phonemic spelling influenced her emergent reading and Tamika began to rely more on print and less on picture clues to interpret the printed word. As the semester ended for the winter holidays, Ms. Garcia observed with pride Tamika's marked progress in reading.

Discussion Questions and Activities

1. Visit an early childhood classroom. Pick a child who interests you. What emergent reading and writing behaviors do you observe? How is the teacher facilitating the process?
2. Describe how the emergent reader's awareness of phonological sensitivity develops and how you would scaffold it as a teacher.
3. As the young child becomes immersed in a print-rich environment, she begins to engage in emergent writing. Look at five samples of emergent writing and try to identify the child's stage of spelling.

Additional Web Sites

Center for the Improvement of Early Reading Achievement
http://www.ciera.org
This Web site provides teachers with the latest research regarding emergent literacy.

Reading Online
http://www.readingonline.org
The site provides activities for making and writing words.

Additional Children's Literature

Bandes, H. (1993). *Sleepy river.* New York: Philomel.

Base, G. (1987). *Animalia.* New York: Harry N. Abrams.

Boynton, S. (1983). *A is for angry: An animal and adjective alphabet.* New York: Workman.

Carle, E. (1973). *Have you seen my cat?* New York: Philomel.

Cole, J. (1993). *Six sick sheep.* New York: Morrow.

Degan, B. (1983). *Jamberry.* New York: Harper & Row.

De Paola, T. (1985). *Hey diddle diddle and other Mother Goose rhymes.* New York: Putnam.

Maurel, C. (1997). *No, No, Titus!* New York: North-South Books.

Steig, J. (1992). *Alpha beta chowder.* New York: HarperCollins.

Wescott, N. B. (1980). *I know an old lady who swallowed a fly.* Boston: Little Brown.

Additional Readings

Bowman, B. T., Donovan, M. S., & Burns, M. S. (2000). *Eager to learn: Educating our preschoolers.* Washington, DC: National Academy Press.

Holdaway, D. (1986). The structure of natural language as a basis for literacy instruction. In M. L. Sampson (Ed.), *The pursuit of literacy: Early reading and writing.* Dubuque, IA: Kendall/Hunt.

Maclean, M., Bryant, P., & Bradley, L. (1987). Rhymes, nursery rhymes, and reading in early childhood. *Merrill-Palmer Quarterly, 33,* 255–281.

National Research Council. (1998). *Preventing reading difficulties in young children.* Washington, DC: National Academy Press.

Snow, C. E., Burns, M. S., & Griffin, P. (1999). *Language and literacy environments in preschools.* Champaign, IL: ERIC Clearinghouse on Elementary and Early Childhood Education.

Children's Literature References

Gag, W. (1956). *Millions of cats.* New York: Coward-McCann.

Greenfield, E. (1978, 1995). *Honey, I love.* New York: HarperCollins.

Shaw, C. G. (1993). *It looked like spilt milk.* New York: HarperCollins.

Williams, S. (1989). *I went walking.* New York: Harcourt.

CHAPTER 7

Literacy Instruction and Assessment for Early Readers and Writers

Portrait of an Early Reader and Writer

Juan is in the first month of second grade and is 7 years old. He speaks English in school and Spanish at home. He is beginning to read independently and is developing the same independence in writing. Juan's teacher Ms. Miller expects that he will write longer stories and begin writing informational stories as well. In his journal, during independent writing, Juan wrote the following story after having a family party to celebrate his seventh birthday.

I am seven and I had a big partee.
And a big brown cake with
a numbr sevin on it. All my
cuzins came to my partee.
And my frends came. They
sang happy bithday, Juan and how
old ar you.

Juan's story is focused on a single topic—the celebration of his birthday with his family and friends. He begins with an introduction telling the purpose for the party, and the middle of his story describes who was at the celebration. Finally, Juan writes a delightful conclusion to his story. From his writing, Ms. Miller describes Juan's literacy development as approaching the early stage in writing and moving into the transitional stage for spelling development.

In this chapter, you will read about a variety of instructional plans that include literacy activities aligned with assessment strategies for children like Juan who are at the early stage of literacy development. Children's home and school literacy experiences, their interests in reading and writing, as well as their personalities vary widely. Therefore, children's journeys in becoming literate may take different paths. Some children experience periods of intense growth in learning certain literacy concepts or skills whereas in other areas of literacy, they may lag behind and, for a while, they may go through a slow to moderate growth phase (Clay, 1998). For example, a teacher may observe a child making rapid progress from September through November; then suddenly, the child's growth slows for a month or two, picking up after the holiday season. This is not unusual for young children who are in the first stages of literacy development, because development is dynamic (Katz, 1995). Therefore, the very nature of children's development makes tracking and monitoring language and literacy quite complex for the classroom teacher, yet it is *essential* for effective student learning.

As in previous chapters, the emphasis in this chapter is on aligning instruction and assessment. You will read how instructional plans are designed for children who are moving from the emergent stage yet standing at the threshold of early literacy development. The instructional strategies and the assessment tools presented in this chapter target children who are at the *early stage of literacy development.*

To design an instructional plan, it is important to first focus on the literacy behaviors already acquired by the reader and writer. The literacy skills and concepts that children have acquired at the emergent stage of literacy development become the springboard for teachers as they work with children at the early stage. Thus, the blueprints for literacy instruction and assessment are linked to what children already know and what they need to learn to become literate, thereby preparing instruction that is developmentally appropriate. Accompanying each instructional strategy is an assessment tool that is aligned to the literacy activity and may be used to monitor children's progress as they attempt to reach the benchmarks for the early stage of literacy development. Throughout this chapter, instructional strategies and assessment tools are presented within a framework of a balanced literacy program. Following the pattern in previous chapters, each instructional strategy and accompanying assessment tool is designated as a *modeled, shared, guided,* or *independent* literacy experience. The chapter concludes with specific ways for classroom teachers to promote connections with families that focus on ways to extend literacy at home for early readers and writers.

As you read this chapter, reflect on the following topics:

- What children at the early stage of literacy development already know about reading and writing
- How benchmarks within the early stage of literacy development help us to think about what literacy concepts and skills children need to learn
- How benchmarks for literacy guide instruction rather than dictate a specific plan of instruction
- How each instructional plan is part of a balanced literacy program
- How an instructional plan facilitates children's meeting specific benchmarks at the early stage of literacy development when it is aligned with assessment
- How teachers may modify each lesson based on an individual child's needs
- How teachers may support parents in helping their children who are at the early stage of literacy development

Using Benchmarks to Prepare Instruction

Teachers need to have certain expectations for children's learning. As discussed in previous chapters, what children need to learn at a given level may be expressed as benchmarks or performance standards. In organizing instruction for student learning, teachers need to identify what the children know as well as the literacy performances that they need to learn designated by the benchmarks at their level. The benchmarks for children at the early stage of literacy development shown in Table 7.1 are organized around book sense, story sense, and literacy behaviors. *Book sense* refers to concepts that readers and writers need to know about books—the structure of a book as well as its format and organization. Concepts within the category of *story sense* refer to the children's understanding of stories. Such concepts include the parts of a story or the internal story structure, remembrance and understanding for stories, an interest for stories, and so on. The last category, *literacy behaviors,* refers to the skills and concepts required by children to read and understand text. These include literacy strategies, the use of the three cueing systems for reading or decoding unknown words in text, writing new words, and the ability to make predictions using information that was read in the story.

Table 7.1
Developmental Benchmarks for the Early Literacy Stage

Book Sense	Story Sense	Literacy Behaviors
Knows the book parts and can talk about them	Engages in independent reading for longer periods	Participates during book introductions and begins to initiate questions and responses to stories Participates during book discussions
Distinguishes among different authors and illustrators	Asks for specific books to be read aloud or to be shared	Reads left to right with a fast sweeping return to the next line
Uses the table of contents when directed to do so	Retells a story that includes (a) the setting, (b) the theme, (c) the story problem, (d) most story events, and (e) the resolution	Increases rates of reading and writing
Finds the index of the book	Responds to stories read and heard and makes connections to personal experiences	Engages in visible word-to-word matching while reading
Makes comments on their contributions	Appropriates and uses the "book language" in story discussions	Begins to use multiple sources of information—semantic, syntactic, visual cues as well as pictures—to decode unknown words
	Writes more complete stories and reads them back	Reads and writes words using more letter–sound relationships
	Composes written stories using familiar stories as models	Spells more sight words correctly
	Writes nonfiction books	Begins to use punctuation marks in writing

Developmental Benchmarks for the Early Literacy Stage

The three categories in Table 7.1—book sense, story sense, and literacy behaviors—were designed to plan instruction more effectively and to analyze children's growth. It is important to note that these three categories are interrelated. When teachers engage children in a literacy activity such as writing a story, the children may be developing skills and concepts in all three areas. For example, children who have a strong story sense may also possess strategic literacy behaviors for reading and writing text. As they use their sense of story to construct meaning from new stories or to solve words that are unknown to them, they progress in both categories. To monitor children's growth and progress toward meeting the literacy benchmarks in a more systematic way, it is necessary to isolate the skills and concepts for greater accuracy.

Book Sense: What Early Readers and Writers Know and Need to Learn

By the time children have reached the middle of the first grade, many may be entering the early stage of literacy development. They may have had several book experiences because they have been read to both at home and at school. For some children, trips to the library and bookstore are routine. Through these experiences, they have acquired knowledge of books or book sense.

By the early stage, children have had the opportunity to develop some of the following concepts and skills about books: books contain a story and convey meaning, a book has front and back covers, readers use page-turning techniques when reading, books have titles and authors that are found in a certain location in the book, stories begin and end at specific places in a book. These are basic concepts about books that are indeed required by children who are receiving guided or formal instruction in reading.

Children who are at the early stage of literacy learning are continuing to develop concepts about books, building on what they already know. Teachers encourage children to talk about different parts of the book. Children learn about book jackets, for example, and begin to see their relationship to the story contents. They further their conceptual knowledge of authors and illustrators through writing and illustrating their own books. Because children at this stage are reading more nonfiction books, they begin to use the table of contents and the index of a book.

Story Sense: What Early Readers and Writers Know and Need to Learn

Children entering the early stage of literacy come with a developing story sense. At home and school, they hear stories from books as well as from storytelling. They read short narrative stories independently, and many children begin developing an interest for nonfiction books. They can retell stories to include the major story elements, and they can also compose their own stories. Children who are early writers are competent in composing simple narratives that have a beginning, middle, and an ending.

Like Juan, children who are at this point are ready to move into writing more complex stories. Juan's teacher Ms. Miller has an expectation for him to begin to write more complete stories, and to extend his writing to include expository text. His sense of story can be further measured by his story retellings. Ms. Miller includes instruction designed at developing children's retellings so that the children include more details related to the elements of a narrative, and she will monitor the progress of story concepts through oral retellings. Ms. Miller uses the benchmarks for children at the early stage by developing instructional strategies that target text comprehension, showing them how to make personal, text, and world connections with text.

Literacy Behaviors: What Early Readers Know and Need to Learn

When children start to approach the early stage of literacy development, they are beginning to read text and write stories. They write short sentences, and their words on the page are few. There are many pictures and repetitive text to help early readers understand the story and decode the unknown words. By the time they enter the early literacy stage, they have developed a small body of sight words and know their letters with some of their sounds. They are beginning to use letter knowledge for reading unknown words, although their word-solving strategies are indeed limited. The expectation for children at this stage is to bring them to reading and writing fluency. That is, teachers want children to be word solvers so that they may increase their independent reading. Because of this expectation for children, phonics plays a

The alphabetic principle refers to the concept that each sound of the language is represented by a graphic symbol. When children grasp this concept, they are on their way to decoding unknown words.

major role in the early stage of literacy, and this stage is frequently referred to as the **alphabetic stage of reading.**

Learning the alphabetic principle is fundamental to successful reading and writing in the early stages of literacy development. This is one of the most critical benchmarks developed at the early stage of literacy, for the primary goal for children who are moving into this stage is to further develop and refine the literacy strategies that support their independent reading and writing.

Teachers organize instruction within a balanced literacy program, so children learn decoding or word-solving strategies that engage them in many different types of literacy contexts. Teachers take many opportunities to demonstrate or model how to apply the principles of phonics to reading and writing, they work together within shared literacy contexts on developing decoding skills, and they offer opportunities for children to practice decoding through independent literacy experiences. Within guided literacy, children receive direct or explicit instruction on phonics as well as decoding and comprehension strategies as they learn the specific applications to reading and writing. A systematic plan for teaching children phonics as well as explicit instruction in decoding strategies is needed to bring children to the stage of fluent reading (Adams, 1990). It is no wonder Fountas and Pinnell (1996) refer to guided reading as the heart of a balanced literacy program.

As children are learning the alphabetic principle, they are also developing other aspects of literacy behaviors. For example, when children begin to move toward reading fluency, they have a greater control over text and their rates of reading increase. Another benchmark within this category relates to their responses to reading and the levels of questions they ask during book introductions, demonstrating a developing comprehension of text. Within writing instruction and practice, children further develop their alphabetic knowledge as they learn how to spell new words and develop strategies to write unknown words. Their correct use of language conventions, such as punctuation marks and capital letters, also develops.

As already stated, because of the complexity in becoming literate, the early stage of literacy is best served through a balanced literacy program that is carefully designed and systematically assessed. What follows is a set of instructional plans aligned with assessment strategies to meet the needs of readers and writers as they progress toward the benchmarks of the early stage.

Developing Literacy in Early Readers and Writers Through Modeled Activities

Teaching Through Different Types of Modeling

Children's first exposures in learning to read and write occur within interactive contexts. In Chapters 1 and 2 we discussed how children first learn about reading and writing through authentic and natural experiences occurring within the home environment. They carefully observe adults reading and writing and begin to construct the concepts about print. Scaffolding or modeling the literacy process is an important type of instruction that is especially required by beginner readers and writers (Dole, Duffy, Roehler, & Pearson (1991). Providing effective literacy instruction includes demonstrations to children on how reading and writing work, an aspect of the bal-

Types of Modeled Literacy Instruction	Examples of Modeled Literacy Instruction
Indirect modeling involves a literacy experience that is not directly identified as a teaching event	Reading aloud Writing aloud Storytelling
Direct modeling involves showing and telling children how to do something	Writing aloud while showing children where to put the author's name in writing a story Demonstrating changing voice intonation when reading dialogue and telling the children how and when to change voice intonation

Figure 7.1
Types of Modeled Literacy Instruction

anced literacy program called modeled literacy. There are different ways to demonstrate or model the literacy processes (see Figure 7.1). When teachers read aloud to children, they model how effective reading sounds. This type of literacy activity is an *indirect type of modeling.* The teacher does not describe how reading sounds; rather, the children listen to the teacher read them a story. A *direct type of modeling* of literacy occurs as the teacher shows and tells the children how to perform a particular skill. Roehler and Duffy (1991) have identified think-alouds as a type of direct modeling.

Thinking aloud about the story. The teacher models to the class how to make a prediction in the story based upon what the children read in the story and using the picture as clues in predicting what will come next. The teacher makes the prediction by thinking aloud to the class how she arrived at the prediction. The sequence progresses as follows:

1. First, I will think about what I read. This is what I know from reading the story . . .
2. Next, I will search the picture for clues to help me find out what will happen. I notice that . . .
3. I predict that . . . because I know . . . from what I have read and from the picture.

The kinds of modeled literacy instruction addressed in this section include (a) modeling how to listen to stories that are being read aloud through the use of **Directed Listening Thinking Activity (DLTA),** (b) modeling **expository writing** through the use of the wall story, and (c) modeling the use of **spelling strategies** for early writers.

Modeling Reading and Listening

Directed listening thinking activity (DLTA). This instructional strategy is a modification of Stauffer's (1975) Directed Reading Thinking Activity (DRTA). The teacher combines the benefits of *reading aloud* to children with the important element of *critical listening* and by directing the listeners' focus on aspects of the text that are significant to understanding the story. The instructional plan aims at focusing children's attention on specific aspects of the story and then in a small group discussing the focus of their listening.

The teacher models to the children how to make predictions by using the information from the story and clues from the pictures.

The use of this strategy in early childhood classrooms is indeed powerful. When teachers carefully select children's literature to be read, they are providing the best models of language for children to hear with stories that have structure and appeal, as they demonstrate the read-aloud process to their listeners. Through books, both narrative and informational, children's conceptual knowledge is deepened. Stories help them to learn about human behavior as well as understand diverse cultures, furthering children's interest for reading books by varying the contexts in which the stories are presented to include literature activities that are pleasurable. Within this activity, the goal for children is to develop their oral language and literacy, using children's literature as a language catalyst.

Although reading aloud to children demonstrates expert reading, there is an added benefit of using Directed Listening Thinking Activity. Children are encouraged to focus on specific aspects of the text, they must think more deeply about the story, talk with a small group, and continue to listen to the story that is being read. Using DLTA will encourage children to become engaged listeners and critical thinkers by the teacher's guidance through the story and discussion with their peers. The teacher's guidance comes in the form of critical thinking questions. They talk with their small group about the question, share their ideas with the larger group, and continue to listen to the story. Let us walk through the procedure for combining DLTA strategy with a group read-aloud.

Procedures for Using DLTA

1. **Select a Story:** Select a story that is appropriate for *listening* by children at the early stage of literacy and a book that encourages problem solving and predicting story events.
2. **Prepare for Instruction:** Divide the story into two parts for a shorter book and three parts for a longer book. When using this strategy for the first time, stop only once for the guided listening discussion.

- The divisions of the story should be guided by the story itself. That is, an appropriate juncture in the story might come at a natural place for the reader to make a prediction, or a place where the main character must solve a major problem.
- Divide the children into small groups of three or four.

3. **Give Directions to the Children:** First, provide the following general instructions to the children.
   - Tell the children that they will listen to a story. Emphasize that they should listen carefully to the story so that they can help the main character solve a problem, or predict what might come next.
   - Explain to the children that they will work in small groups of three or four, and one person will be a reporter.
   - Tell the children that after they listen to the story they will work together, talking about "what will come next in the story" (or solving a story problem) within their small groups.
   - Inform the children that they will have a short time to discuss their predictions and then to decide on the best prediction from the group, giving a reason for their choice.
   - After the group discussions are complete, explain the "sharing session": The reporter from each group shares the group's prediction, stating the reason for their selection.
   - After the sharing session, focus children's listening on the end of the story. Tell the children to listen for a confirmation or rejection of their prediction as the teacher continues to read the story aloud.

One of the genres of children's literature that promotes thought and develops conceptual knowledge is **biography.** At the early stage of literacy development, children are beginning to read informational books. To further their reading interests, teachers can use the read-aloud time to introduce children to a variety of nonfiction literature. David A. Adler's *A Picture Book of Sojourner Truth* (1994) from his *Picture Book Biography* series may be used for DLTA as a way to introduce children to reading a series of biographies.

The teacher begins with a thorough book introduction, starting with the meaning of the words *sojourner* and *truth.* For many children who are unfamiliar with the concept of slavery, the teacher conducts a discussion to provide background knowledge for children to understand the story. As children listen to the story, they are learning about the concept of slavery, about time, and about the laws of the 18th century related to slavery. They also will come to understand the plight of the slaves through the experience of one—Isabella Hardenbergh—who later changes her name to Sojourner Truth. The life of Sojourner Truth has many turns; however, one logical juncture in the story is when Isabella changes her name. At this point the teacher might stop reading to ask the children:

> Think about what the name *Sojourner Truth* means and why she changes her name from Isabella Hardenbergh. What do you think she will do in her life that is connected in some way to her name?

After children discuss their predictions, and after they share their group predictions, they are again directed to listen to the story to confirm or reject their predictions.

Student talk focused on question			
Student talk showed an understanding of the text			
Practiced good listening behaviors and turn taking			
Demonstrated an interest in the story through engaged discussion			

KEY

H	**High** level of engagement	L	**Low** level of engagement
M	**Moderate** level of engagement	NO	**No** level of engagement

Figure 7.2
Checklist for Assessing Guided Listening and Discussion of a Read-Aloud

Assessing Children's Listening and Discussion During Modeled Reading

Assessment will focus on the student outcomes related to the instruction. Because the goal of the instruction is to encourage children to be critical listeners, this is what will be assessed. Critical listening means listening for understanding. Were the children in the small group talking about the prediction that the teacher posed? Was the discussion focused on the question and on the story to support their choices? Were the members of the group able to come to a consensus on a prediction and tie it to the text?

As the teacher observes each small group during the discussion, she will listen in on the children's discussions to determine how the talk is going. At times, the teacher might have to refocus the discussion with a single comment. Using a clipboard and the checklist found in Figure 7.2, the teacher may record observations of one or two groups' discussions. The checklist's key may be used to indicate the level of each child's engagement in the group discussion.

Writing Aloud: Modeling Expository Writing

The wall story. The wall story is an excellent instructional strategy to expand children's writing to include informational text. Children who are at the early stage typically begin to read more informational books—that is, literature that is written with different text formats than narrative. Therefore, learning to write using varied text patterns is consistent in their sequence of development. The wall story provides an instructional context to model how to write nonfiction or informational text using expository text formats (Iversen & Reeder, 1998).

A review of the five types of text formats that are used in expository writing with examples of each type appears in Figure 7.3. The examples of expository writing come from the familiar children's book *The Great Kapok Tree: A Tale of the Amazon Rain Forest* by Lynne Cherry (1970). The author combines narrative or a story with a variety of expository text formats. This is a common feature of many informational books written for young children. Although some children's science and social studies textbooks do not include a story context to present information, writers use a variety of expository formats, not just one type of text format. For instance, most textbooks include a combination of descriptive, compare-contrast, time-order, and other text formats to convey the author's meaning.

First attempts at teaching expository writing to young children should focus on a single text format, one that is commonly used and is therefore more familiar to early writers. The different formats can be seen in the text pattern examples in Figure 7.3.

Text Patterns in Informational Literature

A Review

The purpose of expository writing is to inform or explain. It often provides the reader with facts and information about one or more topics. Many children's books are nonfiction or informational texts and are written using expository writing. The authors of these texts usually use more than one type of expository text formats. Although many informational books are purely nonfiction, others are written as tales or stories, and facts and information are presented.

Informational Text Format	*Examples from* The Great Kapok Tree
Descriptive patterns are employed through a list of characteristics or features as well as examples	"The man looked about and saw the sun streaming through the canopy. Spots of bright light glowed like jewels amidst the dark green forest. Strange and beautiful plants seemed to dangle in the air, suspended from the great Kapok tree."
Comparison patterns are used when there is a comparison and/or a contrasting of a topic or a person	"*The Great Kapok Tree* is about the Amazon Rain Forest—a tropical rain forest—but we have a temperate rain forest in the Pacific Northwest of the United States."
Sequential patterns are easily recognized through a sequence of events that are ordered. The signal words such as *first, second, then,* and so on are often used.	"The larger man stopped and pointed to a great Kapok tree. Then he left. The smaller man took the ax he carried and struck the trunk of the tree. . . . Soon the man grew tired. He sat down to rest at the foot of the great Kapok tree. Before he knew it, the heat and hum of the forest had lulled him to sleep."
Cause-and-effect patterns are found in writings with a cause-and-effect relationship; the author wishes to show that one or more phenomena is caused by another.	"You chop down one tree, then come back for another and another. The roots of these trees will wither and die, and there will be nothing left to hold the earth in place."
Problem-and-solution patterns occur in informational books when an author states the problem followed by one or more solutions to the problem.	"I wrote *The Great Kapok Tree* to let the world know what happens to the rain forest creatures and the entire planet when rain forests are destroyed. . . . Please care for Mother Earth. Together we can make a difference!"

Figure 7.3
Text Formats in Expository Writing
Source: From Cherry, 1990.

Demonstrations and modeling how to write are part of effective teaching.

For instance, **descriptive patterns** list characteristics or features. Because descriptive patterns would be the most familiar to children due to their frequent use in books, teachers may begin with them when teaching young children about writing informational text.

In Cherry's *The Great Kapok Tree,* the information about vanishing rain forests is written with a combination of several text formats to convey meaning. Many other informational books have a similar format because there is no formula for writing, and informational books often use more than one or two formats. For example, a writer may choose to describe an animal using a descriptive text format and write a number of sentences listing the animal's features. The author may then conclude by comparing and contrasting the animal to another.

The need for instruction in expository writing. To understand expository writing, or informational books, children develop a *schema* or concept for different text formats. Pappas (1998) emphasizes that the informational genre has a very different structure than the stories that children are familiar with. As children develop a schema for narrative stories, they do so for expository writing as well. Children become familiar with text formats—or ways of presenting information—through reading informational books. Learning about the variety of text formats will help children become better readers and writers (Calkins, 1994; Fletcher, 1993). When children write informational text, their schema for expository text formats is further developed, thereby deepening their understanding for reading informational books. Therefore, teaching children how to write about ideas and concepts using expository text patterns will increase their understanding for reading and writing expository

Involving Families: Encourage children to read more informational books in the classroom. Suggest to parents the benefits of nonfiction literature, and offer some reading suggestions of informational books that relate to the topics that are being studied as part of the curriculum.

text. Nonfiction plays an important role in helping children in their academic writing as well as in their life careers: "nonfiction is probably the most usable kind of writing for school and a lifetime of work" (Graves, 1994, p. 313).

Providing children with a model or a demonstration of how to organize their ideas when writing expository text is indeed an efficient approach. The wall story is an instructional strategy that may be used to demonstrate the writing process to young children. Let's read how Joanne used the wall story in an integrated unit titled "Let's Eat!" The topic of the unit integrates science, social studies, health, and mathematics curriculum with literacy. During a 2-week unit of study, the children in Joanne's first-grade class read many informational texts on healthy foods that included the importance of eating healthy, on keeping healthy teeth, the basic food groups, and classifying healthy and junk foods.

Below is a description of how Joanne modeled expository writing to her first graders using the wall story. What type of modeled instruction did Joanne use to demonstrate expository writing to children?

Joanne began her wall story by gathering the children around the rug and showing them the books they read. She asked the children which books they enjoyed most. As the children selected their favorite books and began to look at the illustrations, the discussion grew lively. The children talked about healthy foods and junk foods, how each food was important to the body's health, the importance of getting into a habit of eating good food, and some healthy snacks that they may eat. It was after the discussion that Joanne invited the children to write a group story on what they had discussed—healthy foods. They all agreed, and Joanne introduced the children to a new format for writing a wall story. Their wall story would be the culminating literacy activity of the unit.

After agreeing on the topic, Joanne suggested that they focus the story on healthy snacks. They discussed the facts that they could include in their story and how each fact related to their topic. Joanne told the children that all good informational books or stories should begin with a sentence that tells the reader what the book is about. She showed them the first pages of two books and explained how the writer introduced the book with the lead sentence. Joanne made sure to select books that had good introductory sentences that stated explicitly what the reader could expect to read. They talked about writing a good lead sentence for their story.

Joanne decided that she would use a descriptive text format throughout the wall story without combining it with different text formats. On the first of the five large sheets of paper that Joanne taped to the wall, she began to write the introductory or lead sentence. Again, she reminded the children why they begin the story this way. She asked the children what to write next. Jimmy eagerly told everyone that his mother gives him carrots because they are good for his eyes. Joanne paraphrased Jimmy's contribution and wrote on the large chart paper: "Carrots are a healthy snack. They are good for your eyes." Joanne continued until all the large pages were filled.

After she completed modeling how to write descriptive text, Joanne called on individual children to read the story. For each page of the wall story, a team of two children was asked to draw an illustration that would go with the story on the page. After the illustrations were completed and displayed, Joanne read the story and asked the children for a title. They responded with "Healthy Snacks." "Wonderful, the title tells about the story, and it is a great beginning." Joanne then talked about the importance of making the title more focused and demonstrated how she could take "Healthy Snacks" and make it tell more about the story by telling who would be eating the healthy snacks. Joanne altered the title, saying, "Healthy Foods for Healthy Kids," as she carefully wrote it above the wall story. She reread the wall story, and invited each team of two illustrators to read their page.

THE WALL STORY

Healthy Foods for Healthy Kids

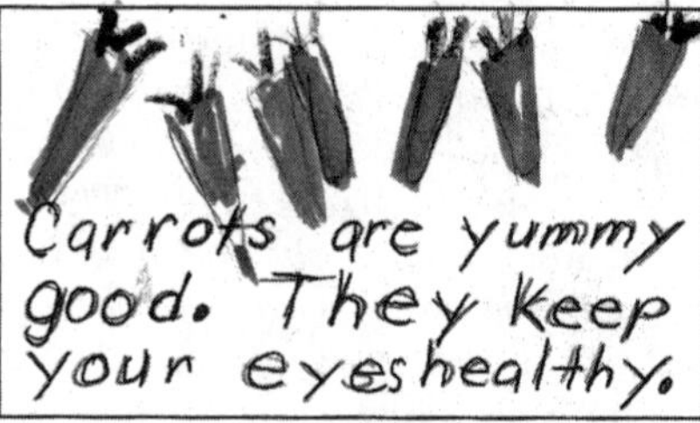

Procedures for Using a Wall Story

1. Identify a broad topic area to write about. An appropriate topic is one that the children know through their reading and is part of an integrated unit of study.
2. Conduct a discussion with the children about that topic, referring to books that they have read. Review the ideas from the books, and use the illustrations in the books to stimulate the discussion.
3. Tell the children that you will write a wall story together, explaining to them what a wall story is.
4. Select a topic and show the children how to narrow down the topic.
5. Conduct a discussion on the topic. Have the children suggest ideas and concepts that should be part of the story. Tell them this is what good writers do before

writing about a topic—they think about the story contents and verify the facts. You may use a web during the discussion to jot down their ideas.

6. Decide on what ideas will be used, and show the children how to organize their ideas—for example, which idea will go first, second, third, and so on.
7. With approximately five large squares of paper taped to the board, write simple factual statements. The placement of the text, one or two sentences, should be at the bottom half of each large sheet of paper, leaving the top half for the illustrations.
8. Model how to write informational text. Take time to model the first sentence, or the lead sentence, that introduces the topic or the contents of the wall story. Explain its importance to each sentence in the story.
9. The top part of each page has been left blank for illustrations to be drawn by the children who worked on the wall story. Direct the children to work in pairs, selecting a page to draw the illustration that represents the sentence.
10. After the children have illustrated each page, have the children read the wall story. Demonstrate how to write a title of a story, and then write a title together. Show them how the title helps readers make predictions on what they will read.
11. When the story is complete, invite the children to write their names under the title to show authorship. Remind the children that this story is telling facts about a topic and giving information to readers.
12. Finally, read the story with the children to determine if it conveys the meaning that they want, or if they left out any important facts. Review the concept of coherence, that all the facts support the main topic. Invite each child to read a page of the wall story.

If this is the first demonstration of expository writing, the teacher may wish to use a more explicit type of modeling. The teacher will also need to model how to think about the contents of the story before writing and how to organize the ideas that will be included. As the teacher models writing informational text through the wall story, another important focus is on other aspects of writing, such as the use of a capital letter at the beginning of a sentence, the use of punctuation marks, and how to write the title of a story.

Assessment of Modeled Literacy: The Wall Story

An excellent assessment strategy to use with modeled literacy is observation or kidwatching, as referred to in earlier chapters. Goodman (1985) noted that effective teachers have always observed children's learning, but what they have failed to do was to systematically record or *document* students' literacy behaviors during instruction and learning. We now know that such documentation of children's performances over time offers useful information about the growth and development of their literacy as well as other forms of learning.

When the teacher observes children during modeled instruction, the focus may be on the degree to which the children participate in a literacy activity. In the wall story activity, Joanne documented children's specific responses to content-related questions to be included in the story. The teacher may also wish to document how children respond to specific types of instruction.

Student's Name	Participates in Discussion	Contributes Ideas for Writing	Reads Back the Story Upon Request	Participates in Illustrating Assigned Page

KEY

H	**High** level of engagement	L	**Low** level of engagement
M	**Moderate** level of engagement	NO	**No** level of engagement

Figure 7.4
Annotated Checklist for Modeled Writing: The Wall Story

How can busy teachers document their observations of groups of children during modeling the wall story? The annotated checklist is a useful assessment form that permits teachers to focus their observations on specific areas of learning intended for small-group instruction. An example that has been designed for use with modeled instruction of the wall story is found in Figure 7.4. The children's participation may be coded very easily. The level of engagement (see the key) for each of five categories can be recorded, denoting each child's progress. In addition to documenting levels of participation, the teacher may add annotations or comments that are especially insightful about a specific child's response to instruction or student learning.

Modeling Spelling Strategies During Writing

Spelling development. At the early stage of literacy development, children write more and more, and as a result, they are learning more about spelling words. As we have mentioned in Chapter 2, children move through stages of spelling development as their experiences with print increase. Children typically begin to use conventional forms of language to a greater degree. Just as in the literacy stages of development, however, the stages of spelling development are not clearly defined within children (Gentry, 1999). For example, one piece of writing may indicate that a child is at the **transitional stage,** whereas a second piece of writing may indicate that the same child a week later is at the **phonetic stage.** This is especially true when children are between stages or when they attempt to spell new and more difficult words.

Most early writers are moving from the phonetic stage toward the transitional spelling stage. Children who are transitional spellers adhere to basic conventions of English orthography. Their writing samples show that they use vowels in every syllable, vowels with consonants, vowels before syllables that contain an *r*, vowel diagraphs *(sheet)*, the silent *-e*, and inflectional endings (*-s* and *-ing*; Gentry, 1982).

Indeed, transitional spellers are moving beyond the single "sounding-out strategy," as they take advantage of visual memory as well as the meaning of words or word parts for developing their own spelling strategies. Teachers target their spelling development when they design spelling instruction to build upon what they already know to "nudge" children along toward the conventional spelling stage.

Modeling spelling instruction. Short lessons to demonstrate new strategies to transitional spellers are offered below. The instruction may be incorporated as mini-lessons through the use of a wall story, a poem, or a set of directions. Modeling spelling strategies may also be used as mini-lessons to small groups of children in writing workshops. In any case, spelling instruction should be connected to authentic writing contexts and take into account the child's stage of spelling development. For instruction, it is important to select the specific spelling strategy that the children are beginning to develop and then select the target words that relate to the context of the children's writing.

Mini-lesson #1: Inflected endings. Build on what children already know. At the transitional spelling stage children begin to use **inflected endings;** therefore they need help to develop this skill. Inflected endings are added to the end of words but do not change their meaning, only their number, case, gender, tense, or form. Common inflected endings are *-s, -ing,* and *-ed.* Model to children how to build ongoing lists of words by adding word endings to a known word, showing them changes in spelling when adding some endings. For example,

- **Happy:** happier, happiest, happiness
- **Carry:** carries, carried, carrying
- **Lucky:** luckier, luckiest
- **Play:** plays, playing, played, player

Mini-lesson #2: Word sort. Help children become aware of the differences in sounds of vowels that are spelled with the same letter(s). In this way, children will further develop their visual strategy that they already use to spell words. Use a **word-sort** to model how words with the same vowels (visually alike) may be sorted by the differences in their vowel sounds. That is, the words *loose* and *flood* have the same vowels but not the same vowel sounds. A word sort provides an opportunity to classify words that have the same feature or characteristic. In this case it would be the sounds in the vowels. Two different sounds that the vowels *oo* make have been used to sort six different words with the same vowel spelling. Model the word sort for children by having them first listen to the two different sounds in words that are represented by the same vowels and placing each word in the appropriate pile. As you say the word *took,* drag out the sounds in the word and then isolate the vowel sound of *oo.* Do this again for the word *flood.* Give the children a set of words containing the vowel *oo* printed on cards. Tell them to listen to the sound each

Meeting Diverse Needs: For second language learners, help children connect the words to their lives and experiences not only through discussions of word meanings but also through pictures of the words. For example, use picture word cards for the word sort.

vowel makes and sort the words by their vowel sounds. Place the words that sound like the word *loop* in one pile, and place the words that sound like the word *took* in a second pile.

Words for sort

cook, loop, brood, book, moose, soothe, took, loot, loose, tool, foot, loom, soot

Mini-lesson #3: If I can spell . . . spelling patterns. Demonstrate to children that they can use words they know to spell words that they do not know through the use of spelling patterns. Present three words to children that have the same spelling patterns and tell them that the words may look and sound the same way. Show children the following words:

bean lean clean

Say each word. Then track the familiar pattern with your finger or with a marker. Tell children that if they know how to spell *-ean* in the word *bean,* they can also spell *lean* and *clean.* Draw the chart in Figure 7.5 on the board, and then model to children how spelling patterns help to spell other words (Taberski, 2000). Change the spelling patterns on the chart in Figure 7.5, and have children work on new spelling patterns. Once they become familiar with the task, they may do this activity independently.

Spelling patterns you know

-at	*-ake*	*-ook*
	will help to spell new words	
________	________	________
________	________	________
________	________	________

Figure 7.5
Worksheet for Using Familiar Spelling Patterns to Spell New Words

Mini-lesson #4: Word detective. Finding words within words promotes children's skill to use visual analysis of words for word parts and then to use familiar patterns within words to spell new words. Tell children that they will be detectives looking for small words in large words. Present them with a word that contains many small words. Depending on the familiarity with the task of visual analysis of words, you may start with a familiar word with only one or two word parts to model the task. Make a chart like the one in Figure 7.6 and model how smaller words may be found in larger ones.

Mini-lesson #5: The family word tree. Help children continue to develop their use of morphemic knowledge (meanings in words) to spell new words. Use a mini-lesson to model the relationship between spelling words that have similar

Satisfaction	Favorite	Mountain	Something
sat	favor	mount	so
action	or	in	some
at	it		me
fact			met
is			thing
faction			thin
on			in
act			hi

Figure 7.6
Chart for Word Detective

Make a Family Word Tree

Skate	Eighteen	Ate	Eighth
Eighty	Twenty-eight	Mate	

"Eight" asks, "Who are my word relatives?"

meanings. One way of doing this is to show children how words belong to a family, and then build family word trees. Each word that is placed on the tree is related by meaning. For example, engage children in a discussion about how words belong to the "eight family" and may be put on the family tree. Demonstrate that two words are related when they both contain word parts that are spelled the same and have similar meanings.

Discuss the meaning of the word *eight.* Ask children to read the words aloud with a word part that sounds like "ate" or "eight." Point to each word with the word part spelled "eight," telling how they are related by meaning. Ask children to place words on the tree that belong to the "eight family tree." After children have placed the words on the "eight family tree," ask them if they know any other words that could be added to the tree. This strategy for spelling words using the meaning parts found in words needs to be further developed at this stage of spelling development.

Assessing Children's Spelling

One method used to determine the developmentally appropriate spelling instruction for students is to analyze children's spelling within their writing. Knowing a child's stage of spelling development will help the teacher select the appropriate teaching strategy. It is important to use children's writing samples that have not undergone revision or editing. In other words, to determine a child's level of spelling development, use the first draft of his writing. Analyzing children's writing samples over time allows teachers to see the progression of spelling development as well as the specific strategies that each child is using while spelling unknown words. This type of assessment may be used to inform the teacher's spelling instruction with individual children and document how children progress through the stages of spelling development.

According to Gentry (1982, 1985, 1999), the typical sequence in spelling development moves from the prephonetic stage to the standard stage. Figure 7.7 shows a list of the characteristics of all of the stages of spelling development. Note how each behavior is expressed in children's writing samples and what it tells about the child's knowledge of spelling. This helps in analyzing children's writing to determine their stages of spelling development. Because effective instruction builds on what children already know, using spelling analysis of children's writing to plan for their instruction ensures good teaching.

Children who are early readers and writers are most likely to be at the beginning or well on their way in the *transition stage of spelling development.* This means that they know how to read and write many sight words, they are using their knowledge of consonant sounds and vowel sounds to spell words, and they are aware of word endings and use them in their spelling. At this stage, children's spellings show overgeneralizations, and they are using visual memory in spelling words—seeing if a word "looks right."

Analyzing Maria's spelling. To analyze Maria's spelling in the story in Figure 7.8 about camping, the first step is to chart the spelling characteristics of her writing. Figure 7.8 shows Maria's original writing sample that was taken from her journal. The entry was made during independent writing and was not edited for spelling errors. Use the stages checklist shown in Figure 7.7 to track a child's spelling development. Note how the qualitative analysis is holistic in nature as we search for patterns and strategies that the child is using to spell unknown words are identified. The spelling analysis of Maria's writing sample shown in Figure 7.9 indicates that she has spelled many sight words correctly. Unknown words that she attempted to spell are represented by initial, medial, and final consonants. Her writing also reveals that she uses most of the consonants correctly, indicating her knowledge of most consonant sounds. There are two words where Maria used inflected endings, adding *-s* to the word *cat* and attempting to add *-ing* to the word *camp.* Although the error on the word ending *-ing* may be developmental, this spelling pattern indicates that Maria is beginning to use inflected endings. Indeed, with continued monitoring she will learn

Prephonetic Stage of Spelling Development—Random Letters

Characteristics of Writing
- Scribbles and draws shapes that look like letters
- Makes random letters and shapes
- Uses no spaces between words
- Draws pictures to express meaning

Knowledge of Spelling
- Lacks letter-sound relationship
- Begins to copy small words

Writing Sample

Early Phonetic Stage of Spelling Development—Consonants

Characteristics of Writing
- Begins to show letter–sound relationships
- Uses invented spelling
- Uses initial consonants
- Spells words with consonants
- Uses spaces between words

Knowledge of Spelling
- Knows longer words have longer spellings
- Matches some consonants with correct sounds
- Begins to decode words when reading

Writing Sample

PZ

Advanced Phonetic Stage of Spelling Development—Letter Sounds

Characteristics of Writing
- Spells words using letter–sound relationships
- Spells words based on how they look
- Begins to use long vowels in spelling words

Knowledge of Spelling
- Knows how to spell some sight words
- Knows most consonant sounds
- Sees distinctive features in words (i.e., the extenders in *yellow*)

Writing Sample

PBT WZF

Transitional Stage of Spelling Development—Vowel and Consonant Combinations in Words

Characteristics of Writing
- Spells words using more standard forms of spelling
- Relies more on visual memory, how words look, to spell words
- Spells more sight words correctly
- Spells words using familiar letter patterns
- Spells words representing all syllables

Knowledge of Spelling
- Knows and applies basic spelling rules
- Knows and spells some words with their endings (e.g., *-s*, *-ing*, *-ly*)
- Knows short and long vowels and begins to use them correctly in spelling
- Knows correct spelling of more sight words

Writing Sample

MI DG

Standard Stage of Spelling Development—Correct Spelling

Characteristics of Writing
- Spells most words using standard or correct spelling
- Begins to spell words that have multiple spellings (e.g., *their, there, they're*) correctly
- Relies on meaning and syntax as well as phonics to spell words

Knowledge of Spelling
- Knows compound words, root words, affixes
- Knows more rules and applies them to spelling
- Knows compound words and contractions

Writing Sample

I LIK MILK

Figure 7.7
Stages of Spelling Development

Figure 7.8

the correct spelling of the word ending *-ing,* which the teacher may use for a minilesson. Spelling analysis also shows that Maria is beginning to use visual memory, which she demonstrated in the errors she made in spelling the words *cooked* and *brother.* To summarize, Maria is developing spelling strategies typical at the transition stage, uses standard spelling of more sight words, shows spelling of familiar spelling patterns, and is moving closer to conventional or standard spelling, indicted by the quantitative analysis. Out of 17 words that she wrote, 10 or 59% were correct. Indeed, Maria is entering the transitional stage of spelling development.

Using the analysis of Maria's spelling, her teacher can infer what Maria knows about spelling words and can then use this to make instructional decisions. Figure 7.10 shows the correspondence between what Maria knows and how to prepare instruction so that learning is developmentally appropriate, proceeding from the known to the unknown.

Name: Maria

Date: January 25, 2004

CHILD'S SPELLING	BEGINNER WRITER	CONSONANTS			VOWELS		WORDS		STRATEGIES		
	Scribble/ Random Letter	*Initial*	*Medial*	*Final*	*Used*	*Not Used*	*Sight*	*Endings*	*Meaning*	*Visual*	*Phonics*
Me							X			X	
and							X			X	
my							X			X	
bruthr		X		X	X						X
wnt		X	X	X		X					X
campng		X		X	X			X			X
We							X			X	
cookted		X		X	X			X		X	
Ar				X	X						X
fuud		X		X	X						X
in						X				X	
the						X				X	
fier		X		X		X				X	X
We							X			X	
had					X					X	X
hot		X		X	X					X	X
dogs		X		X	X			X		X	X

QUANTITATIVE ANALYSIS

Total Number of Words = 17	Correct Words = 10 (59%)	Incorrect Words = 7 (41%)

Figure 7.9
Analysis of Writing for Spelling Development

What Maria Knows About Spelling	***Spelling Instruction for Maria***
• Most consonant sounds • The use of vowels in some words • The correct spelling of many sight words • The use of some word endings • The use of familiar spelling patterns • The beginning development of other spelling strategies (e.g., visual)	• Mini-lesson on word endings • Mini-lesson to increase the use of familiar spelling patterns for spelling unknown words • Mini-lesson on spelling word endings • Mini-lessons on the use of vowels in spelling

Figure 7.10
Using Assessment for Planning Instruction

Student's Name ______________________ **Date of Birth** ________

Prephonetic Stage of Spelling Development—Random Letters

Date:

__________ Scribbles and draws shapes that look like letters

__________ Makes random letters and shapes

__________ Uses no spaces between words

__________ Draws pictures to express meaning

Grade _____

Early Phonetic Stage of Spelling Development—Consonants

Date:

__________ Begins to show letter–sound relationships

__________ Uses invented spelling

__________ Uses initial consonants

__________ Spells words with consonants

__________ Uses spaces between words

Grade _____

Advanced Phonetic Stage of Spelling Development—Letter Sounds

Date:

__________ Spells words using letter–sound relationships

__________ Spells words based on how they look

__________ Begins to use long vowels in spelling words

Grade _____

Transitional Stage of Spelling Development—Vowel and Consonant Combinations in Words

__________ Spells words using more standard forms of spelling

__________ Relies more on visual memory, how words look, to spell words

__________ Spells more sight words correctly

__________ Spells words using familiar letter patterns

__________ At the end of the stage, words are spelled representing all syllables

Grade _____

Standard Stage of Spelling Development–Correct Spelling

__________ Spells most words using standard or correct spelling

__________ Begins to spells words that have multiple spellings (e.g., *their*, *there*, *they're*) correctly

__________ Relies on meaning and syntax as well as phonics to spell words

Grade _____

Figure 7.11
Student Profile of Spelling Development Form

Teachers will also want to track children's spelling over the school year, documenting their growth in learning to spell words and showing when they have reached certain stages in spelling development. After the teacher has analyzed the children's spelling, their progress is documented at different periods of the school year. Our suggestion is to record children's progress at least four or five times a year or when progress reports are sent to the parents. The student profile of spelling development form found in Figure 7.11 can be used as a guide in monitoring the stages of growth in spelling over a period. This form has been developed from the research on children's spelling development by Gentry (1982, 1985, 1999). These forms should be kept in each child's literacy portfolio to review spelling development over the course the year, and may follow the child into the next grade.

Shared Literacy

Shared Reading

Webs and maps during reading. A common trait of early readers is that they begin to read series books (Taberski, 2000). During shared reading teachers can encourage children by developing their interests in series books as well as extending their preferences to include more informational books. Leon, a second-grade teacher, used David A. Adler's *Picture Book Biography* series to introduce early readers to a new genre—biographies. *A Picture Book of Thurgood Marshall* (1994) is one that Leon used during shared reading.

Using maps to construct meaning. Leon knew that the children's language and concepts would need to be developed to understand this biography. He used webbing to introduce the critical vocabulary in the story that would help children understand what was being read. "Webbing serves as a tool for structuring classroom talk about stories and books that can broaden thinking and deepen responses to literature" (Bromley, 1995, pp. 90–91). His prereading discussion included building prior knowledge of the major concepts about which the children had little or no knowledge, but needed for constructing meaning when listening to the biography of Thurgood Marshall. During the discussion, Leon modeled the concept of webbing. He started with critical concepts such as *segregation, U.S. Supreme Court,* and the *Constitution.* As children talked about the concepts, more information was written on the web. Lines were drawn to show a relationship between ideas. The result was the web shown in Figure 7.12.

Leon introduced the book to the children. He carefully conducted a short book introduction. He then read the book through showing them the pictures, stopping at difficult words to give a brief explanation. After the reading, Leon returned to the concept map to integrate the experiences from the life of Thurgood Marshall that the children remembered. Leon helped the children make the connections from the story to the concepts that were discussed prior to the reading. During the discussion, Leon jogged the children's memory through the use of open-ended questions about the events from

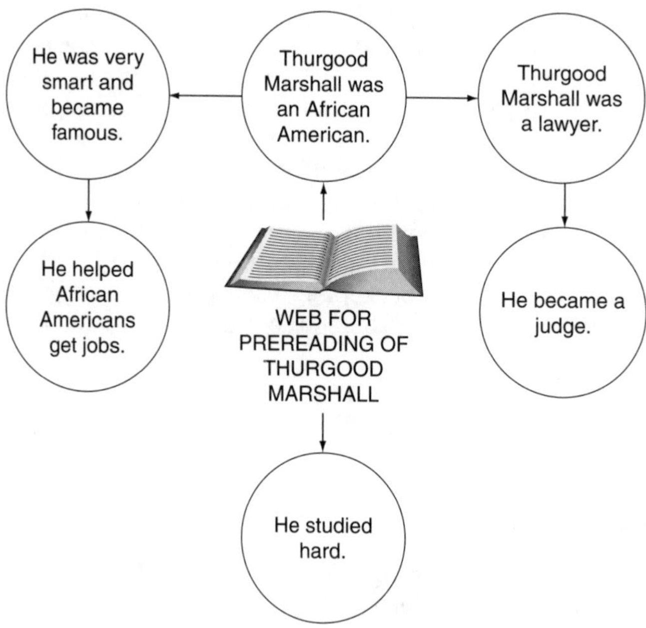

Figure 7.12
Prereading Concept Map of Language and Concept Development

the biography. The postdiscussion concept map in Figure 7.13, shows how much children remembered from the story. It also demonstrates how the experiences from the life of Thurgood Marshall are organized around important concepts and vocabulary from social studies. The use of the concept map to facilitate children's organization of knowledge is indeed important, but *without the guided discussion* that led to the development of the web, the children would find little use for the concept map.

The following day, Leon returned to the biography of Thurgood Marshall. He conducted a short review of the book. He then turned the children's attention to the postdiscussion web or concept map. Together they reviewed all of the information about Thurgood Marshall. Leon emphasized the importance of placing these ideas in the order in which they happened in the person's life. Presenting another form of graphic organizer, the biography map, Leon demonstrated how it may be used in thinking about a person's life—the beginning, middle, and end. He directed the children to use the biography map to think about three important life events that happened when Marshall was very *young,* three when he was *growing up,* and three toward the *end of his life.* The children were also asked to decide on Thurgood Marshall's major contribution.

Lionetti (1992) suggested a graphic organizer for helping the children to organize the many events that they may have learned from reading a biography. The map in Figure 7.14 shows a time frame and encourages children to think of the person's

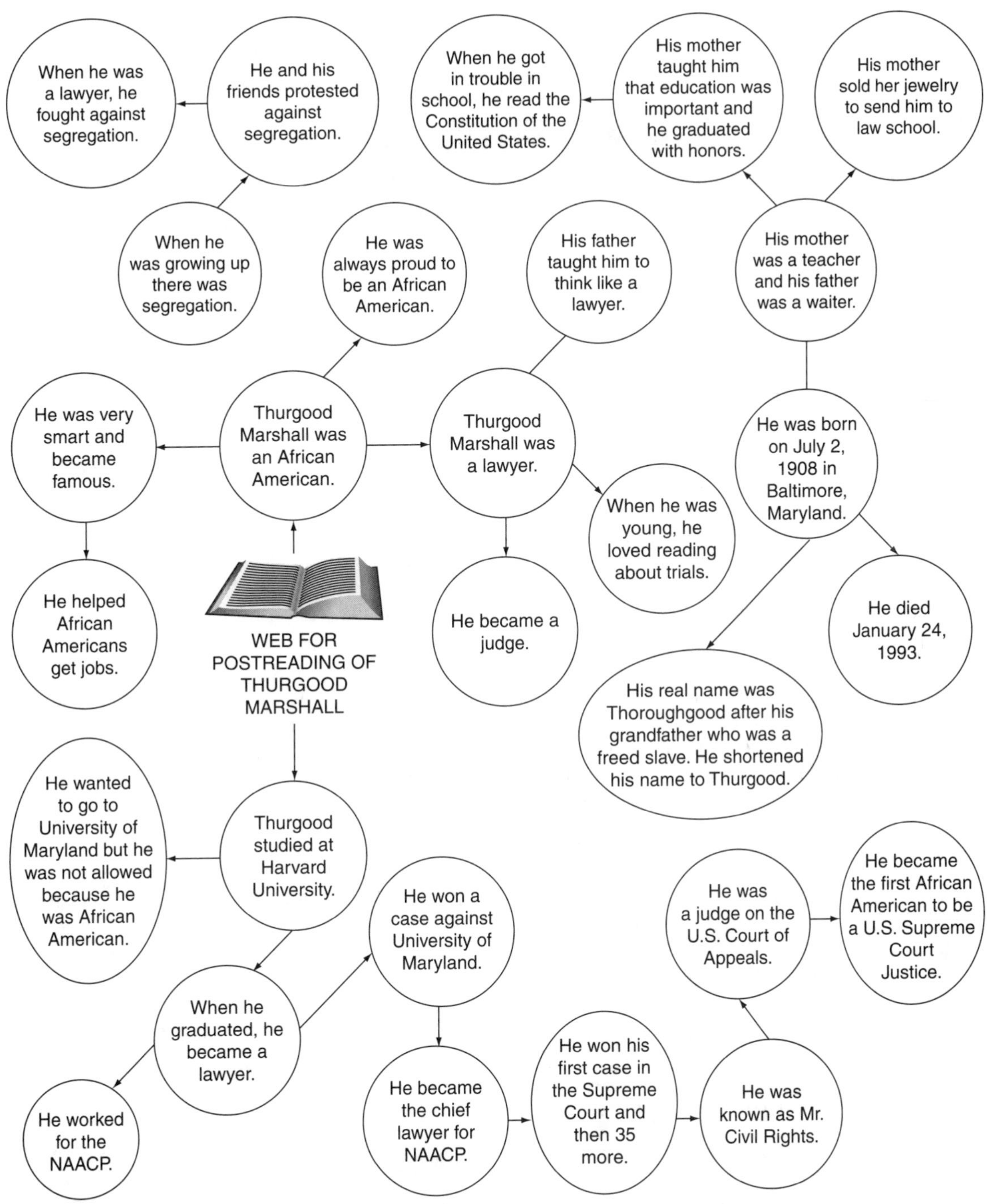

Figure 7.13
A Postreading Discussion Concept Map

A Picture Book of Thurgood Marshall
by
David A. Adler

What we learned about the life and times of Thurgood Marshall

When Thurgood Marshall was very young . . .	When Thurgood Marshall was growing up . . .	When Thurgood Marshall was older . . .
1.	1.	1.
2.	2.	2.
3.	3.	3.

The most important contribution that Thurgood Marshall made to the world was . . .

Figure 7.14
Biography Map

life theme by focusing on a major contribution. The biography map may be adjusted for the book or for the children and the goal of the lesson.

Leon placed the children in his class in small groups and gave them a biography map to help to guide their discussion. He told them to use the postdiscussion concept map in Figure 7.13 and the book to decide the time frame for the occurrence of the life experiences in Thurgood Marshall's life. Each group selected a moderator of the discussion and wrote down the decisions made by the group using the biography map in Figure 7.14 as their guide.

Assessment of the biography map. Assessment of the biography map tells whether the small group understood the biography. It also indicates the amount of assistance or teacher support the children need as well as the level of responsibility for this genre that may be given to the children at the early stage of literacy development. Leon used the assessment checklist found in Figure 7.15 to analyze the children's biography retellings.

Shared Literacy: Writing

Language Experience and Group Stories

The *language experience approach (LEA)* may be familiar from one's own experiences as a student in elementary school. The LEA was introduced in the seventies (Allen, 1976; Veatch, 1978; Veatch, Sawicki, Elliott, Barnette, & Blakey, 1973) and was used widely by classroom teachers as well as reading specialists. It is still used today in its original form as well as in modified formats because it is such a powerful

Name:									Date:			
Key Y = Yes N = No	Childhood			Youth			Adulthood			Person's Contribution		
	Fact			Fact			Fact			Fact		
	#1	#2	#3	#1	#2	#3	#1	#2	#3	#1	#2	#3
Accurate												
Clearly Expressed												
Significant Event												

Figure 7.15
Assessment Checklist for the Biography Map

instructional approach for young readers and writers. In the LEA, the children's experiences are used as well as their own language and their vocabulary to develop a story that they dictate to the teacher. After the story is composed and written, the teacher reads the story to the children, and the children read it back to the group. The LEA has been criticized for being limited by the children's experiences. Because of this limitation, teachers have modified the approach to include a variety of language catalysts such as children's literature, thereby extending topics for writing.

Group experience stories. The group experience story has elements of the language experience approach. Stories are composed by a small group of children with the teacher, and the topics arise from the group's shared experiences. Starting with a discussion of a shared experience, the group composes a story with the teacher through interactive writing (Vukelich, Christie, & Enz, 2002). The experience may be a curricula event such as hatching duck eggs, or it may be a class field trip to an apple orchard where children engage in apple picking. Additionally, a language catalyst—a piece of children's literature that has been read to the group or that the children read together—may be used to initiate the group's discussion on the topic of their story and to help children make connections to their personal experiences.

Like the LEA, group experiences begin with a rich discussion focused on the children's shared experience that becomes the topic of their story. The teacher acts as the scribe, writing the children's story. While the children compose the story, the teacher takes the opportunity to develop language and literacy concepts and skills. For example, the teacher may talk about the spelling of certain words, ask the children for a "million dollar word" to enhance the story and increase their vocabulary, vary the sentence structure, and incorporate the conventions of print. After the story is completed, the teacher reads the story aloud to the group and asks the children to read it back.

Group experience stories are excellent ways for teachers to show children how to use "book language" in writing their own stories.

Because group stories may be used with children at varying literacy levels, what makes it a valuable instructional tool is the way the teacher targets the literacy needs of the group while they compose the story together. The materials needed for conducting the **group experience story** are an easel, large chart paper that is lined and securely fastened to the easel, and markers for writing the story. The steps for developing a group experience story are described in the following section.

Procedures for group experience stories. The following procedures may be used to implement the group experience story as a shared writing process. The two aspects of the instructional strategy are the group discussion and the writing. The group discussion is valuable because children need time to talk about their shared ideas related to the topic or central theme of their writing that may be considered a prewriting phase. The second aspect is the writing phase, which gives the teacher the opportunity to use the children's ideas and to compose the group story with them. While writing, the teacher makes instructional decisions targeting the needs of the children.

- **Preparation Phase:** Discussion is the major aspect of this phase. Before writing the story, children need to be prepared by discussion as they "warm up" to the writing phase. This phase begins with the teacher gathering the children in a small group on a rug or around a circular or kidney-shaped table. The teacher decides on the shared experience that the children will talk and write about, and begins by asking open-ended questions. As the discussion proceeds, the teacher uses prompt questions, asking for elaboration on specific aspects of the topic, for developing an idea, or for more ideas related to the topic. The discussion continues until all aspects have been exhausted. At the end of the discussion the

Discussion about the writing topic promotes thought and clarifies ideas.

teacher summarizes all of the ideas that were discussed and tells the children that talking and thinking about their ideas are good ways to get ready for writing.

- **Writing Phase:** During this phase, the teacher elicits the ideas that were part of the discussion, asking the children to think about the major topic so they would know how to begin the story. After the first sentence is decided upon, the teacher may begin to write and instruct the children on the need for a sentence that would make a good beginning to the story. As the teacher writes the sentence, help is requested from the children. Their participation may be in the form of telling how to spell a word, whether a word needs a capital letter, the punctuation marks demanded by the type of sentence, and so forth. The teacher continues acting as scribe as the children make their contributions to the story.
- **Reading and Rereading Phase:** After the story is completed, the teacher reads it aloud. She asks for volunteers to read certain parts of the story or to read it together as in choral reading. The chart is then placed in an area so that the children may have access to it when they have free reading time. In the application, Shondra and a small group of second-grade children are writing a group story.

The Preparation Phase: A Discussion on *Brave Harriet* and How the Children Might Be Brave in Pursuing Their Own Goals

Shondra, a second-grade teacher, gathered a small group of early readers and writers around the writing table. The group had recently finished reading *Brave Harriet* by Marissa Moss (2001), a biography of Harriet Quimby, the first American woman to receive a pilot's license and the first woman to fly solo across the English Channel. Their reading consisted of a book discussion that focused on the obstacles that Harriet Quimby had to overcome to achieve her goals. The children are eager to talk about one of their favorite books. Indeed, they have many responses to share and some questions to ask. Shondra uses the biography as a language catalyst to talk about bravery and the children's own ambitions.

Shondra: Harriet Quimby was very brave. What were some of the things that made her so brave?

Jenna: She was a lady and she flew a plane and no ladies flew planes then.

Tanya: Her friends thought she was crazy and she didn't care. She wanted to fly.

Marc Anthony: A long time ago planes weren't safe. Planes had no roof on the top of the pilot. And it was cold.

Shondra: Can you think of any other reason that Harriet was very brave?

Juan: I don't think people wanted her to fly alone. Maybe they didn't think she could because she was a lady.

Shondra: That's a good point. Sometimes people think we can't do certain things. And maybe we haven't even tried. We won't know until we try. Can you think of one thing that you might want to do that would make you a "brave Harriet"?

Tanya: I want to be a police lady and help people. I think that is brave.

Keisha: I saw an animal doctor in the zoo with the lions. She was brave. I want to be a vet and help animals.

Marc Anthony: I told everybody that I want to drive right on the top of the fire truck and rescue people in the flames.

Juan: I want to drive cars really fast.

Shondra: You mean like a racecar driver.

Jenna: I think that I could be just like Brave Harriet and fly an airplane.

Shondra: We talked about how Harriet was brave, and how she wanted to learn to fly an airplane even when no woman flew long ago when Harriet Quimby lived. We also talked about the planes built during that time. They were not as safe as today's airplanes. They also had an opened cockpit where the pilot flew the plane. Each of you said how you want to be as brave as Harriet.

The teacher gets ready to write a story with the children. The group experience story is written on large chart paper with a marker. Many teachers use a large spiral-lined pad to save the group stories for later reading. The teacher and the children write together, often sharing the marker as they compose the story. During this time the teacher will take the opportunity to teach parts of the writing process as well as certain conventions of print that the children need. Note how Shondra focuses on developing the concept of a good lead or opening sentence that is needed to begin a story.

The Writing Phase: Using the Discussion to Write the Group Story

Shondra: Let us begin to write our story about bravery. Remember the importance of the first sentence. This is the sentence that tells our readers or audience what the story is about; it is like a window into our story. Does anyone have any ideas how we can begin?

Juan: I want to be like Harriet. I am going to drive a racecar.

Shondra: That is a fine sentence, Juan. We will save your sentence to write after the opening sentence. First, let us think of a sentence that tells why Harriet was so brave before we tell how we are going to be like Brave Harriet.

Shondra continues through the composing process. Together they write a story. Once Shondra elicits a sentence from the children, she "shares the pen" with them just as the group shared their ideas to write the story. Let's listen in on how Shondra shares the pen during the group story.

Shondra: Tanya, that is a perfect opening sentence to start the story (Shondra repeats the sentence): "Harriet Quimby was brave because she flew an airplane a very long time ago when ladies did not fly airplanes. I want to be a brave Harriet." Let us start to write our opening sentence at the top of the page. Who knows how to spell "Harriet"?

Shondra: Fine, Juan. Come to the chart and write the first word. Remember how names begin and how first words of sentences begin.

Shondra continues to write the group story with the children, sharing the pen during the entire composing process, asking the children to come and write the first word of a sentence, to write a word, or to put a punctuation mark in the story. After the story is completed,

Shondra hands markers to the children to write their names showing joint authorship. The date is then added.

The Reading and Rereading Phase: Reading the Story to Revisit Learning

When the group finishes penning the story, Shondra reads it aloud with expression. She then revisits some aspects of instruction that she feels need to be highlighted.

Shondra: (Shondra points to the first sentence.) This is a good lead or opening sentence. Can anyone tell why stories need an opening sentence?

Jenna: Because the first sentence is the one that tells what we will write about.

Shondra: Yes, and our lead sentence tells us that we will read about how you will be brave like Harriet.

Shondra will continue to revisit some aspects of instruction to highlight what the children have learned and see the application to their own writing. The story is then read together, as the teacher points to each word. Shondra takes the group storybook and places it in the reading area where the children may reread their stories during independent reading time, or the teacher may select one of the stories to be read during shared reading.

Assessing the Group Experience Stories

There are three phases to the group experience story, and within each phase the teacher has a set of expectations for children's learning. Each of the expectations or student outcomes may be assessed within the instructional context. In the first phase, the children are expected to participate in a lively discussion, offering their experiences related to the topic of discussion. In the second phase, the children and teacher share the pen, and they are expected to work together to compose the story and to write it down on paper. In the final phase, the children take turns reading the story they have written together. The expectations are the learning outcomes for the children that can be assessed through observation and documented through the use of an annotated checklist. Shondra used an annotated checklist to document the children's level of participation during the group experience story like the one in Figure 7.16. An alternative to the annotated checklist is to use sticky notes on a clipboard.

Guided Literacy

Guided Reading

There is a reason why Fountas and Pinnell (1996) have called guided reading the heart of a balanced literacy program. Within the context of guided reading, the teacher uses direct or explicit teaching to help children as they learn how to read. All other instruc-

The Group Experience Story

Student's Name	*Participates in Discussion*	*Contributes Ideas for Composing the Story*	*Shares Pen During Writing of the Story*	*Reads Back Story to Group Upon Request*

KEY

H	**High** level of engagement	L	**Low** level of engagement
M	**Moderate** level of engagement	NO	**No** level of engagement

Figure 7.16
Annotated Checklist for Shared Writing

tional pieces of the balanced literacy program work to support the most critical goal of guided reading—to help children become independent and strategic readers.

Working with small groups of children who are at similar stages in reading development and have the same skill needs, the teacher instructs the children on how they are to use skills and strategies to read and to construct meaning from text. Because instruction is directed at their skill and strategy needs, an important part of guided instruction is *grouping for children's instructional needs.* Therefore, the teacher needs to monitor or assess children's progress in reading development to group them appropriately for effective instruction.

When teachers work within children's capabilities of reading, they are teaching within the children's zone of proximal development (ZPD). That is, they mediate reading strategy development (Antonacci, 2000). Such types of teaching are developmentally appropriate and are based on students' instructional needs. Within this section, you will see an application of Vygotsky's theory that was discussed in Chapter 2. Vygotsky (1978) maintained that the best teaching occurs within the learner's ZPD—the area of learning where the child develops the skill, concept, or strategy through the careful assistance of the teacher. It is the area of development where the child is ready for learning but needs the assistance from an expert to perform successfully. For example, when children are reading a book where they can be successful only if the teacher provides the necessary support and assistance, the level of the book is within their ZPD. The teacher provides direct instruction of the skills and strategies that the children in the small group need in order to read and understand the book. As the children are reading, the teacher is waiting, ready to offer assistance and feedback when each child needs it. Thus, guided reading provides the context where the child will receive such careful mediation or assistance. Below is a review of the background and procedures for guided reading that effective teachers use in planning and implementing this aspect of a balanced literacy program.

Background for Guided Reading

The purpose of guided reading. A primary feature of guided reading is the formal nature of the instruction in reading that the children receive. During guided reading, teachers offer direct instruction to teach highly specific skills that are targeted for the needs of the small group of children with whom they are working. The type of instruction that children receive—instruction that is intentional and designed for their needs—is quite effective in developing fluent reading in young children. Guided reading provides children with guidance and immediate feedback in developing word-solving and comprehension strategies that fluent readers need to gain independence in reading.

Designing an effective guided reading area. Guided reading is taught in small groups of approximately six to eight children. To accommodate the focused instruction, a special space in the classroom needs to be set aside for guided reading. The teacher may choose to have a teacher's chair set at the edge of a small area rug where the children sit. Another way to design the area for guided reading is through the use of a small, round or kidney-shaped table that the children sit around with the teacher at the center. In both cases, the children sit close to the teacher who guides them through reading the text. Within the guided reading area, the teacher should be able to monitor the children's reading by carefully assessing and documenting their growth. The materials used for guided reading instruction should be organized for easy access and placed close by to the guided reading area. Such materials might include magnetic letters and the accompanying board, sentence strips and a pocket chart, an easel with chart paper and markers or a whiteboard with markers and an eraser, and records for assessing students' oral reading and comprehension.

Managing time for guided reading. For children to become strategic readers, they need sufficient time for instruction at their levels of reading development. Therefore, all children ready for guided reading need from three to five sessions per week in 25-minute blocks of time. Although there is no uniformity with respect to class size in schools, most school districts target their primary grades for smaller class size. Therefore, in many school districts, the class size in the primary grades ranges from 20 to 25. Teachers take advantage of smaller classes by offering guided reading to all children five times per week.

Selecting materials for guided reading. Because the purpose of guided reading is to provide instruction pitched at the development of the children within the small group, the materials must be developmentally appropriate as well. Therefore, "a critical aspect of guided reading is matching books to individual children" (Fountas & Pinnell, 1996, p. 107). Effective teachers view the process of material selection as a critical aspect of the instructional plan and a way to make instruction developmentally appropriate. For guided reading, among the most tried and tested materials that work well are the small, leveled books. Teachers invest much time in collecting these books and organizing them by levels for guided reading. Leveled books are bundled in groups of six to eight, because children need their own copies for reading during and after instruction. A great source of extensive lists of leveled books to start with is *Guided Reading: Good First Teaching for All Children* by Irene C. Fountas and Gay Su Pinnell (1996).

Grouping children for guided reading. In a balanced literacy program, children are grouped in many different ways related to the goals of instruction. Such grouping patterns may include small groups of children at the same skill level, small or large groups with the same interests, or large groups to include a whole-class grouping for a class project or a read-aloud.

For guided reading, children are grouped primarily according to *literacy level* and *instructional needs.* The groups are dynamic in nature because learning and development are dynamic in young children. Children do not develop at the same rate; therefore, some children who are grouped together this month or week for guided reading may be in a different group next month or next week. Because one of the aims of guided reading is to provide children with developmentally appropriate instruction, it is necessary to pay considerable attention to the children's progress in skills and strategies related to reading when grouping for instruction. As mentioned, the size of the group is usually six to eight, six being an optimum number. However, there may be instances when one or two children need special instruction. This is the case when children need extra help in strategy development and skill instruction or their levels do not match any of the groups.

Procedures for the Teacher During Guided Reading

As in many instructional plans, a lesson may be defined in terms of what comes *before* the lesson, what happens *during* the lesson, and finally, what occurs *after* the lesson. Therefore, the procedures for planning a guided reading lesson are divided into these three phases.

Before-the-reading lesson. The teacher selects a developmentally appropriate book that is short and may be finished in one sitting. Each child has a copy of the book. Before reading, the teacher prepares the children for reading with a book introduction. Within this aspect of the lesson, the teacher strives to connect the children's personal and other book experiences with the story they are about to read. The teacher calls the children's attention to the title and author, asks them to make a prediction about the book based on the title and the illustrations on the cover, and conducts a story walk. During the story walk, the teacher engages the children in a discussion about the story events as they "walk through the book." The conclusion of the story or the solution of the story problem is not revealed in the book introduction. It is used to establish a purpose for reading by encouraging the children to make a prediction about how the story will conclude.

Within this aspect of the lesson, the teacher anticipates the words that may provide difficulty to the children. The teacher offers mini-lessons of specific phonic skills as related to words that children do not know how to decode. The lessons may also include word-solving strategies for unknown words.

The book introduction is a critical piece of instruction because the teacher prepares the children to use specific cues to solve words that may be unfamiliar to them. Thus, the teacher is "setting the stage" for the children to use their cueing systems in the following ways:

- **Semantic cues:** The discussion about the content of the book helps children to make personal and text connections so they can use their semantic or meaning cues to solve words with which they are unfamiliar. They are looking for a word that makes sense.

- **Graphophonological or visual cues:** The word work that the teacher presents before the reading is meant to prepare the children to use alphabetic knowledge to decode words with which they may be unfamiliar. The children are looking for a word that "sounds" or "looks" right.
- **Syntactic cues:** When the children are talking about the vocabulary and word meanings from the story, the book language will become more familiar to the children, thereby allowing them to use the familiar word order to select the most accurate word in word solving. They are looking for a word that fits the correct word order.

During-the-reading lesson. After a thorough book introduction, the teacher encourages the children to read the book independently. If the children made many predictions before reading, the teacher asks the children to read to confirm their predictions. While the children are reading, the teacher is "listening in" to provide encouragement, support, and guidance that the children may need. When children are experiencing trouble and are unable to decode a word, the teacher offers help by guiding them with prompts that are built on strategy language rather than telling them the correct word. Fountas and Pinnell (1996, pp. 160–161) suggest that teachers provide children with prompts to help them use different sources of information to aid them in word solving. Young readers need to construct and use a flexible word-solving system of strategies as they encounter new and more difficult texts. An example of such prompting may be found in Figure 7.17. The teacher furthers the child's processing system or strategy use to solve words and understand text by prompting the child who is having difficulty by using appropriate strategy language.

After the reading lesson. When the children have finished reading the story, the teacher may conduct a mini-lesson related to some of the difficulties the children experienced while reading. For example, if all or most of the children had a problem reading a word, the teacher will show them a useful strategy to decode that word.

- Does it make sense?
- How does the word begin?
- How does the word end? (When the child ignores word endings)
- Read to the end of each word.
- You noticed your mistake; that was good. (When a child self-corrects)
- Read the sentence again. (After the child makes an error)
- Read it again and watch for the tricky word.
- Watch for the mark at the end of the sentence.
- You read _______. What letter would you expect at the beginning and end of that word?
- Try that again and think about what might make sense.
- Check the word. Does it look right? Does it sound right?
- You made a mistake. Can you find it?
- Try that again.
- Can you read this again, just more quickly?

Figure 7.17
Prompts for Using Strategy Language

The teacher may take another minute to reinforce some of the strategies that the children were using to figure out words by drawing attention to a word that was being decoded and highlighting the strategy that the children used to figure out the word. During guided reading, this "kind of help is critical. *Making it easy to learn* does not mean simply *making it possible for the child to get it right*" (Fountas & Pinnell, 1996, p. 162). The teacher's task is to help children develop a system of strategies in getting words right. That is, children need to become problem solvers of new words, and teachers need to assist young readers by helping them develop the most effective strategies for achieving this goal.

Assessing Children's Oral Reading Through the Use of Running Records

The term *running records* was used in assessing a student's oral reading within the context of the classroom, because the classroom teacher literally takes a record of the child's reading "on the run." The name of this assessment strategy is not to minimize its potential power. Clay (1985, 1993) encouraged the frequent monitoring of children's oral reading through the use of running records. The running record is a valuable assessment tool that provides documentation of how a child is reading text. Frequent use of running records of the beginner reader provides rich information about the child's reading development and will aid the teacher in planning reading instruction for the child.

The information that the teacher learns from monitoring the child's oral reading behavior is both **quantitative** and **qualitative.** Quantitative results provide the teacher with the following information about a child's reading: (1) the number of words read correctly, (2) the number of errors or miscues, and (3) the number of self-corrections. In short, quantitative analysis of children's reading is limited to a description of a child's reading using numerical results.

Quantitative analysis of oral reading provides information that helps the teacher to determine whether the text was appropriate for the child. If the text is too difficult, the child will make many errors. If the child's accuracy level of reading is less than 90%, the text is inappropriate for either instructional or independent reading by the child. If a child's accuracy rate is 90% to 95%, the text may be considered appropriate for guided reading; if it is greater than 95%, the child will need a more difficult level of text to practice the strategies for word solving. Thus, using quantitative data from running records will help the teacher in selecting developmentally appropriate texts for guided reading instruction.

The information that may be derived from **qualitative analysis** is far richer, for it reveals how the child is using different sources of information or the cueing systems—semantic, phonologic, and syntactic—to decode a word; that is, it tells us about strategy use by the child. In other words, an analysis of the child's errors or miscues reveals how the child is sampling the text, or using the text cues as he attempts to decode a word. To do this, teachers examine errors or self-corrections children make to determine if they use the meaning to make sense, the structure of the language (syntax or word order) so that it "sounds like we talk," and visual or graphophonological information so that it sounds or looks right when attempting to read an unknown word. As teachers analyze the errors, they look for patterns of errors that indicate a set of strategies that children are developing.

Running records are used within the context of a guided reading lesson. When children are directed to read their books, the teacher monitors each child's reading to provide them with necessary support or assistance where needed. The teacher then asks them to reread the text for additional practice. At this time, the teacher will take a running record on one child's oral reading behavior.

Procedure for taking a running record. The following procedure is frequently used for recording a child's oral reading:

- The teacher has the following materials available: a clipboard, a form for taking a running record, and a pencil.
- The teacher and child sit next to each other in a quiet area so that the teacher may see the child reading and the text at the same time.
- The teacher asks the child to read the book, and during the reading, the teacher uses the code to record the child's oral reading. Figure 7.18 shows the code to record different types of oral reading behaviors.
- The teacher uses quantitative analysis to determine the percentage of words the child has read correctly (see Figure 7.19 for an example).

Running records provide much information on a child's reading growth, including the development of strategies.

The Type of Literacy Behavior	*Code*	*Scoring*
Accurate reading: The child reads the word correctly. Write a check for each correct word.	✓	**No error**
Substitution: The child substitutes a word for the one in the text. Write the substitution over the word in the text.	for / from	**1 error**
Told: The child does not attempt to read a word, and the teacher tells the child the word. Write a **T** next to the word or words that the teacher told the child.	— / from T	**1 error** for each word
Omission: The child omits a word while reading. Write a horizontal line over the omitted word.	— / from	**1 error** for each omission
Insertion: The child inserts a word that does not appear in the text. Draw a symbol for insertion and write the insertion that the child read.	the / —	**1 error** for each insertion
Self-Correction: The child reads the word incorrectly and corrects his mistake. Write the child's miscue and **SC** next to it.	for / from SC	**No error**

Figure 7.18
Scoring Oral Reading Behaviors

Quantitative Analysis of Sasha's Oral Reading	
Accuracy Rate—91%	With a 91% accuracy rate, Sasha reads 91 out of 100 words correctly. This accuracy score of 91% indicates that the book Sasha was reading was at her instructional level. Because *Cookies Week* is at level F, this level is an appropriate level for guided reading for Sasha.
Self-Correction—8:1	Sasha corrected 1 out of 8 miscues. Although Sasha indicated that she was able to correct an error, cross-checking strategies need further development to improve the self-correction ratio.
Error Ratio—11:1	An error ratio indicates in how many running words an error appears. Sasha makes 1 miscue for every 11 running words.

Figure 7.19
Quantitative Analysis of Sasha's Oral Reading

Running Record Assessment Form

Name Sasha Howard Date April 5 Grade 1
Literacy Level Early Teacher John Gray
Text Title *Cookie's Week* by Cindy Ward

Quantitative Analysis

Running Words 80 # Correct Words 73 # Errors 7 # Self-Corrections 1
Accuracy Rate 91% Error Ratio 11:1 Self-Correction Rate 7:1

Quantitative Analysis

Coding of Child's Reading	Words	Errors	Self Corrections	Cue used for Attempt Error/Self-Correction		
				M	S	G
✓ ✓ ✓ ✓ ✓ ✓ bowl On Monday...Cookie fell in the toilet.	7	1		✓	✓	
✓ ✓ ✓ pushed ✓ ✓ ✓ ✓ ✓ On Tuesday...Cookie knocked a plant off the windowsill.	9	1		✓	✓	
✓ ✓ sand ✓ There was dirt everywhere!	4	1		✓	✓	
✓ ✓ ✓ ✓ ✓ ✓ ✓ On Wednesday...Cookie upset the trash can.	7	0				
✓ ✓ trash ✓ There was garbage everywhere.	4	1		✓	✓	
✓ ✓ ✓ ✓ ✓ ✓ ✓ ✓ ✓ On Thursday...Cookie got stuck in a kitchen drawer.	9	0				
✓ ✓ ✓ ✓ ✓ ✓ ✓ all over SC There were pots and pans and dishes everywhere!	8	0	1	✓	✓	
✓ ✓ ✓ ✓ ✓ ✓ ✓ ✓ ✓ ✓ ✓ On Friday...Cookie ran into the closet before the door closed.	11	0				
✓ ✓ Cloths ✓ There were clothes everywhere.	4	1		✓	✓	✓
✓ ✓ ✓ ✓ ✓ drapes On Saturday...Cookie climbed the curtains.	6	1		✓	✓	
✓ ✓ ✓ ✓ And Cookie went everywhere!	4	0				
✓ ✓ ✓ — ✓ ✓ ✓ Tomorrow is Sunday...Maybe Cookie will rest!	7	1				
TOTALS	80	7	1			

Figure 7.20
Qualitative Analysis of Sasha's Oral Reading

- The teacher uses qualitative analysis to analyze the types of errors. Analyzing a child's errors or miscues will provide insight into the strategies that the child uses while reading (see Figure 7.20 for an example).
- An error is a semantic miscue (M) if it destroys the meaning of the text, as when a child reads *dog* for *dark.* Figure 7.21 presents the form used in taking running records and analyzing errors or miscues.
- An error is classified as a syntactic miscue (S) if the child ignores the syntax or word order of the language, as when the child reads *from* for *frog.*
- An error is classified as a graphophonologic or visual miscue (G) if the child does not use letter–sound relationship knowledge or how the word looks, as when the child reads *bake* for *long.*

Running Record Assessment Form

Name ____________________ Date ____________ Grade ________
Literacy Level ________________ Teacher ____________________
Text Title ____________________________ Level ____________

Quantitative Analysis

Running Words _____ # Correct Words _____ # Errors _____ # Self-Corrections _____
Accuracy Rate _________ Error Rate __________ Self-Correction Rate ____________

Qualitative Analysis

Page	*Coding of Child's Reading*	*# Words*	*# Errors*	*# Self-Corrections*	*Cue Used for Attempt Error/Self-Correction*		
					M	*S*	*G*

Figure 7.21
Form Used in Taking Running Records and Analyzing Errors or Miscues

Quantitative Analysis of Oral Reading

After coding a child's oral reading, the teacher analyzes the miscues or errors the child makes. The teacher may determine the accuracy rate of the child's reading and the error ratio. The **accuracy rate** reveals the percentage of words the child reads correctly. For example, if the child reads 100 words and makes 3 miscues, the accuracy rate would be 97%. That is, the child reads 97 words correctly out of 100 running words. The **error ratio** reveals the ratio of words read as errors to the words read correctly. The error ratio of 1:33 is interpreted as the following: The child reads 1 error in every 33 running words. Another ratio that may be calculated is the self-correction ratio. If the child has 8 miscues and self-corrected 1, the ratio of errors to self-corrections is 8:1, interpreted as follows: Out of 8 errors, the child self-corrects 1 error that he makes. Figure 7.19 shows a quantitative analysis of Sasha's oral reading.

Staying Informed With the Running Record Analysis

The running record is a rich source of information about the developing strategies of the young reader. The two categories of data, quantitative analysis and the qualitative analysis, provide us with information about how to help children further their reading development. One valuable use for quantitative data is for an accurate selection of books for children's reading. Sasha read a level F book with 91% accuracy, which shows a good match for her instructional level. At the instructional level, she can read the book with the assistance of her teacher. If Sasha's accuracy level was 95% or above, the book would be appropriate for her reading independently.

Qualitative Analysis of Oral Reading

To determine how children sample text or use word-solving strategies as they read, teachers analyze miscues or children's errors identifying patterns within their oral reading. **Patterns of errors** are determined by finding the predominant types of errors or miscues that children make while reading. For example, a child's errors may be all related to his not using graphophonological knowledge or cues. Therefore, the pattern is easy to determine, and the conclusion is made about the child's lack of strategy use related to phonic knowledge and sight word knowledge. If a child has one error related to the lack of graphophonological knowledge, there is no pattern of errors, and the teacher cannot draw a conclusion with respect to the type of knowledge the child is using for decoding words. Figure 7.22 shows a qualitative analysis of Sasha's oral reading.

Qualitative Analysis of Sasha's Oral Reading

Semantic cues	An analysis of Sasha's errors showed that she read errors while using the semantic cues. All of the seven errors were good semantic fits; that is, no error destroyed the meaning of the text. So we can say that Sasha reads for meaning.
Syntactic cues	All miscues that Sasha made during oral reading preserved the author's syntax. Therefore, this pattern shows that Sasha was using language cues to read unknown words.
Graphophonologic or visual cues	Only one of Sasha's errors revealed that she was using visual word analysis to determine unknown words in the text. When Sasha read *cloths* for *clothes,* it demonstrated her use of visual cues to determine unknown words. Sasha's other miscues did not show that she consistently used phonic knowledge or visual cues to decode new words. This is the strategy that the teacher will target to help Sasha read unknown words using all cues.

Figure 7.22

Guiding Children Through Writing

Writing workshop. The format used in guided writing is very similar to writing workshop. In writing workshop, teachers use direct instruction with small groups of children. Children within the small group are at the same literacy level and have the same instructional needs. Therefore, small groups for guided writing will not always be the same because children's instructional needs differ over time.

In the primary grades, within a balanced literacy program, teachers allot at least 45 minutes each session, 4 days per week to writing workshop. It is within this instructional context that most teachers include guided writing. There are a variety of instructional formats that teachers may use for direct instruction of writing skills and strategies, but they often find writing workshop most appropriate to teach small groups of children the conventions of language as well as the writing processes that are needed to become successful writers. During writing workshop, children are working on their own stories and are confronted by writing challenges that make apparent their specific instructional needs. The teacher uses this information to group children for writing instruction using the **mini-lesson.**

Teachers may conduct three or four mini-lessons during one session. Mini-lessons are short and focused and last no more than 5 minutes. The teacher carefully observes children who are experiencing the same skill needs, and groups them for a mini-lesson on a skill related to their writing that helps them to complete their stories. Similar to the guided reading lesson, the instruction is focused on some small aspect of writing tied to the context of their writing. A mini-lesson may focus on the development of an idea through descriptive details or on the conventions of print such as beginning each sentence with a capital letter and ending each sentence with the appropriate punctuation mark. The teacher is cautious not to overteach—that is, to include too many skills in one lesson. The following are key to an effective mini-lesson: (a) The teacher directs instruction at the level and the skill needs of the small group of children; (b) the teacher uses a mini-lesson to focus instruction on a small aspect of writing; and (c) the teacher monitors the children's writing for their immediate application of the skill that was taught, providing appropriate feedback to each child.

After the mini-lesson, the children continue to work on their stories, applying the skills they have just learned. The teacher monitors the children's writing and encourages them to check their writing for correct applications of the skill they have learned through 1-minute individual conferences. The teacher is cautious to guide the children through their writing. As they work on their writing, the teacher prompts children with *strategy language* that will help them apply the skills they have learned in the mini-lesson. In turn, the children are expected to appropriate such prompts while writing independently. Children eventually internalize strategy language, developing their own strategy for writing. For example, when a teacher sees that a child does not use punctuation marks at the end of the sentence he is writing, the teacher asks the child to look at the end of the sentence. "Do you remember what goes at the end of each sentence?" The teacher may continue, "Read the sentence. Do you know how to tell what mark goes at the end?" Eventually, while writing independently the child will look to the end of the sentence, asking the same question of himself.

There are times when children experience difficulty working through a piece of writing. A child may stop writing, not knowing how to continue. The teacher may respond with a set of prompts. The following are frequently used questions or prompts used by teachers to help children through difficult parts during their writing.

- Tell me about what you wrote. What do you think should come next?
- Can you say any more about that idea?
- You talked about ___________. Tell more about that character. How does he or she look? Act?
- When and where does this story takes place?
- Is there anyone else who should be part of this story?
- That is a wonderful story. Can you think of an ending?

Assessment of story writing. Guided writing needs to be a strong part of the balanced literacy program. The expression "Guided reading is the heart of a balanced literacy program" can be applied to guided writing as well. Whereas children need time to gain fluency in writing through independent writing activities, they grow as writers and develop strategies for effective written communication through direct instruction and guidance through the writing process.

Guiding children's growth in writing does not happen through instruction alone. It is linked to a well-thought-out assessment program. Effective teaching of writing views the assessment of writing as a blueprint for guiding writing development, a goal that simply grading children's writing does not achieve (Tchudi, 1997). When teachers assess children's writing, they look at the children's development to determine a teaching response. After the teacher analyzes a story, a series of questions related to the child's progress toward literacy benchmarks surface. Because writing assessment looks at a child's development over time on each standard, the teacher's questions relate to the most effective ways to move the child toward the standard.

Teachers may use the writing rubrics found in Figure 7.23 to assess the stories of children who are at the early stage of writing development. They include the writing benchmarks in two major categories, the message and the use of language conventions. The **message** refers to how the children composed the story. The **language conventions** refer to the way children use the conventions for using the Standard English language while writing. A description for each of the three levels of performance for each benchmark is also provided. To use the rubrics, the teacher will assess the child's story on each benchmark and make a decision with respect to the level at which the child performs—the beginning, the transition, or the developed level. For example, the teacher reads the story to determine if the sentences are related to the same topic. If all of the sentences within the story are related to the same topic, the child has acquired this writing skill at the developed level. After assessing the story for all of the skills and concepts within the message and language conventions, the teacher is ready to record the child's literacy performance within the portfolio. The teacher then uses a writing profile (see Figure 7.24), for monitoring children's writing development for narratives in documenting their progress for each of the benchmarks over a period. This profile may be part of the child's literacy portfolio.

Guiding Children Through Oral and Written Retellings

Using narrative text frames. At the early stage of literacy, children have a developing sense of story. That is, they know the parts of a simple narrative. When teachers encourage children to retell what they have read, they do more than monitor or assess their story concept. Research reports the power of retelling a story. The value of retellings lies in improvement of children's comprehension, the growth of

THE MESSAGE			
Sentence Sense	***Beginning***	***Transition***	***Developed***
• Sentences are related to a topic	Sentences are not related to a single topic	Sentences are related somewhat to a topic	Sentences are coherent, focused on a single topic
• Sentences convey meaning	Sentences do not convey meaning	Most sentences convey meaning	Meaning is clearly stated
• Story is organized with a logical sequence	Ideas are not connected; there is no logical sequence	Sentences have some sequence	Story shows a logical sequence of events or ideas
• Story contains some detail	Story has no or very little detail	Story contains detail	Ideas and events are developed through details
• Vocabulary shows development	Vocabulary growth is not apparent	Story shows some vocabulary growth	Rich story vocabulary is consistent throughout
• Illustrations convey meaningful content	No illustrations or the illustrations do not connect to the story	Illustrations show a sense of meaning	Illustrations convey meaning and are carefully placed
LANGUAGE CONVENTIONS			
Punctuation	***Beginning***	***Transition***	***Developed***
• Uses a period at the end of a sentence	May use a period in one or two sentences	Uses periods correctly in most sentences	Consistently uses periods correctly in sentences
• Uses a question mark at the end of a sentence	May use a question mark in one or two sentences	Uses question marks correctly in some sentences	Consistently uses question marks correctly in sentences
• Uses quotation marks in writing	Rarely uses quotation marks	Uses quotation marks appropriately sometimes	Consistently uses quotation marks correctly in sentences
• Uses commas	Rarely if ever uses commas	Is beginning to use commas	Uses commas frequently
• Uses apostrophes	Rarely if ever uses apostrophes	Is beginning to use apostrophes	Uses apostrophes frequently
Capital Letters	***Beginning***	***Transition***	***Developed***
• Uses capitals at the beginning of sentences	May use a capital letter to begin one or two sentences	Uses capitals at the beginning of sentences sometimes	Consistently uses capitals at the beginning of sentences
• Uses capitals for proper nouns	Rarely uses a capital letter for a proper noun	Uses capitals for proper nouns sometimes	Consistently uses capitals for proper nouns
• Uses capitals for titles of books	Rarely uses a capital letter for titles of books	Uses capitals for titles of books sometimes	Consistently uses capitals for titles of books

Figure 7.23
Rubrics for Assessing Stories for the Early Writer

Directions for assessing children's stories: Use the writing rubrics to determine the child's level of development for each writing benchmark found in the two major categories. Mark the date that the story was written and the level of development using the following code:

B: Beginning
T: Transition
D: Developed

Writing Profile for Children at the Early Stage of Writing Development
Narrative Stories

Name ______________________ Grade ________

THE MESSAGE

Sentence Sense	***Story #1 Date***	***Story #2 Date***	***Story #3 Date***	***Story #4 Date***	***Story #5 Date***
• Sentences are related to a topic					
• Sentences convey meaning					
• Story is organized with a logical sequence					
• Story contains some detail					
• Vocabulary shows development					
• Illustrations convey meaningful content					

LANGUAGE CONVENTIONS

Punctuation	***Story #1 Date***	***Story #2 Date***	***Story #3 Date***	***Story #4 Date***	***Story #5 Date***
• Uses a period at the end of a sentence					
• Uses a question mark at the end of a sentence					
• Uses quotation marks in writing					
• Uses commas					
• Uses apostrophes					
Capital Letters	***Story #1 Date***	***Story #2 Date***	***Story #3 Date***	***Story #4 Date***	***Story #5 Date***
• Uses capitals at the beginning of sentences					
• Uses capitals for proper nouns					
• Uses capitals for titles of books					

Figure 7.24

story sense, the encouragement of students' critical thinking, and the development of oral language (Brown & Cambourne, 1990; Hu, 1995).

When teachers ask children to retell a story, they are providing them with an opportunity to think more deeply about the story. Retellings demand children to think through the story and use a logical sequence in rearranging the events within the story. They also provide an opportunity for children to analyze the story characters for the roles and relationships that they play within the narrative. It is no wonder that when children are guided through a retelling, their concept for story further develops. When children hear or read a story and then retell it, they are more likely to use book language in their eagerness to reconstruct the story events. Thus, retelling of stories leads to children's appropriation of book language, thereby facilitating language growth.

Bensen and Cummins (2000) state that the true power of retellings appears when they are part of a balanced literacy program. They further define the three important assumptions of retellings as instruction:

1. **Retelling as meaning:** When children retell a story in their own words they go beyond simple recall of a story: "It (story retelling) is the child's construction of meaning" (p. 9).
2. **Retelling as language:** Language and thought are related. When children construct meaning through story retelling, they search for and find the appropriate language to label their thoughts and ideas. Oftentimes, they will use the language of the text. Good children's literature provides the best models of the English language. Thus, retellings facilitate in laying the foundation of oral language development.
3. **Retelling as developmental:** Bensen and Cummins (2000) provide a developmental model of retelling because of the assumption that retelling is a process that is developmental. Therefore, children's story retellings can and should be monitored. Teachers also need to use their knowledge of each child's development to provide them with an appropriate type of retelling experience that is aligned to each child's literacy level.

For the students at the early stage of literacy, guided retellings and story maps aid children in retelling a story and provide them with an experience to match their development. The learning outcome for early readers is to further develop their story sense—that is, to heighten their awareness of the literary elements so that they may use them to comprehend stories at a deeper level.

Teachers frequently use questions as a way to guide children in their construction of meaning. During guided retellings, teachers may use specific types of questions that encourage children to think about the story elements in deeper ways. Figure 7.25 lists a set of generic questions that may be used in guiding children through their story retellings. The questions are arranged around each of the elements of the story. In developing a concept for story, it is best to begin by focusing the retelling around one element at a time. This provides a framework for children to use later on in their spontaneous retellings.

Procedure for Guided Retelling

Select a story for guided retelling that has a well-developed plot or has one aspect of the story that is developed and explicit in nature. For example, a story may be

Generic Questions to Guide Story Retellings Using Literary Elements

The Setting
Place and Time

- Where did the story take place?
- Would the story change much if there were a different setting? What if it took place many years ago or in the future?
- When did the story take place? (Time)
- Did the pictures give you any clues about the setting? Did the author use special words to tell about the time and the setting?

Character Development

- Can you describe the characters in the story? Which character would you pick as the most important and why?
- Did the main character change in any way? If so, what story events made the character change?
- Did any of the other characters change during the story? If so, what made them change?
- Have you ever felt like the main character in this story?
- Do you know of any other story with the same kind of character?

The Plot
Story Problem, Story Goal, Story Events, Solution to the Problem

- What was the first thing that happened in the story?
- What was the problem in the story?
- What was the first thing that the main character did to solve the problem?
- Tell all of the things that happened in the story that helped to solve the problem.
- How did the main character feel about the solution to the problem?

Theme

- What kind of main lesson were you taught through reading and thinking about the story?

Figure 7.25

dependent on the setting for the story line, and another story may be an excellent selection for character analysis. Patricia Polacco's *Babushka's Doll* (1994) is an example of a story that would be a good choice for character analysis. *William's House* by Ginger Howard (2001) takes the reader back to 1637 when William and Elizabeth are leaving England for a new life in the New World. The plot in this story is dependent on the setting, and it would be an excellent selection for examining the setting through a form of guided retelling. In William Steig's *Doctor DeSoto* (1986), the sequence of story events is very important to plot development and to the solution of the story. This book is excellent for helping children make predictions during the story.

Using props to facilitate guided retellings. Guided retellings with props are excellent ways to facilitate children in their retelling of stories. The use of flannel board with cut-out pictures that represent the story elements, pasted on oak tag with felt backings, make excellent props for children to begin retelling stories. The props serve as prompts for the children as they talk about the various literary elements. The following is a simple set of directions for guided retelling with flannel board:

- Read a story to the children, or have the children read a story. Begin by a thorough introduction of the story. Ask the children what they think the story will be about from an examination of the title and the illustrations.
- After the children have heard or read the story, discuss the elements of the story. In the discussion, have children make connections to the story. **Personal connections** are made by talking about similar experiences they may have had. Help children make **text connections** by asking them about similar events, characters, and story problems that they may have read about in other stories. Finally, you may wish to facilitate children's **world connections** by talking about story events that were similar to those events that happened at home, school, in the community, or in the world.
- After the story discussion, invite a child to come up to the flannel board. Handing the child the props, identify each one as it relates to the story elements. Direct the child to use the props to retell the story. When children do not know how to begin because they lack the experience of retelling stories, model the retelling of a story with props before asking the children to engage in this activity. As the child is retelling the story, he may stop, forgetting a story part. You may wish to use the appropriate generic questions in Figure 7.25 to prompt the child's memory.

Assessing Children's Retellings of Narrative

Assessing children's retelling of stories is an excellent check for comprehension. Children who understand and interpret the story will have a greater recall for the elements of the story. A child with a well-developed schema for story will recall not only the story elements but also the details. For busy classroom teachers, to document a child's story retelling, a checklist may be used as the child is retelling the story. The teacher may use the checklist in Figure 7.26 to mark the story elements that the child was able to recall and to annotate other kinds of expressive behaviors occurring during the retelling. For example, in retelling the story, the child may begin to use "book language." Teachers may want to note new vocabulary that the child has acquired, the development of conceptual knowledge derived from reading or listening to the story, or any interesting characteristic the child uses in story retelling such as using expression while retelling. When a child makes an inference during the retelling—that is, provides an explanation that did not appear in the text—the child is thinking more deeply about the text. Such text interpretation deserves to be annotated.

Directions in using the retelling checklist. The following are a set of directions that the teacher may use in assessing a child's retelling of a story within an instructional context, while he retells the story to a small group of children.

- Have the small group of children sit around the flannel board during the retelling.
- Select one child to retell the story.

Child's Name ____________ Grade ____ Date ____________
Title of Story ____________ Author ____________

	Recall +	*Recalls With Prompt* ±	*Does Not Recall* –
Setting			
• *Main character(s)*			
• *Secondary character(s)*			
• *Time*			
• *Place*			
Story Problem			
• *States the problem*			
Story Events			
• *States important events*			
• *States details related to story events*			
• *States events in sequence*			
Story Ending			
• *States the story ending*			
Total Number	*Recall* ___/out of 9	*Recalls With Prompt* ___/out of 9	*Does Not Recall* ___/out of 9
Teacher Observations			

Figure 7.26
Assessment of Story Retellings

- On the flannel board, have cut-out figures that represent the characters and the place(s) that the child may use in retelling the story.
- As the child is retelling the story, complete the retelling checklist form found in Figure 7.26 including the child's name, date of retelling, and story that is being retold.
- Be consistent in marking the story elements that are retold. For each story element that a child retells, use the (+) symbol; for each story element that the child retells with a prompt, use the (±) symbol; for each story element that the child fails to retell, use the (−) symbol. Write in annotations that you have observed during the child's story retelling.

Independent Literacy

Independent literacy activities provide time for children to practice the reading, writing, and language strategies they have learned as part of modeled, shared, and guided instruction. To optimize the time that children spend reading and writing independently, it is important that teachers structure and vary the activities as well as monitor the children's progress.

Contexts for Independent Reading

Many opportunities are available to children throughout the day to engage in independent reading. Routman (2000) suggests that teachers need to make a commitment to independent reading and offers the following principles as guideposts to promote independent reading:

- A sustained period is set aside each day for independent reading.
- Everyone reads, including the teacher.
- Students choose their own reading materials.
- The reading environment is quiet, relaxed, and comfortable.
- Students keep a record of books and genres read.
- Written responses are rarely required.
- There is a time for sharing and recommending books.
- Students must have books with them at all times. (p. 45)

Teachers become committed to providing time for independent reading to children on a regular basis when they themselves have a passion for reading and they are aware of the effects that establishing such a routine has on children's literacy and overall achievement. Research strongly supports children's need for independent reading. The amount of independent or free reading that children do correlates with their reading achievement (Anderson, Fielding, & Wilson, 1988).

We have discussed and emphasized the importance for the need of planning instruction that is developmentally appropriate for children with respect to literacy. It is just as important to think about the development of **dispositions** toward literacy in young children. Katz (1995, 1999) highlights the development of dispositions in children as one of the four learning goals: knowledge, skills, dispositions, and feelings. "Dispositions can be thought of as habits of mind or tendencies to respond to certain situations in certain ways" (Katz, 1995, p. 6). It is possible for children to have acquired literacy skills and knowledge, but have no disposition to read or write.

Can dispositions for engaging in independent reading be taught? Formal instruction is not an effective approach to develop a disposition toward reading. Modeling dispositions for reading is one way that children may begin to develop a love for reading. Remember that attitudes are caught, not taught. Further, Kohn (1993) suggests that the way dispositions are strengthened is by using them effectively and by being appreciated rather than rewarded.

What does this mean for developing dispositions or habits of reading in young children? To develop effective dispositions toward reading and writing, teachers need to plan effective literacy strategies and demonstrate a real, not superficial, appreciation for reading and writing. This can be applied to each part of the literacy program as well as to strategies for independent reading.

Independent reading is an important part of a well-balanced literacy.

Indeed, children need independent reading, and a structured time for this literacy activity will ensure the opportunity. However, it is just as important to promote independent reading throughout the day. A classroom environment can enhance and foster independent reading. Areas in the classroom where there is easy access to reading material will encourage independent reading. For example,

- A classroom library that is overstocked with good children's literature
- Open-faced bookshelves for highlighting featured books
- Walls that are "dripping in print" to include wall stories, reading charts, children's stories, etc.
- Labels on objects around the classroom
- Book boxes that organize books at specific reading levels
- Poem boxes that include familiar poems and songs that were read during shared reading

Guidelines for Independent Reading

The following guidelines promote structured independent reading for early readers:

- **To develop reading routines for young children, be consistent with the time.** Place independent reading in the schedule daily, allotting the same amount of time to the children each day.
- **Ensure success at independent reading by helping children select material of interest at their independent reading levels.** Some teachers or-

My log for independent reading

Name ______________________ Grade __________

DATE AND MINUTES	TITLE OF BOOK	AUTHOR	MILLION $ WORD	PAGES READ

Figure 7.27
Independent Reading Log

ganize book boxes that are especially coded for children's reading levels. Children can select a book from their level.

- **Engage in book talks to stimulate children's interest in books.** A book talk is informal and lasts for a few minutes. The purpose of a book talk is to introduce books to children by giving them a preview—brief information about the characters, the problems, the story events, a glimpse at the illustrations, and maybe even a brief discussion of the authors if the children are familiar with their works.
- **Highlight books on open bookshelves.** Keep an open bookshelf by the classroom library. An open bookshelf provides a convenient way to show the cover of a book, and is used by teachers to attract children to some of the favorites.
- **Have children become accountable for their time spent during independent reading.** Using the log in Figure 7.27, let children write down the number of pages read in school during independent reading time. Encourage children to look for words that are especially interesting, recording them on their logs.
- **Have a sharing time.** At least once a week, encourage children to share the stories that they have read using informal book discussions. They, too, can engage in book talks and recommend books that they especially liked to a friend. Have the children sit in a circle with their books. Ask them to talk about the stories they have read. Encourage the children to make book recommendations, to ask questions for clarification. This might be an opportunity for children to read favorite parts or share interesting words and illustrations. There are no limits or boundaries.

At this age, children begin to account for what they do. Let children enter the routine of systematically monitoring their own independent reading. This may be

Directions: Observe the child during independent reading to determine growth in different reading concepts and dispositions for reading. Use the following code to assess a reading concept or reading disposition:

Shows a **High** Level of Growth and Development = **4**
Shows an **Above-Average** Level of Growth and Development = **3**
Shows an **Average** Level of Growth and Development = **2**
Shows a **Minimal** Level of Growth and Development = **1**
Shows **No** Level of Growth and Development = **0**

Name ______________________ Grade ________

	Date	Date	Date	Date	Date	Date
Selects books based on a developing interest						
Reads independently for an extended period—about 20 minutes						
Demonstrates an eagerness for independent reading						
Shows enjoyment through facial expressions while reading						
Shares books with others showing an enthusiasm for stories						
Talks about stories with ease						
Begins to develop an interest for certain genres						
Shows development in handling books and caring for them						

Figure 7.28
Annotated Checklist for Early Readers During Independent Reading

done through keeping a log of their free reading during the block of time for independent reading. Figure 7.27 shows a sample form for accounting for time spent during independent reading.

Assessing Independent Reading

The teacher may assess the student's independent reading through the reading log that the student keeps. Assessment of the reading log is done each week to determine the quantity of books that are being read, book selection, and any vocabulary words recorded. During independent reading, it is suggested that the teacher observe children's behaviors using kidwatching techniques, documenting observations on sticky notes and later recording them on the annotated checklist found in Figure 7.28.

Because there may be a large group of children reading at the same time, select one or two children per day to observe. Some children may have problems sitting for 15 or 20 minutes of independent reading and may be at a lower level of engagement. These children's behaviors need to be documented more than those children who can read for longer periods.

Buddy reading. Another context for independent reading is buddy reading where children may be paired or partnered to read together. One child is the reader, while the other listens to the story. After the reader completes the story, the listener becomes the reader and reads his book. Book selection is important. When children select their own books, the books should be at their independent reading level. At the independent level, the child can read at least 95% of the running words with accuracy. Remember, the purpose for buddy reading is to provide a pleasurable context for children to practice reading and to develop positive dispositions toward reading. Children may select their own books to read or they may read the same books, taking turns on each page.

Teachers may pair two children for additional instructional reasons. A stronger reader may be partnered with a child who is just beginning to read independently. For example, a child at the emergent level may be paired for buddy reading with a child at the early level of reading. In this context, the early reader supports the emergent reader by modeling the process of independent reading.

Buddy reading provides authentic contexts for children to practice their reading strategies.

Contexts for Independent Writing

It is clear that young children learn about print through writing. Through independent writing contexts, teachers provide children a time to construct meaning around literacy concepts. It is the time when children are able to think about what they have learned through modeled and guided writing and apply it to their writing. Many educators emphasize the benefits of independent writing time that incorporates meaningful experiences, noting that children who are engaged in authentic writing experiences learn phonics, spelling, the mechanics of writing, and the functions of print (Edelsky, Altwerger, & Flores, 1991).

Message boards. In most, if not all, school districts that use language arts standards as the guideposts for developing literacy, children are expected to use language for multiple purposes. Reading and writing for social interaction is one purpose or function of language that traditionally has not been part of the formal language arts curriculum. Children are expected to be able to write to interact with others. Message boards provide children with the opportunity to write to other children in the classroom for social interaction. Indeed, it is an authentic context for writing!

When one author was teaching the first grade, she had read about Carolyn Burke's success with message boarding, and she decided to give it a try with her first graders. She found it was successful not only as a learning tool but also as a motivator. Through their participation, the children learned more than multiple functions of language; that is, writing for another purpose, social interaction. Aside from the many literacy concepts and skills they acquired, they learned how to read and spell the names of each child in the classroom as well as the author's, they began to understand the importance of using standard spelling as well as correct mechanics of language, and they discovered that if they wanted to receive messages, they had to write them. Here are the author's suggestions for using a message board in the classroom.

- **Preparing for message board writing:** To get started, use a bulletin board within the reach of the children. Each month decorate the bulletin with a seasonal theme. For example, during the month of February, the bulletin may look like the one in Figure 7.29. Arrange oak tag pockets with children's names written clearly on the front so that the messages could be slipped in by the writers.
- **Getting started:** Introduce the message board to the children explaining what it is used for. Let the children examine the message board to find their names and to identify the names of the children in their classroom. Tell the children that in writing a message to another person there are rules to follow. First discuss the rules with the children, eliciting from them the need to respect others in their writing. Then, take chart paper and write out the rules. Have the children read the message board rules, and ask if there are any other rules that may be needed. The message board may be used whenever a child has free time to write. Now watch the children use the message board!

Message Board Rules

- Whenever you get a message, write one back.
- Sign your name at the end of the message.
- Do not use bad language.

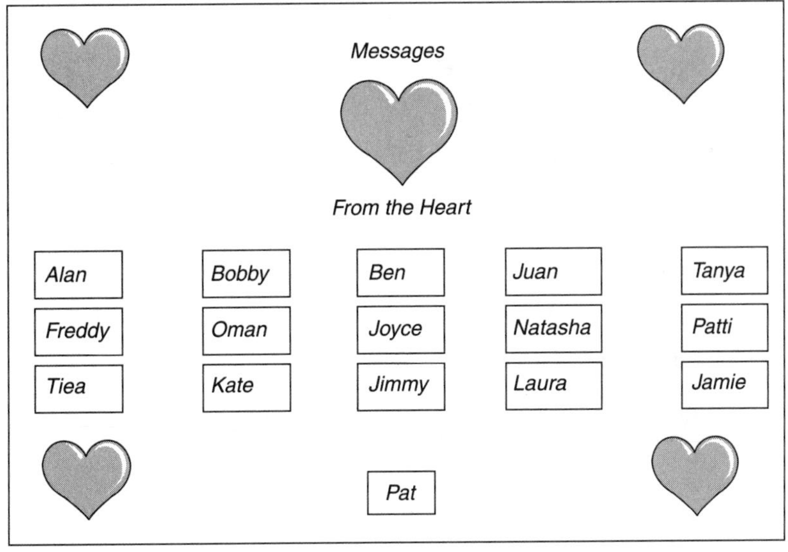

Figure 7.29
Sample Message Board

When children write for authentic purposes, their fluency in writing increases.

When I first used the message board in my first-grade classroom, I was hoping that because it was an authentic writing context, children would enjoy it. Indeed they did! When I introduced the message board and how to use it, I placed a message in each of the children's pockets. They were so eager to read their messages that they all dashed to the board at one time. (After this experience, I found that after lunch recess, we would have quiet time for reading our messages.) Because my name was on the message board, they felt they needed to write a message back immediately.

I observed the children's enjoyment of personal interaction in the form of writing. Each morning when they came into the classroom, they immediately opened their backpacks and took out a pile of messages that they had written at home and began to deliver their mail.

The power of the message board was apparent in one student who came to the class later in the year and could not read or write. She was homeless for 6 months in her kindergarten year and was in and out of foster care in three different states. She began to write her own name and could read it after a week in school. Tiea was able to take care of herself on the playground, and she loved to play games that required physical strength. This meant that there was a group of boys who respected her for her physical prowess. One day, after lunch, the children went to the message board to retrieve their messages to read. Tiea received a message from Jimmy and could not read it. She took the letter and rushed to my desk, opened it, and demanded for me to read it to her. I responded, "Tiea, let's read it together."

Dear Tiea,

Your are the best girl in the class to play with. The boys would really like you if you did not call us names. You are cool because you like to play football.

Love,
Jimmy

After reading the message together, Tiea took it from my hand and clutched it close to herself. She sat down alone and tried to read it. A short time later, Tiea was standing next to me, putting a paper and a pencil in my hand. Looking up, Tiea demanded, "Let's write to Jimmy." At that moment, I knew that Tiea understood the concept of writing for social interaction. While the children were busy reading their messages, Tiea was writing her first message.

Assessment of writing independently—message board writing. In assessing literacy, teachers think about the purpose for the literacy activity and the related student outcome. Within the context of independent literacy, the goal for children is to promote fluency. Message board writing allows children to develop fluency and control over their writing. Although it is important to monitor children's growth in writing such as story development, the mechanics of writing, and spelling, the student performance that should be monitored here is the children's level of engagement in writing messages. This may simply be in the form of a checklist or an observation of the frequency in which children engage in writing messages.

Discussion Questions and Activities

1. Below is a sample of a story that a first-grade child has written. It has not been corrected for spelling errors. Analyze the child's spelling to determine the level of spelling development. Make suggestions to further the child's spelling at his stage of spelling development.

pal is mi
Frnd and
tls strs to
mereds bks wh
me
Juan

2. Observe a primary-grade classroom during literacy instruction. Describe the instructional strategy and the assessment strategy that was used by the teacher to monitor literacy development. If no assessment strategy was used, suggest one that you would use to align instruction and assessment.
3. Observe a child during independent reading. Describe the child's behaviors while he is reading. What behavior indicates engagement in reading and interest in reading? Describe the child's book behaviors while reading.

Additional Web Sites

Ready to Read
http://www.ed.gov/pubs/startearly/ch_2.html

A chapter from *Start Early, Finish Strong* underscores the importance of a strong literacy program in the early years.

Additional Readings

Bolton, F., & Snowball, D. (1993). *Ideas for spelling.* Portsmouth, NH: Heinemann.

Clay, M. (2000). *Running records for classroom teachers.* Portsmouth, NH: Heinemann.

Edwards, S. A., Maloy, R. W., & Verock-O'Loughlin, R. E. (2003). *Ways of writing with young kids: Teaching creativity and conventions unconventionally.* Boston: Allyn & Bacon.

Feldgus, E. G., & Cardonick, I. (1999). *Kid writing: A systematic approach to phonics, journals, and writing workshop.* Bothell, WA: The Wright Group.

Hadaway, N. L., Vardell, S. M., & Young, T. A. (2002). *Literature-based instruction with English language learners, K–12.* Boston: Allyn & Bacon.

Iversen, S. (1997). *A blueprint for success: Building a foundation for beginning readers and writers.* Bothell, WA: The Wright Group.

McCarrier, A., Pinnell, G. S., & Fountas, I. C. (2000). *Interactive writing: How language and literacy come together, K–2.* Portsmouth, NH: Heinemann.

Shea, M. (2000). *Taking running records.* New York: Scholastic.

Additional Children's Literature

Brown, M. (1992). *Arthur meets the president.* Waltham, MA: Little Brown.

Clymer, E. (1947). *The trolley car family.* New York: Scholastic.

Hayward, L. (1987). *Noah's ark.* Westminister, MD: Random House.

Lundell, M. (1995). *A girl named Helen Keller.* New York: Scholastic.

Polacco, P. (1992). *Mrs. Katz and Tush.* New York: Bantam Doubleday.

Rylant, C. (1992). *Appalachia? The voices of sleeping birds.* Orlando, FL: Harcourt.

Steig, W. (1992). *Doctor De Soto goes to Africa.* Scranton, PA: HarperCollins.

Children's Literature References

Adler, D. (1994). *A picture book of Sojourner Truth.* New York: Holiday House.

Adler, D. (1994). *A picture book of Thurgood Marshall.* New York: Holiday House.

Cherry, L. (1990). *The great kapok tree.* New York: Scholastic.

Howard, G. (2001). *William's house.* Millbrook.

Moss, M. (2001). *Brave Harriet.* Orlando, FL: Harcourt Brace.

Polacco, P. (1994). *Babushka's doll.* New York: Simon & Schuster.

Steig, W. (1986). *Doctor Desoto.* New York: Scholastic.

Ward, C. (1997). *Cookie's week.* New York: Scholastic.

CHAPTER 8

Literacy Instruction and Assessment for Fluent Readers and Writers

Portrait of a Fluent Reader and Writer

Robert is a fluent reader who is in the third grade. When he was asked to take out his mathematics book from his desk, he had a difficult time finding it. His desk was filled with at least five different library books. Robert was reading two Harry Potter books at the same time. As he was finishing one, he had started a second, making sure it was the one he really wanted to read. Robert also belongs to the class Dinosaur Book Club, and its members were reading Pinocchio *by C. Collodi and Ed Young (1996). There were two more books squeezed into his desk; one was* The Magic Cooking Pot, *a folk tale from India that was retold and illustrated by Faith Towle (1975). Robert was part of a team that was engaged in a writing project. The team was rewriting the folk tale to be performed as a class play. The fifth book in Robert's desk was a nonfiction book. Robert recently developed an interest in birds from his parents who both are birdwatchers. He used the field guide to northeastern birds published by the National Audubon Society to read about birds that he had spotted with his parents. He kept a log on the kinds and numbers of birds he saw, and when and where he sighted them. He loved to share his expert knowledge with his friends.*

Robert's literacy behaviors are benchmarks for children at the fluent stage of reading and writing. He demonstrates a developing interest in reading from the wide range of books he is reading. Robert chooses chapter books that are both fiction and nonfiction, and his developing pursuit in reading is not without discrimination: He knows different authors, and prefers some works to others. He is also aware of the kinds of books that he can read on his own with understanding, those that are at his independent reading level. Reading instruction occurs through membership in a book club, where discussion is a featured element. Robert actively participates in book talks and oftentimes initiates discussion through self-generated questions.

Robert's writing development is paralleling his reading development. He engages in writing longer texts and chooses different genres when given a choice. He enjoys working with others on literacy projects that last over long periods. He engages in revising his stories, and his sense of audience is showing development. As with independent reading, Robert also engages in independent writing. He enjoys writing in his reading journal, he sends e-mail on a regular basis, and occasionally he tries his pen at poetry. This chapter will explore ways to further literacy development in children like Robert who is at the fluent stage of literacy development.

The goal that early childhood teachers set for young children is to help them become fluent readers and writers. As we have discussed in previous chapters, children's journeys on the path to becoming literate varies, each taking different routes to the same goal. As children leave the early stage of literacy development, they move into the beginnings of fluency, sometimes called a *transitional stage,* then on to the *fluent stage.* This chapter describes specific instructional and assessment strategies that teachers may use with children in helping them to reach the benchmarks for the fluent stage of literacy development. Teachers of the fluent reader and writer plan their instruction around the children's literacy development. They build instruction on what readers and writers already know and the concepts and skills that they expect them to learn. Therefore, we begin this chapter with a review of the benchmarks for fluent readers. As you may recall, the benchmarks will determine what teachers' expectations are for children who are entering a specific stage of literacy development. The benchmarks will also direct teachers to look closely at what children already know and what they need to learn or the **student outcomes** for the instructional sequence. Knowing the student outcomes is important because the outcomes determine what the teacher will assess.

As you read this chapter, reflect on the following topics:

- How the literacy benchmarks that identify fluent readers and writers are used to design instruction
- What vocabulary development means and its significance in understanding text
- The relationship between readers making connections—personal, text, and world connections—to their becoming literate thinkers
- Using literature circles as a different context for teaching reading and writing to children at the fluent stage of literacy development

Establishing Developmental Benchmarks for Fluent Readers and Writers

Although we continue to promote a balanced literacy program for fluent readers and writers, within this chapter we organize strategies for literacy learning around some of the larger areas for extending literacy development and learning for fluent reading and writing. Within each of those larger areas, instruction and assessment are balanced to include modeled, shared, guided, and independent instructional contexts. The following areas of learning for fluent readers and writers are addressed in this chapter: (1) vocabulary development; (2) responsive understanding of narrative; (3) literacy across the curriculum: reading and writing nonfiction; and (4) strategies for effective learning. Within each of the major areas of learning, balance is achieved through the approaches that are used within instruction. For example, in the area of vocabulary development, strategies are offered for teaching through modeling and demonstrations, direct and guided instruction, shared approaches as well as providing ways to develop independence in learning. Table 8.1 shows the developmental benchmarks for fluent readers and writers.

Developing Literacy in Fluent Readers and Writers

Fluent reading means faster and smoother reading, and reading with expression when reading aloud. As young children move into the fluent stage of literacy, their independent reading becomes silent. Many of the literacy accomplishments of the child at the fluent stage are benchmarks that correlate with such fluent and effortless reading. Children entering this stage are reading more and developing their unique interests in literature genres as well as in topics in reading.

Vocabulary Instruction and Assessment

Vocabulary development is key to literacy development in young children. To understand why vocabulary instruction is the cornerstone of a literacy program, you will read about definitions of vocabulary, what scientific research says about children's learning of new words, instructional strategies that foster vocabulary development in children, and approaches to monitor its growth.

What is vocabulary development? A radio commercial promoting vocabulary-improvement tapes began this way: "You are judged by the words that you speak!" That opening sentence seemed very powerful. The commercial promised that if you listened to the tapes, your vocabulary would change dramatically and that you would be using words that would make you more successful. The assumption is that people judge you by your language, by your vocabulary, and that if you use a more advanced vocabulary, you will be considered intelligent and successful. Although the assumption may be partially true, the underlying premises related to language development that are implied in this commercial are rather simplistic.

The term *vocabulary* refers to the words that you may know and use. However, consider the aspects of word knowledge. Chall (1987) has categorized the two aspects of vocabulary development as **word recognition** and **word meaning.** Word recognition refers to the ability to identify or recognize the words to which you listen or

Table 8.1
Developmental Benchmarks for the Fluent Literacy Stage

Book Sense	Story Sense	Literacy Behaviors
• Requests a wider variety of authors, genres, and chapter books • Uses different parts of the book (e.g., table of contents and index) to help find information • Makes own books that are longer and contain more complex parts of the book • Integrates authors' and illustrators' styles into own books	• Chooses to engage in independent reading for extended periods • Reads and selects a variety of genres • Writes a wide variety of genres • Maps the sequence of story events and shows the relationship of story elements • Discusses the different parts of the story • Begins to make connections between books from the same genres by 1. Comparing and contrasting story elements 2. Comparing stories for style 3. Comparing informational books for content 4. Critiquing stories for personal response 5. Understanding stories that may not relate to personal experiences 6. Connecting stories with personal experiences 7. Connecting different texts 8. Connecting story events with world events 9. Comparing stories for content and style • Demonstrates within narrative and expository writing different connections: personal, text, and world	• Demonstrates an increased desire to read and write independently • Writes longer texts over a period • Uses revising strategies • Selects appropriate books for reading independently • Continues to increase rate of reading • Adjusts reading rates for different purposes and difficulty levels of the text • Reads orally with expression • Uses the three cues—semantic, syntactic, and visual—with ease for decoding unfamiliar words • Continues to increase reading and writing vocabulary • Challenges the story content • Questions the authors' assumptions • Knows when able to understand and unable to understand text • Possesses and uses a variety of strategies when confronted by text not understood • Conducts book discussions independently WORD-SOLVING STRATEGIES • Uses varied strategies (usually unobservable) to read and write unknown words • Reads and writes a large bank of sight words automatically • Writes many words using standard spelling • Uses base words, inflections, plurals, and affixes in reading and writing • Manipulates base words to make new words • Uses base words to derive meaning from unknown words

read. The second aspect of vocabulary refers to one's knowledge of the meanings of words. Vocabulary at this level is far more complex because meaning is multilayered. When you first learn a word, you may know the word at its simplest meaning, or you may know a single reference for the word. With a limited knowledge of the word's meaning, you will find that word difficult to use, especially in your writing and speaking. As you use the word in listening, reading, writing, and speaking, and as you hear the word applied to a variety of contexts, the meaning you have of the word grows, develops, and expands. Now you can use the word in many different ways and you understand when you hear the word or when you read it in text. In this sense, we can think of vocabulary as **labels for conceptual knowledge.**

Go back to the claims of the commercial. You know that one's acquisition of multiple meanings surrounding words does not develop overnight. One's ability to use the word in speech or in writing in varied contexts takes even longer. Such knowledge does not happen simply by listening to words on a tape. The type of vocabulary acquisition gained through listening to words on tapes is at the first level, word recognition—recognizing the word and knowing one or two meanings. Unless we use the word over and in many different contexts, the word will not belong to us, and we do not gain ownership of the word. At the very least, we may gain an understanding of the word and our use of the word may be restricted to a single context. Therefore, vocabulary is the ability to recognize a word and use the word in multiple contexts. Children who develop vocabulary will also develop conceptual knowledge related to the word.

Types of vocabulary. Research shows that there are four types of vocabulary (Armbruster, Lehr, & Osborn, 2001):

- **Listening Vocabulary:** When we hear a word and we recognize it and understand what it means, it is in our listening vocabulary.
- **Speaking Vocabulary:** When we use a word in a meaningful way, the word is in our speaking vocabulary.
- **Reading Vocabulary:** When we come to a word in print, recognize and understand the meaning, the word is in our reading vocabulary.
- **Writing Vocabulary:** The number of words that we use in our writing designates our writing vocabulary that is usually smaller than our reading vocabulary.

During the first years of young children's lives, their listening vocabularies increase followed by their speaking vocabularies. Researchers (Loban, 1976; Maxim, 1989; McCormick, Loeb, & Schiefelbusch, 1997; Papalia & Olds, 1998) have found that children who are 6 years and older have a speaking vocabulary of approximately 3,000 words. Further, children understand twice as many words and respond to even more. Therefore, children's **listening vocabularies** are larger than their **speaking vocabularies.** When children are in the emergent and the early stages of literacy, they are reading books that contain words that are in their listening vocabularies. The teacher focuses instruction for the emergent and early readers on facilitating recognition of words in print (Chall, 1987). However, when children advance to the fluent stage of literacy, they begin to read more complex stories that contain more difficult words that may not be in their listening vocabularies. The fluent readers may be able to decode the more difficult words, but the word meanings often present a challenge.

The importance of vocabulary instruction. Meaning is central to language use and language learning. There are many teachers in Grades 2, 3, and 4 who are challenged by children who may appear to be fluent readers. That is, when these children are asked to read aloud they sound like any fluent reader, having no errors in decoding, reading with expression, maintaining smooth phrasing, and reading at a rate that is consistent with fluent readers at their grade level. Yet, these same readers do not comprehend what they read. They cannot recall parts of a story, retell a story, or summarize a major story part. Studies reveal that there is a positive relationship between the readers' understanding of words and their comprehending of complete text (Anderson & Freebody, 1981; Graves, 1994; Johnston, 1981). To comprehend text, the reader must know the meanings of the words that are being read. It makes sense for teachers of readers at all literacy stages, especially at the fluent stage, to systematically provide for balanced vocabulary instruction.

How children learn new word meanings. Good readers learn the meanings of many new words. To cope with the increased reading throughout the child's academic life as well as the literacy needs for a successful life in a competitive society, understanding of text is a requirement. Therefore, placing an emphasis on vocabulary development should be a goal for all teachers. However, when researchers have estimated the size of children's vocabularies, their findings reveal that they are too low (Nagy & Anderson, 1984). To reach a competent level of understanding all text types by senior high school, the average number of words that they need to learn is 40,000. This means that the child needs to learn at least 3,000 new words per year (Beck & McKeown, 1991).

What is the most effective way to facilitate word growth in the primary grades? To answer this question we must turn to the children and determine how they acquire meanings of new words. Studies show that children learn most words indirectly through everyday experiences with oral and written language. It is clear that some new words must be taught explicitly (Armbruster et al., 2001). We follow the view based on research that children need *multiple approaches to the acquisition of word meanings:*

- Listening to stories that are read aloud offers a rich source for learning new words (Elley, 1989; Sternberg, 1987).
- Children who read extensively will develop rich vocabularies (Nagy & Herman, 1987; Sternberg, 1987).
- Children may learn from listening to and reading words in context, but for some words, they will need explicit instruction for using such strategies as the use of contextual clues to determine the meaning (Armbruster et al., 2001).

Foundations for Developing Vocabularies

Prior knowledge and text comprehension. Text comprehension is an interactive process. As children engage in reading text, they use what they know that is related to the meaning of the story so they can understand what they are reading. This is a constructivist approach to meaning or comprehending text. Those who consider reading from this point of view place importance on prior knowledge (Spivey, 1997). Some of the information that they read is *new,* and the information they have already acquired or bring to the text is considered *old* knowledge or information. Old information is often referred to as *prior knowledge.* In comprehending text, readers use what they know (old information) to understand the novel ideas found in the text (new information). As children read, they make connections between the old and the new information—that is, they bridge what they already know with what they are learning. This explanation of the reading process is based on schema theory (Pearson & Johnson, 1978) and emphasizes the importance of readers bringing text-based information to their readings for a greater understanding of text. Without such information, or prior knowledge, the reader will not be able to comprehend the text, she will not be able to recall what she has read, and she will not be able to engage in story retellings.

Schema theory and vocabulary development. Schema theory suggests that we store knowledge in *schema* or schemas. Our schema is never fully developed. As readers interact with print and media, and as they engage in discussions, they learn new information. The readers' new information is connected to the old, and as a result, their schemas are changed or *restructured* to include the new information. Schema theory emphasizes the importance of preparing children to read by (1) activating prior knowledge that is related to their reading before they read, (2) building children's knowledge for comprehending text when it is lacking, and (3) helping children make connections between the old information and the new information. As teachers help children to develop conceptual knowledge, they also teach the words that label the concepts or the vocabulary words.

Activating prior knowledge. Strategic readers use what they know to make sense of new ideas they read in the text. They are activating prior knowledge so that they can use it for interpreting text. Prior to reading, effective teachers help children to activate prior knowledge. Many immature readers have knowledge that is related to the text they will be reading, but they may not know they must use it to understand new concepts or information about which they are reading. Through the use of questioning strategies with children prior to reading, the teacher activates children's prior knowledge necessary for comprehending text. When teachers remind children to think about the ideas as they read, they are training children to activate and to use prior knowledge for understanding stories. This is a strategy that is used by strategic readers.

Developing prior knowledge. Other children may not know the concepts and ideas related to the story they will be reading, or they may have *misconceptions* of the concepts—inaccurate or undeveloped concepts. For children who do not have prior knowledge related to text they are about to read and for those with misconceptions, it is critical that the teacher builds the prior knowledge needed for the child's comprehension of text. For example, the children may be getting ready to read a book about bears going into hibernation. The effective teacher will determine what the children already know about bears and the concept of hibernation. The teacher is aware that some children in the classroom may be from diverse cultures where the concept of hibernation is not relevant and bears do not exist. When children do not have the prerequisite information related to their reading, the teacher decides to build it through a systematic discussion, pictures, and stories, using the vocabulary they will read about. Without prior knowledge, children cannot make sense of what they are reading. Further, when children have misconceptions about the ideas they are reading, their lack of understanding may lead to the development of inaccurate concepts (Chinn & Brewer, 1993).

Making connections. Finally, many of the ideas and concepts within children's readings appear as isolated facts or fragments of information. In order to make this knowledge useful to children, effective teachers help readers make connections. Making connections means that the teacher will help children to understand how two sets of facts are related. Teachers help their students make connections between what they read and their prior knowledge and personal experiences. For example, some children are working on a unit of study in science about weather. After they have read a nonfiction book about hurricanes, the teacher guides the discussion on characteristics of hurricanes. She then helps them see the connections between a hurricane and a thunderstorm, a type of weather system that they just finished studying. She helps them to relate hurricanes and thunderstorms to the weather they know and have experienced. She also compares and contrasts the features of the two systems, an excellent approach to help children *build connections between facts and integrate knowledge.* Connecting ideas is especially important to develop concepts or to restructure schemas—that is, to add to the knowledge that children have. When children possess well-developed concepts, they learn the vocabulary that is attached to their knowledge, the goal vocabulary development.

Making Connections

The children in one literature circle were discussing Somewhere Today *by Bert Kitchen (1992). Their teacher, Jim, was listening in. The children were talking about a fish, the archer from Australia, that was looking for insects just below the surface of the water in the "overhanging vegetation." Suddenly, Jolie asked, "What's that?" Jim waited for a response from the small group. After a minute of silence, Jim jumped in, "Do you like vegetables?" "Oh!" exclaimed Jolie. That one question helped to make a connection. They continued to talk about the word* vegetation *and what it means in several different contexts and what it means within the context of the story. Jim helped the group make a connection between what they already knew and what they learned. Developing vocabulary is learning about new ideas and connecting them to old ones!*

Instructional Strategies for Representing and Building Knowledge to Develop Vocabulary

Mind maps for vocabulary development. Mind maps or semantic maps are visual representations of knowledge. Mapping has been defined as "a categorical structuring of information in graphic form" (Heimlich & Pittelman, 1986, p. 1), because they provide ways to illustrate the connections among meanings within text. Perhaps because of the visual aspect of semantic maps, they have become one of the most widely used strategies with numerous applications to different areas of learning, particularly to that of reading comprehension, prewriting techniques, and vocabulary development. Over the years, semantic maps have been known by many names; among them are mind maps, semantic webbing, semantic networks, and idea maps, all having the same purpose—the visual representation of knowledge.

Preparing to use mind maps. **Mind mapping** is used to develop vocabulary in young children, to facilitate their comprehension of text, and to prepare them for writing. To help them understand what they are reading, it is important that children are able to recognize the words they read as well as possess prerequisite conceptual knowledge related to the vocabulary in the text. The objective of the strategy is to activate children's knowledge related to their reading, to build the required knowledge that prepares them for reading, and to facilitate children's learning new ideas from their reading by helping them make connections. What must the

Children learn new vocabulary when teachers help them make connections between the new words and their own experiences.

teacher do to prepare for using this strategy so that the objectives are reached? Buehl (2001) suggests the initial step-by-step preparation for the teacher that includes the following:

- Analyze the passage or book to be read.
- Think about the children who will read this passage and what they already know about the topic.
- Determine the main ideas of the passages, and select only the key words and ideas that support and extend understanding of the passage.
- Organize key ideas and words into a mind map that depicts the vocabulary, the ideas, and the relationships. Wherever it is possible, create a pictorial that will further illustrate the ideas.

The map is a source of knowledge; therefore, it will include the ideas that the children will bring to their reading, the ideas that are needed for understanding their reading, and new information that they have learned from reading the passage. Let us take a look at a fourth-grade teacher who used mind maps with his class.

Follow the strategy below that Doug used to activate and develop knowledge *before* reading, to facilitate children's comprehension *during* reading, and to work with children to help them make connections *after* reading.

BEFORE READING

1. Before reading the article, Doug began with a discussion on snowy owls by asking, "What do you know about snowy owls?"
2. Doug pointed to the large mind map and continued to discuss with the children their connections to snowy owls, what they knew about the snowy owl.

Portrait of Vocabulary Instruction for Fluent Readers and Writers

The children finished several different Harry Potter books. All the children were familiar with Harry Potter's lovable messenger and pet, the snowy owl. Doug connected a current news story about the alarm among animal advocates who feared a surge of interest in keeping owls as pets to science and social studies. Researching this event, Doug was led to a story in *National Geographic News,* http://news.nationalgeographic.com/news/2001/11/1116_harrypotterowl.html. He decided that this would be part of the children's reading. The following shows what Doug did *before, during,* and *after* the children's reading.

Doug had prepared a mind map of snowy owls (see Figure 8.1). He developed the mind map by reading the passage "Harry Potter Owl Scenes Alarm Animal Advocates" by John Roach for *National Geographic News,* November 16, 2001. While he read, he selected the main ideas and words that children needed to know to read the article with understanding. Doug drew a mind map of snowy owls on very large paper that covered one chalkboard. He made individual copies for each child.

3. As the children contributed their ideas on the snowy owl, Doug added them to the mind map.
4. He then asked the children about having the snowy owl as a pet. "Would it be easy to take care of? What kind of care would it need? Would it be fair to the pet to keep it in captivity?"
5. The children had a discussion of the snowy owl, what type of bird it is, its habitat, the need for preserving the snowy owl's habitat, and the relation of the snowy owl with the life cycle of its food, lemmings. Each time that Doug used a new vocabulary word in guided discussion, he explained it and then showed the word in print, demonstrating how to decode the new word.
6. The children were now ready to read about the article. Doug passed out the mind maps as well as the passage to be read.

Explain how Doug activated children's prior knowledge about snowy owls before they read the article. What else did Doug do to develop the children's vocabulary?

DURING READING

1. Doug previewed the article with the children, telling them that they were going to read about what they had discussed and how the information was organized around different topics.

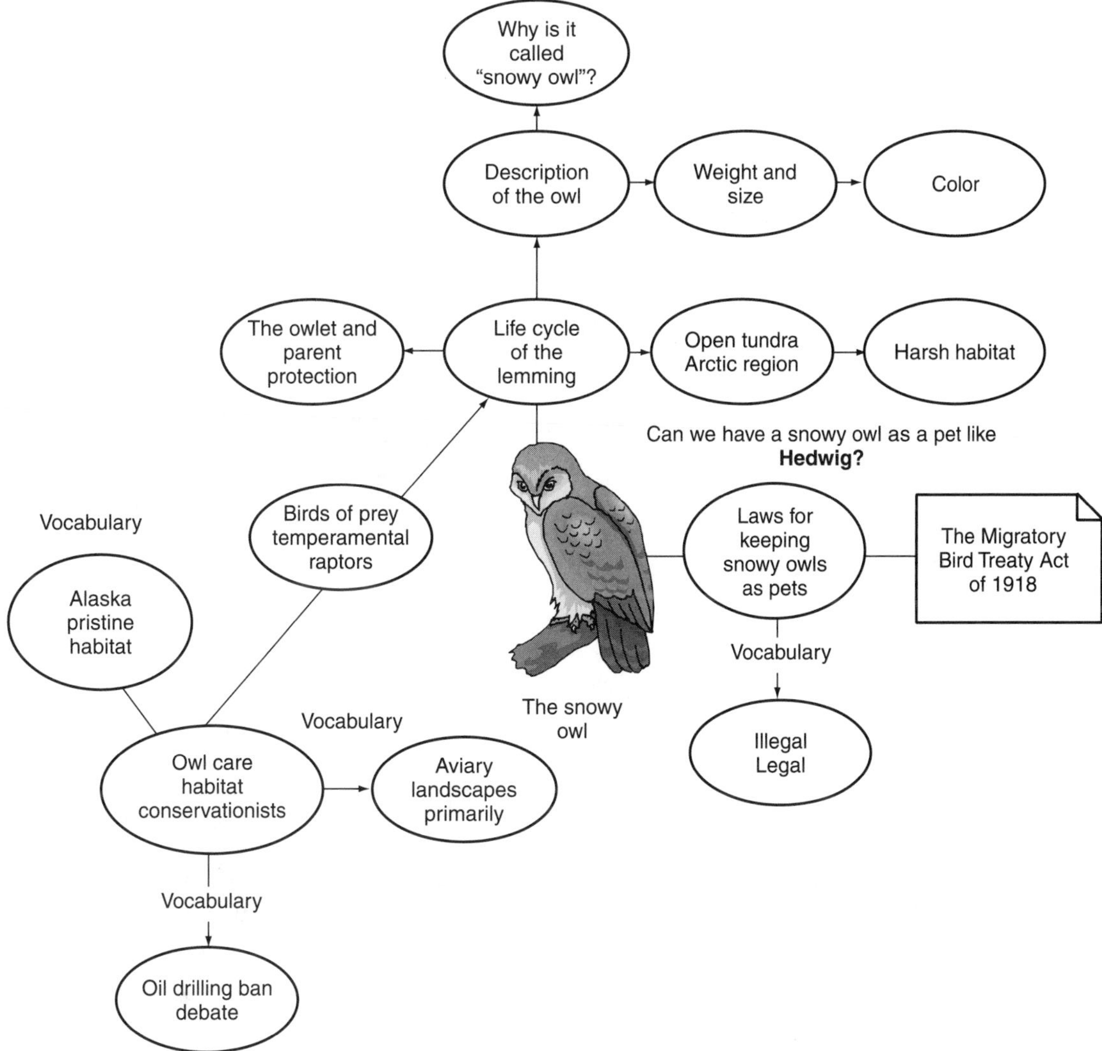

Figure 8.1
Mind Map for Reading About the Snowy Owl

2. Doug asked the children what they would expect to read under these subtopics:
   - Legal to Keep Owls in the U.K.
   - Owl Care
   - Conservation Symbol
   - Hedwig May Raise Awareness of Refuge
   - Snowy Owl: Vital Statistics
3. Doug directed the children to read the entire article and write down on their mind maps interesting facts they had learned.

In the second instructional sequence, Doug helped the children set a purpose for reading by setting specific expectations for what they were to read. How was he developing vocabulary as part of this instructional sequence?

After Reading

1. Doug directed the children's discussion around the article following the topics.
2. The children compared what they added to their maps and discussed why they thought their ideas were important.
3. Doug told the children to use their maps to write a paragraph on one of the following topics:
   a. The Snowy Owl: Where It Lives and How It Survives
   b. Is It Possible to Keep a Snowy Owl in Captivity?
   c. Conserving the Habitat of the Snowy Owl

Doug's instructional sequence focused on vocabulary development. Indeed, his objective was clearly met: to develop knowledge of the words that were key to understanding the passage that was read and to help children connect their knowledge to the new information they learned. During the instructional sequence, Doug encouraged the children to construct knowledge around the new vocabulary they learned, oftentimes asking, "What do you think that means?"

Identify the parts of the instructional sequence where the children developed a listening, speaking, reading, and writing vocabulary.

Thematic word study. When teachers use a thematic approach to literacy development, they integrate subject areas such as social studies, language arts, science, and mathematics around a theme or a broad topic. Children bring to the unit of study many experiences and ideas that they already know. Effective teachers begin such units of instruction with guided discussion to *activate children's prior knowledge.* Through a discussion approach, similar to brainstorming, teachers solicit experiences, knowledge, ideas, and words that children know about the topic. They record this information, and they will use it later to help children make connections to the new information. As the children learn about new ideas, words, and facts during their unit of study, teachers and children keep a record of what they have learned. Teachers use their written record of the children's prior knowledge and their new understandings to make connections.

The Sequential Roundtable Alphabet (Ricci & Wahlgren, 1998) has been suggested for older children as a systematic way to represent knowledge and vocabulary. The authors of this strategy suggest that the chart be used with cooperative groups, whose members brainstorm associated terms that they know are related to the topic and record them on the chart. Another similar strategy for use with younger children in second, third, and fourth grades who are fluent readers and writers is the thematic vocabulary chart, where the teacher plays a more directive role in developing vocabulary around a theme. The children are provided with a chart that contains 26 boxes, each box representing a letter. As they learn a new vocabulary word, they are instructed to record it in the appropriate box.

Materials

1. A large thematic vocabulary chart, shown in Figure 8.2, so that children may see the words that are being recorded by the teacher
2. A copy of the thematic vocabulary chart for each child

The thematic word chart should be sized to 8½" x 11" paper for children and on large chart paper for the class chart.

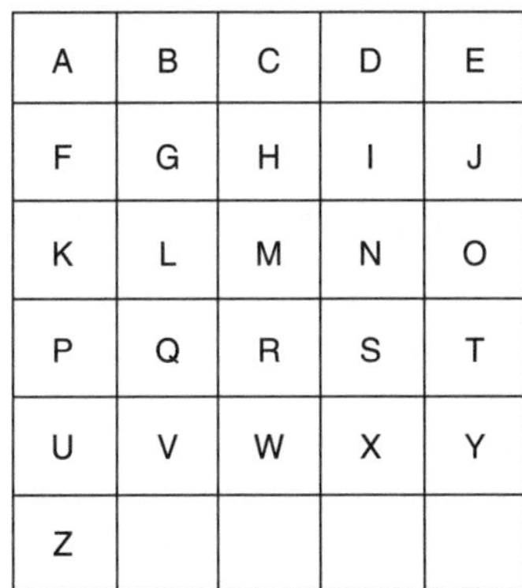

Figure 8.2
Thematic Word Chart

PROCEDURE

1. Introduce the theme or topic to be studied through guided discussion supported by a reading and visuals related to the topic.
2. Explain to the children that you will collect all their ideas and words related to the theme—words that they already know and words they will study—by recording them on the chart.
3. Give the chart a name related to the theme. For example, if third-grade children are engaged in a thematic unit on *time,* what creative title might they call their unit of study?
4. Conduct a discussion on the major ideas related to the theme about which the children are expected to read and write.
5. As the children respond with ideas or personal experiences, provide a vocabulary word that labels the concept or idea. Redefine the word to fit the study if it is necessary.
6. Write the word in the appropriate box on the thematic vocabulary chart. Have the children write the new word on their charts.
7. During the course of the thematic unit, the large chart may be used to add new vocabulary that children have acquired during their reading and discussions.
8. Children may be encouraged to add new words to their own charts as they read and discover new ideas related to the theme.
9. Encourage children to use their new words for writing topics during the thematic unit of study. Praise their attempts!

Within the sequence of instruction for using the thematic vocabulary chart, what type of approach did the teacher use: modeling, shared, guided, or independent? Support your choice(s) with an explanation.

Vocabulary Activities for the Fluent Reader and Writer

Direct instruction in vocabulary words is important to ensure that children learn new words. Like all kinds of learning, vocabulary development will need practice. It is important to remember that vocabulary instruction and practice include developing children's skill in word recognition and word meaning; therefore, teachers will balance the activities to extend both areas of skill. Below are several word study activities that are intended to encourage word recognition, build concepts, look for word parts, and develop an interest in words.

Word bank activities that promote word study. As children learn words, they collect them by making word banks. Most teachers have children make their own word banks by decorating cardboard canisters that have the easily removable plastic tops, for example, those that hold the popular potato chips. As children learn words, they carefully print them on small 1 × 2-inch cards, and they store them in their word banks to use for different word activities. Sometimes teachers set 10-minute blocks of time, or longer, for a word bank activity. Word bank activities may be part of center time, where children bring their personal word banks to the table and select activity cards guiding them through, from beginning to end.

A quick warm-up activity: Children can work together with partners who are at the same reading level. Using their own words, they can take turns selecting words from their banks and reading them to each other.

Word chains: Working independently or with partners, children can create word chains from the words they find in their word banks. Students select a word from their word bank and search for related words. For example, *eagles, talons,* and *feathers* are three words that can be chained (Tompkins, 2003).

Vowel sound activity: Children can find as many words in their word banks with a specific vowel sound. For example, the teacher may direct the children to find words with a short *a,* or a long *o.* At another time, the teacher may ask children to sort words with all the short sounds of the vowels; at other times, the teacher will let the children sort their words by a sound that they select. This vowel sound activity is often accompanied by a worksheet on which the students keep a record of the words they find having a specific sound like the ones shown in Figure 8.3.

Alphabetical order: Children play together in partners or small groups of three or four. One child selects a word from her word bank, shows it to her partner, reads the word, and says "before" or "after." The partner must find a word in his word bank that comes before if his partner said "before," or a word that comes after the word that was read if his partner said "after."

Sort by word function or parts of speech: At the fluent stage of literacy, the children are learning the functions of words. For example, teachers help children to understand that certain words are nouns when they name persons, places, or things. They also teach children about action words or verbs, and descriptive words or adjectives. When children have received sufficient instruction on the function of words, they may do a word sort. For example, the children may be asked to find all of the nouns, the words that name persons and have an ending of *-er* or *-or (teacher)* and those words that name persons and do not end with *-er* or *-or (captain).*

Name ______________________ Date ______________

Words From My Word Bank

Short *a*	Short *e*	Short *i*	Short *o*	Short *u*

Figure 8.3
Worksheet for Word Sort by Short Vowel Sounds

Word bank activities that promote word meaning. We have demonstrated how word bank activities may focus on word study. A critical area of vocabulary development is learning the meaning of words. The following activities may be used to develop conceptual knowledge that is related to the meaning of words.

Concept/definition mapping: The concept/definition map is a method of focusing children's attention on the meaningful features of a word. Concept/definition mapping (Schwartz & Raphael, 1985) offers children a frame to slot the information that they know about a word. The purpose is to engage children in thinking about the meanings of a word. Before concept/definition maps are used as independent activities, the teacher should have used the strategy several times as part of an instructional sequence modeling to children how it is used. When children use concept/definition mapping as an independent activity or with a partner, they should know the words that they will use: their meanings, uses, and pronunciations.

The children may work in pairs and select a word for study. During the study, they determine the semantic category or classification of the word (What is it?), the

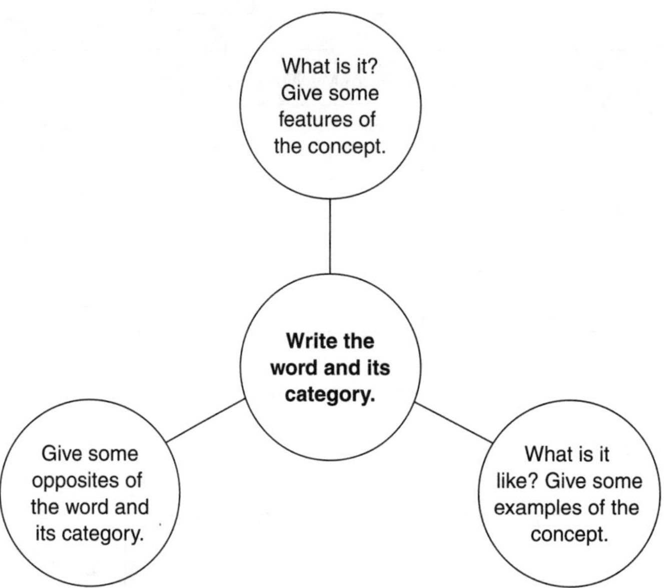

Figure 8.4
Sample Map for Concept/Definition Study

general features of the word (What is it like?), and some specific examples of the word. After the children complete their concept/definition map, they can use the information to write their own definition of the word. Figure 8.4 shows an example of the graphic organizer.

Word bank riddle: Friday is "Riddle Day." Children write riddles using the words from their word bank. Each clue to the riddle should be related to the meaning. Children can use their concept/definition maps of the word to help them develop a riddle. For example, the children may write the following riddle:

I am a bird of prey.
I cannot be kept as a pet.
An example is a snowy owl.
I begin and end with an *r*.
I am a ___________.

After children read the article about the controversy over snowy owls, and learned that the snowy owl is a raptor, a bird of prey, they added the word *raptor* to their word bank.

Word bank sentences: Children can arrange the words into sentences using those in their word banks. For example, the teacher may ask

- "Write one sentence using at least three words from your word bank."
- "Write a sentence using one verb, one noun, and one adjective from your word bank along with any other words."
- "Write a sentence that has no adjectives in it."

Student's Name ______________________ Date __________

Directions: Put words that belong together in separate groups. Decide on a name for each group. Write the category name and each word that belongs to it in the column.

Category Name	Category Name	Category Name	Category Name	Category Name

Figure 8.5
Categorizing and Classifying Words

Teachers can be as creative as they wish and focus on what children need to learn about words in their word banks.

Word sorts: Children can be asked to use their words from their word bank to classify words by meaning. For example, the teacher may ask the children to do the following: "Read all the words in your word bank and think about their meaning. Find as many words as you can that name animals or that describe the features of animals."

Children may be asked to sort words into groups and tell what each group is. In other words, the children must decide on the *semantic category* and the set of words that belong to it. Using the chart found in Figure 8.5, children may record their words and the name category to which they belong. This activity is especially effective with words from a specific unit of study.

Assessing Vocabulary Knowledge

Assessing vocabulary knowledge for fluent readers means determining how well they understand the meaning of words. Assessing children's word recognition skills—being able to say or decode words in print—is emphasized with assessing emergent and early readers for vocabulary development. At the fluent stage of literacy development, teachers focus on the word meanings, although they are mindful of monitoring children for word recognition.

Do you remember when you took a vocabulary test, and you had to write the definitions of words? This approach to vocabulary assessment is no longer widespread, especially in the primary grades. Most teachers rely on informal methods for vocabulary assessment, and effective teachers of literacy use multiple ways to assess children's vocabulary development. What teachers want to know is, do children understand the meaning of the words when they are used in a variety of contexts? Do children *use* the new vocabulary words as they discuss the story in literature circles? How do children use the words they learn in their writing? *How* teachers assess vocabulary is dependent on *what* will be assessed. Below are different examples of assessing vocabulary.

Observation. The role of observation in assessing language use is powerful and should not be underestimated. As we mentioned in previous chapters, good teachers have always used observation for assessing children's growth for all areas of learning, from their cognitive to physical and social-emotional development. What most teachers did not do was to accompany observation with documentation. This aspect of assessment makes growth and development visible to teachers who are accountable for student learning, who prepare lessons based on development, and who communicate with children's families, resource staff, and administrators about the progress that each child makes. Figure 8.6 is a form that will facilitate the teacher's attempts at the documentation of children's vocabulary use during conversations, small-group discussions, and writing that was observed and analyzed.

Cloze Procedure to Assess Comprehension

Cloze passages. The **Cloze** procedure, traditionally used as a test of comprehension, was developed and introduced by Wilson Taylor in 1953. Since then, it has been used in its original form as well as with a variety of modifications. A Cloze passage is a paragraph of approximately 250 words that contain deletions or missing words. The assumption of Cloze testing is that readers who know and understand a passage will be able to fill in the missing words. This is an application of the gestalt notion of "closure," where the mind tends to bring closure by supplying the missing parts to form a whole. The more the reader knows about the contents of the passage, the easier it is to fill in the deleted words.

The original procedure to make a Cloze test uses a passage of approximately 275 to 300 words. Every fifth word is deleted, even if the word is a simple word such as *a* or *the.* The first sentence is left intact, and the deletions begin at a random spot in the second sentence. Usually there are 50 deletions made throughout the passage. The test is typed with the missing words, using a blank line of the same size for every deletion. The exact word that was deleted is the correct answer. When students are given the Cloze passage, they are allowed to take as much time as needed to fill in the deleted words. The teacher scores the test using the exact words from the passage that were deleted as the scoring guide. The percentage of correct responses allows the teacher to determine whether the reader understood the passage. For example, students who score above 61% fully understood the passage, and it could be read without guidance from the teacher; for students who score between 40% and 60%, the passage posed a few problems related to comprehension and could be read with instruction or assistance by the teacher; and for students scoring below 40%, the assumption is that the passage is too difficult for them to read, even with assistance by the teacher.

Name: ______________________________ Grade: _______

Language Context	Date	Ratings and Comments
Conversations Context of conversation		1 Very limited vocabulary; frequently uses words incorrectly 3 Developing vocabulary; attempts to use new words 5 Developed vocabulary use of idioms; uses new words correctly **Rate student's growth and give examples of vocabulary used in conversations.**
Book Discussion Title of Book Type of Discussion		1 Very limited vocabulary; frequently uses words incorrectly 3 Developing vocabulary; attempts to use new words 5 Developed vocabulary use of idioms; uses new words correctly **Provide examples of vocabulary used during the book discussion. Did the child appropriate the language of the book discussed? What new and interesting words from the story were used?**
Informal Writing • Journals • Reading logs • Letters and messages to friends • E-mail • Other		1 Very limited vocabulary; frequently uses words incorrectly 3 Developing vocabulary; attempts to use new words 5 Developed vocabulary use of idioms; uses new words correctly **Cite examples of new and interesting words found in the child's writing.**

Figure 8.6
Documenting Observations of Vocabulary Growth

Adapting the Cloze procedure to assess word meaning. The use of the Cloze test for evaluating reading comprehension of young children would not be as appropriate as using a modified Cloze for assessing word meaning. We suggest that the Cloze test to assess vocabulary be used *after* the children are familiar with the vocabulary through a variety of reading and writing activities. That means the children have read the words several times, the teacher has taught the new vocabulary words, the words appear on the word wall and in word banks for use in writing, children have used the words in discussion, and they may have recorded the vocabulary words on their reading log record under "New and Interesting Words." A Cloze passage to assess vocabulary may be very useful after a prolonged study of a theme or a unit. For example, when the class studied the rain forest or desert life in the United States, the specialized vocabulary that grew out of the units may be used to assess children's knowledge of word meanings. The teacher expects that after reading, discussing, and writing about related topics to the theme, the children know the meanings of key words. Therefore, at the end of the unit, the teacher develops a test to measure the children's understanding of the words. The following procedure is an adaptation of the original Cloze test to be used with younger children (Grades 2–4) to assess word meanings. In the original Cloze test procedure, the teacher would delete every fifth word, even if the word were *an* or *the.* For the modified Cloze test, the teacher makes one deletion per sentence, and the deleted word is the target vocabulary word you are assessing. A target vocabulary word is a content word directly related to the unit of study, one that has been the focus of instruction, and a word that was part of the children's independent word activities. If the children know the word's meaning, they should be able to supply the deleted word. Therefore, in the modified Cloze test, it is important to supply as much information about the word from the context of the sentence or surrounding sentences so that readers can fill in the correct word when they know the meaning of the word. Figure 8.7 shows a sample assessment of vocabulary using the adapted version of the Cloze procedure.

PROCEDURE FOR PREPARING AND SCORING A CLOZE PASSAGE FOR ASSESSING VOCABULARY

1. List the words that you wish to assess for their meaning. These are the key words that children learned in a unit of study. For young children, test no more than 10 words.
2. Write a paragraph in which you use the target words in the context of their meaning that the children studied. Use only *one target word for each sentence.*
3. Take out or *delete the words that you are targeting* for assessment.
4. *List the targeted words* above or below the Cloze passage so that the children may choose from them to fill in the deleted words.
5. Check to see that
   - You have only one deletion per sentence.
   - You have no deletions in the first two sentences.
   - You have given the reader enough information to supply the missing words.
6. For scoring the Cloze passage
   - Give 10 points to each word.
   - If you have 10 deletions, each correct response is worth 10 points.
   - The total score may be changed easily to a percentage of words correct.
   - The benchmark for a child's growth in vocabulary is between 70% to 100%. The assumption is that the children were learning the targeted words during the thematic unit of instruction. Therefore, if a child knows how to use at least seven words, achieving 70%, we can say that the child's vocabulary knowledge is developing.

The Instructional Context

During a 2-week unit titled "Life in Colonial America," the children read many informational books on how life was different than it is today. The children spent time reading and talking about the major differences between how people of Colonial times and the people living today got their clothes. In Colonial times, people made their own outer garments. If they wanted a cloak, like the one that Charlie wanted in the book Charlie Needs a Cloak *by Tomie dePaola (1973), they would need to make the wool from shearing the sheep, washing, spinning, dyeing, and weaving it. Only then was it ready to be made into a cloak. Figure 8.7 is a modified Cloze passage to assess the children's acquisition of vocabulary after they learned about the process of wool making within this unit through discussion, reading, and writing. Children's vocabulary knowledge is assessed only after reading and discussing as well as writing about the topic.*

A Sample Cloze Passage to Assess Vocabulary Knowledge

How to Make Wool

If you lived long ago and wanted a wool coat, you would have to make it yourself. Wool comes from sheep, and you would first need to clip or to __1__ the wool from the sheep. The next step is to wash the wool and __2__ it to straighten it out which may be done using a brush. After the wool dries, you would need to __3__ or twist it into yarn. Certainly, most cloth has color, and you simply add __4__. To get color from plants, you simply __5__ it from berries and other plants. For example, the color red can be taken from __6__ berries. The next step is to place the strands on the __7__, a large wooden frame. To make the cloth, you would take each piece of yarn and pass it over and under one another that we call __8__. When you have finished the cloth, it would be ready to make into a piece of clothing or __9__. If you lived a long time ago, you would probably be making a coat without sleeves called a __10__.

Words to Use

loom	weaving	cloak	extract	pokeweed
spin	garment	dye	shear	card

Figure 8.7
A Sample Cloze Passage to Assess Vocabulary Knowledge

Developing Comprehension of a Story

Responsive Understanding of the Narrative

As children advance to the fluent levels of literacy, they begin to read longer books that are more difficult. Because children at this level are well on their way to mastering decoding skills, it does not mean word recognition ensures comprehension. It is true that knowing how to decode difficult or unfamiliar words will support comprehension, because children fluent in decoding can be free to think about what they are reading, not stopping constantly to figure out an unfamiliar word. However, some children may read every word correctly and not understand what they have read; they simply have a difficult time comprehending text. This section focuses on supporting fluent readers and writers in understanding longer text through the use of different comprehension strategies.

In every instructional strategy that we use with children, we need to ensure that children are engaged in reading the text. Engaged readers are more likely to understand what they are reading. To guarantee that children are interested and engaged in the story they are reading, the teacher helps them to make connections to the story. Connecting to the text is what strategic readers do automatically. Indeed there are a wide variety of instructional strategies, any one of which may be used to foster the reader's engagement through text connections. Therefore, before we describe individual instructional strategies that promote readers' engagement in text, let us first review the concept of connecting with text.

Making Connections Promotes Story Understanding

Connecting to literature—character study. Good literature will capture children's imaginations. At the heart of excellent fiction is the interesting character that helps children to *personally connect to literature* (Monson, 1992). Personal connections to stories make reading pleasurable to children, while building understanding about the world in which they live.

Harvey and Goudvis (2000) describe how strategic readers construct a variety of connections before, during, and after reading and how these connections work to create a deeper understanding of what was read. Building connections between a story and a personal event will indeed help the reader understand the story at a deeper level. Remembering that readers need prior knowledge to comprehend what they read, making connections helps to further develop their knowledge base. Making connections while reading is a strategy that is worthwhile; however, most children need to learn such strategies. To help children build connections, it is important to review the types of connections that readers make. Personal connections, or **text-to-self connections,** occur when readers relate their own experiences to those within the text. As children read and talk about stories, they begin to make connections between two or more texts. For example, they may compare three different versions of *The Mitten* (Brett, 1989). Children in a second-grade classroom talked about three different versions with respect to the animals that appeared in each version. They also saw the differences among the main characters other than the animals in the different versions. Some children pointed out the dramatic differences among the illustrations that appeared in the three versions. This is a type of **text-to-text connection** that strategic readers make instinctively. The third type of connection occurs when children connect events in the story to real-world events, those that occur in their school, their community, their country, or their world. When Doug had the children read "Harry Potter Owl Scenes Alarm Animal Advocates" by John Roach and encouraged them to think about whether they could keep a snowy owl as a pet, he was helping children connect the Harry Potter stories to world events. This is the third type of connection, **text-to-world connections,** that may foster critical thinking and problem-solving

Text - to - Self Connections	Text - to - Text Connections	Text - to - World Connections
	Definitions of Text Connections	
Readers connect their personal experiences and their own lives to what they read in the text, or they connect background knowledge to the concepts in the text.	Readers relate the events in one text to those that they have read in another. They may also connect the themes, characters, plots, literary style, etc. from two or more texts.	Readers connect events in the story to world events.
	Examples of Text Connections	
Text - to - Self Connections	Text - to - Text Connections	Text - to - World Connections
In Paula Danziger's book *Amber Brown Goes Fourth* (1995), Tanya made a personal connection when she responded during a discussion about how she felt the same way as Amber when she moved, and how she lost her two friends Annie and Lizzie.	When children read *Yeh-Shen: A Cinderella Story from China* (Louie, 1982), they compare all of the elements of this version to those in *The Talking Eggs,* the French Creole version. This is a text-to-text connection because children look at similarities and differences between the stories.	In the story by Eleanor Clymer, *The Trolley Car Family* (1947), the Parker family must make their home in a trolley car because the father loses his job when trolley cars are replaced. This book deals with the issue of homelessness as well as the loss of a job as a result of changes made by inventions—two examples of world connections.

Figure 8.8
Types of Text Connections

Presenting different versions of a story to children will help them understand taking different points of view and writing from different perspectives.

strategies in young children. The chart in Figure 8.8 provides the definitions and examples of three types of text connections. Some stories lend themselves to text-to-self connections because there are so many events within the story to which children can relate. Many stories share similarities with others and may be suitable to making text-to-text connections. Text-to-text connections may be made within an individual story as well. The children may compare an author's description of one character with the description of another. Other stories are appropriate in helping children relate story events to those events that are happening in their own world.

Questions and text connections. Developing comprehension of text in young children through text connections may be achieved through questioning strategies. However, traditional types of questions that have been part of instruction targeted assessing of literal comprehension of the text. Unfortunately, most questions were not used to promote understanding and critical thinking. Although teacher questioning is an important strategy to help students make connections and construct knowledge, questions that students pose are also critical. Student-generated questions leading to construction of meaning are those that emerge from curiosity.

> Curiosity spawns questions. Questions are the master key to understanding. Questions clarify confusion. Questions stimulate research efforts. Questions propel us forward and take us deeper into reading. Human beings are driven to find answers and make sense of the world. (Harvey & Goudvis, 2000, p. 81)

The kinds of questions that promote critical thinking and thoughtfulness help children to reflect deeply about what they are reading. They are the questions that children ask of themselves as they are engaged in reading and writing. Teacher-driven questions that ask students about what they read to assess and evaluate their comprehension simply do not encourage thinking. The key to fostering children's curiosity, thinking, and learning is to promote student-generated questioning strategies. How do we get children to ask themselves and others questions about what they read? Teachers need to *model and demonstrate good questioning* to children and to *use explicit instruction* to show students how to question the author to construct meaning. Children will begin to ask authentic questions about stories when teachers provide opportunities to them to share their questions about texts and to promote questions through independent reading and writing contexts.

Changing the Context for Teaching Fluent Readers

For children who have acquired and use the alphabetic principle for decoding and for word-solving strategies and who are moving into the fluency stage, instructional approaches will further their independence in reading. The teacher continues to engage in explicit instruction, but the instructional focus takes an emphasis on developing children's comprehension for different text types, increasing their sustained silent reading, developing self-monitoring strategies during reading, and promoting a positive disposition toward literacy. Because the goals for children at the fluent stage of literacy have changed, the context of instruction must change to accommodate children's literacy needs and development. To promote their independence in reading, the teacher needs to slowly release the responsibility to the children by giving them greater autonomy in the literacy process. This means providing more time and widening the choices for reading and writing. In guided reading at the emergent and early levels, books were deliberately chosen for children based on their specific reading levels, critical to effective learning. Although this consideration is just as important for the fluent reader—children need to read books that are within their instructional level—their choices in book selection need to extend beyond independent reading time. The teacher's aim is to develop strategic readers who know how to select books they can read. If children are not given opportunities to select their reading materials with teacher guidance, they will not have difficulty when they have the chance to choose a book for reading on their own. Further, self-selection of books will deepen children's interests thereby developing positive dispositions toward reading. To meet this goal, the classroom teacher needs to have several sets of books at the children's levels of instruction so that such choices may be made.

Recall that during guided reading most questions are initiated by the teacher with a few posed by the children. It is important that the fluent readers begin to initiate discussions around the texts they are reading. Discussions become rich when they emerge through student-generated questions. During guided reading, children read shorter texts and practice reading on leveled texts. Fluent readers need longer pieces of text such as chapter books that will help promote sustained periods of reading. Because children are moving toward chapter books that will take longer to read, they may be reading a book over several days. Additionally, instructional blocks of time need to be longer to accommodate reading, response writing, and discussion.

Literature Circles: Promoting Independence in Literacy

Literature circles are intended to meet the literacy needs of the fluent reader by engaging children in reading and writing about children's books for longer periods, by promoting choice, and by furthering student-initiated discussions. Children in literature circles read the same book and then respond to the text through writing and discussion. Teachers further children's understanding of the text through extension or follow-up writing projects or other types of activities. Literature circles provide the most effective context for helping children to generate questions about text. Children will learn to ask types of questions that promote critical thinking. Because the literature that is used is selected by children on the basis of interest and is developmentally appropriate, the text will stimulate the self-generated questions rather than questions posed by the teacher.

Daniels (2002) emphasizes that the two powerful aspects of using literature circles with children are that they promote independence in reading and develop learning through group cooperation. As children move from a guided reading group to a literature circle for their literacy instruction, they will experience dramatic changes in their own learning. They will learn to engage in longer periods of sustained reading and initiate and sustain discussions about aspects of the topics within books they are reading (Samway, Whang, Cade, Gamil, Lubandina, Phommachanh, 1991). This learning outcome is not surprising for children who meet on a daily basis to discuss a piece of literature in depth, who are taught, encouraged, and rewarded for self-generated questions, and who are given blocks of time to read and to formulate a written response to prepare for group discussions. Before discussing a specific procedure for setting up literature circles, it is important to think about selecting the *core books* that children will read to extend their literacy levels.

Providing and Selecting Literature for Fluent Readers

As we look at the many books displayed in children's libraries and on the shelves of bookstores, we find an overwhelming number of books for young children to read. Not all of these books are worthy of classroom time and children's effort in reading and writing about them. Therefore, when selecting books for literature circles or for the classroom library, it is important to be guided by criteria that will help judge the quality of each book. Routman (2000) suggests the following guidelines that teachers may use in selecting books for classroom use:

- Literary excellence (includes writing style, visual presentation, organization, and content)

- Depth of subject matter (teacher guidance required for full appreciation and understanding)
- Reading level and interest level appropriateness
- Age appropriateness

Anchor books, which ground the literature program at each grade level, are texts that

- Display exceptional literary (and artistic) merit
- Reflect the diverse population of our district as well as our multicultural world
- Connect to students' lives and values
- Comprise mostly current literature (published within the last decade) as well as "classics"
- Challenge the reader to think deeply about important concepts
- Support thoughtful discussion, analysis, and understanding
- Can be used to teach students how to read (as long as the book is at the students' instructional level)
- Can be utilized to highlight literary elements, such as setting, point of view, theme, and character development
- Can be used for examining the author's style and as a model for writing
- Connect to district objectives across the curriculum (Routman, 2000, pp. 66–67)

Preparing for Literature Circles

- **Setting up groups for literature circles:** Create groups of six to eight children for each literature circle based upon their levels of reading. When setting up groups, think about the *interests* of the group and about the *literacy needs* of the group.
- **Selection of books for a literature circle:** Because the books need to be at their instructional level of reading, children should be able to read most of the words in the book—at least 90%.
  - Select at least three sets of books for children to choose from. Children need their own copies of the book.
  - Consider the quality of the material (review the guidelines above).
  - Consider the length of the book and appropriate divisions within the book. Because discussion is an important part of literature circles, children need to read a section, respond to that section, and share their responses through discussion.
- **Response journals:** When children are placed in literature circles for the first time, they need to have a structured routine. Part of the routine should include the children responding to the readings by writing in journals. It is important for the teacher to review their journal responses so that their growth in understanding may be monitored.
- **Classroom environment to support literature circles:** What worked well for the guided reading group will work well for literature circles. Children need to meet around a table to hold their discussions. Oftentimes, the group will work at the table on projects that are related to the book. The table needs to be located in a quiet place, out of the way of other class activities.
- **Scheduling blocks of time for literature circles:** Teachers who begin literature circles in the primary grade need to *think of the children's development*

as well as their previous experience with literature circles. When designing the schedule, a literature circle block might include time for the following:

- Time for silent reading: 20 minutes
- Response writing in the journal: 15 minutes
- Discussion time for sharing responses: 10 minutes
- Mini-lesson on reading, writing, discussion strategy: 10 minutes
- Extension projects: 20 minutes
- Self-assessment and reflections: 5 minutes
- Organizing and clean-up: 5 minutes

At first, the schedule should be highly structured to enable the children to enter a routine. When the groups are set in place and when the children become aware of their roles and responsibilities, more flexibility is needed and change may be dictated by the nature of the book, the time needed to finish a discussion, or other classroom or school events of the day.

- **Suggestions for organizational structures for classroom management:** In order to stay on schedule and make optimum use of instructional time, classroom management is strongly suggested. Following are some tips to keep materials and books together:
  - Keep all materials for one literature circle in an appointed place. For example, colorful plastic crates that are marked with the name of the groups are especially helpful.
  - Keep books for reading, response journals, and extension activities organized in separate student folders.
  - Have children date entries in their response journals, and help them to organize their responses to each book in its own section. Dating journal entries is easy and inexpensive when a date stamp with an ink stamp pad is made available.
  - Be prepared for literature circles, having their assignments ready for each group based upon their progress.
  - Have self-assessment sheets available that are aligned with the goals and objectives of the process that is needed to keep the group working effectively. For example, you may focus the group's attention on role responsibility, giving each member a certain task to keep the discussion lively and to ensure group participation. As an alternative, the focus may be on taking turns, not interrupting others, as well as listening and responding to others during the discussion. The questions for student reflection and the self-assessment sheet need to focus on the specific goals and objectives that are being developed.
- **Follow-up activities or extension activities:** Follow-up activities or extension activities allow children to think deeply about the book or an aspect of the book. The teacher may wish to have children work in small groups, pairs, or individually to complete projects. The type of activity emerges from the nature of the book as well as the interest and literacy levels of the children. Just as children were given a choice for reading, provide them with the opportunity to choose from a variety of projects.
- **Children's experiences with literature circles:** When implementing literature circles for the first time, it is indeed important to think of the children's prior experiences of working in longer blocks of time or reading independently for extended periods. Children who had no experience of reading on their own, responding in their reading journal, and conducting their own discussions around

books by using self-generated questions will need more support and guidance by the teacher. A group of children who lacks experiences with literature circles will benefit at first from a highly-structured context. As children become more accustomed to the routines of literature circles, the teacher becomes more flexible in setting up the routines for the literature circles. Gradually, the teacher releases responsibility for conducting the routines of the literature circle to the group.

Guidelines for Integrating Mini-Lessons in Literature Circles

There are many different reading, writing, and language strategies that can be integrated in the form of mini-lessons or longer instructional sequences to follow the literature circle period. As with all effective instruction, *let the children lead or inform instruction.* In other words, what must children know to successfully understand what they are reading now? What do they already know? What are the learning needs of children within each group? Another guide for the teacher's instruction is the book itself. Is its focus on character development? If the author develops the character, the instructional strategy needs to target character analysis and evaluation. Is there a series of events that is especially complex and must be understood to comprehend the plot and the theme? Have the children in the group read a book by that same author? All of these questions and more will facilitate the teacher in preparing his mini-lessons as well as developing the focus questions for responding in the journal or developing the extension activities.

Before reading in literature circles. The literature circle is not independent reading but categorized more as guided instruction. Within some aspects of literature circle, as in the mini-lesson, the teacher may use direct or explicit instruction. What the teacher does before reading to prepare the children for reading the book is critical. Think of how the teacher prepares children to read during guided reading through intense book introductions and story walks. Preparation for reading in the literature circle is crucial as well. Children need to set purposes and to make connections to the story, and their imaginations need to be stimulated so they may read the text for longer periods.

In preparing children to read, the teacher takes into account how much children need to know to comprehend the text. The teacher will consider the children's prior knowledge by asking: How does the children's conceptual knowledge match the concepts that are presented in the book? If the children lack the conceptual knowledge that is needed to understand the information in the book, the teacher will need to develop the prerequisite knowledge through the use of a mini-lesson prior to children's reading the book. Another aspect of prior knowledge includes children's experiences reading a certain genre or literary style. For example, if the book chosen for the literature circle is an autobiography and most of the children in the group have not read this genre, the teacher needs to develop a mini-lesson around autobiographies. The teacher may connect this lesson to the children's writing in writers' workshop by having the children write their autobiographies. A thorough preparation before reading the book gives children a firm footing and the self-confidence that is needed to read for longer periods.

During reading. Children read silently for approximately 20 minutes or longer. During that time, much is happening within each reader. For example, some children may be delighted and entertained as they read, they may be learning new ideas, or they may be following the author develop the character in a story. Other children may come across a word that is unfamiliar, a word they think they know from its usage in the story but need to check when reading time is over. Children may experience a bit of confusion about a certain area of the text. These types of text engagements create the kinds of questions that strategic readers know to ask. Therefore, children need to be encouraged to note areas of delight as well as areas of concern while they are reading. Teachers may model or demonstrate what to do when confronted by an unfamiliar word or when confused by a part of the text.

Immediately after reading, children should have time to write in their response journals. The teacher needs to monitor children during response time. Some children have no difficulty getting started, whereas others do not know where to begin. The blank page may seem quite intimidating. Teachers may help reluctant writers in several ways:

- Before children begin to read, have children use sticky notes to mark the areas in their reading. Model the process for marking areas in their reading. Depending on the story, you may suggest one or two ways to mark places for their responses.
  - **Mark the part you find exciting.** Ask: Why did you like this part of the story? What part would you like to share with the group in the literature circle? Do you think others may have found this part as interesting? Can you think of questions you want to ask the group?
  - **Mark the part you find most confusing.** Ask: Which part did you understand, and which part caused you concern? What question could you ask others that may help you understand the confusing area? What would you like to ask the author?
  - **Mark words that are interesting.** Say: Sometimes words in the story may delight you as much as a sentence or a paragraph. Mark a word that you especially liked in the part of the story you just finished reading. Tell the group why you thought the word was a good choice.
  - **Mark words that are new to you—Be a word wizard!** Encourage children to use a sticky note to mark each new word they read in a book. Direct them to write down what they think the word means, then look up the word in the dictionary to see if their definition was correct. Finally, have them add the new word to their personal word walls, their word banks, or the classroom word wall.
- Ask children to respond to the story they are reading by
  - Writing about a character they like or dislike.
  - Writing about how the story is connected to their own lives.
  - Drawing a picture response with a caption or explanation on how the story made them feel.
  - Writing a letter to a family member about what they felt about today's reading.
  - Writing a poem to respond to the story.
  - Writing and illustrating a comic strip to respond to part of or the whole story.

After reading. Children need time to share with the group what they have read. Their discussion is determined by the book they are reading and by their experience and maturity in conducting discussions. Children may ask questions before and during their reading that promote understanding of the text. After reading, literature circles are kept lively through discussion that emerges from self-generated questions posed for further understanding and clarification. At first, children may be reluctant to ask questions of their peers because literature circles present a new context for instruction. When children lack such experiences, the teacher may use modeling and demonstrations to encourage questioning strategies, because "questioning [is] the strategy that propels readers forward" (Harvey & Goudvis, 2000, p. 18). Teachers may also share with children questions that they ask of themselves while reading novels and nonfiction. Mini-lessons that incorporate explicit instruction, modeling, and sharing are appropriate for developing questioning strategies in young readers. To expand children's thinking, help children to ask **sincere questions.** Harvey and Goudvis (2000) describe them as the questions that are reserved for recess or lunchtime. Unlike the assessment questions to which children are expected to know the answers and are used by the teacher to monitor comprehension, sincere questions are those to which one does not know the answer, to which we ponder and think about, and they are the questions that often demand further research. These questions are most likely to be described as heuristic in nature. Halliday (1975) refers to this function as one of the purposes or functions of language. It is the function of language that we use when we are trying to solve "real problems." Most language used in class does not fall into this category, because the problems are already solved. When teachers ask questions, they have the answers. Sincere questions often appear in inquiry-based learning, which is described later in this chapter.

The global question. One way to help children use questions to expand their thinking is through the use of a **global question** about a topic that they are reading. The global question relates to the main topic of their reading. Using the form of semantic webbing, the question is written in the center. Children then use the global question to think of related questions. The teacher needs to encourage the children to develop the questions around the topic. Children's questions may be written in the circles around the global question. Their questions are a guide that directs them during and after reading. When they find answers or information about the question, they add it to the question web. Figure 8.9 shows a sample of question webbing.

Using the question web before reading will encourage children to read with questions in their minds. During reading, children may use the question web to organize information by writing it next to the question to which it relates. The question web may also be used after reading to expand their knowledge on a topic through extension projects. The global question promotes discussion and sharing by children related to the information they found to be important around the "big" topic.

Structured discussions. There are many stories for young children that promise a lively discussion after reading. Books that promote different points of view will foster a discussion with little encouragement from the teacher. Early fluent and fluent readers are beginning to develop opinions and have different views on issues. Using a strategy similar to Alvermann's (1991) discussion web will promote a systematic dialogue on opposing views. As we know from experience, the most convincing opinions in discussions are those that are organized and supported by a set of arguments. Therefore, using a strategy for discussing books that raises issues or controversies encourages participants to support their viewpoints. In the process of preparing for the discussion, children use a graphic organizer that will help them prepare to present their viewpoints on a question. A discussion strategy may be used after reading a story that promotes differing opinions. Figure 8.10 presents a graphic organizer for leading a structural discussion.

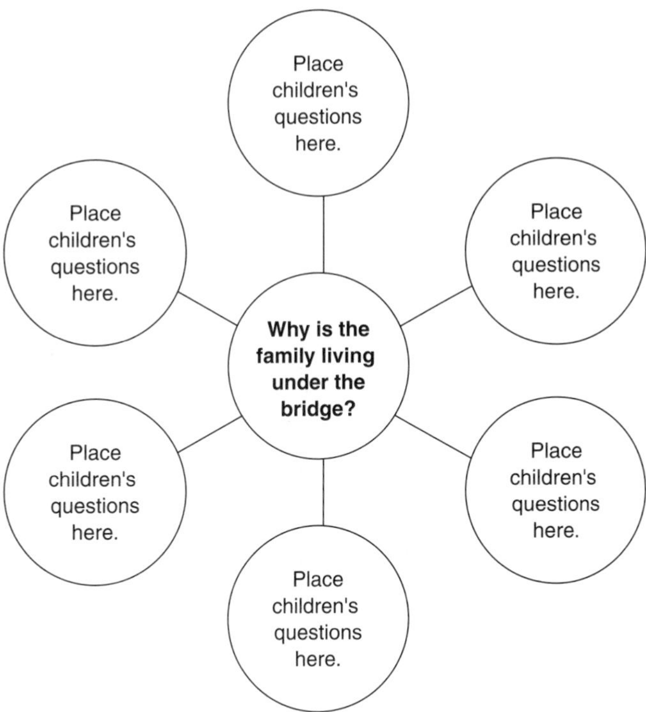

Figure 8.9
Question Web

PROCEDURE

- After children have read the book and are ready for a discussion, present them with the question that encourages different opinions.
- Have them break into groups based upon their point of view.
- Help children to express the controversy in a question format. For example, "Should children be allowed to vote?"
- Model how a point of view should be supported by reasons. Show children how to find text that supports their opinion.
- Distribute the graphic organizer (Figure 8.10) and ask the children to find at least two reasons to support their point of view. Have them write their reasons in the appropriate opinion side, "We agree" or "We Disagree."
- After children have written their reasons, show them how to draw a conclusion. Have them write their conclusions in the appropriate frame.
- Prepare the groups to present their opinions.

Extension and Follow-Up Activities for Literature Circles

Thinking about story events. The story pyramid. The story pyramid is a good follow-up activity to be used after a story is read and discussed. This activity is suitable for a story that has a plot that is explicit. Because it is a follow-up activity, it should be used *after* the events of the story were discussed during literature circles.

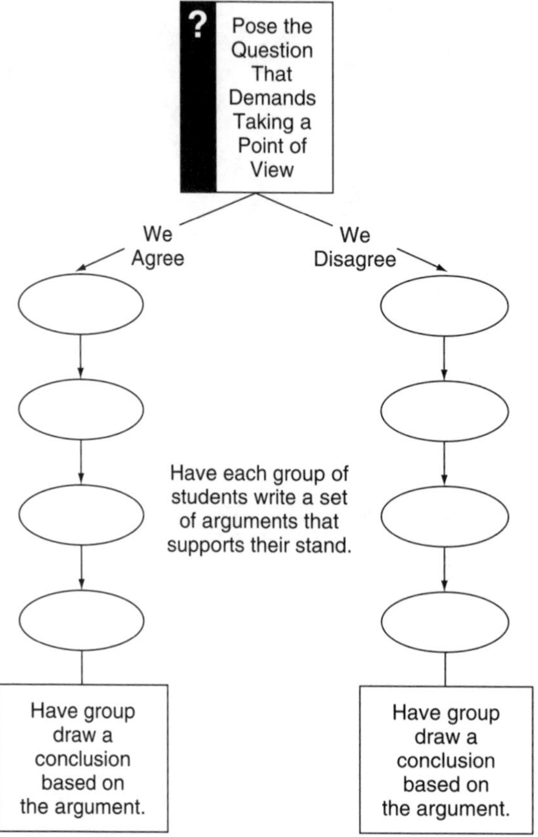

Figure 8.10
Graphic Organizer for a Structured Discussion

The use of graphic organizers such as the story pyramid help children in the primary grades to understand new and complex concepts about literacy (Brunn, 2002; Robinson, 1998). Especially useful for children with special needs as well as for students whose language is not English, visual organizers scaffold their understanding of intertextual relationships through a spatial presentation of information (Dye, 2000).

Materials

- A graphic organizer, shown in Figure 8.11 for children to use for their written responses
- A set of directions accompanying the graphic organizer

Procedures

- After children have discussed the story, have them work in pairs.
- Children work in pairs to read the directions to complete the story pyramid.
- After the completion of the story pyramid, children from different groups may share, compare, and discuss their responses. When there are different responses, groups should be able to support them with a set of reasons.

Story Title: ____________________

Author(s): ____________________

Story Pyramid

1. ________
2. ________
3. ________
4. ________
5. ________
6. ________
7. ________

Directions for the Story Pyramid

1. Name the character.
2. Write two words to describe the character.
3. Write three words that tell about where the story took place.
4. Write four words that tell about the problem that the main character faced.
5. Write five words that tell about how the main character solved the problem.
6. Write six words to describe how you felt about the main character and the story ending.
7. Write seven words to describe a person you know who is like the main character in the story.

Figure 8.11
Story Pyramid

Character study. There are many excellent stories in which the author focuses on the main character. These stories provide an opportunity to help children understand the author's craft of developing the character through the story problem and events. Further, many stories have two characters with very different personalities and characters. Such stories offer children an opportunity to compare and contrast character traits. Graphic organizers may be used to facilitate children as they discuss the characters in the story and gather information from the story they just read (see Figure 8.12). The visuals may offer a scaffold to children who need a way to organize their thoughts before they present their character within a group or write about their character.

Sketch to stretch. Sketch to stretch provides the children the opportunity to use visual literacy skills to capture the story they read and discussed. The sketch to stretch (Harste, Short, & Burke, 1988; Whitin, 1996) strategy engages children in interpreting their readings through drawing or sketching their ideas as well as using their words. **Stretching** the children's retellings or responses through their sketches encourages children to go beyond literal interpretations to more creative ways of thinking about stories, both fiction and nonfiction.

Procedure

- After the children complete the reading and the discussion, have them make a sketch of what the story meant to them.
- Explain to the children that the purpose is not on the illustration but on individual interpretations of the story.

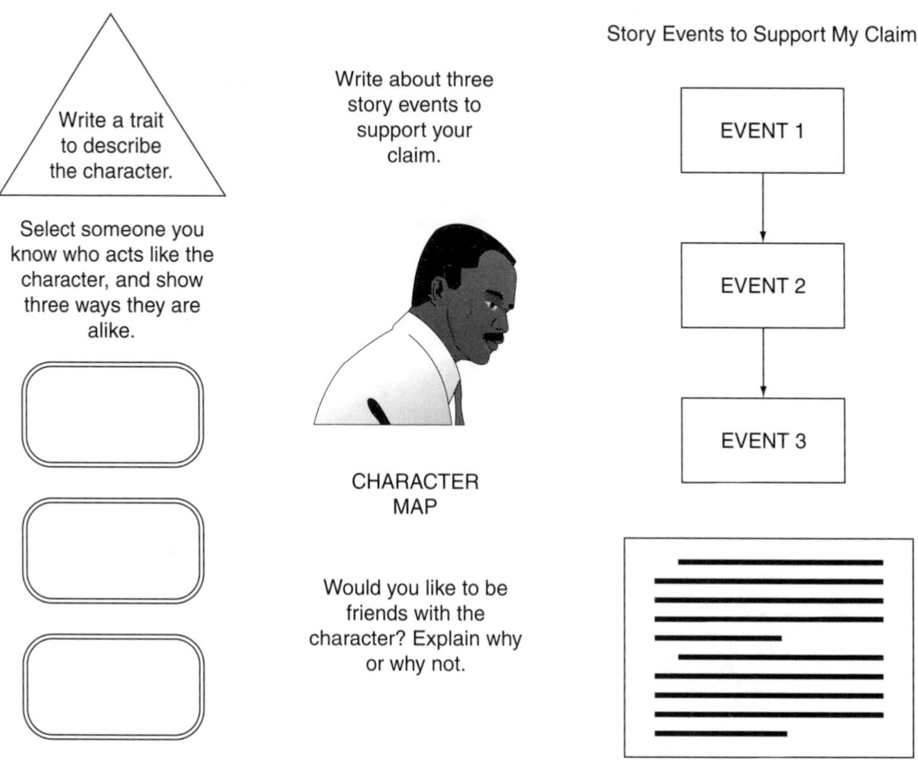

Figure 8.12
Graphic Organizers of Character

- Returning to the group, each child shows her own story sketch and interprets the story to the group through her illustrations.
- The group's discussion may then focus on the different interpretations of the story by group members.

The purpose of using this strategy is to promote children's creative thinking through art. Many different modes can be used to express meaning. Applying Gardner's (1993) theory of multiple intelligences, the use of art to express a response to a text would be an appropriate medium for children who possess superior spatial abilities over verbal skills, and who would be more inclined to incorporate art into their responses. Using sketch to stretch is one way to help students go beyond literal meaning and to understand that there are multiple ways of knowing and different forms to express insights.

Responding to Literature Through Drama

Teachers have the opportunity to "enhance children's experience of a good story and let them live a little longer in the spell of a good book" (Galda & West, 1995, p. 183). Simple reenactments of story parts will promote children's thinking at the story's deeper levels by entering into the author's portrayal of the saga of human life. Such dramatic activities around stories will promote text-to-person connections.

Types of drama for stories. There are several formats of dramatic performances that may be used to respond to or interpret an episode in a story, a whole story, or a character within the story. Some drama activities listed below may be used with fluent readers:

- **Reenactment:** After the reading of the story and a thorough discussion, children focus on the most significant story parts. They use these parts to plan their presentation of the story. Although their reenactment of the story is spontaneous, with no written play nor props and costumes, children must know the story, the characters, and the sequence of events. After the children have planned their presentation through retellings, they reenact the story with no script.
- **Readers' Theatre:** Readers' theatre is much like reenactment in that the children need to know all of the story elements and the sequence in which they occur. They know the characters and their personality traits. The difference, however, is in the delivery of the story. In readers' theater, children write their own script and read from the script they have written. Unlike reenactment, it is not spontaneous. There is a narrator who describes the scene and the actions, and meaning is also conveyed through the characters in what they say. Unlike acting, where lines are memorized, readers' theatre requires children to read with natural expression without acting, costumes, or props.
- **Improvisation:** In improvisation, children go beyond the story to enact an original scene. In other words, after the story is over, what happens next? Children answer the question by thinking about the main character(s) and what that character would do to respond to the problem.
- **Pantomime:** Children act out through gestures and movements, facial expressions and body language the personality traits of the character(s) in the story. This means that the children involved in pantomiming the story characters must know their characteristics, and the audience responding to the pantomiming engages in the meaning that is being conveyed.
- **Role Playing:** Role playing is a dramatic performance that is appropriate for stories that develop characters. Children are encouraged to "take on the life of the character" they read about in the story. After learning about the character's interests, language, actions, and perspectives, the children then use role playing to interpret the characters.

Procedures for Developing and Assessing Reading Fluency

Why Develop Fluency?

Fluency in reading is related to reading proficiency. The lack of fluency is a mark of a struggling reader. Therefore, most teachers would agree that a major goal of the literacy program is the development of fluency in the young, yet fluency instruction is not given much attention (Rasinski and Zutell, 1996).

Fluency in reading is associated with reading achievement, referring to the "reader's ability to read accurately, quickly, in appropriate syntactic phrases or chunks, and above all, with meaningful and appropriate expression" (Rasinski & Padak, 2001, p. 162). Therefore, when teaching and assessing for reading fluency, the following factors will be the focus: accurate word recognition, rate of reading, accuracy in chunking, and reading expression.

- Model to children how to read with expression.
- Show children what correct phrasing sounds like, and then demonstrate choppy reading.

- If children need to be helped with return-sweep eye movement, show them how to use a marker to guide their eyes from getting lost on the page.
- Time children's reading occasionally.

Activities for Developing Fluency

Paired and shared reading for developing fluency. Paired readings are very powerful instructional tools that may be used in a variety of ways and within a number of instructional contexts that support reading fluency. It is the beneficial alternative to "round robin reading"—when students spend instructional reading time taking turns reading aloud. Such oral reading practices like round robin reading were found to be inefficient and boring by children (Opitz & Rasinski, 1998). Teachers need to find alternatives to round robin reading for developing fluency in oral reading. Strategies that are used for fluency development should fit children's developmental needs and be appropriate for the instructional sequence. We have discussed the use of paired reading after guided reading as a way to practice the words and the word-solving strategies that were learned during instruction. For children moving into the stage of fluency, the teacher's major objective is to develop children's fluency in oral reading, their rate of reading, their reading expression, and syntactic phrasing during reading. Children at the fluent stage of literacy may be asked to time their reading during partner reading. The partner or the teacher may keep a record of their rate of reading over a 6-month or 10-month period on a line or bar graph as they monitor their speed of reading. For the fluent reader, paired reading may be a part of the instructional sequence of literature circles. When paired reading is part of literature circles, the teacher builds in time after silent reading, discussing, and writing responses to stories. When children are paired for oral reading, the children take turns reading selected parts of the story that they have already read and discussed. After the paired reading, they may retell the selection they have read to their partners. Below are the procedures for paired reading that may be used as part of the instructional sequence within literature circles.

Procedures for Paired and Shared Reading Activity

- After the group of children have read, discussed, and written about part of the book, they engage in a structured time for reading in pairs a selection from the book. The time block for reading and retelling is about 8 to 10 minutes.
- Prior to the reading, the following decisions are made:
  - *Who* will read together in a pair
  - *What selection* will be read by each person
- Children paired for reading sit together, out of earshot from others, and follow a set of rules that may be similar to those below:
  - The students sit side by side.
  - While one of the students is reading, the second is listening and following along.
  - As in guided reading, the reader needs ample time to self-correct and to engage in word-solving strategies whenever necessary. The partner offers suggestions or clues to figure out the word, and gives the word only when the reader cannot solve the unknown word.
  - The partners must respect each other and not criticize or laugh at the partner's errors.
- After oral reading, partners retell the parts that have read. They may wish to respond to their parts as well as their partner's selection.
- Partners should congratulate each other on a good read.

While paired and shared reading strategy is one way to practice reading aloud for the purpose of increasing children's reading rates, there are others. Remember that round robin reading is not an effective approach to increasing fluency. Children need to practice their reading with others in contexts that are purposeful and authentic. Some excellent alternatives to round robin reading are

- **Radio Reading:** Children pretend they are on a radio show. The audience gathers on one side of a large sheet, so they do not see the readers who are on the other side of the sheet. Children read their stories or read the announcements for the day. The readers' focus is on expressive, natural, and accurate reading so that the audience can understand the message.
- **Choral Reading:** Poetry is excellent for choral reading. Small groups of children practice reading in unison one stanza of the poem. The entire poem is read through a class choral reading. Variations of choral reading are as many as the teacher may create.
- **Echo Reading:** The echo reading strategy is appropriate for the teacher who needs to model fluent reading. The teacher demonstrates to the students oral reading changes in stress and pitch, chunking the text for appropriate syntactic phrasing, and when to take brief pauses or longer ones. The approach is quite simple: The teacher models or demonstrates fluent reading, one sentence or part of a sentence at a time and the children echo what the teacher has read. To implement echo reading, follow the procedure below:
  - Select a part of the children's reading with which they are familiar. The children should have read the passage and discussed it.
  - Explain to the children the importance of chunking text and model what it means. Show them why you need to put words together, pause briefly after commas, and make a full stop after a period or question mark. Show children how to read dialogue in natural ways. This mini-lesson is followed by practice with the echo reading strategy.
  - Each child has a copy of the reading and follows the text. The teacher reads part of the sentence or the complete sentence and stops. The children echo or repeat the teacher's reading, trying to use similar stress and pitch, using the same syntactic phrasing, and making the same pauses within the reading.

Assessment of Oral Reading Fluency

When teachers assess children for reading fluency, they will determine if the children can say each word accurately. They will also be interested in timing children to determine their rate of reading. Assessing whether children have the skill of reading with appropriate syntactic phrases, teachers will need to determine whether they read using correct phrasing. Finally, when children read with expression, similar to speech expressions, it is a clue that they understand what they are reading. The results of assessing children's oral reading fluency may mean that the teacher will need mini-lessons to develop areas of fluency. Figure 8.13 presents the rubrics for assessing stages of fluency in oral reading.

Aspects of assessing oral reading fluency. Teachers may assess children's reading for accuracy, rate of reading, syntactic phrasing, and reading expression.

Proficient Stage	Developing Stage	Beginning Stage
The child reads in *meaningful phrases.* Any repetitions or digressions do not detract from the meaning of the text. The child's oral reading keeps the author's syntax intact and she reads with expression that demonstrates meaning. Reading is smooth and effortless.	The child reads in *three- to four-word* phrases and some small groupings. Most phasing is consistent with meaning, with the author's syntax preserved. The child reads with some expression.	*The child reads some text with two- or three-word phases.* Word-by-word reading is present. The child's oral reading does not preserve the author's syntax and does not contribute to the meaning. The child's reading is choppy and lacks expression.

Figure 8.13
Rubrics for Assessing Stages of Fluency in Oral Reading

- **Accuracy:** How many words the child reads correctly out of 100 running words
- **Rate of Reading:** How many words a child reads in one minute
- **Syntactic Phrasing:** How the child groups the words together in meaningful units—syntactically appropriate phrases
- **Reading Expression:** How the child raises and lowers her tone of voice to demonstrate natural language use

In the first assessment strategy, all of the above factors are included while observing a child for oral reading fluency. Teachers may also wish to focus on a single factor such as the child's rate of reading—as in the second assessment strategy—by measuring how many words a child reads in 1 minute. Below is a list of materials as well as a set of procedures used for assessing reading fluency.

Assessing word accuracy, reading rate, phrasing, reading, and expression.

Materials

- Stop watch.
- A selection from the child's book that is marked for 100 words.
- A form for recording the child's reading fluency.

Procedures

- Sit with the child who is being assessed.
- Ask the child to read to you a part of the selection that was read and discussed during the literature circles. Point to where the child should begin.
- For your guide to monitor the child's reading, use a copy of the book with a selection marked for 100 words.
- Ask the child to begin to read, and when the child begins to read, start the clock. Mark where the child begins and ends reading after 1 minute.
- Observe the child's reading for syntactic phrasing and reading expression. Using the rubrics in Figure 8.13, determine the child's stage of fluency in oral reading, and mark the stage on the form. Note important strengths and areas of improvement in oral reading on the assessment form.

Comprehensive Assessment of Children's Fluency in Oral Reading

Name ______________________ Grade ________

Observer ______________________

Date	**Rate of Reading**	**Automatic Word Recognition** Accuracy Level: # of Words Correct Out of 100	**Stage of Oral Reading: Proficient, Developing, and Beginning**	**Additional Comments**

Figure 8.14
Profile of a Child's Fluency in Oral Reading

- While the child is reading, record the number of word recognition errors and record the number of errors on 100 words.

It is important to note that children's oral reading is not the only predictor of success in reading. Indeed, teachers need to monitor comprehension as well as children's dispositions for reading. Along with comprehension of text, the effortless and smooth oral reading has been found as a strong predictor for children's overall reading proficiency in Grades 3 and 5 (Rasinski, 1985). For a more comprehensive assessment of fluency in the child's oral reading fluency, we suggest word accuracy and reading rate, along with syntactic phrasing and reading expression. To document children's performances in oral reading, follow the procedure suggested above and record assessment results on the form shown in Figure 8.14.

Teachers may monitor children on a regular basis for their fluency in oral reading, simply focusing on their rates of reading. It is not time consuming, and it can be easy and fun when other children are involved. The assessment of five children for their reading rates may be accomplished in 10 to 15 minutes because the teacher takes a 1-minute sample of the children's readings. The five children may sit together and listen to their friends read as the teacher monitors their rates of reading. Teachers may record the children's reading rates on the form shown in Figure 8.15.

Assessing reading rate.

MATERIALS

- Stop watch.
- Copies of the book for the child and the teacher.

PROCEDURES

- Select a story that the group of children have read and discussed.
- Have children read a selection of the story.
- When each child begins, begin the stop watch and mark the area where the child begins.
- After 1 minute of reading, mark where the child has finished.
- Count the number of words read, and record the total on the chart in Figure 8.15.
- Using a line graph procedure, mark the number of words that the child has read within 1 minute on the graph in Figure 8.15 and in the Appendix.
- Keep a record of the child's reading to compare the rate of reading over time.

As we measure children's rates of reading, it is important to have benchmarks that will help to understand how children's reading rates are progressing. Rasinski and Padak (2001, p. 198) suggest that the following are estimated reading rates for materials that are at children's instructional levels within the second part of the school year.

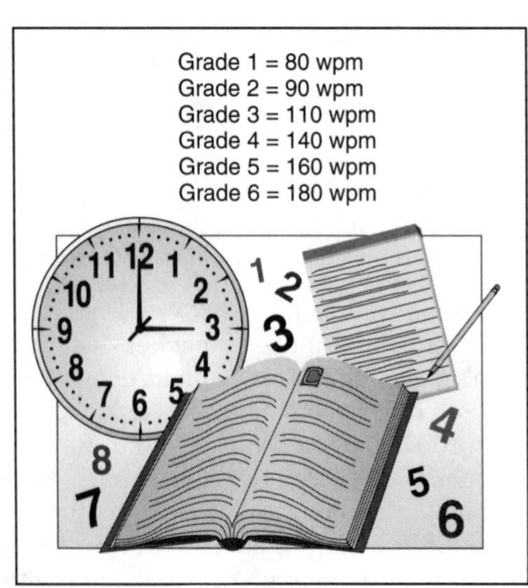

Assessing Children's Reading Rate
Timed Reading Chart

Name ______________________ Grade ________

Beginning Date ______________________ Ending Date ______________________

Number of Readings and Reading Rate (WPM)

# of Words	0	1st	2nd	3rd	4th	5th	6th	7th	8th	9th
150										
145										
140										
135										
130										
125										
120										
115										
110										
105										
100										
95										
90										
85										
80										
75										
70										
65										
60										
55										
50										
45										
40										
35										
30										
25										
20										
15										
10										
	0	1st	2nd	3rd	4th	5th	6th	7th	8th	9th

Number of Readings

Summary of Readings

Date	Reading	WPM	Date	Reading	WPM	Date	Reading	WPM

Figure 8.15
Assessment of Children's Reading Rate

Developing Literacy for Informational Text in Fluent Readers and Writers

Narrative text is fundamentally different than expository text. Two major differences discussed in previous chapters are the way that fiction and nonfiction texts are written; that is, the structure of the text. Another significant difference is the contents within the fiction and nonfiction. A further consideration is the assumption about stories: Stories are prominent in our culture, and children, having heard many stories, have developed a schema for story. Because of their schema for stories, children can follow them when they listen to them, read them, or write them. They use their knowledge of stories to reconstruct a story after reading one (Wells, 1986). Therefore, many teachers feel that the beginner readers learn how to decode faster and easier with fiction over narrative text. Yet young children do show a developing interest for informational books, those that are written with expository text features. Research demonstrates that children understand nonfiction as well as stories. As early as kindergarten, children have shown a preference for informational text over narrative (Pappas, 1993). Therefore, effective teachers use what they know from children's interests and research to help their students learn from informational text.

Benefits of Using Informational Books with Young Children

Informational books include a vast genre that encompasses true stories—textbooks, references, maps, newspapers, magazines, Web sites, biographies, autobiographies, reports, journals, and so on. There are interesting pieces of information with new concepts and ideas to be learned as well as the specialized vocabulary and graphics that depict all sorts of information. In spite of their rich contents, many of the literacy classrooms find little room for exemplary nonfiction (Moss, Leone, & Dipillo, 1997). Researchers made a case for promoting fluency in reading informational text. They found that the more children and adults read nonfiction, the greater an increase in their vocabulary knowledge, verbal fluency, spelling, knowledge of general information as well as history and literature (Cunningham & Stanovich, 1997, 1998).

Prereading Strategies for Informational Text

Anticipation guides. The anticipation guide is a prereading strategy that forecasts to children what they will be reading so that they reflect on or anticipate the text. Developed by Herber (1978), the anticipation guide engages children in their reading by helping them to focus on the major ideas or concepts in the text. The teacher develops a set of statements and asks the children to think about them. Then they agree or disagree with each statement based upon their prior knowledge as well as background experiences related to the text. Their response to the statement encourages discussion around the topic(s) to be read.

Head and Readence (1992) suggest that one of the major contributions of using the anticipation guide as a prereading strategy is that it identifies *misconceptions* that children have prior to their reading. Misconceptions may be incorrect notions or beliefs that children have related to conceptual knowledge. A common misconception that children have is "clouds are soft and made of cotton." Knowledge of children's misconceptions enable teachers to correct them while preparing children for reading the text. Further, because each statement in the anticipation guide encourages students to respond with an experience-based statement, lively discussions are promoted (Readance, Bean, & Baldwin, 2000).

Procedures for Developing and Using an Anticipation Guide

1. Identify the concepts within the text that the students will be reading.
2. Identify the children's personal beliefs about the concepts within the text.
3. Develop general statements about the concepts within the text and the children's personal beliefs that will serve as the anticipation guide. Each statement should have the following qualities:
   - They should reflect children's beliefs prior to their reading the text.
   - Their beliefs within each statement should be challenged and changed through their reading.
   - Some statements need to be aligned to children's personal experiences as well as concepts to be read in the text.
4. Write the statements in the anticipation guide on a transparency for an overhead projector or on the chalkboard.
5. Engage children in a discussion about what will be read through the use of the statements in the anticipation guide by asking them to agree or disagree with each statement. Each response should be supported by a reason.

After children respond to the statements in the anticipation guide, they read the text. They return to each statement and discuss it further. Some statements may need more clarification through discussion than others. Teachers may use minilessons to clarify ideas or address children's misconceptions.

Questioning the Author (QtA) Strategy. Whereas the **Questioning the Author (QtA) Strategy** (Beck, McKeown, Hamilton, & Kucan, 1997) encourages students to read with questions in their minds, it is an approach "for text-based instruction that is designed to facilitate building understanding of text ideas" (p. 5). Beck and KcKeown (1999) indicate that when readers are actively engaged in text and have a sense of the world, there is an intense impact on their comprehending of what they are reading. QtA strategy assumes that the meaning of the text is somewhere between what readers know and what the author writes. Very often, the author does not explain everything to the audience, assuming that the readers already know something about the content within the text. This may lead to confusion for some readers who may not have prior knowledge of the topic. Therefore, the purpose of the strategy is to train the readers to question the author in terms of what the author meant to say in the text. Such questions encourage children's active reading as they think through the text. In another sense, children are constructing meaning as they go beyond the words of the author to understand the passage. Through the use of QtA, the readers' conceptual knowledge and comprehension of what is read are developed, because the strategy encourages them to consider the more sophisticated aspects of the text to which they respond.

Flynn (2002) used QtA strategy with third-grade boys and found that not only did students' questions about the text increase during discussions but also the types of questions that they raised changed dramatically. Children began to ask questions that promoted higher order thinking. Most compelling among the findings were the effects that the use of the QtA strategy had on students with special learning needs. Although all students' comprehension improved, students with special needs demonstrated greater gains in comprehension scores on both standardized measures as well as on an informal assessment measure—the retelling procedure.

Procedure for the QtA Strategy

PLANNING THE LESSON

- The teacher prepares for the use of the QtA strategy by reading the children's text to identify ideas and concepts that may be confusing to younger and less-skilled readers. This is a key feature of the planning stage for the teacher because each group of children is quite different, bringing their prior knowledge, skills, and interests to the topic. The teacher decides the major ideas and the problems the students may encounter while they figure out the meaning of the ideas in the text.
- Each text is different; therefore, the teacher segments the texts into areas that are natural to stop for a discussion. Within each segment, there should be a major idea that will promote a discussion for clarifying meaning of the text. Thus, segmenting text means "determining where to stop reading to initiate and develop discussion toward construction of meaning" (Beck et al., 1997, p. 53).
- The next step in planning the lesson involves developing the questions. Unlike traditional questions used by teachers to determine how much and what the student remembered after reading, the questions that are used in the QtA strategy are meant to promote discussion and to engage children in thinking about the text. Therefore, the authors of the strategy refer to the questions as **queries.** The heart of the strategy is the query used to promote understanding. The three types of queries identified below will aid the teacher in promoting an active discussion:
  - **Initiating queries** are prompt questions to make the ideas within the text public to launch a discussion. For example: What is the author trying to say? What is the author's message?
  - **Follow-up queries** are proposed at getting at the ideas within the text. The goal is to facilitate students in making connections with the ideas, which is needed to construct meaning around the text. For example: What does the author mean here? Does the author explain this clearly?
  - **Narrative queries** are the third type of questions posed. Although the first two types are used with expository text, the third type is especially designed for narrative text. Such questions are aligned to the structure of narrative to include the elements of setting, problem, goals, events, resolution, and theme. For example, a query that relates to a story character might be: What did the author tell about the character in the beginning of the story, and does the author tell you more later on?

IMPLEMENTING THE LESSON

- The teacher and children are seated in a circle. Each has a copy of the book that will be read.
- The role of the teacher is to *use queries during the reading* to facilitate children's understanding. The teacher has planned for the reading and the dis-

cussions and knows the kinds of queries that need to be asked. However, there are times during the lesson when the children will inform the teacher about what they know or do not know related to the text. The flexible teacher knows to take an *instructional detour.* That is, the teacher makes a decision to modify the lesson on the spot to address the developmental needs of the children.

- The teacher provides *an introduction to the text* that the children will be reading. Children are motivated and prepared to read through a brief introduction where the teacher helps the children make connections to the text.
- The teacher encourages the children to read the first segment of the text. When they have completed the reading, the discussion begins. The initiating queries posed by the teacher open the discussion. Follow-up queries are used to help children "get at the meaning of ideas" not clarified by the author. As the teacher and children engage in questioning the author through the discussion, the teacher makes a decision to close the discussion and move to the second segment when he feels confident about the students' understanding of the text.
- The teacher and students continue reading and discussing the text guided by the queries.

Using QtA strategy with children offers promising results. For one, children begin to understand that many times authors write texts that are not clear, and authors may make errors in their descriptions of ideas by simply failing to mention important pieces of information. Children begin to understand that they are not powerless when they fail to understand a passage on its first read. They know they can go back to question the author's writing to try to gain meaning from the text. A second benefit for using this strategy with young readers and writers is that they begin to think like authors. The results may carry over to their own writing in trying to state their ideas clearly for the benefit of their readers. Finally, strategic readers read with questions in their minds. Using the QtA strategy fosters strategic reading in students.

Developing self-monitoring strategies in children. One of the characteristics of strategic readers is they can monitor their own reading. As children become efficient learners, they develop a number of cognitive skills. One such skill is the ability of children to monitor their own learning and thinking, a metacognitive skill. Metacognition is thinking about your own learning; it is knowing when you know and when you do not know, and knowing what to do about it. Metacognitive strategies are extremely important, especially as children advance through the grades where their learning becomes more reliant on the textbook.

The purpose of the **SMART strategy** (Vaughan & Estes, 1986) is to help children think about their own reading—that is, to help them think about how much they really understood while reading the text. The assumption is that strategic readers recognize when they understand and do not understand and have a plan to deal with it. Teachers may use strategies that foster and develop metacognitive skills in young readers and writers. Below is a procedure for using the SMART strategy with younger students:

- ***Read:*** The teacher directs the children to read a short selection, one or two paragraphs. Children think about the meaning of the selection they read. If they understand the paragraph, they place a sticky note with a check mark **(✓)** on it next to the paragraph. For the paragraphs that they do not understand, they put a sticky note with a question mark **(?)** on it next to the paragraph.

- **Retell:** After reading the selection, children are asked to go to the first paragraph with a check mark and retell it in their own words, using a brief summary. If large sticky notes are used, children may write a one-sentence summary on it. Teachers check each summary statement for accuracy.
- **When I just don't know:** Children are then asked to go to the paragraphs that are marked with a question mark. The teacher works with individual children to identify the areas of difficulty by asking the following questions:
  - Is there a word that you do not understand? How can you find the meaning of the word?
  - Is there a sentence in the paragraph that may be especially difficult to understand? Is it the language in the sentence that causes difficulty?
  - Is there an idea in the paragraph that you never heard about? What can you do to understand this new idea?
- **Explain and get help:** The teacher asks each child, after targeting the areas of difficulty, to explain in her own words what is the cause of the problem. They work together to identify specific ways for the children to get help when they do not understand the text. These might include asking a friend for the meaning of the word or using a dictionary for further clarification; rereading the sentence one more time, and then reading it to a friend and talking about the meaning, and looking up the word in the glossary.

Developing self-monitoring strategies does not happen in one lesson. The SMART strategy can work only if the teacher uses demonstrations and think-alouds with the children to present each aspect of the procedure. Although young children continue to benefit from the support of their teacher, the advantages of developing metacognitive skills early in their literacy development are many. When children in the primary and elementary grades do not comprehend what they have read and when they do not have self-monitoring skills, they are likely to dismiss the text as being beyond their understanding. Additionally, children who fail to comprehend text may develop negative strategies that interfere with their learning and take a long time to remediate.

Developing Informational Literacy With Technology and Inquiry Practices

How should technology be used to support literacy and learning in today's classroom? Technology is such an essential mediator for accessing information, and its role in the classroom can no longer be overlooked. A natural fit for the effective use of technology is in an inquiry-based classroom. Both concepts—technology and inquiry—are powerful tools that may be integrated to foster understanding and learning, thus should not be overlooked. Research has demonstrated that inquiry projects supported by technologies affect students' learning outcomes in positive ways (Owens, Hester, & Teale, 2002).

Let us begin to explore the concept of inquiry. One of the greatest natural resources that teachers most often waste is the constant stream of questions that are submitted by young children. Eager to learn and overflowing with energetic questions, children blurt out: "How long will it take that duck egg to open? I saw the moon last night, are we moving around it? I was wondering . . . will the dinosaurs ever come back to Earth?" It is unfortunate that as children get older the questions cease. In the sixth grade, such questions are a rarity. These types of questions are the "natural resources" in the world of learning and research. Inventors follow their questions to answers and solutions. It is the authentic questions of children that generate inquiry-based learning. In inquiry projects, children's interests and curiosity drive learning. Why does children's natural quest for learning fade; why do their questions stop coming? Traditional curriculum is designed where the questions come from the teacher and the children provide the answers. However, "two people cannot have a dialogue with each other if only one of them is asking the questions and demanding all the answers" (Copenhaver, 1993, p.6). Genuine dialogue is prerequisite in constructing knowledge (Wells & Chang-Wells, 1992). Therefore, inquiry-based approaches provide a context that engages children in their learning by tapping their curiosity and quest for learning new ideas.

Inquiry approaches further develop informational literacy by connecting children to authentic reading and writing. Harvey (2002) asserts "nonfiction is the genre most likely to spur children's passion and wonder for learning" (p. 12). She continues that teachers can promote inquiry and lead children to deeper learning and understanding by doing the following:

- Sharing their own passions and wonder about the real world
- Surrounding children with compelling nonfiction of every type and form
- Matching the reading to the writing
- Emphasizing short text for nonfiction reading and writing instruction and practice
- Engaging in the inquiry process ourselves—modeling instruction, showing our thinking, demonstrating how we do things, and giving our students time to practice
- Building long blocks of time for children to explore their thoughts and questions, to read text of their choice, to research topics of interest and to practice reading and writing strategies (pp. 13–14)

Inquiry-based curriculum demand an extended time period for planning. Part of the planning needs to focus on the developmental needs of young children to meet the benchmarks within their literacy stage. In addition, the teacher needs to be concerned about the mandated district curriculum. One suggestion for approaching inquiry learning is to start small. Begin with one strategy that addresses both the developmental needs of all children as well as the curriculum needs. The **Inquiry Chart (I-Chart)** is a good place to begin, because it helps students to generate meaningful questions that may be used to focus on research and organize their writing.

Inquiry Charts

By now, most teachers are very familiar with the K-W-L (what I know, what I want to know, and what I learned) strategy. The I-Chart (Hoffman, 1992) is a great follow-up to the K-W-L chart. In the I-Chart (see Figure 8.16), the children learn to generate questions around a topic of exploration, they use what they know about the topic to answer some of the questions, and they explore different sources to use in doing research on self-generated questions.

Procedure for Using I-Charts

- Together select a topic familiar to the students. Think of the questions that children ask, their topics of interest, and the curriculum for the grade.
- Discuss the topic with the children. You may wish to do a read-aloud of an informational text related to the topic. Work with the children to develop about three to four questions that will provide them with direction for inquiry into the topic area.

Topic: Pilgrims	**Q 1:** ***Who were the Pilgrims?***	**Q 2:** ***Why did they leave their homes?***	**Q 3:** ***Who were some famous Pilgrims?***	**Q 4:** ***Where did they come from and where did they settle?***	**Other Interesting Facts**	**New Questions**
Source: Books						
Source: Magazines and news articles						
Source: Web sites						
Source: Expert on the topic						
Source: Media						
Summaries:						

Figure 8.16
I-Chart for Topic "Pilgrims Coming to America"

- **Model the use of the I-Chart:**
  - Provide each child with a blank I-Chart.
  - Have an enlarged I-Chart on paper along with markers on which to record responses.
  - **Show children the organization of the I-Chart:**
    - Indicate where to record the topic of study.
    - Indicate where to record each of the questions related to the topic they want to explore.

- Discuss each question at length focusing on what source would be most helpful in finding the information. Include technology as a major source for information. Use newspapers and magazines as sources when they are appropriate. If there is an expert on the topic, consider a group interview.
- Brainstorm for information that students already know on the topic. Demonstrate where to place that information. When children offer information about a topic, let them determine which of the questions on the I-Chart that their facts answer, writing it in the appropriate box. For information that does not fit the questions, place it under "Other Interesting Facts" category.
- Assign children to small cooperative groups, and let each group research one question.
- Provide students with multiple sources of information on the topic: books, maps, lists of Web sites, magazines, newspaper articles, illustrations, charts, and so on.
- Demonstrate to the children how to use their question as a guide to find their information by modeling to the children how a question may direct them to the appropriate information and lead them away from irrelevant facts.
- As children read the material and discuss it in small groups, help them to record the facts on the I-Chart.
- Children may find that there are new questions that need to be asked. Help them to develop new questions for research. At the conclusion, children should look at each question and the information generated by the question. Have them synthesize it to form a summary statement. Students will write their summary statements at the bottom of the I-Chart under each question.
- Direct the children to write about the main topic of research. Each question may be transformed into a paragraph. The details will come from the answers to the questions.

The I-Chart shown in Figure 8.16 is for the third grade. It is incomplete. Complete the I-Chart for use with children at the fluent stage of literacy. Find informational books, Web sites, magazine articles, and other sources for each question.

In summary, helping young children to reach the benchmarks for the literacy stage of reading and writing should be an important goal of the balanced literacy program. Indeed, it may be thought of as the target of the primary grades. To be able to decode words and read with expression is only one aspect of fluency. Children at the fluent stage of literacy development read with meaning, engage in lively and logical discussions about text, and are literate thinkers whose ideas are readily expressed in writing. We hope that the instructional and assessment strategies found in this chapter will provide readers with a basis for a balanced literacy program for children moving into the fluent stage of development.

Discussion Questions and Activities

1. Work with a child who is at the fluent stage of literacy development. Select one aspect of reading fluency to measure and compare the child's fluency over several oral readings.
2. Select a piece of children's literature appropriate for teaching reading at the fluent stage. Prepare questions that facilitate children's making connections: (a) personal

connections, (b) text connections, and (c) world connections.

3. Observe a primary classroom during mathematics, social studies, or science lesson. Describe the possibilities for integrating reading and writing instruction within the lesson.

Additional Web Sites

Potato Hill Poetry Online
http://www.potatohill.com
This site provides creative teaching ideas including a regular "poem of the week."

International Reading Association
http://www.reading.org/publications/rt/rteacherdirections.html
RTEACHER is the official listserv for readers of *The Reading Teacher.* Members participate in online discussions about issues of literacy and technology.

American Library Association
http://www.ala.org
The ALA Web site provides an annotated list of notable children's videos to assist in the selection process.

Additional Readings

Ada, A. F. (2003). *Magical encounter: Latino children's literature in the classroom.* Boston: Allyn & Bacon.

Beck, I. L., McKeown, M. G., Hamilton, R. L., & Kucan, L. (1997). *Questioning the author: An approach for enhancing student engagement with text.* Newark: DE: International Reading Association.

Blevins, W. (2001). *Building fluency: Lessons and strategies for reading success.* New York: Scholastic.

Daniels, H. (2001). *Looking into literature circles.* Portland, ME: Stenhouse.

Dorn, L. J., & Soffos, C. (2001). *Shaping literate minds: Developing self-regulated learners.* Portland, ME: Stenhouse.

Hill, B. C., Noe, K. L. S., & Johnson, N. J. (2001). The literature circles resource guide. Norwood, MA: Christopher-Gordon.

Hoyt, L. *Make it real: Strategies for success with informational tests.* Portsmouth, NH: Heinemann.

Miller, D. (2002). *Reading with meaning: Teaching comprehension in the primary grades.* Portland, ME: Stenhouse.

Opitz, M. F., & Rasinski, T. V. (1998). *Goodbye round robin: 25 effective oral reading strategies.* Portsmouth, NH: Heinemann.

Routman, R. (2002). *Reading essentials: The specifics you need to teach reading well.* Portsmouth, NH: Heinemann.

Smith, P. G. (Ed.). (2001). *Talking classrooms: Shaping children's learning through oral language instruction.* Newark, DE: International Reading Association.

Szymusiak, K., & Sibberson, F. (2001). *Beyond leveled books: Supporting transitional readers in grades 2–5.* Portland, ME: Stenhouse.

Additional Children's Literature

Aardema, V. (1997). *Anansi does the impossible! An Ashanti tale.* New York: Atheneum.

Alphin, E. M. (1996). *A bear for Miquel.* New York: HarperCollins.

Bunting, E. (1997). *December.* Orlando, FL: Harcourt.

Clymer, E. (1947). *The trolley car family.* New York: Scholastic.

Danziger, P. (1995). *Amber Brown goes fourth.* New York: Putnam.

DePaola, T. (1973). *Charlie needs a cloak.* New York: Scholastic.

Fritz, J. (1993). *Just a few words Mr. Lincoln.* New York: Grossett & Dunlap.

George, J. C. (1997). *Arctic son.* Hyperion.

Kitchen, B. (1992). *Somewhere today.* Cambridge, MA: Candlewick Press.

Louie, Ai-Ling (1982). *Yeh-Shen: A Cinderella story from China.* New York: Philomel.

Penner, L. R. (1996). *Twisters.* New York: Random House.

Wroble, L. A. (1997). *Kids in colonial times.* Rosen.

CHAPTER 9

The Role of Phonics in Literacy Development

Chapter Overview

No one will argue that one of the most important functions of the school is to teach young children how to read and write. In the process of facilitating each child's journey to a literate life, educators view learning phonics as playing a primary role. Two polls taken with parents and teachers validate this assumption, both having demonstrated the priority that reading plays in education. When Hart Research Associates polled parents in 1992, 62% indicated that reading was the most important skill their children needed to learn. In 1994 the Chrysler Foundation polled teachers with a similar question; 70% had the same response. Indeed, the momentum is gaining ground. A decade later, teaching all children to read by the end of the third grade has become a national priority. Therefore, giving children access to knowledge through learning to read must be viewed, at the very least, as part of every school's mission.

As you read this chapter, reflect on the following topics:

- The relationship between phonics and reading and writing: How does the knowledge of phonics help children to read and write?
- What phonic concepts and skills children at the emergent, early, and fluent stages of literacy development acquire and need to develop for successful reading and writing
- The stages of phonological development and how teaching and learning differ at each of the stages
- The "layers of learning" in acquiring alphabet knowledge
- Sight word development

The Role of Phonics in Achieving Academic Success

Early reading is critical to a child's learning life. The lack of good reading skills can have severe consequences. Children who are poor readers at the end of the first grade are most likely to be poor readers by the fourth grade (Juel, 1988). Stanovich (1986) refers to the negative effects on overall academic performance of not knowing how to read by the end of the first grade as the **Matthew Effects:** the rich get richer, and the poor get poorer. To understand the Matthew Effects, compare children who are fluent readers when they enter the second grade with those who cannot read. The children who are independent readers learn more in each of the content areas such as social studies and science. By reading children's literature in a variety of subject areas and books with increased difficulty levels that naturally have more information, children are learning about exciting ideas, increasing their vocabularies, and advancing in literacy skills. Simply put, young fluent readers are "getting richer with information," and at the same time, they are developing their literacy skills through frequent use and practice. Conversely, children entering the second grade who are struggling to read are denied access to information in texts because of their inability to read more challenging books that expose them to new ideas. With their lack of proficiency in reading and learning, their self-esteem and their motivation to achieve in school also decrease.

Why does phonics knowledge play a critical role in preventing failure for most young readers?

Children who are classified as readers and writers with disabilities often have difficulty grasping basic word identification and spelling skills (Aaron & Joshi, 1992). These skill deficits are due to children's limited understanding of the phonological and orthographic structures of words (Levy & Carr, 1990). This means that children who find it difficult to read lack the required phonic skills needed for decoding unknown words. Even when readers with disabilities begin to develop a *memory for sight words*—the ability to recognize words by sight without decoding them—their phonic skills are usually underdeveloped (Stahl, 1998). Clearly, beginning readers need well-developed phonological skills when faced with unknown words. When children are reading new words in text, they need to use skills in phonics; that is, make letter–sound associations. With efficient decoding strategies, reading becomes effortless (Adams & Henry, 1997). It seems clear that learning the correspondence between letters and sounds—or phonics—is keenly important for young children learning to read. Research also suggests that direct instruction in phonics during the early years may prevent needless cases of reading disabilities.

From the discussion above, we can understand why teachers in early childhood classrooms maintain a goal that is clear and direct—to help children become fluent readers as early as possible. Therefore, this chapter focuses on *phonics instruction in a well-balanced literacy program* for the young children. As in previous chapters, we integrate instruction and assessment. Beginning our discussion with the background of children's *development of phonological knowledge,* we then present phonics instruction and activities for a balanced literacy program in an early childhood classroom. Because assessment and instruction need to be aligned, we suggest ways to track children's progress in phonological development.

Teaching and Learning Phonics

Clearly, it is the early childhood teachers who are challenged with "getting children started" in their reading lives. For most of these teachers, one key to a good start in literacy is building a base of phonological knowledge and the skills for its use. As you have read in Chapter 2 and other previous chapters, prior to their entering school, many children have begun to develop numerous *concepts about print.* To review, when children possess concepts about print, they know that books contain stories that may be read and listened to over and over, that the pages contain printed words, and that the words are made of letters. As parents, caregivers, and teachers read with children, their concepts about print expand to include associations between letters and sounds, an aspect of phonological awareness and alphabet knowledge. Therefore, we can understand how children's developing concepts about print facilitate their process of learning to decode words. Effective teachers are responsive to children's *prior knowledge* of books and print. They are especially cautious not to assume that all children have similar literacy experiences and interests; therefore, they know there will be varying levels in children's phonological development.

Learning the Alphabetic Principle Is Key in Phonological Development

When young children begin to use their knowledge of sounds and letters to read words in print, they are **decoding.** Decoding is generally thought of as sounding out the printed word into the spoken word. Therefore, at the emergent and early stages of reading and writing, teachers are involved in helping children learn how to use the alphabetic principle. As you recall, the alphabetic principle refers to the written letter or group of letters (grapheme) that represent a speech sound (phoneme). Children need to have some fundamental concepts and skills about print before formal instruction on how to apply phonics to decode words. In *The Portrait of First Graders Acquiring the Alphabetic Principle,* you will read a short lesson in phonics that is embedded in a guided reading lesson.

Thinking About a Phonics Lesson

Children's first lessons in phonics for learning how to decode words must be built on many concepts about print they already know. Note that the children in Brian's guided reading group have a similar level of phonological development. Brian would not be successful if the children did not know the letter names. The children also needed to know the sound or sounds that a letter or group of letters make. Alphabet knowledge is critical to instruction in phonics for decoding words. When Brian asked for the children to read *sat* and then *-at* in that word, the children demonstrated they knew words contain smaller sounds (phonemes) within them. The foundation for this concept lies in phonemic awareness. Remember that phonemic awareness relates to the speech sounds in spoken words. For children to decode or to map sounds onto the printed words, they first need to be able to grasp the basic understandings

As you read this brief lesson, think about the portrait of the children in Brian's small instructional group: What do they already know related to phonological knowledge and what do they need to know? Identify Brian's learning outcomes for the students.

Portrait of First Graders Acquiring the Alphabetic Principle

Brian sits at the table for guided reading with a group of eight children who are at a similar level of phonological development. After he finishes the story walk with the children, he conducts a word study or a mini-lesson in phonics that is related to the new words that the children will see in print. Brian begins instruction by asking the group to read the word *sat,* a word that the children already know. He points to the letter cluster or pattern *-at* in the word and the children read it in unison. Brian then introduces the consonant blend *spl-* to the children. He says each letter, and as he points to each letter, he slowly stretches out the sound that each letter makes. He then asks the children to do the same. Brian uses plastic magnetic letters to demonstrate how to decode an unknown word by using part of a word they know. He demonstrates how to put together two parts of a word, *spl-* with *-at,* to make a new word. The children read the new word by recognizing the part *(-at)* in it they already know. Brian finishes the mini-lesson by talking with the children about the meaning of the new word, *splat.* After the mini-lesson in phonics, Brian resumes the guided reading lesson.

in phonemic awareness—that words contain sounds, that sounds may *blend* into a word, that a word may be *segmented* into its smallest sounds, and so on. In Brian's lesson, the specific phonic knowledge the children learned related to the sound of a consonant blend, *spl-*. When Brian told the children and demonstrated how to use a word they know (*sat*) to read a word they do not know (*splat*), he taught them a **word-solving strategy,** using words you know to decode unfamiliar words. Brian also pointed to *-at* in the word *sat*, helping children to see patterns in words that they can use to decode unfamiliar words with similar letter clusters or patterns. Because he explained and showed them the strategy, he used *direct or explicit instruction*. Brian realized the strategy he taught to the children does not ensure that children will learn and use it. He provides the children with ways to practice their strategy, and he will monitor their use of the skill that the children were taught. Children's practice of this word-solving strategy will lead to their constructing more knowledge of its use. This approach to teaching is *indirect or implicit instruction*.

Strategic readers use a number of different ways to figure out a word they do not know. Helping children learn how to use varied word-solving strategies is key to helping them become fluent readers.

Therefore, instruction in phonics, like all teaching and learning, must build upon what children already know. *Phonics is developmental*: Certain concepts, skills, and strategies for using letters and letter sounds are learned before others and are connected to what is already known. As children learn a decoding strategy, its frequent use and application within different contexts and on more difficult text will further develop the strategy. When the word-solving strategy is fully developed or learned, its use will become effortless.

We can, therefore, think about the development of phonics in children as a dynamic progression through the acquisition of various phonic skills or word-solving strategies for decoding unfamiliar words. This means that the building of phonological knowledge is more than a linear progression of learning a series of small pieces of information about decoding. Rather, like all strategy learning, it is a multidimensional complex process. In acquiring word-solving strategies, children learn the multiple facets to a strategy through use and practice of it in a variety of literacy contexts.

Phonics Is Developmental

Stages of Phonological Development

Throughout this text, we have referred to the three stages of literacy development—*emergent, early*, and *fluent.* These three stages refer to broad literacy concepts. When teachers observe children's decoding as they read and their spelling as they write, they may use another useful classification related to their development of phonological knowledge. Children's *stages of phonological development* help the teacher to focus on a specific area of literacy concepts needed to decode and to spell. Indeed, these stages are aligned to the broader stages of literacy development—emergent, early, and fluent—as aligned in Figure 9.1. As with all stages in learning, growth in phonological development is complex and dynamic (Gunning, 2001); therefore, the stages provide a rough guide to track children's progress in this aspect of their reading development. Just as with other ways to categorize developmental benchmarks, one must be cautious in their use. At times it may seem that children are fully developed on a set of learning behaviors and have reached the benchmarks within the particular stage. However, oftentimes for one or two literacy skills or behaviors, a child may then seem to have lost his level of achievement of that skill. This is to be expected. Following is a description of the stages of phonological development.

The logographic stage. Within this stage of phonological development, children do not use their knowledge of letters and sounds to decode words. Oftentimes, when we observe young children reading predictable texts, it does seem that what they are doing is sounding out or decoding words when they read. However, children who are logographic readers do not decode or sound out words. According to Ehri (1994), logographic readers do not map sounds onto print; rather, they use the nonverbal visual cues from the printed word to make an association with the spoken word. For example, they may see the word *look* and associate the two letters *oo* in the middle of the word with eyes that "look" or "see" to remember this word. A child who is at the logographic stage is an early emergent reader. Within this stage, children are learning about letters and sounds as they develop phonemic awareness; they have yet to acquire the alphabetic principle, the ability to map sounds onto words to decode them.

At this stage, teachers support children's development by providing them with a strong foundation in phonemic awareness as well as alphabet knowledge—recognizing uppercase and lowercase letters along with knowing individual letter sounds. The

Emergent Stage	***Early Stage***		***Fluent Stage***	***Advanced Fluent Stage***
Logographic	***Alphabetic Stage***	***Word-Pattern***	***Multisyllabic***	***Morphemic-Analysis***
• Reads a few words through memory **(logographic reading)** • Knows letter names • Recognizes the uppercase and most lowercase letters • Knows sound matching • Knows sound isolation • Knows sound blending • Knows rhyming words • Knows sound isolation • Knows sound substitution • Knows sound segmentation	• Uses letter–sound relationships to decode words **(alphabetic reading)** • Begins to use initial and then final consonants to decode words • Begins to use word parts to decode it • Increases the number of sight words recognized • Knows all the sounds of letters	• Uses patterns to decode • Uses multiple word-solving strategies (**phonic skills**) for decoding words • Uses short vowels with consonant blends or diagraphs *(**dr**op, **ch**at)* to decode words • Uses final markers in words (*mak**e***) to decode words • Uses vowel diagraphs (*tr**ai**n, st**ea**m*) to decode words • Uses the controlled *r* vowel pattern *(b**ar**k, j**ar**)* • Increases rate of reading slowly • Has an increased growth of recognition for sight words	• Shows ease and fluency in the use of multiple word-solving strategies to decode new words • Shows progress to decode more difficult words with more syllables: • Begins with easy inflectional syllable patterns (*jump**ing***); • Moves to compound words (*firehouse*), then to multisyllabic words that incorporate patterns already known (*women*) • Learns patterns that occur only in multisyllabic words (*action*). • Reading rate and fluency increases • Makes a rapid and increased growth of recognition for sight words • Is aware of syllable junctures	• Learns to decode words that are not in listening vocabulary • Uses prefixes, suffixes, and root words to derive meaning from words • Begins to see semantic or meaning connections in words (***sign** and **sign**ature*) • Demonstrates an increased interest in words • Benefits from learning the origin of word roots • Learns to apply prefixes to root words to change their meaning • Learns the limitations of prefixes to determine the meaning of an unknown word

Figure 9.1
Comparison Between Literacy Stages and Stages in Phonological Development

children learn beginning and ending sounds in words. Typically, children in kindergarten and at the beginning months of first grade are in the logographic stage of phonological development.

The alphabetic stage. At the alphabetic stage of reading, the child begins to use a more systematic approach to decoding the printed word. The child at this stage is learning to use the alphabetic principle—the relation between spoken sounds and letters or combination of letters. It is clear to the teacher who observes the child learning to map sounds onto printed words the importance of a strong foundation in phonemic awareness—the understanding that speech is composed of a series of individual sounds (Juel, Griffith, & Gough, 1986; Yopp, 1992). To young readers, entering the alphabetic stage is the hallmark of reading: As they start to decode unfamiliar words, children begin their journey to independent reading. The phonic strategy that children use widely at this stage is the "sounding out," letter-by-letter approach to decode unfamiliar words. Many children in the first grade, at the beginning months, embark on this stage of phonological development. Children will need to learn more efficient word-solving strategies as their phonological knowledge develops.

The word pattern stage. We read that at the alphabetic stage, children learn the consistent relationships between individual letters and sounds. It is within the word pattern stage that children advance to an understanding of the consistency in the patterns in words that are derived from word parts. That is, children learn to *detect familiar word parts*—such as *-at, -ay, -en*—and use them to decode unfamiliar words. Therefore, it is quite reasonable that children quickly advance in their phonological knowledge and its use at this stage.

What children need to learn at the word pattern stage is the sound of the beginning letter or cluster of letters—the **onset**—and the word pattern at the end of the word: the **rime**. Figure 9.2 shows an example of one word pattern with varying beginning letters, a word pattern often referred to as a word family—*at*—that teachers use frequently to help children see parts of words. They then use the word parts to decode unfamiliar words with the same word parts.

When children are learning onsets and rimes, teachers demonstrate how to find the small word pattern in the larger word, then how to put the onset together

ONSET *Initial letter(s)*	RIME *Word pattern*	WORD *Word families*
c	-at	cat
m	-at	mat
ch	-at	chat
p	-at	pat
r	-at	rat

Figure 9.2
Examples of Onsets and Rimes in Words

with the rime to decode the new word. Through this type of instruction, children learn an additional word-solving strategy to the sounding out strategy they have learned at the alphabetic stage. Many children in the middle of the first grade use word patterns to help them read unfamiliar words. Because children at this stage have an additional word-solving strategy to use when reading, they can decode more unknown words. This means that the time spent reading independently by children at the alphabetic stage increases. Further, more practice in reading provides children with greater exposure to print that will lead to an expanded sight word vocabulary.

The multisyllabic stage. At this stage, children are reading more difficult texts with longer, multisyllabic words. They are becoming proficient in using different word-solving strategies to decode unfamiliar words, and oftentimes, use more than one word-solving strategy to figure out an unknown word. When they are reading and come to a word they do not know, they will be able to draw upon varied sources of information and methods to go about decoding unknown words. They may think of the meaning of the surrounding text (semantic), or they may examine the word for sound–symbol relationships including word parts, onsets, rimes, and affixes. At this stage, children are beginning to use multiple word-solving strategies effortlessly.

Children within the multisyllabic stage are capable of reading books that have an increased difficulty level because they are reading longer words that contain more than one syllable. They learn to read multisyllabic words in a progression of lower to higher difficulty levels. Children in the earlier part of this stage begin to read such words that include the easier inflectional syllable patterns, such as *jump**ing***, *look**ing***, and *mak**ing***. They also read compound word patterns that include words like *doghouse, airplane, firehouse*, and *baseball.* Within this stage, children learn to read more varied multisyllabic words that incorporate single-syllable patterns that they already know such as *manner, chatter*, and *butter*. They also read words with affixes—prefixes and suffixes—patterns that occur only in multisyllabic words such as ***trans**form*, ***in**form*, and ***trans**port**ation***. Children no longer rely on their first strategy of mapping sounds on words, letter by letter. Rather, they are scanning words for word patterns that they already know. Their rates of reading increase, as do their sight word vocabularies. Some children in this stage are at the end of the second grade and many are in the third grade.

The morphemic analysis stage. This stage begins in the fourth grade and continues throughout the lifetime of a reader and writer (Gunning, 2001). Readers of this textbook are in the morphemic analysis stage of phonological development. When you do not know a word that you are reading, most likely it will not be in your listening vocabulary, a word that you have never heard. Therefore, you will first examine it for *meaningful parts* rather than first decoding the word. Then you may sound out the word parts so that you may hear it.

A **morpheme** is the smallest unit of meaning in a word. Some words contain more than one morpheme. For example, words with one morpheme are *cat, happy,* and *love.* These morphemes are called **free morphemes** because they can stand alone as words. Another type of morpheme is **bound morphemes** because they

Children's learning of phonics is developmental; therefore, teachers need to consider children's development in preparing for phonics instruction.

are bound or attached to another morpheme. For example, bound morphemes are *re-*, *-ly*, and *-tion*. Bound morphemes must be attached to others to acquire their meaning such as *repay*, *quickly*, and *attention*.

Students in the morphemic analysis stage use prefixes, suffixes, and root words to derive meaning from unfamiliar words. If you did not know the word *psycholinguistic*, what are the morphemes within the word that would provide you with clues to figure out its meaning?

Planning for Systematic Phonics Instruction Guided by Children's Development

Although it is clear that children need systematic instruction in phonics—including word-solving strategies—to be successful readers and writers, the attributes for effective teaching and learning must be considered. Let us begin by reviewing some of the principles that guide all successful literacy instruction for young children and apply them to phonics instruction (see Figure 9.3).

- Have a systematic plan for teaching phonics throughout the year guided by children's phonological development and special needs.
- Be flexible in executing your plan.
- Build on the children's phonological knowledge by knowing each child's level of development.
- Use informal assessment throughout the year to track children's stages of phonological development, determining the benchmarks that they have reached.
- Use assessment results to prepare developmentally appropriate instruction.
- Do not depend on workbooks as a form of instruction. They may be useful for reinforcement, but remember that worksheets are not a teaching tool.
- Provide daily phonics instruction throughout the day, using mini-lessons that are fast paced and focused on a single skill or two.
- Use different models of teaching phonics and word-solving strategies including direct instruction, modeled instruction, and shared instruction.
- Be diligent about developing children's word-solving strategies alongside of teaching phonic knowledge.
- Provide time for the children to practice their newly acquired word-solving strategies on appropriate-leveled books.
- Provide authentic forms of practice for children to use their new word-solving strategies.
- Teach phonics in multiple contexts of reading and writing.
- Develop children's curiosity and excitement for new words.
- Think of writing and spelling as a vehicle to enhance phonic knowledge.
- Create a learning environment that fosters phonological knowledge and development.

Figure 9.3
Do's on the Teaching of Phonics

Phonemic Awareness: The Foundation of Phonics

Why Assess Phonemic Awareness?

Children's growth in phonemic awareness plays a critical role in their ability to decode new words. A growing body of research supports the strong correlation between a child's knowledge of the separate sounds in words and their learning how to read (Adams & Bruck, 1995; Beck & Juel, 1995; Foorman, 1995). Additional support from research by Stanovich (1991, 1992) shows that children who have low standardized scores in reading also have low phonemic awareness. Studies also reveal that direct instruction in the tasks related to phonemic awareness may be necessary for some children. Although many preschool and kindergarten teachers have paid attention to children's developing awareness for sounds in words, most have not engaged in explicit or direct instruction of phonemic awareness. These studies are among many that have provided the impetus to teachers to provide instruction and assessment for young children in monitoring and developing their phonemic awareness.

Because research has demonstrated such a strong connection between the knowledge of the phonemes and reading achievement, phonemic awareness ought to be included as an important part of the literacy program for young children. Many children may not need an intensive program in phonemic awareness tasks due to their rich language experiences. However, children who score consistently low on related tasks in phonemic awareness need special instruction. Without the ability to hear sounds in words, children will not benefit from developing and using word-solving strategies to decode unfamiliar words. Therefore, for some children, direct training in phonemic awareness will provide the foundation needed for decoding skills when they enter the alphabetic stage of phonological development.

In Part II on oral language development, we gave considerable attention to the development of phonemic awareness, providing direct instructional strategies as well as a variety of independent activities at all stages of literacy development. Therefore, in this chapter we will focus on a systematic approach to assess phonemic awareness. Assessing and monitoring children's development in phonemic awareness provide the teacher with a starting point in planning appropriate instruction.

Assessment of Phonemic Awareness

When children are involved in formal instruction in reading, it is critical that they have a strong foundation in phonemic awareness. As previously discussed, such knowledge ensures a foundation for their learning about phonics and the development of word-solving strategies. Especially for teachers in kindergarten and first grade who engage children in guided reading, it is crucial to know about areas of children's development related to phonemic awareness. Indeed, it is a required starting point in learning about children's literacy development. Using the assessment results, teachers may plan for instruction and for grouping children based on their development.

What follows is a set of assessment tools that the teacher may use to begin to determine the children's development of phonemic awareness. The areas of phonemic awareness that are assessed include the following:

- Rhyming words
- Segmenting words in sentences, in compound words, and in syllables

Student Name ____________ ***Grade*** ______ ***Age*** ______			
Teacher ____________ ***Examiner*** ____________ ***Date*** ______			
Rhyming Words: Examiner says: Today we will rhyme words. Remember, when words rhyme they sound like each other. *Cat* and *sat* rhyme so I will say, "Yes." Say the word *yes* to any two words you think rhyme, and say the word *no* to two words you think do not rhyme.			
tan, ran (yes)	______	**plate, late (yes)**	______
sock, tock (yes)	______	**clap, clock (no)**	______
help, flood (no)	______	**let, met (yes)**	______
Jill, hill (yes)	______	**said, jump (no)**	______
		Total # Correct	______
Segmenting Words in Sentences: Examiner says: You will listen to words in sentences. Each time I say a word, tap the pencil only once. Listen to me. "Today is Monday." (3 taps).			
______ **I ride on the bus. (5 taps)**			
______ **I have one brother and one sister. (7 taps)**			
______ **My name is very long. (5 taps)**			
______ **Today we will play in the gym. (7 taps)**			
______ **I can jump rope. (4 taps)**			
______ **How old are you? (5 taps)**			
		Total # Correct	______
Segmenting Compound Words: Examiner says: I will say long words that have two parts. Please say each part of the words. Listen while I say a word: *firehouse.* Now tell the two parts: *fire house.*			
Superman	______	***goldfish***	______
doghouse	______	***beehive***	______
hairbrush	______	***anything***	______
firefly	______	***bluebird***	______
bedroom	______	***backpack***	______
		Total # Correct	______

Figure 9.4
Student Profile of Phonemic Awareness Development

- Segmenting sounds in words: first sound, last sound, and each sound
- Blending compound words and syllables
- Phoneme identification

Assessment Procedures

Figure 9.4 contains a set of assessment tools with directions. As a teacher assesses a child, she uses the profile sheet to code each response as right or wrong and then tallies the number of correct responses. Whereas the number of correct responses

Segmenting Syllables: Examiner says: I will say long words that have one or more parts or syllables. This time listen to each word and then say and clap each part of the word. Listen while I say a word: *baby.* Now say and clap the parts you hear in the word *ba-by* (2 claps).

candle (2 claps)	______	**strawberry (3 claps)**	______
boy (1 clap)	______	**peanut (2 claps)**	______
father (2 claps)	______	**man (1 clap)**	______
elephant (3 claps)	______	**lady (2 claps)**	______
yellow (2 claps)	______	**mountain (2 claps)**	______
		Total # Correct	______

Segmenting First and Last Sounds: Examiner says: I will say a word. Listen to the word and say only the first sound. Listen while I say *cat.* The first sound is /c/. When the child has finished identifying the first sounds in words, continue to the last sounds. Now listen to the word for the last sound. The word is *cat.* The last sound is /t/.

First Sounds:		***Last Sounds:***	
1. sat (/s/)	______	**1. met (/t/)**	______
2. big (/b/)	______	**2. ran (/n/)**	______
3. not (/n/)	______	**3. sad (/d/)**	______
4. fun (/f/)	______	**4. miss (/s/)**	______
5. candle (/c/)	______	**5. hope (/p/)**	______
6. yellow (/y/)	______	**6. leaf (/f/)**	______
Total # Correct	______	**Total # Correct**	______

Segmenting All the Sounds Within a Word: Examiner says: I will say a word. Listen to the word and to each sound in the word. Then say each sound you hear. Listen while I say *cat.* I hear /c/, /a/, and /t/.

1. me (/m/ /e/)	______	**4. so (/s/ /o/)**	______
2. sit (/s/ /i/ /t/)	______	**5. pet (/p/ /e/ /t/)**	______
3. bike (/b/ /i/ /k/)	______	**6. game (/g/ /a/ /m/)**	______
		Total # Correct	______

Figure 9.4
Continued

Involving Families: The student profile of phonemic awareness development assessment may be shared with parents as a way of talking about the children's development in this aspect of literacy growth. The teacher may use the profile to provide specific ways that parents may offer assistance to their children based upon their areas of need.

provides information on a child's development of phonemic awareness, it is also important to look for patterns within the child's responses. Determining patterns within the child's responses helps the teacher to go beyond a *number* of right or wrong responses to determine areas of strengths and areas that need to be developed. The teacher may also look for answers to questions. For example, she may ask: "Maria had one wrong response within the rhyming words assessment strategy; what did she hear? I know that she knows the concept of rhyming, but why did she miss this one?" Asking questions like these forces the teacher to think more deeply about the child's learning needs.

Blending Compound Words and Syllables: Examiner says: I will say parts of a word. Listen to each word part. Then put the parts together to say one word. Listen while I say it: *Fruit cake. Fruitcake.*

Compound Words		***Syllables in Words***	
1. air plane	______	***1. can dle***	______
2. dog house	______	***2. bak ing***	______
3. door bell	______	***3. fas ter***	______
4. blue berry	______	***4. mo ther***	______
5. base ball	______	***5. boys***	______
6. bull dog	______	***6. child ren***	______
Total # Correct ______		**Total # Correct** ______	

Blending Phonemes: Examiner says: I will say some sounds. When you put them together they make a word. Listen to each sound, and then put them together to make a word. Listen: /c/ /a/ /t/. The word is *cat.*

1. b–e (be)	______	**4. m–o–p (mop)**	______
2. g–e–t (get)	______	**5. h–u–g (hug)**	______
3. h–a–nd (hand)	______	**6. b–u–n–ch (bunch)**	______
		Total # Correct ______	

Phoneme Deletion: Examiner says: I will say a word. Then I will say it without part of the word: *baking.* Now I will say it without *-ing. Bake.*

1. Say the word *carried.* Now say it without *–ed.* (carry) ______
2. Say the word *happy.* Now say it without *–py.* (hap) ______
3. Say the word *mat.* Now say it without *–t.* (ma) ______
4. Say the word *lamp.* Now say it without *–l.* (amp) ______
5. Say the word *boat.* Now say it without *–b.* (oat) ______
6. Say the word *return.* Now say it without *–turn.* (re) ______

Total # Correct ______

Figure 9.4
Continued

Alphabet Knowledge

One of the expectations that first-grade teachers have for beginning students is their knowledge of the alphabet. Throughout the school year, kindergarten teachers spend many hours developing letter knowledge with children using a wide variety of activities. Research has made a strong case for children's early acquisition of letter knowledge (Spear-Swerling & Sternberg, 1996). Adams (1990) points out that knowledge of the alphabet is a strong predictor of early reading. Further, Snow and Burns (1998) emphasize that among the many predictors to reading success, letter knowledge stands out as the strongest. Moreover, with the importance in letter recognition as an early predictor to reading success, the speed at which children can name letters and know their names is of equal importance. "By the end of kindergarten, children should be able to name most of the letters of the alphabet, no matter what order they come in, no matter if they are uppercase or lowercase. And they should do it quickly and effortlessly" (Burns & Snow, 1999, p. 78). What leads children to fluency in alphabet knowledge? The response is rather complex. Children's prior experiences with print used in multiple contexts lead to their ability to name letters. Practice with a wide variety of letter activities throughout the course of the year greatly increases children's fluency in letter naming as well as their knowledge of the sounds for each letter.

Alphabet knowledge includes

- Knowing the names of the letters
- Recognizing uppercase and lowercase letters both in and out of sequence
- Knowing the sounds of each letter
- Knowing how to write each letter

Kindergarten teachers take stock of children's letter recognition throughout the year; that is, they monitor children's alphabet knowledge through ongoing assessment. It is important for first-grade teachers to determine the children's letter recognition skills at the start of the school year. In this section, we will present ways to instruct and develop alphabet knowledge and monitor its development in young children.

Learning Letter Names, Letter Recognition, and Letter Sounds

The alphabet song. Many children enter kindergarten and even preschool knowing the names of the alphabet because they know how to sing "The Alphabet Song." Children enjoy the song, and it may be used in a number of different ways to help children connect the name of each letter with its visual representation. As children sing the song, let children take turns pointing to each letter as the letter is named in the song. Children like to act out the alphabet song holding cards with a letter on it and waving the letter name as they sing it. Another way to promote letter recognition is suggested by Cunningham (2000) who describes the use of "The Alphabet Song" when lining up to go someplace. The teacher passes out letter cards randomly, and as the song is sung, each child lines up in the order in which he holds the card.

ABC books. Alphabet books are an appealing way for children to learn letter names as well as the sounds that letters represent. Because a wide variety of alphabet books have become part of children's literature and because of the number of ABC books available, they are often used with older children who are at the emergent stage of literacy development (Chaney, 1993). Teachers should have a variety of alphabet books in the classroom library so that children may select them for independent reading. Children may even write their own ABC books if given the opportunity, or they may write a group alphabet book. Using a topic such as weather, food, or animals, each child selects a letter and creates a page in the group ABC book. The possibilities for using alphabet books are endless. What are some other ways that teachers may use alphabet books?

Using Technology: ABC Gulp (http://www.brainconnection.com/teasers/?main=bc/gulp) provides an activity on the Internet designed to help students practice letter–name knowledge.

Learning letters through games. There are many games that children may play to promote letter recognition for both uppercase and lowercase letters. Once children know most of the uppercase letters, have them learn the lowercase letters

Alphabet knowledge is development and begins when children are able to say the letters of the alphabet.

through matching with the uppercase letters. You may use two separate sets of index cards, each set a different color. Designate one set for the uppercase letters and the other set for the lowercase letters. With five children playing the game, pass out the lowercase letters. Randomly place one uppercase letter on the table so that all children see the letter and say it. They then look in their set for the matching lowercase letter and put them together.

Letter toss. An appealing game for children that provides practice with letter names and sounds is letter toss. On an 8 × 8-foot piece of paper or white sheet, make large boxes with a magic marker. In each box, write one set of the uppercase and lowercase letters in random order. Fill a cloth bag (a heavyweight plastic bag may be used) with beans and secure it so it will not break open. Give each child a turn to toss the bag into a box. The child should say the name of the letter and the sound that is associated with it. You may wish to keep a checklist of children with the letters they can name and letter sounds they know.

Bluebird redbird match. For a center time activity, have children match uppercase and lowercase letters. Divide a large piece of oak tag into 26 boxes, using it to make an alphabet board game. In each box, paste a picture of a bluebird and write an uppercase letter under its picture. For durability, laminate the oak tag board game. In a shoebox, have pictures of redbirds on small cards with lowercase letters written under the picture. The pictures can be laminated as well. The child pulls a lowercase letter card (the redbird card) from the shoebox, finds the matching uppercase letter (the bluebird box) on the game board, and places his redbird card on the bluebird card calling out the letter name.

Alphabet spin. On a large cardboard circle, write the 26 uppercase letters on its outer edge. Fasten a spinner in the center of the circle. On small cards, write the lowercase letters of the alphabet and place them on the table. Have children take turns, spinning the pointer so that it stops at an uppercase letter. The child says the letter and finds its match from the set of lowercase letters. For each letter the child names, he holds the letter indicating one point earned.

Alphabet snack time. Bring to class a large box of alphabet cereal for snack time. Place a napkin on each child's desk and a handful of cereal. Have the children sort the letters, name them, and count the letters in each pile (have them do this before they eat the cereal!). After children are finished sorting, naming, and counting, invite them to enjoy the snack.

Learning to write the letters. Children also learn the letter names by writing them. During guided writing or independent writing, children will try to spell words they do not know. At the emergent stage of literacy, the teacher encourages the use of invented spelling. Observing that the child cannot write the word, the teacher might prompt the child with the following:

Teacher: Do you know how the word begins? What is the first sound that you hear when you say the word *cat*?

Child: *Cat.* It begins with a /c/.

Teacher: Good. What letter stands for /c/?

Child: *C* says /c/.

Teacher: Very good. Can you write the letter *c?* Find it on your alphabet line.

Child: (The child points to the letter *c,* and writes the letters *c-a-t.*)

Teacher: That is very good. You know how to write the letters *c-a-t* in the word *cat.*

There are times when children know the initial sound in a word and the letter that stands for the sound, yet they do not know how to write the letter. Learning letters because of a specific need—for example, writing a story—is an intrinsic motivator. Thus, writing stories is an authentic context that provides children with an excellent motivation for learning letters.

Picture sorts. Pinnell and Fountas (1998, pp. 137–138) suggest sorting pictures as an ideal activity for children who are learning sounds. Primary-grade teachers should have many pictures for children. One source of pictures is magazines, and a second source is clip art software programs that provide a wide variety of pictures that can be accessed instantly. Cut out each picture and paste it on an index card. Children may sort the pictures using a variety of sound categories shown in Figure 9.5.

This type of activity is quite different from a worksheet where children circle the answer that is either right or wrong. A picture sort *engages children in active learning*, because they are required to tell why they have sorted the pictures into certain piles. When children are not familiar with the activity, the teacher should first

Sort By	Examples of Picture Sorts
• ***Initial or beginning sounds in words***	• ball, boys, box, bell • fire, fence, fork
• ***Final or ending sounds in words***	• bat, gait, eight, cat • hen, pan, phone, ten
• ***Medial or middle sounds in words***	• cat, fan, rat, bat, man • pin, pig, six, fish, dish
• ***Numbers of syllables***	• One syllable: boy, girl, ten, school, books • Two syllables: teacher, children, candle, pictures, penny
• ***Rhyming words***	• fan, tan, man, pan, can, van • ham, clam, jam • band, sand, hand

Figure 9.5
Picture Sorts

demonstrate the steps in the procedure to the children. It is very important that the pictures that are used are familiar to the children who are doing the sorting. At first, the teacher may select the type of picture sort the children will do; for example, sort by initial or beginning sounds. Children may, and often do, suggest other picture sorts; for example, final or ending sounds.

Magnetic Letters in Letter Recognition and Learning Letter Sounds

Children at the logographic stage of phonological development are learning the letter names, learning how to write letters, learning the sounds of letters, and beginning to recognize some words by sight. Plastic magnetic letters are fun to use, easy for children to manipulate, and inexpensive as well. Another benefit is that children get to touch them and feel their shapes. Using magnetic letters on a cookie sheet to build small words is an excellent way of learning letter names, letter recognition as well as letter sounds. Children also may begin to learn how to put the letters together to make words based on the letter sounds.

Here is an example of using magnetic letters in a classroom. The teacher is sitting with a small group of children around the table. On the table is a cookie tin with magnetic letters placed out of order.

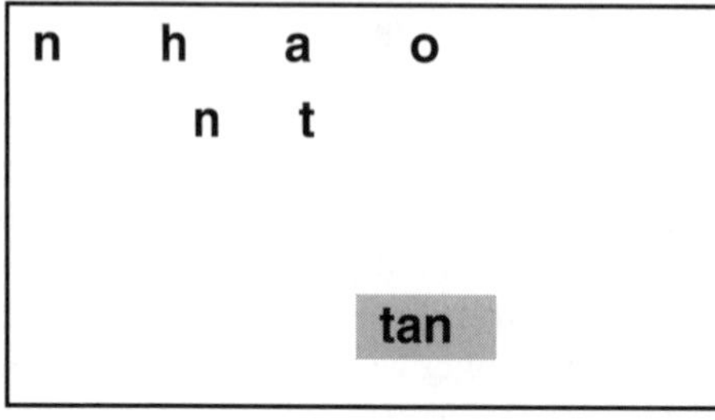

Teacher: (Pointing to each letter) Name the letters that I point to. (After the children name each letter) That was very good.

Teacher: I want to make the word *tan*. Listen as I say each sound in the word *tan*. /t/—/a/—/n/ (stretching out the sounds).

Teacher: What letter stands for /t/? Very good. Jon, find *t* and start making the word. What letter stands for /a/? Very good. Where does it go? Yes, that's right, after the *t*. What is the last sound you hear in *tan?* That is right. Find the letter that stands for /n/. Now put it at the end of the word. The teacher points to each letter and says the separate sounds in the word, then shuffles the letters around and asks: Make the word *tan* with the letters. The teacher then scrambles the letters and gives each child a turn to make the word.

In the making-words lesson, children were learning the names of letters, the sounds of letters, and how to put together the letters to make a word based upon their sounds, not on the visual cues alone.

Word boxes. Another approach to further develop the concept of letter–sound correspondence is the use of word boxes (Clay, 1993). Using word boxes with children allows them to understand the relationship between each spoken sound (the phoneme) and the corresponding letter or letters (the grapheme) within a word. Joseph (2002) suggests the word boxes may be used to hear the sound, to see the relationship between the sound and the letter(s), and to write the sounds within a word. The children engage in the following three smaller activities that are part of the larger activity:

- Activity I: They *segment the sounds* within a word.
- Activity II: They *match the letter(s) to each sound* within the word.
- Activity III: They *write the letters that represent the sounds* of the word.

Activity I: Segmenting Words Into Sounds

Purpose

- The purpose of the lesson is to help students to separate or to segment a word into its individual sounds or phonemes.

Materials

- Prepare a magnetic board drawn with rectangles. Each rectangle should be divided into boxes according to the number of sounds in the word presented. For example, for two sounds within words, draw a rectangle with two boxes; for three sounds within words, draw a rectangle with three boxes; and for four sounds within words, draw a rectangle with four boxes.
- Use a small magnet as a counter for tracking the sounds in words.
- For each word that will be segmented, have a picture that illustrates the word.

Procedure (Before children engage in the procedure, model the process for them)

- Show the picture of the word to be segmented, and have the children name the picture. Let them repeat the name, saying it slowly.
- Next, help children say the name one more time, stretching it out, so that the individual sounds or phonemes may be heard clearly.

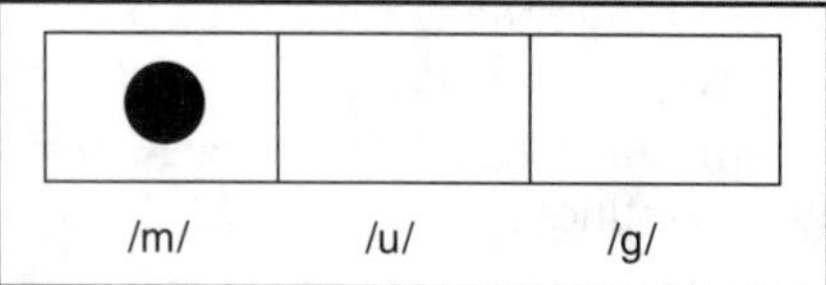

- Last, give each child a counter to move from one box to the next while the rest of the children articulate the individual sounds in the word very slowly, segmenting the word into its individual phonemes.

Activity II: Matching Letters and Sounds

PURPOSE

- The purpose of this activity is to help students match the correct letters and sounds within letters.

MATERIALS

- For Activity II, matching letters and sounds, use the same materials for Activity I, but replace the magnetic counters with magnetic letters that are arranged out of order.

PROCEDURE (DEMONSTRATE THE PROCEDURE TO THE CHILDREN)

- Follow the same steps as above, using magnetic letters.
- Have the children say the name of the picture. Help children say the name one more time, stretching it out, so that individual sounds may be heard.
- Have each child put the magnetic letter into the appropriate box while the rest of the children in the group articulate separate sounds or phonemes in the word.

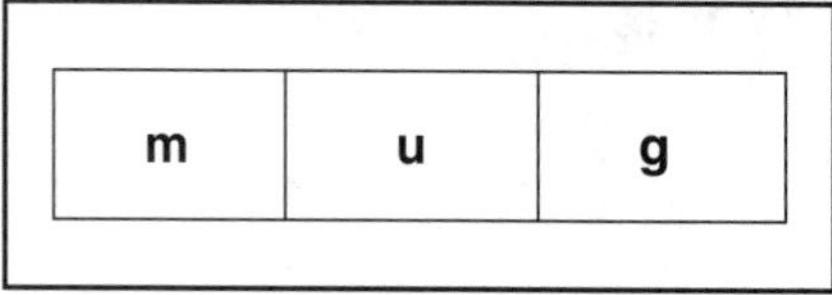

Activity III: Writing the Letters That Represent the Sounds

PURPOSE

- The purpose of this activity is to help children learn to spell the word that they hear by listening to each sound (phoneme) and writing the appropriate letter(s) (grapheme).

MATERIALS

- For this activity, each child needs a paper and a pencil.
- The papers have boxes similar to those on the magnetic board. Figure 9.6 shows a writing sheet that may be used for this activity.

PROCEDURE

- The teacher holds up a picture of the word and says the word. The teacher repeats the word, saying it slowly so that each phoneme is heard distinctly.

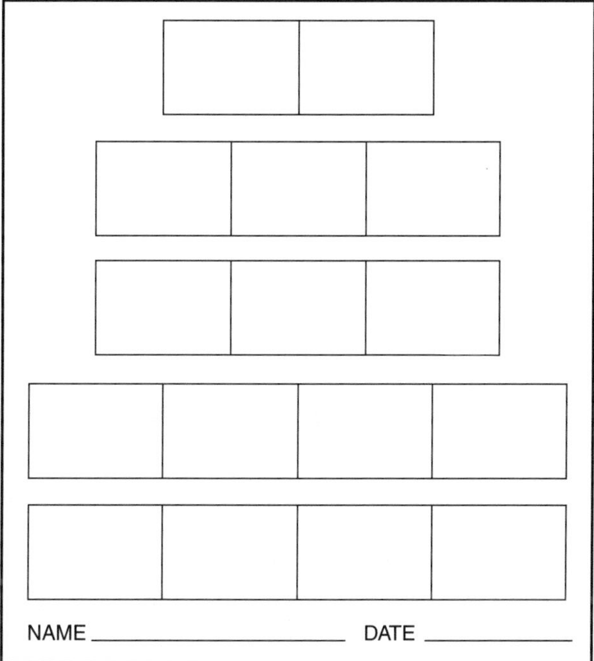

Figure 9.6
Writing Activity Sheet for Sound Box

- The children then say the word, stretching out the word, so they can hear the individual sounds or phonemes within the word.
- The teacher says the word slowly again and directs each child to write the letters that stand for the sounds they hear in the word. It may be necessary for the teacher to stop after saying each individual sound.
- When the teacher finishes checking each word, the children say and spell the word aloud.
- Continue with each word in the same way.

Instructional Contexts to Teach Alphabet Knowledge

Teachers use a variety of instructional contexts to teach letter names, letter recognition, and letter sounds. Mini-lessons or mini-reviews of letter names and letter sounds may be incorporated into regular reading and writing lessons or activities that occur throughout the day.

Shared Book Experience

Shared book experiences are excellent contexts for teaching phonic skills. For kindergarten and first graders, it is best to use big books for shared reading. At the end of sharing the book, focus on one or two pages for review and practice of letter names or sounds. For example, the teacher might ask one child to come up and find a word that begins with the letter *a*, or find a word that begins with the same sound as *ball*. A simple review would be to point to a letter on the page and ask a child to give its name. When introducing the book, you might point to the author's name on the cover or title page and read it. Follow it up with a question, "What is the first letter in the author's first name and in the author's last name? Who has a first name that begins like the author's first name? Who has a last name that begins like the author's last name?" Note how this type of instruction is not explicit or direct; rather, the teaching of the letter names is embedded into the context of shared reading and is considered *indirect* or *implicit* instruction. Such instruction allows for practice and review.

Handwriting

Handwriting should play an important part in the primary classroom schedule. Teachers need to take time to teach children the standard formation of the letters of the alphabet. Therefore, they schedule time for the explicit teaching of letters—remembering that children are at different developmental stages, and therefore, they may need varying amounts of time in learning correct formation of letters. Many teachers feel that while children are learning the sound of a particular letter, it is a good opportunity to focus on teaching how to write that letter. In addition to direct instruction of letter formation, in the balanced literacy program, teachers take many opportunities to demonstrate or model how to write letters in the context of shared writing and engage children to demonstrate to others how to write a letter. For example, within the instructional context of the interactive writing strategy shared pen (detailed in Chapter 7), teachers frequently ask individual children to write a targeted letter or a complete word while the teacher and children work together to compose a story or a message. Therefore, a balanced literacy program includes direct instruction of the standard formation of the letters, and it also relies on modeling or demonstrations, and independence in the use of letters as part of authentic reading and writing tasks.

Key Words for Sounds

Typically when children begin to learn letter sounds in preschool and in kindergarten, teachers establish a systematic approach in teaching and tracking children's knowledge of letter sounds. Knowing the sounds of the letters is an aspect of alphabet knowledge, and it is key to learning how to map sounds onto letters to decode words. Once children know most of the letter names and some of their sounds, direct instruction in learning all their sounds and using them to decode is the next step.

A systematic approach in beginning instruction in letter–sound knowledge is to establish the key word for the letter sound. A *key word* is a familiar word that represents the letter sound. For example, a key word often used for the letter sound /b/ might be *ball* or *banana*. Cunningham (2000) strongly suggests that the teacher with the children establish their own key word for each letter sound rather than rely on the publishing companies for standard key words. For children with cultural and linguistic differences, certain words are not as familiar as others. Therefore, they will not be able to retrieve an unfamiliar word to help them with a letter sound. The key word is also used with a picture and the spelling of the word. The following is a basic procedure in working to establish key words with children:

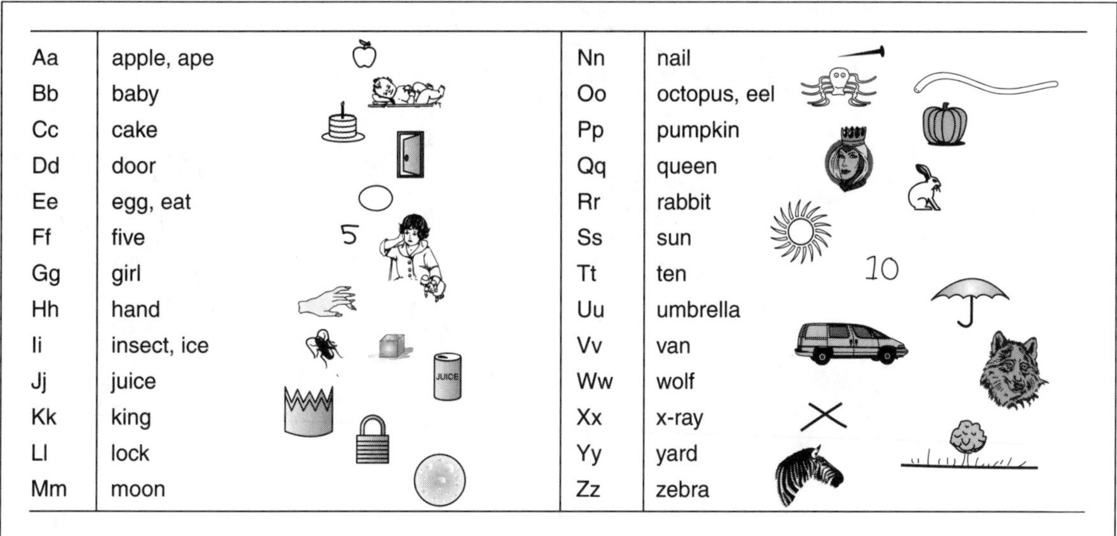

Aa	apple, ape	Nn	nail
Bb	baby	Oo	octopus, eel
Cc	cake	Pp	pumpkin
Dd	door	Qq	queen
Ee	egg, eat	Rr	rabbit
Ff	five	Ss	sun
Gg	girl	Tt	ten
Hh	hand	Uu	umbrella
Ii	insect, ice	Vv	van
Jj	juice	Ww	wolf
Kk	king	Xx	x-ray
Ll	lock	Yy	yard
Mm	moon	Zz	zebra

Figure 9.7
Key Word Chart for Letter Sounds

- Work with the children to establish the key word(s) for each of the letter sounds.
  - The teacher might begin using alphabet books, showing children examples of how each letter has a number of pictures that stand for the letter because the word begins with the sound the letter makes.
  - For vowels, use two key words, one for the long vowel and one for the short vowel.
  - For each key word, draw or cut out a picture to represent the word.
- Take several sessions to complete the key words for the letter sounds. Indeed, it would be impossible to complete the entire alphabet in one, two or even three sessions. Establishing key words may be part of direct instruction for letter names and letter sounds. Therefore, it will proceed over time.
- Make the key words accessible to children. Make a full-sized wall chart of the letters and the key words that represent their sounds. Provide each child with a laminated desk chart of the alphabet and the key words to be used for reading and writing throughout the day. The type of chart that worked for one of the authors was the alphabet line, much like a number line. The alphabet line contains each letter, uppercase and lowercase, written across the line with the picture of the key word and the word under each set of letters. The alphabet line may be laminated and taped at the top of each child's desk. It is easy to use pictures from clip art for key words for both the wall chart as well as the individual student alphabet line. Remember that pictures from clip art software may be resized so that they may be enlarged for the wall chart and made very small for the individual alphabet line. When children have access to the key words, they will use them. An example of a key word chart developed by one class is illustrated in Figure 9.7. The teacher may ask the children to use the key word chart in a variety of ways:
  - Read each letter
  - Read every other letter

Children need to be actively engaged in learning about letters.

- Read only the vowels; read only the consonants
- Read the pictures
- Read the beginning sound of each picture
- Read the words under the pictures

Sound Books

Creating sound books is an enjoyable way for children to learn letter sounds while they collect pictures of the words that represent the sounds. Sound books may be made from simple notebooks with child-decorated covers. Each page of the notebook is used for one sound of a letter. If a letter has more than one sound, as in the letter *c,* the two sounds should be on different pages. At the top of the page, guide children in writing the uppercase and lowercase letter for the sound.

Teaching the letter sounds through the sound book activity. The use of the sound book should be accompanied by the teacher's *explicit* instruction of the letter sounds. When teaching the sounds of letters, it is important to provide children with the *context of the sound* before the sound is used in isolation. Teaching the letter sounds in isolation, apart from words, may be especially problematic for children who are linguistically diverse or for children with regional dialects. The context of the sound is derived from a word in which the sound appears. This is achieved through a discussion of the key word that represents the letter sound as well as the discussion of other concrete words that have the same initial sound as the key word. Show children a picture of each word that you target for the discussion, and use several alphabet books to show the many words that begin with the same sound of the letter you are teaching. Below is a summary of steps for using sound books:

- Select a target sound, the key word for the sound, and pronounce it very slowly, articulating each sound.
- Tell the children to listen to the first sound of the word. Emphasize the first or initial sound of the word.
- Say the sound in isolation; that is, the single sound without the word.
- After the children know the initial sound of the word, make a connection between the sound and the letter. Tell children what the first letter of the word is and explain that this letter makes the first sound we say in the word. Let us look at an example of explicit or direct teaching of the sound of /c/ in the word *cat*.

Teacher: Look at the picture of the cat. Listen while I say each sound in *cat:* /c/ /a/ /t/. (The teacher uses the word *sound* rather than *letter* when helping children to understand the beginning sound of a word.)

Teacher: Listen to the first sound in the word *cat*: /c-c-c-c/. Say it with me and stretch out the sound. (The teacher puts a rubber band around two fingers and stretches it as she stretches out the sound.) Let's say that sound one more time.

Teacher and children: /c/ /c/ /c/.

Teacher: The word *cat* begins with the letter *c,* because the first sound you hear in *cat* is the same as the sound that the letter *c* makes. It makes a /c/ sound.

Teacher: (The teacher displays the picture of a cat on the board and writes a letter *c* under it. While the teacher writes the letter *c*, the teacher says:) The word *cat* begins with the /c/ sound, and we write *c* for that sound.

The teacher continues with several words that begin with the sound of /c/ and words that are spelled with the letter *c*. (Be cautious not to use examples of words that are spelled with *c,* but have an initial sound of soft sound of the letter *c,* /s/.) The children are directed to open to their sound book and find the page with the uppercase and lowercase letters of *Cc.* The children once again go over the sound of letter *c* and find the picture of the cat. They are directed to paste the picture next to the uppercase and lowercase letters of *c.* The teacher tells the children that cat is the key word that will help them to remember that words that begin with the sound /c/ also begin the letter *c*. The children are given a page with several pictures on it such as pictures of a man, cat, dog, horse, cake, table, candy, lamp, television, carrots, book, and car. The children say the name of each picture and find the ones that begin like *cat* and that begin with the letter *c.* They cut out each picture of the word that begins with the sound of /c/ and paste it in their sound books on the *Cc* page. They write the uppercase and lowercase letters of *c* under each picture with the initial sound of /c/. The children may take their sound books home to continue practice finding pictures of words that have the initial sound of /c/.

Children's Names and Alphabet Knowledge

Capitalize on what children know best, their names. Use their names as a source of knowledge for learning letter names and letter sounds. During the course of the day, teachers call out children's names for a variety of reasons. For example, when children are lining up to go to recess, the teacher might ask the children whose names begin with the sound of /n/ like the sound we hear in the word *nail* to line up. As the children line up, each might say, "My name is Nan, and it begins with the sound /n/."

In Chapter 7, we discussed the use of the message board as a way to promote writing for social interaction. In addition to developing this important language function, the message board may be used as a source for developing alphabet knowledge, learning the names and sounds of letters as well as helping children to learn how to read and write each other's names. You will recall how the message board is set up with each child's name clearly printed on a card and secured on the board with a space under the name for posting the message. When it is time for the children to take their messages from the board, the teacher may call them up by their initial or final letters in their names or their initial or final sounds in their names. Once children know how to read their classmates' names, children may play postal clerk and call out children who have mail by reading their names. Children's names are also excellent for use as key words on the key word chart for letter sounds (Figure 9.7).

Assessment of Alphabet Knowledge

In kindergarten and first grade, teachers will continuously and systematically assess alphabet knowledge including the following aspects of this important concept:

- Say or recite each letter of the alphabet
- Recognize uppercase and lowercase letters out of order
- Write uppercase and lowercase letters
- Know the sounds of each letter

Assessing Children's Ability to Name the Letters

There are a number of ways to monitor and assess children's ability to say the letters in the alphabet. The teacher may ask the child to say each letter in the alphabet. If the child is hesitant or does not understand, the teacher may ask the child to sing the ABC song. When a child is able to say all of the letters correctly, the date should be recorded on the profile chart of child's alphabet knowledge shown in Figure 9.8.

Assessing Children's Letter Recognition and Letter Sounds

Children need to recognize the uppercase and lowercase letters of the alphabet. Most children can do this by the end of kindergarten. Teachers monitor their progress in kindergarten, and they also determine mastery of this skill at the end of the year. Teachers will also need to know whether each child entering first grade has **automaticity** for letter recognition. That is, does the child automatically recognize a letter immediately when it is shown to him? A child has automaticity for letter recognition when he says a letter correctly within a 3 to 5 second response time after the letter has been shown to him.

Directions: Write the date the child has demonstrated the performance of each skill in the appropriate column next to the letter mastered. Under the summary section, indicate the total numbers of letters known by skill area with the summary date.

Name ______________________ *Grade* ________ *Age* ________

Teacher ______________________ *Examiner* ______________________

Can recite the alphabet or sing the ABC song: Date ______________________

Letters	Recognizes Uppercase Letters	Recognizes Lowercase Letters	Knows the Letter Sounds	Writes the Uppercase Letters	Writes the Lowercase Letters
Aa					
Bb					
Cc					
Dd					
Ee					
Ff					
Gg					
Hh					
Ii					
Jj					
Kk					
Ll					
Mm					
Nn					
Oo					
Pp					
Qq					
Rr					
Ss					
Tt					
Uu					
Vv					
Ww					
Xx					
Yy					
Zz					

Summary of Alphabet Knowledge

Date					
Total Score					

Figure 9.8
Profile Chart of Child's Alphabet Knowledge

There may be times when teachers will assess children's letter recognition of a few letters during instruction. Within this practice, the assessment of letter recognition ought to be systematic and documented. Teachers need baseline data at the beginning of the year to determine whether children have reached literacy benchmarks. Therefore, the teacher needs to assess each child for letter recognition for all uppercase and lowercase letters, at the end of kindergarten and at the beginning of the first grade. Those children who do not know their letters when they enter first grade need to be monitored for their achievement of this skill until they have acquired full letter recognition.

Testing children for letter recognition and the sounds of letters is an individualized assessment. One way to assess letter recognition and knowledge of letter sounds is to play a letter game with the child. This game may take 15 to 20 minutes. Therefore, assessing the uppercase and lowercase letters and their letter sounds should be completed in separate sittings for most children. Testing for uppercase and lowercase letters may be accomplished in one sitting for those children with longer attention spans and who may be expected to have quick responses or automatic letter recognition skills.

- **Materials:** Print the uppercase letters on one set of index cards and the lowercase letters on a second set of index cards.
- **Procedure:** Assess the uppercase letters first, and then the lowercase letters. The letter sounds may be assessed using the same procedure and deck of cards.
    - Take the deck of alphabet cards and shuffle them so that the letters are not in order. Tell the child that he will play the letter game.

For Letter Names

- Tell the child that you will show the letter card to him, and he will name the letter.
- Explain that when he names the letter for the card, he will hold it until the game is finished.
- Flash each letter to child, giving the child approximately 5 to 8 seconds to name the letter. If the child names the letter within the designated time, give the letter card to him and write the date next to the letter in the appropriate column in Figure 9.8.
- If the child does not name the letter within the given time, tell the child the letter and place the letter card in your pile.
- At the end of the session, tally the number of correct responses and record it at the end of the column with the date of the assessment.
- Use the same procedure for lowercase letters.

For Letter Sounds

- Tell the child that you will show him a letter card with one letter on it, and he will say the sound that the letter makes. If the letter has two sounds, ask the child for the second sound.
- Explain that whenever he can say the sound or sounds the letter makes, he will hold the letter card.
- Flash each letter to the child, giving him approximately 5 to 8 seconds to respond. If the child says the correct sound of the letter within the given time, indicate the child's accurate response by writing the date next to the letter in the appropriate column in Figure 9.8. Give the letter card to the child to hold until the end of the session.

- If the child does not respond correctly within the allotted time, tell the child the sound of the letter, and put the letter in your pile.
- At the end of the session, tally the number of correct responses and record it at the end of the column with the date of the assessment.

Assessing Children's Ability to Write Letters

One way to monitor children's skill in writing uppercase and lowercase letters is simply by analyzing their writing samples. A problem in working with work samples is that the teacher may not be sure whether the child asked the assistance of another child or looked at the alphabet line on his desk or on the bulletin board when writing a particular letter. Another difficulty is that the child may not use all of the letters in his writing sample.

Another approach that may prove more systematic is simply asking the child to write all of the letters, uppercase and lowercase. The teacher documents the date the child demonstrates knowledge of writing uppercase and lowercase letters.

Word Knowledge

Making Words Activity

To support their understanding of the concept of putting letters together to make words, children participate in the making words activity (Cunningham, 2000; Cunningham & Cunningham, 1992). This strategy is used after children have knowledge of letter sounds and understand how letters can be put together to make different words. The making words activity offers children the opportunity to make different words from a set of letters they receive from the teacher, as it encourages active engagement in their own learning. The children begin by making small words, then larger words until the final word is given which is the secret word. The authors of this activity added a final step, which is the word sort, sorting the words that children made into rhyming patterns to decode and spell some new words. The making words activity is not an independent activity; rather, the teacher works with a group of children guiding them in building words from the letters they are given. Below is a sample lesson for the making words activity that uses the procedures suggested by Cunningham (2000).

Materials for the children: A set of letters for each child is required. The consonants are one color and the vowels are a different color and a small teacher-made pocket chart for each child. Each child is given a word holder to display the word that is being made.

Materials for the teacher: A set of duplicate letters large enough to be seen by the children and a pocket chart hanging in front of the children to hold the letters.

Procedures

- Distribute a set of letters to each child. Each child receives the same set of letters. The children have the vowels *a, i,* and *e* and the consonants *p, n, t,* and *d.* The children use word holders to display the word they are making.
- The teacher asks the children to locate and name the vowels and checks to see if all children hold up their red *a, i,* and *e.*

- The teacher guides the children in making each word. "Let's begin by making **three-letter words**. Everyone take three letters to make the word *pin*. Say the word *pin.*" The teacher says the word, stretching out the sounds so that the children can hear the individual phonemes in the word.
- While the children are putting the letters in their holders, the teacher looks to see who needs help. The teacher may select one child who has made the word correctly to go to the pocket chart and spell it out with the large letters.
- The teacher continues to direct the children to make another word: "Change the vowel to make *pan*." The teacher may use prompts for some children who need help. For example, the teacher may say: "Think about the middle sound in the word *pan*. Now change the middle sound /i/ to an /a/. What vowel do you need to change *pin* to *pan*?"
- The teacher continues to guide children to make more three-letter words: *nip, nap, tin,* and *tan.*
- The teacher now guides the children to make **four-letter words,** following the same procedures as with the three-letter words. The children work at making *pain, pint, paid, tied, dine,* and *pine.*
- The teacher then asks the children to make the **five-letter word** *paint.*
- The word-making activity is concluded with **guess the secret word.** "Who can use all the letters to make the secret word?" If the children cannot make the word *painted* with their seven letters, the teacher may guide them through this word giving them clues.
- The conclusion to the lesson is the word sort activity with the words the children made.

Word sort activity. To conclude this word-making lesson, the teacher asks the children to put away their cards and word holders. Their attention is focused on the words that they have made which appear in the pocket chart.

The children may sort the words in several different ways:

- Initial sounds
- Final sounds
- Long or short vowels
- Words with similar word patterns

High-Frequency Words

What are high-frequency words? As suggested by their name, high-frequency words are those words recurring in text. As one reads a newspaper, 100 words account for half of the words that are being read (Fry, Fountoukidis, & Polk, 1985). These words that recur fall into the category of high-frequency words. From among the 250 words that children read and write, 70–75% are high-frequency words (Rinsland, 1945), and 20% of that group comprise the following words: *a, the*, and *and.* As they move through the stages of literacy development, high-frequency words become more familiar, and children's speed of recognition for high-frequency words increases as well. Thus, if the goal for all children is to bring them to fluent reading and writing, it makes sense to include instruction and assessment that focuses on the recognition of sight words within literacy programs.

There are many high-frequency word lists, and one of the easiest ways to find such a word list is in the basal text that is used for teaching children to read. Many of these lists, however, do not rank the words with respect to their level of frequency within print. Instead, the words are placed on the list because of their high-frequency use within the stories being read (Harris & Jacobson, 1972). A very useful list is from the Fry Instant Word List in Figure 9.9. The list offers 300 words grouped for their levels of frequent use. Examine how within each of the 100 word groups, there are categories of 25 words, arranged according to their frequency of use.

Learning Sight Words

Children in the earliest stages of literacy development begin to recognize words that are frequently used in the books they read and in environmental print. With their repeated exposure to words, children remember the most frequently used words, and they do not have to decode them. In the early stages of reading and writing, children have instant recognition of some of the high-frequency words. Therefore, these words are called **sight words** because they are recognized upon sight. Repeated exposure to words builds sight word vocabularies. The goal for beginner readers is to build large sight vocabularies, words that can be instantly recognized. Because of children's repeated exposure to high-frequency words, they are excellent words for developing at sight.

SIGHT WORD

The term *sight word* has several meanings. At times it is used to refer to the high-frequency words whose spellings defy decoding, for example, *the*. Sight words may refer to words that children remember because of a special visual cue. For example, in the word *look,* the two "o's" may be associated with eyes to look, and the reader will use the cue to remember the word. *Sight words* also refers to any word that a reader recognizes instantly. At one time, the reader had to decode the words, but because of repeated exposures through reading and writing, decoding these words is no longer necessary. These words are now in the reader's sight word vocabularies.

Automaticity for Word Recognition

Knowledge of high-frequency words is critical to fluency in reading. Many of the high-frequency words are functional words, carrying little meaning or no meaning when they are in isolation. However, a reader's skill for automatic recognition of function words will permit the easy flow of the text as these words bring meaning when they appear with other words. LaBerge and Samuels (1974) developed a theory of automaticity, referred to earlier, which is the ability to recognize many words as whole units quickly and accurately. Fluent readers possess automaticity for many words they read. Automaticity for words is necessary because a lack of reading fluency affects a reader's comprehension of text (Nathan & Stanovich, 1991). When a reader must stop to analyze each word, reading becomes slow paced and halting. Readers often become frustrated because their attention is diverted from thinking about the text to decoding each and every word. Thus, the development of instant word recognition, along with smooth word-solving strategies, is necessary to support reading comprehension.

Many teachers question whether to teach a bank of sight words prior to working on instruction of phonics, or whether phonics instruction should come first. The answer

Figure 9.9
Fry's New Instant Word List

The Instant Words: First Hundred

First 25 *Group 1a*	Second 25 *Group 1b*	Third 25 *Group 1c*	Fourth 25 *Group 1d*
the	or	will	number
of	one	up	no
and	had	other	way
a	by	about	could
to	word	out	people
in	but	many	my
is	not	then	than
you	what	them	first
that	all	these	water
it	were	so	been
he	we	some	call
was	when	her	who
for	your	would	oil
on	can	make	now
are	said	like	find
as	there	him	long
with	use	into	down
his	an	time	day
they	each	has	did
I	which	look	get
at	she	two	come
be	do	more	made
this	how	write	may
have	their	go	part
from	if	see	over

Common suffixes: *s, ing, ed*

The Instant Words: Second Hundred

First 25 *Group 2a*	Second 25 *Group 2b*	Third 25 *Group 2c*	Fourth 25 *Group 2d*
new	great	put	kind
sound	where	end	hand
take	help	does	picture
only	through	another	again
little	much	well	change
work	before	large	off
know	line	must	play
place	right	big	spell
year	too	even	air
live	mean	such	away
me	old	because	animal
back	any	turn	house
give	same	here	point
most	tell	why	page
very	boy	ask	letter
after	follow	went	mother
thing	came	men	answer
our	want	read	found
just	show	need	study
name	also	land	still
good	around	different	learn
sentence	form	home	should
man	three	us	America
think	small	move	world
say	set	try	high

Common suffixes: *s, ing, ed, er, ly, est*

The Instant Words: Third Hundred

First 25 *Group 3a*	Second 25 *Group 3b*	Third 25 *Group 3c*	Fourth 25 *Group 3d*
every	left	until	idea
near	don't	children	enough
add	few	side	eat
food	while	feet	face
between	along	car	watch
own	might	mile	far
below	close	night	Indian
country	something	walk	real
plant	seem	white	almost
last	next	sea	let
school	hard	began	above
father	open	grow	girl
keep	example	took	sometimes
tree	begin	river	mountain
never	life	four	cut
start	always	carry	young
city	those	state	talk
earth	both	once	soon
eye	paper	book	list
light	together	hear	song
thought	got	stop	leave
head	group	without	family
under	often	second	body
story	run	late	music
saw	important	miss	color

Common suffixes: *s, ing, ed, er, ly, est*

Source: From "The New Instant Word List," by E. Fry, 1980, *The Reading Teacher, 14,* 286–287. Reprinted with permission of Edward Fry and the International Reading Association.

from research (Ehri & McCormick, 1998) is that children need broad-based instruction. Learning phonics will help children learn sight words, and learning sight words will aid their word-solving strategies because word analysis and sight words are interdependent. Consider how a child may know a word pattern *-at*, and he will use it to decode and remember sight words such as *that.* Conversely, a child may use the sight word *and* to decode the word *band.* Phonics will facilitate children's learning of sight words, and children use their knowledge of sight words to decode new or unfamiliar words.

Tips for Teaching Sight Words

- Remember that not all sight words are the same. Some are decodable, whereas others are not.
- When teaching sight words, incorporate phonic cues as much as possible. Children will learn high-frequency words faster when they are given cues.
- Some high-frequency words have patterns. Use children's knowledge of word patterns to learn high-frequency words. For example, if you are teaching the high-frequency words *then* and *when*, you may use words that children already know with the word pattern *-en,* such as *hen, ten, pen*, and so on.
- Once high-frequency words are taught, place them on the word wall to be reviewed and to be referred to within different contexts of the literacy program.

Instruction of Sight Words

There are several approaches that educators use to teach children sight words. Gunning (2001) describes two approaches that are used. The first, the whole-part approach or teaching words in context, *instruction of the sight words comes after reading the story.* The children are introduced to the sight words by reading them within the context of the whole story. The second approach, the part-whole approach, involves *teaching the sight words to the children before they read the story.* A combination of both approaches will support children's word recognition skills.

Whole-part approach. The teacher plans to teach two or three sight words using direct or explicit instruction. When the teacher plans a whole-part approach it means that the sight words will be presented and taught to the children after they have read the story. Let us observe teaching of sight words within the context of guided reading. In Chapter 7, guided reading was presented as the heart of the balanced literacy program because children receive direct instruction in small groups at their own level. Guided reading would be an excellent context to present instruction of sight words after children have read and discussed the story. Instruction of sight words would come as a mini word study lesson.

For example, Sheila selects two sight words from the small patterned book that her class has finished reading. On her small movable chalkboard, she writes the words and underlines the phonic element that the two words share.

then

them

Sheila: Let's look at the two words we read in today's story. Let's read the words together.

Children: Then, them. (As the children say the words, Sheila traces under each word with her finger.)

Sheila: That was very good. Look at the two words and see if you can tell how they are alike.

Paul: They both start the same.

Sheila: Yes, they start with *th-*. Remember the sound that *th* makes. Say it.

Sheila: The first word is *then,* and the next word is *them.* (Sheila emphasizes the ending sounds as she says the words.) How are they different?

Children: They end different.

Sheila: Yes, the word *then* ends with *-n* and you can hear the sound of /n/ at the very end. The word *them* ends with *-m* and you can hear the sound of /m/ at the very end.

Sheila: Now take your slates and write the word *then*, and remember the sound at the end. (Sheila checks the spelling of each child's word.) Now take your slates and write the word *them.* Does it end the way it sounds with an /m/ sound? Check both words. Do they begin the same? Do they end differently?

Sheila: Erase your words and write them without looking at the board. Write the word ***them***. Now write ***then***. (Sheila looks at each child's slate and checks the spelling of the words.)

Sheila: Now let's go to the word wall. Where will we look for the word ***them?***

Tara: Under the ***T.***

Sheila: Yes, under the letter ***T.*** Can you find the word ***them?*** Remember how it begins and remember the last sound. Yes, Tara, please point to it.

Sheila: Can you find the word ***then?*** Thank you, Edwin, you remembered that the words end differently; the word ***then*** ends with an ***n***.

Part-whole approach. In the second approach to teaching sight words, the teacher selects the words from the story that the children will read and presents the new words to the children *before* they read the story. If Sheila's word study of the sight words *then* and *them* occurred before the children read the story, the lesson would be considered a part-whole approach to teaching sight words.

> What approach to teaching sight words would be more effective for young children? Why?

Activities to Support Sight Words

Teachers know that children need many exposures to words before the word becomes a sight word, one that they can instantly recognize. There are many games that children can play after they have been taught sight words. In addition to the practice they receive from their independent reading, these games provide supplementary exposure to high-frequency words that is necessary for automatic word processing.

Bean Bag Toss is an easy game that provides children with fun while practicing sight words. Children should have had instruction in the sight words that will be used in the game. Below are a list of the materials and a simple set of procedures to use in playing the game.

Purpose

- The purpose of the bean bag toss is to provide practice in sight words that will lead to children's instant recognition of the words.

Materials

- Using a shower curtain liner, carefully draw about 20 boxes with a marker. Spread the curtain on the middle of the floor.
- Carefully print sight words on cards that you wish the children to practice, and place one card in each box.
- Place beans in a small plastic bag and secure the bag with a knot or a tie.

Procedures

- Have the children sit on the floor around the "plastic floor of words."
- Give each child a chance to toss the bean bag onto a word.
- When the child recognizes the sight word, he may pick it up and hold it until the end of the game.
- When all the children have had a chance to play and the words have been picked up, the game is over.

There are many other activities to support the development of sight words. In Go Fish, you simply use a deck of cards with pairs of sight words. Another activity for children is WORDO using boards with sight words like the one in Figure 9.10. WORDO is played like BINGO. Children may also be collectors of words, storing them in their word banks. A small plastic storage box may serve as the container to hold the words. Children use 2 × 2-inch cards to write down the words they know as sight words to store them in their word banks. Word banks have numerous uses: Children may work with each other to review their words; children may

W	O	R	D	O
THAT	AND	THEY	WHEN	DOES
BUT	AN	ON	PLAY	DAD
SAID	MAKE	IN	BUT	MAN
YOUR	WORK	COME	HAPPY	PART

Figure 9.10
Sample Game Card for WORDO

pull out three words to build a story around them; or children may sort the words into designated categories. Each activity provides more exposure to the words and will reduce the number of seconds needed to say the word, thereby increasing fluency. Word searches are excellent activities to give repeated exposure of words to children.

Assessment of Sight Words

Teachers need to have confidence in children's developing sight word vocabularies. Assessing children's knowledge of sight words often occurs during a number of instructional or assessment contexts. To determine children's achievement of sight words with reference to specific benchmarks—what sight words should they know at specific points—Rasinski and Padak (2001) suggest the use of the Fry Instant Word List for sight word assessment (see Figure 9.11). They have selected a sample of 20 words for each group from the Fry list of high-frequency words for use as a diagnostic test. This test provides a rule-of-thumb type of monitoring for children's sight word vocabularies in the primary grades. Automaticity for word recognition (instant recognition of words) of 90% of Group I in Figure 9.11 should be achieved by the end of first grade; Group II by the end of second grade; and Group III by the end of third grade. By the time the children enter fourth grade, they should have a "fairly accurate and automatic command of the first 300 words in the Fry Instant Word List" (Rasinski & Padak, p. 190).

Purpose

- The purpose of assessing sight words is to determine if the child can recognize the most important sight words and if his recognition is instant or automatic.

Materials

- Print each sight word on an index card.
- Keep each group of sight words separate for assessing the varied levels.

Procedure

- Tell the child you are going to play a word game. Tell the child that you will show the card with the word, and if he can say it right away, he gets to keep it.
- During the game, mark those words that the child had instant recognition in the column marked *A* with a +, and mark those that the child had to decode in the column marked *R* with a + (see Figure 9.11).

Word Walls

Designing the Classroom Word Wall

If you are not familiar with a word wall, your first glance would make you think of "a bulletin board of words." Word walls are more than that. Indeed, they have come to be powerful functional tools for both the children and the teacher. For the chil-

Directions: Have the child read each word. Place a "+" in the first column, *R*, if the child recognizes the word, and place a "+" in the second column, *A*, if the child can say the word automatically; that is, before the lapse of 4 to 5 seconds. Leave a blank for any word a child fails to recognize.

Name ______________________ Grade ________ Age ________ Date ________

Teacher ______________________ Examiner ______________________

Group I			Group II			Group III		
	R	A		R	A		R	A
1. the			1. give			1. city		
2. have			2. sound			2. country		
3. was			3. work			3. earth		
4. you			4. sentence			4. saw		
5. they			5. know			5. thought		
6. were			6. where			6. few		
7. your			7. through			7. group		
8. their			8. around			8. might		
9. each			9. follow			9. always		
10. said			10. show			10. important		
11. would			11. another			11. children		
12. about			12. large			12. white		
13. them			13. because			13. river		
14. time			14. went			14. carry		
15. write			15. move			15. second		
16. people			16. picture			16. enough		
17. water			17. play			17. almost		
18. who			18. animal			18. mountain		
19. down			19. mother			19. young		
20. over			20. America			20. family		
Total			Total			Total		

Figure 9.11
Child's Profile of Automatic Recognition of Sight Words.
Source: Adapted from Rasinski & Padak (2001, p. 191).

dren, they are a resource of words that they have learned and rely on as they engage in varied reading and writing tasks throughout the day. For the teacher, word walls have become teaching tools that may be used with varied instructional approaches for developing children's phonological knowledge and their sight word vocabularies.

Word Wall and Children's Development

Although there is no one way to use the word wall, when starting one, it is important to think of the children for whom the word wall is intended. Their stage(s) of phonological development will help to clarify the teacher's purposes for using the word wall. For example, for children at the logographic or alphabetic stage, or for those at the multisyllabic stage of phonological development, word walls will have different purposes. For instance, for the logographic reader, the focus of the word wall is to develop alphabet knowledge—that is, learning letter names and sounds as well as building sight word vocabularies. At the logographic stage of development, children do know some sight words, but only a few. If the word wall contains many more words than what the children know, it will be confusing for them and they will not find it useful. The focus of word walls for readers and writers at the multisyllabic and morphemic analysis stages is quite different. Word walls for them will spotlight their expanding interest in words as well as their developing vocabularies required for reading and writing in broader areas of learning. Therefore, word walls need to suit the children who use them, and they should be adjusted to the children's changing literacy needs as well as interests.

Getting Started With a Word Wall

There are some considerations that teachers should keep in mind when designing word walls to maximize their benefits for children.

- Where the word wall is placed is very important. The word wall should occupy a bulletin board or a wall that is an area where children typically gather for instruction and for use while reading and writing. A word wall should be at eye level so that children are able to see the words.
- The words need to be written legibly and in large print so that children may see them. Remember, writing on the word wall is a model for children to use.
- Using different colors for beginning letters of words (red for all *b* words and green for all *c* words) may be useful for children at the logographic stage, but it will not assist children at the multisyllabic or morphemic analysis stages.
- Writing different word patterns (rhymes or word chunks) in different colors may be useful in helping children to remember and recognize words that belong to word families. This type of word wall would be best suited for children at the alphabetic and the word pattern stage of phonological development.
- Cutting out the words to show word shapes, that is, words with extenders like *book, yellow,* and *they*, may help children's visual memory for spelling words. This approach is especially helpful to alphabetic readers recognizing sight words.

- Building daily and varied activities around the word wall will keep children's interest for using word walls at high levels. For example, activities with word sorts and word families of words from the word wall promote interest.
- Because the word wall is designed for the literacy levels or phonological stages of the children who are using it, build it gradually each day based on the needs of the children. Cunningham (2000) suggests that five words per week be added to the word wall that means *one per day*. This rule of thumb would apply more to

the struggling or the emergent readers and writers, and less to those at fluency levels.

- Encourage children to use the word wall as their *resource*, for group writing, for independent writing, or whenever they need to know how to spell a word. For instance, when they ask you for the spelling of a word, you might direct them to the word wall.
- Finally, let the word walls belong to the children. This is especially true for children in the third and fourth grades whose vocabularies develop rapidly through a wide variety of reading and writing. Encourage children to add their newly discovered words to the word wall.

Word Walls for All Occasions

Teachers are very creative and will often "invent *on* or modify" known and used instructional strategies and approaches. The word walls often reflect different types of strategies for spelling and for recognizing words as well as strategies for building vocabularies. When word walls were first introduced, there was one type. As teachers and children used them, new displays of words were invented and varied ways to use or to interact with word walls evolved. Let us examine a variety of word walls that are designed for different learning outcomes and with children at different levels of literacy development.

Words walls with key words. We learn best when we make connections between what we know and what we have just learned. Children who are learning the beginning sounds in words (logographic readers) need to be able to connect a first letter of the new word to a picture of the word that begins with the same letter and same sound. In this chapter, we have discussed the importance of having children learn the key words for letter sounds by developing and using a key word chart. The word wall with key words is an extension of the key word chart. This type of word wall will help children by having familiar pictures of the key word and the letter it represents. If a child is looking for a particular word on the word wall, he may use the picture of the key word that has the same beginning sound that will narrow down his search. Remember that the key word contains a picture that serves as the key for the beginning letter sound, a cue to help the reader. For logographic or emergent readers and writers, a word wall that contains key words with pictures would be extremely helpful.

The teacher and the children build the word wall together as they learn the words. They are guided to put their words beginning with the same sound of the letter under the key word. One additional way to make the connection of the letters and sounds they represent stronger for children is to have the children's names written under their initials and the key word. Figure 9.12 shows an example of part of a word wall with key words.

Unit word walls. Collecting and harvesting words is especially useful when the words are used by children in their reading and writing. Teachers who use thematic or integrated approaches to teaching use word walls as children learn new words, concepts, and ideas they garner from subject areas in social studies, science, health, foreign languages, art, and other disciplines. One third-grade teacher had an integrated unit of study on the tropical rain forest and used a word wall as children collected a multitude of related words. Instead of arranging the words alphabetically, the teacher

Figure 9.12
Key Words Word Wall

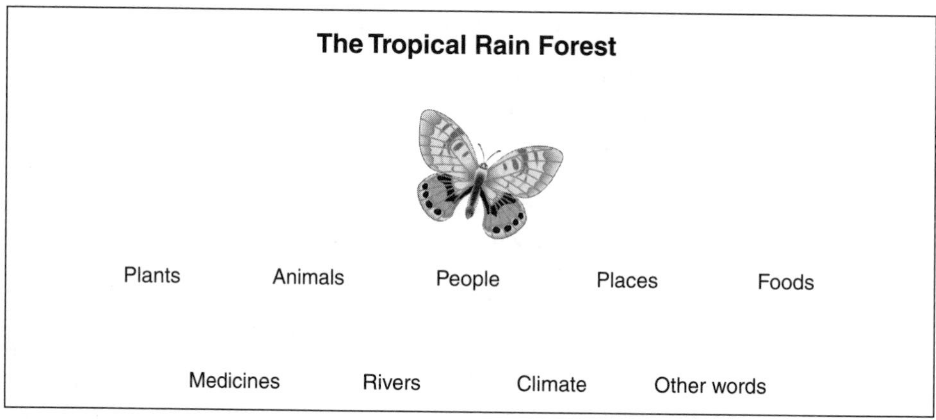

Figure 9.13
Word Wall for an Integrated Unit of Study

and children grouped the words into categories related to the theme as shown in Figure 9.13.

Personal word walls. As children read and write more, they become more fluent, learning words that relate to their special interests. Their reading selections and the topics they write about may differ widely from other children in their classroom. Children are at varying stages of literacy development. This is especially true for children in the third and fourth grades. Teachers encourage children to collect their own words and record them on their personal word walls. It is quite simple to help children to keep personal word walls. Shari, a third-grade teacher, uses personal word walls with children. She uses one manila folder for each child. Each of the four sides of the folder is divided into six columns with a letter at the top of each column, similar to the one represented in Figure 9.14. The last column may be designated for letters beginning with *x*, *y*, and *z* because they will contain very few words.

Aa	Bb	Cc	Dd	Ee	Ff

Figure 9.14
Personal Word Wall

The children have space to record the new words that they have learned and need to remember for their reading and writing. Their personal word walls become a resource for them during writing. When do they collect their words? Children are encouraged to add new words to their personal word walls whenever they are reading and come across a new word, when they are involved in a group activity—such as shared reading or writing or a discussion group—and they learn a new word, when they are writing their individual stories during writers' workshop and come across a new word they use, or on any other occasion when they learn a new word. They become collectors and harvesters of words! Many times children will share with others a word that they have learned. Teachers encourage such sharing of new and big words by setting aside time for talking about children's word discoveries and how they may be used in reading or writing.

Chunking word walls. "The primary goal of chunking walls is to help students read and spell unknown words quickly and efficiently using analogies" (Wagstaff, 1999, p. 40). Decoding by analogy occurs when children use words or parts of words—word patterns or rimes in words—they know to decode an unfamiliar word. This type of decoding is a more efficient method than sounding out the word letter

-ay	-et	-ill	-op
day	jet	sill	hop
say	get	will	top
hay	met	till	mop
play	let	fill	hop
way		chill	stop
		thrill	chop

Figure 9.15
Chunking Word Wall

by letter. Knowing patterns in words helps children to progress from sounding out letter by letter in the decoding process to decoding by analogy. The chunk in the word is the rime or the word pattern. Therefore, on a chunking word wall, words are arranged according to word patterns that the children are learning. The teacher guides the children in using these key words for spelling and decoding.

The chunking word wall is especially useful for children who are in the alphabetic stage moving into the word pattern stage of phonological development. For children to benefit from the use of the chunking word wall, they should already know the letter names and sounds and know some sight words. At this stage, the teacher helps the children to look for patterns or chunks in words rather than simply mapping sounds on to letters. The goal is to help children progress to looking for larger chunks or familiar patterns within unfamiliar words that they are attempting to decode or to write correctly. An example of a chunking word wall used in beginning to teach word patterns for reading and writing is found in Figure 9.15.

Many teachers use word patterns—rimes—to develop lists of word families as shown in Figure 9.15. If children know how to read and spell the most frequently used word patterns they will be able to read and spell so many more by adding on the initial sounds or the onsets (Wylie & Durrell, 1970). Further, as children learn many word patterns or rimes, they use them for figuring out how to spell a word or for **decoding by analogy,** one of the first useful strategies for beginner readers. Because the use of rimes for decoding has been considered very effective, teachers need to use explicit or direct instruction in providing children not only with the skill of reading rimes or word patterns quickly but also with the strategy to use rimes to decode unfamiliar words. Learning the use of word patterns is very beneficial for children who are at the alphabetic stage and moving into the word pattern stage of phonological development, because the approach furthers their development.

Assessing Word Families

Teachers know that when they begin to work with word families, children first need to be able to see similar word patterns within words. Therefore, at the first level, teachers will want to determine whether children can *match* words that belong to a

Directions: Have the child read the words in the first column. Then ask the child to look for the word in the second column that matches the word pattern of a word in the first column. The child should draw a line connecting the two words that belong to the same word family.

boy	**bit**
cat	**let**
top	**fun**
pit	**mop**
bun	**hat**
pet	**toy**

Figure 9.16
Matching Words from the Same Word Family

specific word family. In other words, children need to be able to tell whether two words contain the same rime or belong to the same word family. At the next level, children should *produce* words that belong to a similar word family. That is, the teacher may be talking about the rime in the word *cat* and ask the children to give another word that belongs to the same word family or that rhymes with *cat*.

Informal assessment tools may be used after work on word families with young children. Figure 9.16 shows a simple assessment tool that the teacher may use to determine whether children can find similar word patterns in two words through a matching activity.

Assessing the Production of Word Families

In the next assessment strategy (Figure 9.17), the teacher asks the child to read the set of words and write a word that belongs to the same word family or that has the same word pattern. This is more difficult because the child is required to read the words, identify the word pattern, and think of another word with the same word pattern.

Assessing Manipulation of Initial, Final, and Medial Letters in Word Families

Children who can identify words that rhyme, match words with the same word patterns, and can produce a word in a given word family will be ready for manipulating the initial, final, and medial letters in words. When teachers develop the children's ability to substitute initial and final letters in word families, they will further children's attempts at using chunks or word patterns in figuring out unfamiliar words. Think of what a child may do when reading an unfamiliar word such as *back*. If the child knows the word family *-ack* (rime) and also knows how to manipulate or substitute letters (onsets) before the word family *-ack*, the child can solve the new word

Directions: Have the child read the words in the first column, then write another word that belongs to the word family.

bell, well, tell	________________
take, make, bake	________________
pin, bin, tin	________________
pot, cot, lot	________________
hook, took, book	________________
bug, hug, tug	________________

Figure 9.17
Adding Another Word to the Word Family

Directions: Have the words below printed on cards. Show the child the word *mat*. Say, "Look at the word *mat*. Change the *m* to *h*. Now say the new word *(hat)*." Follow these directions for each word.

Word	Direction	New Word
pot	Change the *p* to *g*	**got**
sun	Change the *s* to *f*	**fun**
cat	Change the *c* to *r*	**rat**
net	Change the *n* to *p*	**pet**
will	Change the *w* to *s*	**sill**
them	Change the *th* to *h*	**hem**

Figure 9.18
Substituting Onsets in Words

in the text he is reading. Indeed, this does become a powerful word-solving strategy. To use this strategy successfully, children must first know about word families and how to read them. They must also know how to substitute letters in words containing word families to make new words. Additionally, they must learn how to apply the strategy in their reading that is most effectively taught during guided reading. Finally, they must be given the opportunity to practice the strategy.

The substitution or manipulation of the final and medial letters in word families will provide children with the opportunity to change a word family that they already know to a new one. This is a skill that will further develop children's word-solving strategies for unknown words. Figures 9.18, 9.19, and 9.20 show the assessment tools to determine the strength of a child's skill to manipulate initial letters in words (onsets) and final letters in words (rimes).

Tracking and documenting children's progress in their knowledge and use of word families is critical. For children to use word-solving strategies to decode unfa-

Directions: Have the words below printed on cards. Show the child the word *mat*. Say, "Look at the word *mat*. Change the *t* to *n*. Now say the new word (*man*)." Follow these directions for each word.

Word	Direction	New Word
cat	Change the *t* to *n*	**can**
but	Change the *t* to *d*	**bud**
set	Change the *t* to *ll*	**sell**
pin	Change the *n* to *t*	**pit**
pod	Change the *d* to *t*	**pot**
them	Change the *m* to *n*	**then**

Figure 9.19
Substituting Final Letters in Rimes

Directions: Have the words below printed on cards. Show the child the word *mat*. Say, "Look at the word *mat*. Change the *a* to *i*. Now say the new word (*mit*)." Follow these directions for each word.

Word	Direction	New Word
cat	Change the *a* to *u*	**cut**
but	Change the *u* to *a*	**bat**
set	Change the *e* to *i*	**sit**
pit	Change the *i* to *u*	**put**
pod	Change the *o* to *a*	**pad**
hem	Change the *e* to *i*	**him**

Figure 9.20
Substituting Medial Letters Within Words

miliar words, they need knowledge of word families and skill to use them. Figure 9.21 shows a profile for tracking a student's knowledge of word families.

Using Meaning to Decode Words

When children look at words and begin to see meaningful parts to help them decode words as well as to understand their meanings, they are moving into the morphemic stage of phonological development. This is the stage at which fluent readers and most adults are reading. Take a word like *sociolinguistics* that may be unfamiliar to many advanced readers. Adult readers may first examine the word for it parts, determining that there are two word parts within this large word. Looking at the first word part, *socio*, they think that this part of the word has something to do with society or

Directions: Indicate the correct response only. Use a "+" to code a correct response and indicate the date of testing.

Name ______________________ Grade __________ Age __________ Date __________

Teacher ______________________ Examiner ______________________

Matching Word With Same Rimes		Producing Another Word Within the Word Family		Substitution: Initial Letter—Onset		Substitution: Final Letter in Rime		Substitution: Medial Letter in Rime	
	Date		Date		Date		Date		Date
boy		-ell		pot (got)		cat (can)		cat (cut)	
cat		-ake		sun (fun)		but (bud)		but (bat)	
top		-in		cat (rat)		set (sell)		set (sit)	
pit		-ot		net (pet)		pin (pit)		pit (put)	
bun		-ook		will (sill)		pod (pot)		pod (pad)	
pet		-ug		them (hem)		them (then)		hem (him)	
TOTAL		TOTAL		TOTAL		TOTAL		TOTAL	

Figure 9.21
Student Profile of Knowledge and Skills Using Word Families

people, because *socio* looks like the word *social*. Then they may look at the second part, *linguistic*, and they continue to think about its meaning, "Ah, I know that this part of the word has to do with language." They think about the word in the context of print and continue to guess at its meaning, probably coming to a general definition—the social contexts of language, the way language is used in social contexts. They used a word-solving strategy based on meaningful elements of the word.

Teaching Affixes: Prefixes and Suffixes

Knowledge of prefixes, suffixes, and root words help readers go beyond decoding by sound to figuring out new words through their meaningful parts. This type of instruction is necessary for children who are fluent readers. Because children at this stage of literacy development read more advanced books, the words are often complex and may not be in the readers' *listening vocabularies*. This means they simply have not heard the word before, and when it is spoken, they do not know the meaning of the word. Therefore, for these readers sounding out the word would not be helpful. As fluent children read more difficult text, their vocabulary increases only if they have strategies to figure out the meaning of unknown words. The goal of instruction for children at this stage of literacy and phonological development should be to help children increase their vocabularies through advanced reading by figuring out the meaning of unknown words. One way to achieve this goal is teaching children to recognize **affixes**, a general term for prefixes and suffixes, and how to use them to figure out unknown words.

What Children Need to Know and Do

- Know what is a prefix and a suffix
- Be able to identify them in a word
- Know that some prefixes and suffixes are meaningful parts and some are not
- Know the meaning of the most frequently used prefixes and suffixes
- Be able to use their meaning to figure out the meaning of unfamiliar words

Children at the morphemic stage of phonological development use meaning to decode unfamiliar words, therefore, knowing and using prefixes would increase their word power. Research shows the importance of learning the most commonly used prefixes and suffixes (White, Sowell, & Yanagihara, 1989). By teaching the following four prefixes—*un-, re-, in-* (sometimes they appear as *im-, ir-, il-*) and *dis-* —all meaning not—children will know 58% of all prefixes added to words. By teaching 16 more prefixes—*over-, mis-, sub-, pre-, inter-, fore-, de-, trans-, super-, semi-, anti-, mid-,* and *under-* —the number that children know will jump to 97%.

The same researchers suggest that the three most commonly used suffixes—*s/-es, -ed,* and *-ing*—account for 65% of all suffixes added to root words. This number jumps to 87% by teaching the following suffixes: *-ly, -er/-or, -ion/-tion, -al, -y, -ness, -ity,* and *-ment*. These studies provide a strong rationale for explicit instruction in learning the meaning of the most commonly used affixes as well as learning how to use them to figure out the meaning of an unknown word in reading text. In Figure 9.22 is a set of the most commonly used prefixes and suffixes, their meanings, and examples of their use.

Instruction in Root Words and Word Endings

Lessons in phonological awareness do not end when children can sound out or decode words. To help children use the affixes of words to further their vocabulary development, teachers need to plan instruction around the meaningful aspects of word parts. The lesson that follows will help children identify the root word and understand how a suffix, or word ending, changes its meaning. This lesson also may be modified for prefixes.

- **Goal of the Lesson:** To teach the meaning and recognition of root words and suffixes and to demonstrate how the root word gives meaning to the word but may be modified by adding a suffix.
- **Student Outcomes:** Children will be able to identify the root word and the suffix, and explain how the meaning of the word is slightly changed by adding the suffix.
- **Materials**
  - *Lon Po Po: A Red-Riding Hood Story from China*, translated and illustrated by Ed Young (1989).
  - The chart shown in Figure 9.23 one for each child.
- **Procedure**
  - Read the story with the children.
  - Discuss the story for its meaning, relating it to the version of Little Red Riding Hood with which they are familiar.
  - Select from the story the words for study. For this lesson choose words that have suffixes. One word is *higher*.
  - Write the word *higher* on the chalkboard. Use this word to point out to the children (a) where to find the root word, (b) where to find the suffix, and (c) how the suffix may change the meaning slightly. Now read the sentence from

Prefix	Meaning	Example of Words
re-	*back*	**remove, replace, repel**
re-	*again*	**recount, redo, resale**
un-	*opposite*	**unmarked, unreal**
in-	*in*	**into, inward, incomer**
in-, im-, ir-, il-	*opposite*	**inhuman, improper**
dis-	*opposite*	**disagree, disengage**

Most Commonly Used Suffixes

Suffix	Meaning	Examples of Words
-s,/-es	*more than one verb form*	**theaters, tables, bushes, brings, carries**
-ed	*past tense of a verb*	**ended, carried**
-ing	*present tense of a verb*	**helping, living**
-ly	*describes a verb or a characteristic*	**quickly, joyfully**
-er/-or	*a person who . . .*	**teacher, creator**
-ion/-tion	*action or process involved with*	**transportation, absorption**
-ible/-able	*capable of or inclined to*	**edible, knowledgeable**
-al	*process of doing the action*	**denial**
-al	*connection with*	**political, social, national**
-y	*condition or quality of*	**watery, cloudy, jealousy**
-ness	*condition or quality of*	**happiness, dampness**
-ity	*a state or quality*	**sanity, security, depravity**
-ment	*shows a product, or a condition*	**measurement**
-er/-est	*used for comparison*	**tall—taller—tallest**

Figure 9.22
The Most Commonly Used Prefixes and Suffixes

the book that contains the word *higher* to demonstrate the slight but real change in the meaning of the word by adding the suffix *-er,* telling the children the meaning of the suffix.

- Discuss what would happen to the meaning of the sentence if only the root word were used instead. Use the root word without the suffix in the context of the sentence to demonstrate the slight difference in meanings.
- Ask the children if they can think of more words with the same suffix.

Now the children pulled the rope with all of their strength. As they pulled they sang, "Hei yo, hei yo," and the basket rose straight up, **higher** than the first time, **higher** than the second time, **higher** and **higher** and **higher** until it nearly reached the top of the tree. When the wolf reached out, he could almost touch the highest branch. (Young, 1989)

WORD Whole Word	ROOT Main Part of the Word	SUFFIX/ENDING Word Ending

Figure 9.23
Words, Root Words, and Suffixes

- Now write the root word and the suffix on the chart in Figure 9.23.
- Write three more words on the chalkboard from the book:
  - *shouted*
  - *delighted*
  - *chicks*
- Ask the children to first write the words on their charts. Then have them find the root in each of the words and write them on their charts under the root word.
- Ask the children to find the suffix in each of the words, and have them write it on their charts in the appropriate place.
- Discuss how each suffix changes the meaning of the root word very slightly.
- Have children work in pairs to find as many possible words from their stories that end with the suffix *-s* and *-ed* within 10 minutes, adding the words, root words, and suffixes to their charts. Assess children's charts to determine if the student outcomes were met.

Mufaro's Beautiful Daughters	*Yeh-Shen*	*The Talking Eggs*
Story Setting	**Story Setting**	**Story Setting**
Character Traits	**Character Traits**	**Character Traits**
Story Events	**Story Events**	**Story Events**
Story Ending	**Story Ending**	**Story Ending**

Figure 9.24
Literature Word Wall for Three Tales of Cinderella

As children begin to grasp the concept of a prefix, suffix, and root word, introduce prefixes and suffixes that are not as common. Help children individually as they apply their skills while they read and write independently.

Literature Word Walls

Children in literature discussion groups read the same books, discuss them, and use journals in writing their responses to aspects of the story. In Chapter 8, we discussed that one way to help them compare the story elements, characters, and language is through literature charts. A literature word wall also may be used to *compare book language* across similar stories. Figure 9.24 shows an example of a literature word wall used by children in the third grade. They found the words in three different versions of the tale of Cinderella: the African version, *Mufaro's Beautiful Daughters* (Steptoe, 1987); the Chinese version, *Yeh Chen* (Louie, 1982); and the French Creole version *The Talking Eggs* (San Souci, 1989).

Children in different literature circles read and discussed the stories. They selected the words the authors used to describe story events and traits of main characters. For example, the children were told to select the words that described the personality traits of the characters, the characters' actions, the setting, and so forth. Then they discussed how the words were used in each story. The groups then discussed the similarities and the differences in the language of the stories with respect to the author's choice of words for each of the story events. This type of activity provides a wonderful way to increase children's vocabulary through the appropriation of book language. As children use the words from literature in their discussion groups, they will *appropriate* the words, using them in other contexts. That is, the children will understand the new word and make it their own, using it in several language contexts. When children talk about the author's writing style or choice of words to express actions, events, and personality traits, they begin to think and act like authors.

Wheel of Fortune

Wheel of Fortune is a TV game show enjoyed by many families including children. Their interest in the game can benefit them by helping them learn to spell and to use the meanings of new and familiar words. The rules of this popular TV game may be very familiar to most children. Teachers can use it in a variety of ways. One way is to provide children practice with words from a set of books that they recently read. For example, consider the vocabulary words on the literature chart from the different versions of Cinderella that the third-grade read. This is an excellent opportunity to provide children with practice for spelling and reading the vocabulary words in the books they have read, and at the same time, the game allows them to think about the story parts of the book they have read. For instance, some categories for vocabulary from stories might include the following: a main character in the story, the setting of a story, a character trait of one of the main characters, an action taken by the main character, or a word that tells about a possible solution. Naturally, the game is intended for the children who have read the books and who have had experience with the vocabulary in the literature.

Procedure

- Divide children into two small teams.
- Tell the children that they will each have a turn at guessing the letter in the word until he misses. The turn is then taken over by the next member of the opposing team.
- Select the secret vocabulary word. Draw a blank line for each letter on the board. For example:

  _____ _____ _____ _____ _____ _____

- Think of an appropriate category for the secret vocabulary word. Then tell the children the category. The children will use the clue from the category and the number of blank letters to make their guess.

- The child whose turn it is guesses by asking the question: "Is there a(n) ____________________?"
- If the child guesses correctly, the teacher or the leader places the letter on the appropriate line and the child may take another turn. The team wins one point for each correct guess.
- When the child does not guess correctly, the opposing team takes over. The player who is next to guess a letter begins to play.
- Whoever guesses the word, whether all or only part of the letters have been filled in, receives five points for their team.
- The team with the most points wins the game.

Compound Words

Children need specific instruction in identifying the parts of compound words—words that consist of two words. Children enjoy figuring out how the two words come together to bring new meaning to the word.

To understand the concept of compound words—how the two words may bring a different meaning when joined to form a compound word—teachers often show children pictures of each word part; then the teacher presents the new picture to illustrate the compound word. Many teachers have children make minibooks of compound words like the one illustrated below. The first box depicts the front cover of the book that opens and closes toward the center. On the cover of the left flap is the first part of the compound word and an appropriate illustration; on the cover of the right flap is the second part of the compound word and an appropriate illustration.

The children are directed to think of the meaning of the compound word. In this case it is *classroom.* The children open the two flaps or covers of their books and write the compound word in the center, draw a picture that illustrates the meaning of the new word, and complete their project by writing a sentence that contains the new meaning.

There are 14 tables and my teacher's desk in my classroom. I just love my classroom.

Inventing compound words. Poets take artistic license when writing, and oftentimes authors of novels do the same. Because language is not static or fixed but changes over time to respond to a changing society, many of the invented words of creative writers become part of our language. Encourage children to invent new compound words that may become part of their creative writing. Some new inventions on words are

electricwriter
snowdog
rockingcar

The teacher can ask the children

- Can you think of what the inventor of the three new compound words wanted them to mean?
- Can you make up a set of compound words, never used before, for a poem? Ask a friend if she knows what the meaning of your words may be.

The front cover of the book has two flaps that close to the center. When the two pages are opened the compound word appears with an illustration of the new word or concept. As children learn new compound words, they can be added to the compound word chart.

Many compound words are derived from the meaning of the two words that form the word. Some words are simple and can be easily figured out (*firehouse, football*). Others are not so simple and take on the meaning of the surrounding words (*however, everywhere*). Still other compounds are not related to the two words that form it (*bulldog, brainstorm*).

Homophone Charts

Children need to learn about words that sound the same but have different spellings. **Homophones** are words that sound the same but have different spellings as well as different meanings. Note that each set of homophones contains the same number of phonemes and graphemes.

Homophones

do—due—dew
their—there—they're
whole—hole

When children understand the concept of letter–sound correspondence and when they have an understanding of word patterns, the teacher may introduce the concept of homophones to them. For some children this may be as early as the first grade. However, the homophones must be within the children's listening and reading vocabularies for them to learn and apply them to their reading and writing. Children who are in the third and fourth grades and who are at the morphemic stage of phonological development will indeed see the relationship between the spelling and the word meanings in homophone sets. Each time a set of homophones is presented to the children, the teacher adds them to the homophone chart. The teacher encourages the children to use the homophone chart when they need it for their writing. During the reading of a story, or during shared book activities, the teacher may notice that a homophone appears in the story. The teacher will call it to the attention of the children and show the children the relationship of its meaning to its spelling.

Summary

The teaching of phonics has been the center of much debate, and most likely, the controversy will continue. What will not be subject to debate is the crucial role that phonics plays in the academic lives of good readers and writers. It is clear that successful readers do know the code; they know multiple strategies for word solving and use them with no effort in decoding new or unfamiliar words; they read more, and as a result, their vocabularies and their world knowledge is positively affected. Effective teachers know the role that phonics plays in becoming literate and use best practices supported by research to develop the skills children need to become successful readers and writers.

Discussion Questions and Activities

1. Lulu is a first-grade student who knows all of her letters as well as her sounds. While she reads orally, her teacher has observed that when she comes to a word that she does not recognize, Lulu sounds out each letter in the word. What instructional strategy would you choose to bring her to look at larger chunks within a word so that her decoding becomes more efficient? What types of activities would help to reinforce her finding patterns in words?
2. Juan knows how to decode words, and he is beginning to read challenging books. You know that advancing his vocabulary will enhance his reading comprehension and may have a spillover into his writing. Suggest some strategies to develop an interest in words as well as strategies that will foster his vocabulary development.
3. You are a teacher in the first grade, and in March, Sheila, a new student, transfers from an out-of-state school district into your class. There are no records on her literacy levels or on her phonological development. After you have introduced Sheila to the class, you have a half hour of free time to begin to assess her. You have decided that you want to find out about her phonological development. List the skill that you will start with to begin to assess Sheila, and tell the assessment strategy with which you will begin. Explain what other assessment tools you will use to gather initial information at subsequent times to determine where Sheila performs in phonological development.
4. Observe an early childhood literacy lesson. Describe the teacher's instruction in phonics with respect to the following:
   a. The approach: Discuss whether the teacher used explicit or or implicit instruction.
   b. The content of the lesson: What were the specific content and skills that the teacher developed within the instructional sequence?
   c. Was the lesson developmentally appropriate? Why or why not?
   d. How did the teacher determine that the children understood the content, concept, and skill that was taught?

Additional Web Sites

LearningPlanet.com
http://www.learningplanet.com/act/abcorder.htm
The LearningPlanet.com Web site provides online activities in a variety of learning areas including ABCs, language arts, and reading and phonics organized by grade level.

http://www.nifl.gov/partnershipforreading/publications/recommended.html
The Partnership for Reading Web site provides recommended readings to implement evidence-based research with children.

Additional Readings

Bear, D., Invernizzi, M., Templeton, S., & Johnston, F. (2000). *Words their way: Word study for phonics, vocabulary, and spelling.* Upper Saddle River, NJ: Merrill/Prentice Hall.

Brunn, M. (2002). Teaching ideas: The four-square strategy. *The Reading Teacher, 55,* 522–525.

Duffelmey, F. A. (2002). Teaching ideas: Alphabet activities on the Internet. *The Reading Teacher, 55,* 631–635.

Eldredge, J. L. (1999). *Phonics for teachers: Self-instruction, methods, and activities.* Upper Saddle River, NJ: Merrill.

Meyer, R. (2002). Captives of the script: Killing us softly with phonics. *Language Arts, 79,* 452–461.

Valtin, R., & Naegele, I. M. (2001). Correcting reading and spelling difficulties: A balanced model for remedial education. *The Reading Teacher, 55,* 36–45.

Wagstaff, J. M. (1998). Building practical knowledge of letter sound correspondences: A beginner's word wall and beyond. *The Reading Teacher, 51,* 298–304.

Zgonc, Y. (2000). *Sounds in action: Phonological awareness activities and assessment.* Portland, ME: Stenhouse.

Additional Children's Literature

Bryan, A. (1997). *Ashley Bryan's ABC of African American poetry.* New York: Atheneum.

Chin-Lee, C. (1997). *A is for Asia.* New York: Orchard.

Ernst, L. C. *The letters are lost.* New York: Viking Press.

Shannon, G. (1996). *Tomorrow's alphabet.* New York: Greenwillow.

Van Allsburg, C. (1987). *The Z was zapped.* Boston: Houghton Mifflin.

Children's Literature References

Louie, A. (1982). *Yeh chen: A cinderella story from China.* New York: Philomel.

San Souci, R. D. (1989). *The talking eggs: A folktale from American South.* New York: Dutton.

Steptoe, J. (1987). *Mufaro's beautiful daughters: An African tale.* New York: Lothrop, Lee & Shephard.

Young, E. (1989). *Lon po po: A red-riding hood story from China.* New York: Scholastic.

PART IV

MANAGING LITERACY INSTRUCTION AND ASSESSMENT IN DIVERSE CLASSROOMS

CHAPTER 10

Teaching All Children: Accommodating Differences in the Literacy Classroom

Portrait of Differentiated Literacy Instruction

Angela Gonzalez's third-grade class has enjoyed repeated readings of Make Way for Ducklings *(McCloskey, 1941). Today everyone is excited as they don their paper hats and grab homemade props to act out their story. "Make way, make way for ducklings," shouts the narrator. The second-grade visitors clap as they watch their friends in third grade attempt to waddle around the classroom.*

Angela Gonzalez's third-grade classroom embodies all of the qualities of a rich literacy environment. The children are exposed to quality literature and respond to the story through constructive activities. The only clue that this classroom has been adapted for special learners is the reading level of the text. The children in Ms. Gonzalez's class have special needs and have been mainstreamed into the regular classroom.

Today's early childhood teacher has to acquire a bank of strategies to accommodate diversity in the classroom. Twenty-first-century classrooms reflect language as well as cultural and behavioral differences. This new model of inclusion embraces the goal of instructing students to accept peers who may not look or sound like themselves and to respect those differences.

As you read this chapter, think of the following questions:

- How would you accommodate cultural, cognitive, and behavioral differences in early childhood classrooms?
- What are some instructional strategies to adapt lessons for differing needs?
- How can you assess children with special needs?

What Is Inclusion?

Inclusion meets the needs of all students within the regular classroom with support services.

Inclusion is the "commitment to educate each student with a disability in the school and when appropriate, in the class that child would have attended had the child not had a disability" (Lombardi, 1994).

The educational journey towards inclusion began with the historic legislation, **Public Law 94-142,** the **Education for All Handicapped Children Act of 1975.** This legislation mandated that all children had the legal right to a free and appropriate public education. In addition, children were entitled to their own individual education.

The inclusion model calls for collaboration among teachers, parents, administrators, special education teachers, and psychologists to address the needs of the child and to offer solutions. This child study team addresses the physical, socioemotional, and cognitive profile of the child and together they generate adaptations for the individual student. In order for the model to run smoothly, educators must be informed about the needs of students with disabilities and research-based instructional adaptations.

Differentiated Instruction

An inclusive classroom strives to meet the needs of all students by using formative assessment to design instructional strategies (National Research Council, 2002). The effective teacher uses the data from running records, retellings, or checklists to identify specific learning experiences for their students, realizing that no one lesson plan "fits all" students.

A differentiated classroom has the following key characteristics:

- Teachers and students respect one another's similarities and differences.
- Assessment is ongoing and used for instructional planning.
- All students engage in learning experiences that are challenging, meaningful, and interesting.
- Flexible grouping is used as well as rotation of individual and group assignments.
- Timing is flexible and pacing is matched to student needs.
- Students are assisted in multiple ways. (Association for Supervision and Curriculum Development, 2002)

The differentiated classroom creates successful learning environments through instructional strategies that are research based and that incorporate how the brain learns (National Research Council, 2002).

An inclusive classroom strives to meet the needs of all children.

Learner Centered —According to cognitive research, a child learns when new knowledge is connected to what she already knows and has personalized (National Research Council, 2002; Tomlinson & Kalbfliesch, 1998). Personalized instruction connects the new concept or skill to their home culture.

Knowledge Centered —In order to create such a learner-centered environment, teachers need to focus on key concepts or skills. Using developmental benchmarks helps early childhood teachers to create activities that focus on the curriculum.

Community Centered —Differentiated classrooms hum with active learning when students see themselves as a community of learners. In addition, their home culture and neighborhood are incorporated into classroom life. This makes instruction personalized and facilitates learning connections.

The Learner With Special Needs

Involving Parents: Share upcoming lessons with parents of children with special needs. This builds the child's self-esteem as the parent prepares the child for upcoming content.

In order to create a learner-centered classroom, the early childhood teacher must especially understand the developmental profile of children with special needs. To illustrate how to differentiate instruction according to developmental needs, this section will discuss the English language learner, the child with learning disabilities, and the child with hyperactivity disorder.

English language learners. As the United States continues to become more diverse, classrooms across the nation enroll children from around the globe. English language learners represent a diverse student population. Some second language learners were born in the United States, but English is not spoken at their home. Others are recent immigrants from China that have learned a pictorial alphabet and now must conquer a phonetic system. The early childhood teacher must be sensitive to the varying linguistic and cultural needs of these learners.

The child's first language is labeled as *L1* and the second is noted as *L2.* There are certain key concepts that should be kept in mind when planning literacy instruction for the English language learner.

- **Children learn a second language in different ways and at their own pace.** A variety of strategies and methods should be used to accommodate children's different learning styles. Also, some children may require a longer period to absorb English before they are able to produce it.
- **Proficiency in L1 supports L2 learning.** Children who are able to read and write in L1 are able to draw upon that knowledge base in learning new words and syntax. Whenever possible, the teacher should try to include signs or phrases in the child's native language so she can draw upon this knowledge. Many school systems have begun *dual language programs* which are two-way immersion programs with the goal of producing bilingual and biliterate programs (Valdes, 1997). The philosophy behind these programs is that all children benefit from learning several languages.
- **Second language learning occurs in stages.** The first stage is absorption or immersion of English. The child is not ready to produce English and should never be forced to speak. The child then moves to early production when she begins to speak English and to read and write in the second language. Gradually, the child becomes more of a risk taker and begins to acquire academic literacy. Finally, the child is able to be more expressive verbally and in written work, although her communication skills may still contain errors.
- **Academic fluency takes time.** Often English language learners appear orally fluent in the cafeteria, playground, and classroom. However, academic fluency entails reading and writing for school learning and takes several years to develop.
- **Language errors indicate progress.** English language learners will make grammatical errors when they are learning English. This is a sign that progress is occurring because the child is aware of basic syntax—similar to the errors that toddlers make as they begin to experiment with oral language. (Wood, 2002)

English language learners will need a supportive, community-based approach to literacy learning. It is important to include their culture and heritage in the curriculum so that they do not feel that learning English is a betrayal to their native culture. Because most teachers have limited experiences with other cultures, this section will discuss how to become more familiar with students' native cultures (Grant, 2001).

The English language learner brings literacy practices from home that may not match school literacy (Xu, 1999). One way to make the children feel more comfortable is to ask them to bring in the newspaper that is read at home that may be in Chinese (Xu, 2003). This shows interest in their native culture and language. It is also

English language learners need a community based approach to instrution.

important to choose instructional texts that reflect their culture and maximize their engagement such as patterned books (Freeman & Freeman, 2000).

It is also important to engage the parents of the English language learner in the literacy process. In order to assess a child's literacy development, the teacher must be familiar with the child's *multiple literacies* or way with words at home and at school (Gee, 2001). One way to accomplish this is to ask the parents to keep a literacy log. This log can have two columns: one column depicting parental literacy activities and the other column noting literacy activities with their children (Paratore, Melzi, & Krol-Sinclair, 2003). Parents may keep this log in their own language which can be translated by another parent or teacher.

Another method for engaging parents of English language learners is to ask them to keep a home literacy portfolio (Paratore et al., 2003). The parents keep any literacy artifacts of their child's and also record literacy activities. The portfolios are brought to parent conferences and the parent shares them with the teacher. The parents also can bring in artifacts from their native language and another parent or teacher can translate the content during the conference. The home literacy portfolio facilitates collaboration between home and school while acknowledging and respecting the literacy practices of the home.

In addition to English language learners, early childhood teachers must be sensitive to the needs of students with learning disabilities.

Students with learning disabilities. About 17–20% of the student population has a learning disability in reading (Alexander, 1999). Children with learning disabilities in reading exhibit slow, hesitant oral reading behavior. Their reading comprehension is impeded by their lack of automaticity in vocabulary or poor decoding skills. In addition, inadequate prior knowledge also leads to vocabulary deficits.

Using Technology: The Web site Learning Disabilities Association of America has ways to adapt instruction (http://www.ldanatl.org).

Reading comprehension for students with learning disabilities is also impacted by processing problems with either visual or auditory discrimination (Wood, 2002). For instance, a student with a learning disability might confuse similar word patterns such as *rat/fat.*

In addition to decoding and comprehension problems, students with learning disabilities may also be inconsistent in their performance. A strategy or skill learned on Monday may be forgotten by Tuesday unless it is reviewed and reinforced. Some students are also disorganized and this slows down their time on task and often frustrates teachers who are trying to keep on schedule. However, as with English language learners, children with learning disabilities need to be supported and praised for their many strengths and talents. Early childhood teachers also need to adapt instruction for children with **attention-deficit hyperactivity disorder (ADHD),** which will be discussed in the following section.

Students with attention-deficit hyperactivity disorder. Children with attention-deficit hyperactivity disorder, or ADHD, have difficulty focusing for long periods (Wood, 2002). Inability to concentrate coupled with impulsive behavior is classified as ADHD. This inability to concentrate for long periods impedes literacy learning for the young child. A child with ADHD typically has problems with the following three behaviors: coming to attention, decision making, and maintaining attention. It is easy to spot the child who is always walking around the room, playing with rulers, and is easily taken off task. In addition, many children with ADHD also have a learning disability that is difficult to identify due to their behavior problems (Rubin, 2002).

Many teachers are also unfamiliar with another attention disorder that is classified as the **hypoactive child** (Stevens, 1997). The hypoactive child is very slow moving and has difficulty completing tasks. The hypoactive child may be sent on errands and not return for 30 minutes, or take 1 hour to complete a task that other children can complete in 15 minutes. The hypoactive child also has focusing and organizational behavior problems.

This chapter will address how to meet the needs of English language learners, children with learning disabilities, and children with attention-deficit disorders within the inclusive classroom. Best practices in literacy instruction are beneficial for all children as all students have individual learning styles and need to be accommodated. The following section describes differentiated instruction and how to modify classroom activities.

How to Differentiate Instruction

A differentiated classroom strives to meet the needs of all students by modifying instructional methods, materials, and the learning environment. The teacher creates a differentiated classroom by adapting four classroom elements:

- Content—subject knowledge
- Process—student learning activities
- Product—student projects
- Environment—classroom setting

Modifying Content. An early childhood teacher can modify content by providing books on tape or CD-ROM, various books on different reading levels, peer reading buddies, or flexible grouping.

Modifying Process. Students' literacy activities can be adapted by providing interest centers, manipulatives, or visuals to accompany an activity. Also, giving children a variety of tiered activities of different ability levels to choose from helps to modify learning activities.

Modifying Product. A literacy project such as a rolled story or diorama could be adapted by allowing students to complete the project with a partner or group. Another technique to modify literacy products is to vary the length of time students have to complete a project. Rubrics for the assignment should be modified to match the ability level of the student. Students should also be allowed to choose which literacy project they would like to complete, increasing student engagement and motivation.

Modifying Environment. Due to varying learning styles, some children need noisy areas in which to work, whereas others prefer quiet. A creative teacher can adapt the classroom setting to meet learner needs by providing headphones for those who need music to work or dividers to create quiet corners. Children with learning disabilities and attention-deficit disorder (ADD) also need routines that are posted and organized materials. A spiral-bound notebook with pockets and attached pencil case can give the student with learning disabilities the necessary organizational framework to complete her assignments. Adapting the environment also entails incorporating the culture of the English language learner and other students to represent American diversity. The key to modifying the environment is to take stock of the students and their needs as well as cultural differences. The resulting data is then used to design and modify the classroom environment (Stevens, 1997; Tomlinson, 2001, 2002).

Where to Begin?

For a novice teacher, the concept of a differentiated classroom may appear daunting. However, as with learning any new skill, the key is to begin slowly and work toward a fully differentiated classroom. The following sequence helps to modify instruction:

- First, mentally visualize the type of classroom you would like.
- Include the parents and students in your vision of differentiated instruction so they understand its philosophy.
- Begin with one subject or even with just one assignment.
- As you feel more comfortable, add another subject area or unit.
- Assess your progress continually and make modifications according to your data.
- Use the resources of the school faculty to help achieve your vision.
- Be patient. It takes time to construct a differentiated classroom. (Tomlinson, 2000)

Teach up. An important component of differentiated instruction is "teach up" (Tomlinson, 2001). Teaching up means enriching the content and providing slightly challenging activities for all students. In order to teach up, assessment must be ongoing so that teachers have a sense of their students' challenge levels. In addition, scaffolded instruction is provided to help the children meet the challenge. Struggling learners such as children with learning disabilities or attention-deficit disorder may need special modifications.

How to Teach Up

- Focus literacy activities on key concepts and skills. Avoid too many details.
- Use literacy products that involve drawing and performing, not just writing.
- Teach mini-lessons using direct strategy or give skill instruction or model tasks as often as necessary for student to master the skill or strategy. (Alexander, 1999; Tomlinson, 2001)

Differentiating Instruction for the Emergent Reader and Writer

This section describes how to differentiate instruction for the emergent reader and writer. It is during the emergent literacy years that young children begin to experiment with letters and sounds. These are foundational years for literacy development as the child develops the concept that print conveys meaning, that letters represent sounds, and that words consist of letters (Clay, 1985). During the emergent literacy stage, emergent readers and writers are also developing their phonological processing skills (Whitehurst & Lonigan, 2001). This means that children are beginning to learn sounds in words and to segment phonemes, a critical skill for future literacy success. In Chapter 6, several activities were presented to scaffold the emergent literacy behaviors of the young reader and writer. This section describes how to modify those selected activities to meet the needs of all students.

Activities for Phonological Processing

Sound stretch. This activity can be used to model phonemic segmentation. This skill may take students a few practice sessions before they are able to master counting sounds in words. Figure 10.1 illustrates the teaching steps for the sound stretch activity.

Modifying Content. Phonemic segmentation can also be practiced with educational software such as Franklin's Word Builder or Reader Rabbit. These titles are especially helpful for English language learners and children with attention-deficit disorder because the visual clues keep them focused and engaged in the phonemic segmentation task.

Another way to modify the content is to pair learners with special needs or students who are struggling with emergent readers who are slightly more advanced.

Modifying Process. Because this activity is primarily auditory, visual learners may need magnetic letters or pocket charts to perform this task. For example, certain reading groups could be given pocket charts and letter cards. As the teacher stretches out the sounds, the children could place the letter cards in the appropriate pockets.

Modifying Product. In order to modify the product, children with special needs may use a keyboard to type out the sounds that they hear. The tactile typing of

- The teacher models a large rubber band how to stretch out a word as she says the word. For example: *MMMM/AAA/NNN.*
- The teacher models with a stretched-out rubber band how to bring the rubber band back to its original length as she says the word quickly. For example, *man.*
- The children pretend to stretch rubber bands as they say the sounds in different words.

Figure 10.1
Sound Stretch

letters and saying the sounds helps the learner with special needs to process auditory information. Children using educational software such as Reader Rabbit may also print out their phonemic segmentation game and present this as their literacy product for this task.

Name that sound. This activity focuses on children identifying the beginning, middle, and ending sounds in words. Figure 10.2 explains how to use the game in the classroom.

Modifying Content. To modify the content of this activity, the teacher may choose to provide a tape of this song for the learner with special needs to listen to independently. This gives the emergent reader and writer familiarity with the content. Also, educational software that focuses on alphabetic sounds, such as Reader Rabbit, may be used.

Modifying Process. Because this activity is primarily auditory, the teacher might choose to show pictures with the alphabet sounds. This provides a visual as well as an auditory cue for the students.

Modifying Product. For English language learners or students with special needs, the children might choose to hold up the corresponding letter card rather than sing the alphabet song.

Rhyming game. The rhyming game may be used to teach children to identify word pairs that rhyme. Figure 10.3 outlines the steps for the activity.

Modifying Content. One way to modify the content of this strategy is to provide audiotapes of *The Cat in the Hat* or another audio-book by Dr. Seuss (1957). The student listens to the rhyming text and can do a follow-up activity selecting rhyming word pairs.

- The teacher begins to the tune of "Old McDonald Had a Farm" by saying: "What's the sound that starts these words—*pig, potato, pot?"* (Waits for children to respond, *p.*)

- The children respond that /p/ is the sound that starts these words—*pig, potato, pot:* "With a /p/, /p/ here and a /p/, /p/ there, Here a /p/, there a /p/, everywhere a /p/, /p/..."

Figure 10.2
Name That Sound

- The children walk around in a big circle taking one step each time a rhyming word is said by the teacher.

- When the teacher says a word that doesn't rhyme, the children sit down. For example: she, tree, flea, spree, key, bee, went.

Figure 10.3
Rhyming Game

Modifying Process. The rhyming game can be made more tactile by providing the students with letter cards. Emergent readers and writers can use the cards to create their rhymes and to identify when a word rhymes, then walk around the circle.

Modifying Product. There are excellent educational software games that focus on rhyming words and creating rhymes that children may choose as an alternative to this activity. Also, CD-ROMs of the *Cat in the Hat* or *Green Eggs and Ham* (Seuss, 1988) are available that include rhyming games.

- On chart paper, the teacher shows the children how to divide their papers to look this way: *C/AT,* with a line after the initial letter.
- The children are asked to write *FAT* underneath *CAT* and to tell what they notice about the words (that they end the same way).
- Then they write *SAT* underneath *FAT* and tell what they notice. After they respond, the teacher comments, "This is how we make word families."
- The teacher asks if they know any other words that would complete the chart. As they respond, he writes them on the chart paper. The students also copy the word *family* onto their charts.
- After the list is exhausted, the children chant the words in the word family. The teacher may call on individual students to identify select words or to read the entire list.

Figure 10.4
Onsets and Rimes

Spelling Activities

Onsets and Rimes. By focusing on word patterns, this instructional strategy increases children's phonological awareness and knowledge of word features. Figure 10.4 details the procedure for the activity.

Modifying Content. One way to adapt this activity to meet the needs of struggling readers is to pair them with slightly more advanced spellers. This will provide peer assistance to generate the onsets and rimes of words.

Modifying Process. For learners with special needs, instructors might choose to provide the students with magnetic letters to complete the task. Another strategy would be to provide color-coded letter cards to give the children a visual cue to create the rimes.

Modifying Product. Another alternative for this activity is to provide students with the CD-ROM game Franklin's Words which includes an activity on creating words using onsets and rimes.

Doing the word wall. Although many versions of this activity exist, the objective of the word wall activity presented in this textbook is to introduce word patterns to the children so that they may internalize their features (see Figure 10.5).

Modifying Content. A word wall containing numerous words can be overwhelming for struggling readers or students with special needs. Therefore, the word wall should be limited to a few word patterns to help the emergent reader and writer process the visual information.

Modifying Process. The word pattern word wall should be color coded to help the learner with special needs to visually recognize the word pattern. Every rime should be in a different color code with the onset a contrasting color. For example, *at* could be in red (*at*) and the onset *c* could be in blue (*cat*). In addition, when students are learning the new words for the word wall, teachers can provide special instruction with tactile tracing of word patterns. For example, instead of writing the new words on their papers, students can trace the word

- The teacher selects a simple word pattern such as the *at* family. After introducing this simple word pattern, he selects high-frequency words the children need in order to read or write such as *the.*
- The teacher cuts around the configuration of the word or color codes it to give the children visual clues to discern the word pattern.
- Before placing the new words on the wall, the teacher dictates the new words in sentences. The students write the words on their papers.
- The students clap out the sounds in the word and discuss its features.
- The drill is repeated the next day. The remainder of the week, the teacher dictates any five words from the word wall as a review for the children.

Figure 10.5
Doing the Word Wall

patterns in cornmeal or clay. This tactile representation of the words helps the young reader and writer to process the written word.

Modifying Product. Instead of using the class word wall, the learner with special needs can create a "portable word wall." This would be changed weekly as the new word patterns were introduced. A blank manila folder is divided into sections for each word pattern. The words are color coded and the child can use the folder as a handy reference tool.

Emergent Writing

Scaffolded writing. This emergent writing strategy allows children to construct stories as the teacher writes down their responses (see Figure 10.6).

Modifying Content. Scaffolded Writing is a wonderful instructional strategy for learners with special needs. Young children love to draw even if they are unable to speak English. If you are working with an English language learner, it is best to pair her with a bilingual student or a paraprofessional who will be able to translate her picture.

Modifying Process. There are educational software games such as Richard Scarry's Wonderful World of Reading that imitate the language experience approach. Children are encouraged to create a drawing and then create sentences. This is a wonderful technique to engage children with attention-deficit disorder in the writing process.

Modifying Product. For children who are just learning to speak English, they might be able to label only a few items in their drawing rather than to describe it. The teacher should write the few words they were able to produce and not push them to speak more English. Another modification would be to allow the English language learner to create a picture dictionary in English as another alternative for this activity.

Interactive writing. Also called shared pen, interactive writing involves both teacher and students in group discussion, retelling or summarizing text,

- Ask the child to dictate the story. Instead of writing words, she puts blanks for each word. for example, if the child says "A cat sat," The teacher would write:

  _____ _____ ______.

- Read the lines pointing to the corresponding sentence as he "reads the sentence."
- Then ask the student to help you write the story. For example, "the first word in your sentence was A, so I'll write 'A' there."
- After each line is written, read it together.
- If the child is ready, ask them to write one letter or put in the punctuation marks.

Figure 10.6
Scaffolded Writing

verbalizing thoughts about an experience, and writing narrative or expository text (see Figure 10.7).

Modifying Content. For this activity, the English language learner might be paired with a bilingual student, parent, or paraprofessional. This helps the English Language Learner to converse about the topic and her writing.

Modifying Process. In order to adapt this strategy, the teacher might choose to allow the learner with special needs to draw instead of write a word or sentence. This creates a rebus that could be used as an instructional text. As the child becomes more comfortable with text, the teacher can write the word below the child's picture as a model for the future.

Modifying Product. The teacher might choose to take a small group of students to do an interactive writing activity on the computer. Different-colored fonts could be used to highlight punctuation or word patterns that the teacher is focusing upon. This use of technology provides a more tactile approach for readers who are struggling.

Storyboards. Storyboards are wonderful activities for independent responses to literacy. After reading a story, emergent readers can retell the story through

- Children are grouped based upon their learning goals.
- The teacher and children discuss the purpose of their written text and the topic.
- The teacher uses conversation to support the process by asking the children how they would like to begin the text.
- The teacher decides when to "share the pen" with the students based upon their instructional needs. They might write one letter, one word, or a whole sentence.
- As the children write, the teacher comments on the features of the word without focusing on too many points, as the children will lose interest.
- After the text is written, the whole group reads the completed work.

Figure 10.7
Interactive Writing

illustrations and sentences about their selected scenes. Once they have finished their storyboards, emergent readers can perform their storyboards with accompanying music and costumes if they so choose.

Modifying Content. Retelling a story through illustrations can be challenging for struggling readers and writers. Therefore, one way to adapt this activity would be to pair the child with a slightly more advanced reader to assist on this task.

Modifying Process. Instead of using illustrations to retell the story, the child might be given the choice of using character stick puppets. The emergent reader draws each of the main characters and glues them to wooden craft sticks. The child uses the stick puppets to retell the story rather than the illustrations.

Modifying Product. To scaffold this strategy for learners with special needs, the teacher might photocopy pictures from the story which the child can use to retell her version of the story. The pictures can be used to scaffold the sequencing of the story which is often difficult for emergent readers who are struggling.

Meeting Diverse Needs: Electronic books such as *Living Books* often have both English and Spanish versions of the same story on a CD-ROM. This is very useful for second language learners.

Differentiating Instruction for Early Literacy Activities

Children at the early literacy stage of development are building upon their concepts of print to focus on decoding. They see themselves as readers and writers acquiring vocabulary words. As decoding becomes more automatic, the early reader begins to focus her attention on comprehension or meaning making. This section explores how to differentiate the instructional strategies that were presented in Chapter 7.

Directed Listening Thinking Activity

Directed listening thinking activity. Figure 10.8 focuses on scaffolding children's listening skills during storybook reading.

Modifying Content. To help early readers with special needs, the teacher can pair each student with a slightly more advanced early reader. Another alternative

- The teacher selects a story that is appropriate for listening by children at the early stage of literacy and a book that encourages discussion.
- He divides the story into two parts for a shorter book and three parts for a longer book.
- The teacher tells the children that they will listen to the story and think about what may come next.
- The children work in small groups of three or four, with one person being the reporter.
- Each group discusses their predictions and reasons for them.
- The reporter from each group shares the group's prediction with the reason for its selection.

Figure 10.8
Directed Listening Thinking Activity

would be to provide the reader who is struggling with a CD-ROM version of the story or audiotape.

Modifying Process. To provide more support in constructing predictions, readers who are struggling can first share their predictions with their reading buddies. Then together they select one prediction and explain their rationale for choosing it. Another alternative would be to provide the children with illustrations of the story to aid in their construction of predictions.

Modifying Product. Instead of writing their endings for the story, children with special needs may choose to draw their version of the story's outcome. They can dictate their ending to the teacher or aide to write or record it on audiotape for their peers to hear.

Early Writing Activities

The wall story. The instructional strategy presented in Figure 10.9 helps children to brainstorm ideas and write informational text.

Modifying Content. In order to participate in a discussion on the rain forest, children with special needs such as English language learners might need reinforcement in the content areas. To build on their prior knowledge base of the rain forest, before the wall story discussion the children can play the "Magic School Bus Visits the Rainforest" CD-ROM (Scholastic) which will provide them with more information that is visual.

Modifying Process. To keep the children with special needs focused during the wall story, portable wall stories may be used. These are blank manila folders with five squares drawn on them. As pieces of the wall story are added, the learners can record them or illustrate the text if they are unable to write.

Modifying Product. If participating in a wall story is too demanding for the child with attention-deficit disorder, an alternative would be to create a diorama. In this activity, the child would create a scene of the rain forest and write about their diorama on index cards. This tactile activity accomplishes the same goal of expository writing but is less auditory.

- The teacher identifies a broad topic area to write about. An appropriate topic is one that the children know through their reading and is part of an integrated unit of study.
- The teacher conducts a discussion with the children about the topic, reviewing ideas from the book.
- Together the teacher and the children write a wall story together.
- The children share their ideas and concepts while the teacher jots them down.
- The class decides on what ideas will be used and organizes their ideas.
- With approximately five large squares of paper taped to the board, the teacher writes simple factual statements on the bottom half of the paper, leaving the top half for illustrations.
- The teacher models how to write informational text.
- When the children have completed the story, they may illustrate the pages.
- Finally, the teacher reads the story with the children and makes editorial corrections.

Figure 10.9
Procedures for Wall Story

- The teacher uses a picture book biography to discuss the major concepts of the person's life.
- The teacher uses a web to focus on critical concepts and vocabulary words as well as the person's life before the children read the story.
- After the story, the children organize the main events of the person's life onto their biography map.
- The children then share their biography maps with the class and discuss the most important contribution made to the world by their subject.

Figure 10.10
Biography Map

Biography map. The activity in Figure 10.10 helps children to organize the major events of a person's life and to create a biography map.

Modifying Content. Similar to the wall story, children with special needs may need preparation by viewing the Encarta Encyclopedia CD-ROM (Microsoft) on Thurgood Marshall's life story. This will broaden their schemas and enable them to participate in the discussion on Marshall's life.

Modifying Process. An alternative to the concept map shown in Chapter 7 would be an illustrated concept map. Students may choose to use pictures they researched on the Internet to create a visual concept map or timeline of Marshall's life. The pictures help the students to generate the main events in Marshall's biography.

Modifying Product. Instead of creating the concept map on chart paper, teachers may choose to create the map with Inspiration software. This software allows the teacher to add to the web as students discuss Marshall's life story. The Kidspiration version allows young children to create their own concept maps using the software.

- The teacher builds on what the children already know about word patterns and sounds.
- The teacher models to the children how to build ongoing lists of words by adding word endings to a known word.
- He shows them changes to spelling when adding some word endings. For example: *happy: happier, happiest, happiness.*

Figure 10.11
Inflected Endings

Spelling Activities for Early Literacy

Inflected endings. The instructional strategy in Figure 10.11 is designed to help children understand how inflected endings change the meaning of words.

Modifying Content. The objective of this instructional strategy can also be implemented through software games such as Grammar Games. Grammar Games has a similar activity on inflected endings that is very helpful for English language learners or children with attention-deficit disorder due to its visual cues.

Modifying Process. To help children with varied learning styles, this activity on inflected endings can be changed into role playing. Children can be paired and are asked to choose a verb to act out. The remaining children in the group must hold up the card that represents the action. Similar to charades, children use agreed-upon hand signals to designate past or future events.

Modifying Product. This strategy on inflected endings can be altered by allowing students to focus on a particular tense or to complete the activity with a partner.

Differentiating Instruction for the Fluent Reader and Writer

The child who has reached the fluency stage of literacy has mastered the intricacies of decoding and can use her attention to focus on comprehension. The teacher's role during this stage of literacy is to facilitate the child's acquisition of comprehension skills such as making inferences. It is also important to help the fluent reader understand readings from the content areas and to organize information into think sheets. This section describes how to differentiate activities for the fluent reader and writer that were presented in Chapter 8.

Modeling Fluency Activities

Questioning the author. The purpose of the activity below is to help children query text and to make connections.

Modifying Content. Children with special needs might find a content area textbook daunting to read. Therefore, a modification for content for questioning the author might be to focus on only one paragraph at a time. This would allow the learner with special needs to become comfortable with the process of querying text before she is responsible for reading the complete chapter. If expository text

The Planning Stage
- The teacher does a careful study of the text the students will read.
- The teacher anticipates any problems that the students might face while they read.
- The teacher identifies key ideas within the text and logical segmented text to create queries that will guide the students as they read.

The Implementation Stage
- Present the reading material to the children.
- While they are reading, have them stop.
- Offer them the query so they will think deeply about what they are reading.
- Have the children tell their responses to the query.

The Discussion Stage
- Engage the children in a discussion of the section of the chapters they read.
- The discussion should raise issues with how the author presented the material for readers and how accurate the author is.
- The discussion should also help children make connections of what they have read to their own prior knowledge and clear up any misconceptions related to the text.

remains too difficult for the children, the teacher might choose a familiar narrative format such as fairy tales to model the process.

Modifying Process. There are several possible adaptations for questioning the author. Students with special needs might need help with tapping their prior knowledge. Therefore, brainstorming on a discussion web before the reading might help the children to recall their prior knowledge regarding the content of the text. Another adaptation might be to provide the chapter on audiotape for the students to listen to before the activity. This gives the child with special needs the confidence to participate in discussions and to generate questions about the text.

Modifying Product. Students with hearing or speech disabilities might have trouble participating in this activity. Therefore, one way to adapt the product for this activity would be to pair them with slightly higher level readers to write down their questions regarding the text. The process is still querying the author; however, the student submits a written product rather than a verbal response.

- Prior to reading or studying about a topic, the teacher asks students to think about what they know related to the topic. Questions that are designed after the three levels of information include: What is the topic? What do we know about the topic? What are some examples that you know?
- During the prereading discussion, the teacher develops a prereading word map.
- After the discussion, the students read on the major topic that was discussed.
- The teacher engages students in postreading discussion. As students discuss, they construct a word map. The teacher demonstrates how to fill in the map.

Figure 10.12
Word Maps

Word map. In the activity in Figure 10.12, children connect their prior knowledge regarding words and create word maps which help them to see associated concepts.

Modifying Content. To do word maps, students need prior knowledge about the concepts being discussed. One way to adapt this activity for children with special needs is to begin with a concept that the children are very familiar with such as television or food. This would allow the students to understand how to construct a word map and to generate their own examples.

Modifying Process. In order to help students with insufficient prior knowledge, the teacher might supplement the list of vocabulary words with pictures or text readings. If the students are primarily visual learners, they might use the Internet or encyclopedia software to learn about the topics that are being studied. This exercise would help them to generate the necessary examples and properties of the topic they need to construct on a word map.

Modifying Product. Because this activity is to help students visualize information in nonfiction text, the teacher may choose to have the students create their word maps with illustrations. This would help the visual learner as well as the student who requires a tactile approach in order to retain information.

Inquiry chart. The activity in Figure 10.13 facilitates students' research of a topic and helps them to organize their research.

Modifying Content. To help students feel confident when first completing an I-Chart, the teacher might choose to focus first on the students' hobbies or areas of interest. For example, if a child with special needs is interested in sharks, she will use that as the focus of her I-Chart. Children usually read about their hobbies or interests and collect facts about them. Therefore, they have already engaged in the I-Chart process, but in an informal way. This will give the child with special needs the motivation to complete her chart and to participate fully in the process.

Modifying the Process. Children with special needs may need to complete their I-Chart on graphics software such as Kidspiration. This tactile, visual approach matches the learning style of the child and helps them to see the connections between facts on the topic. In addition, pictures and videos available on the

- The teacher selects a topic familiar to the students.
- The students select three or four questions that will provide them with directions for inquiry into the topic area.
- The teacher introduces the I-Chart to the children, models and demonstrates its use in researching a topic, then passes out copies of a blank I-Chart. He shows the children the kinds of questions that will provide the best type of information for the research and demonstrates the kinds of sources of information, including technology as a major source.
- The class brainstorms information that students already know on the topic. The students find the question that the information answers and write it under the appropriate box. Any information that does not fit under any of the questions, may be placed under "Interesting Facts."
- The teacher provides students with multiple sources of information on the topic: books, maps, Internet sources, magazines, and so on.
- The children work in small groups, each with a set of resources. The teacher demonstrates to the children how to use the questions in the I-Chart as guides, showing them that the questions may direct them to the material that is appropriate and direct them away from the material that is not appropriate.
- As the children read the material and discuss it with their groups, the teacher helps them to record it on the I-Chart. Children may find that there are new questions that need to be asked.
- At the conclusion, the children look at each question and the information generated by the question and synthesize it to form a summary statement. Students write their summary statements at the bottom of the I-Chart under each question.
- The children write about the main topic of research. Each question may be transformed into a paragraph. The details will come from the answers to the questions.

Figure 10.13
Inquiry Charts

Internet about the topic of study would also help the child with special needs to tap her prior knowledge.

Modifying Product. In order to complete the I-Chart, a child with special needs has to remain focused for a long time. This might be an impossible task for a child with attention-deficit hyperactivity disorder or a learning disability. Thus, one way to modify the product would be to segment the I-Chart into three separate activities that could be spread out over several days. These short segments would allow the child with special needs to stay on task and still complete the assignment.

Adapting Assessment for the Inclusive Classroom

This chapter has discussed how to differentiate instructional strategies for the inclusive classroom. Due to the federal legislation PL 94-142 and the **Individuals with Disabilities Education Act of 1997,** teachers must also understand how to accommodate their assessment system for children with special needs.

Timing of Assessment	*Setting of Assessment*	*Presentation of Materials*	*Student Response*
1. At a time of day best suited for students	In a separate location	Large print or Braille editions of texts	Dictates answers to teacher
2. Rest breaks between items	Room has special lighting or acoustics	Directions or task read aloud by teacher	Responses are audiotaped
3. Extended time to complete task	Student uses a study carrel	Directions are audiotaped	Student uses primer pencils or special writing utensils
4. Additional sessions if child has ADD	Student uses adaptive furniture	Student uses noise buffers	Student uses word processor to type responses
5. Untimed test sessions	Assessment is done individually or in small groups	Place markers are used for students to track print	Students with hearing disabilities may sign their responses

Figure 10.14
Assessment Accommodations

Standards-based assessment that is mandated in many states inquires, "Is the student learning?" In this text, we have been using developmental benchmarks as the guidepost for answering that question. The assessment tools used in this text have emphasized a holistic orientation toward learning (Wiener & Cohen, 1997). A holistic orientation views assessment as promoting learning, not just measuring it (Routman, 2000).

In order to promote learning, this text has used authentic assessment instruments such as checklists, anecdotal records, and rubrics. Authentic assessment instruments are well suited for inclusive classrooms because assessment focuses on typical, daily literacy activities (Allington & Cunningham, 2002). The use of developmental benchmarks also has value for all the stakeholders in the assessment process, such as teachers, students, and parents (Routman, 2000).

What Are Assessment Accommodations?

Due to federal law, children with special needs are entitled to changes in how assessment is presented or how they can respond (Thurlow, 2002). If the student is required to take a standardized test, alternate assessments might be available that the student with special needs could use instead.

How to Accommodate Assessment

Students may need changes in the timing, setting, presentation, or the student response (Landau, Vohs, & Romano, 2002). The chart shown in Figure 10.14 presents some possibilities for assessment accommodations.

Differentiating Assessment for the Emergent Reader and Writer

Differentiating instruction and assessment can be difficult for the experienced as well as novice teacher. Therefore, this section illustrates how to modify assessment for the instructional strategies that were discussed earlier in the chapter. Because most states demand that children with special needs meet the same standards as their peers, the approach of this text has been to modify the assessment process while using the identical assessment checklist or observation sheet that is used with the typically developing child. The first section discusses differentiating assessment for the emergent reader and writer.

Rubber band stretch. The following chart was presented in Chapter 6 as an example of an assessment checklist for phonemic awareness activities.

Directions: Use your observations to identify behaviors demonstrated by students.

Checklist of Phonemic Awareness

Developmental Benchmarks	***Observed—Date***	***Not Observed—Date***
• Identifies words with the same sounds		
• Identifies same-sound patterns		
• Identifies rhyming words		
• Separates sounds in short-vowel words (e.g., *man, cat, dog*)		
• Blends phonemes into words		
• Identifies syllables in two-syllable words through clapping		
• Identifies syllables in three-syllable words through clapping		
• Identifies rhyming words		

Because this activity is primarily auditory, modifications for rubber band stretch that were discussed previously include letter cards and electronic software games. Suggestions for adapting the above assessment instrument are presented in Figure 10.15.

Sound isolation song. The emergent literacy behaviors assessment for phonological awareness form was presented in Chapter 6 as an instrument to use to evaluate a child's performance during the phonetic awareness activities.

Timing of Assessment	*Setting of Assessment*	*Presentation of Materials*	*Student Response*
Children with attention-deficit disorder should be assessed at their most attentive time. For most children, this is the morning period.	Because children with attention-deficit disorder are easily distracted, assessment should be conducted in a study carrel or in another room away from the noisy classroom.	Because this activity is primarily auditory, using letter cards would help the child with ADHD to focus on the task.	As mentioned earlier in the chapter, children using the Reader Rabbit software game could print out their task. This could be used as the assessment instrument for phonological processing.

Figure 10.15
Ways to Adapt the Phonemic Awareness Assessment

Directions: During instructional activities, observe students' literacy performance.

Assessment for Phonological Awareness

Developmental Benchmark	*Observation*	*Interpretation*
Identifies sounds and elements		
Recognizes rhymes and word patterns		
Can sort word patterns		
Orally blends onset and rimes, syllables		
Manipulates phoneme substitutes and deletes phonemes		

The assessment instrument for phonological awareness may be modified as shown in Figure 10.16.

Rhyming word sit down. This activity in its original format is primarily auditory. The children sit down when they hear a rhyming word pair. The instructional modifications for this activity were letter cards as well as audiotapes and electronic software. The phonological awareness checklist shown in Figure 10.17 was presented in Chapter 6 as an appropriate assessment instrument for this activity.

The phonological awareness checklist may be modified as shown in Figure 10.18.

Spelling activities—onsets and rimes. This activity focuses on helping the emergent reader and writer to use word families to build spelling vocabularies. The spelling behavior rubrics (Table 10.1) were presented in Chapter 6 as an example of an assessment tool for this activity.

Timing of Assessment	*Setting of Assessment*	*Presentation of Materials*	*Student Response*
Once teachers have a sense of the child's daily rhythm of behaviors, they should plan assessment tasks at the child's peak performance period.	Because this activity requires music, the teacher should bring the child to another room or hallway for a quieter setting.	In order to accommodate the child with special needs, the teacher might use alphabet picture cards during the assessment.	As mentioned in the instructional strategy discussed previously, the English language learner may respond by holding up picture alphabet cards as an additional prompt.

Figure 10.16
Ways to Adapt the Phonological Awareness Assessment

Directions: During instructional activities, observe students' literacy performance.

Developmental Benchmark	*Observation*	*Interpretation*
Identifies sounds and elements		
Recognizes rhymes and word patterns		
Can sort word patterns		
Orally blends onset and rimes, syllables		
Manipulates phoneme substitutes and deletes phonemes		

Figure 10.17
Assessment for Phonological Awareness

Timing of Assessment	*Setting of Assessment*	*Presentation of Materials*	*Student Response*
Teachers may ask aides to record assessment data during the classroom activity. This might help the children to focus on the task rather than the assessment instrument.	Because this is another listening activity, the child with ADHD should be taken to a quiet place to focus on the task.	As suggested in the instructional strategy, the teacher might substitute the audiotape of *The Cat in the Hat* for this activity. Because most children know this text, it might help the child with special needs to identify rhyming words.	As mentioned earlier in the chapter, children using the Reader Rabbit software game could print out their task. This could be used as the assessment instrument for phonological processing.

Figure 10.18
Ways to Adapt the Phonological Awareness Assessment

Table 10.1
Spelling Behavior Rubrics

Spelling Behavior	Level 3	Level 2	Level 1
Uses knowledge of phonics to encode word	Spells based upon knowledge of phonics	Sometimes uses phonics to spell words	Does not use phonics to spell words
Compares unknown words with familiar words	Uses knowledge of words to spell unknown words	Sometimes uses word knowledge to spell	Does not use knowledge of known words to spell
Uses word wall as a reference	Uses word wall as a reference	Sometimes uses word wall as a reference	Never uses word wall as a reference
Spells words based upon knowledge of syllabication	Uses knowledge of syllabication to spell	Sometimes uses syllabication to spell	Does not use syllabication to spell

Timing of Assessment	***Setting of Assessment***	***Presentation of Materials***	***Student Response***
Children with attention-deficit disorder should be assessed at their most attentive time. For most children, this is the morning period.	The spelling behaviors checklist may be administered during the instructional activity or at a study carrel for a child with ADHD.	As suggested in the activity, color-coded word families may be used to help the child focus on the rimes. Also, magnetic letters with raised bumps may be used to help the child with learning disabilities to trace the onsets and rimes before responding.	Children with learning disabilities might need to type their responses on a computer. The different font choices as well as the tactile act of typing may help to improve their performance.

Figure 10.19
Ways to Adapt the Spelling Behavior Rubrics

The spelling behavior rubrics may be modified for children with special learning needs (see Figure 10.19).

Doing the word wall. This activity is also focused on helping the emergent reader and writer to identify onsets and rimes. A suggested accommodation for the learner with special needs includes using cornmeal to help trace word patterns as well as portable word walls. The student profile of spelling development was suggested in Chapter 6 as an assessment instrument for this activity.

The implementation of the student profile of spelling development may be modified as shown in Figure 10.20.

Student Profile of Spelling Development

Student's Name ____________________________

Prephonetic Stage of Spelling Development—Random Letters

Date:

_____ Scribbles and draws shapes that look like letters
_____ Makes random letters and shapes
_____ Uses no spaces between words
_____ Draws pictures to express meaning
Grade _____/4

Early Phonetic Stage of Spelling Development—Consonants

Date:

_____ Begins to show letter–sound relationships
_____ Uses invented spelling
_____ Uses initial consonants
_____ Spells words with consonants
_____ Uses spaces between words
Grade _____/5

Advanced Phonetic Stage of Spelling Development

Date:

_____ Spells words using letter–sound relationships
_____ Spells words based on how they look
_____ Begins to use long vowels in spelling words
Grade _____/3

Transitional Stage of Spelling Development—Vowel and Consonant Combinations in Words

Date:

_____ Spells words using more standard forms of spelling
_____ Relies more on visual memory, how words look, to spell words
_____ Spells more sight words correctly
_____ Spells words using familiar letter patterns
_____ At the end of the stage, all syllables are represented in words
Grade _____/5

Standard Stage of Spelling Development—Correct Spelling

Date:

_____ Spells most words using standard or correct spelling
_____ Begins to spell words that have multiple spellings (eg., *their, there, they're*) correctly
_____ Relies on meaning and syntax as well as phonics to spell words
Grade _____/3

Emergent writing—The language experience approach. This emergent writing activity used the child's oral language to create the text for an accompanying student drawing. Inclusive modifications to this strategy included allowing the English language learner to communicate through drawings or to use electronic software to create their dictated story. The emergent writing rubrics (Table 10.2)

Timing of Assessment	*Setting of Assessment*	*Presentation of Materials*	*Student Response*
Teachers may ask aides to record assessment data during the classroom activity. This might help the children to focus on the task rather than the assessment instrument.	This assessment can be completed as the child engages in the class activity. If the child is unable to focus, the teacher may have to administer the instrument at the study carrel.	If children are unable to focus, it might be easier to use the portable word wall. The portable word wall helps the child with ADHD or learning disabilities to focus on one word at a time rather than the entire chart.	To make the assessment more tactile, the child with learning disabilities might need to use cornmeal or raised magnetic letters to complete the word wall patterns.

Figure 10.20
Ways to Adapt the Student Profile of Spelling Development

Table 10.2
Emergent Writing Rubrics

Emergent Writing Behaviors	**Target**	**Acceptable**	**Needs Improvement**
Writes uppercase and lowercase letters	Uses both uppercase and lowercase letters	Sometimes uses uppercase and lowercase letters	Uses only uppercase letters
Writes consonants and vowel sounds in words	Writes both consonants and vowel sounds	Writes some vowel and consonant sounds	Writes only consonant sounds
Begins to write sentences and use punctuation	Writes sentences with punctuation	Sometimes writes sentences and uses punctuation	Does not write sentences or use punctuation

were presented in Chapter 6 as an appropriate tool for evaluating emergent writing behavior.

The emergent writing rubrics may be modified as shown in Figure 10.21 to accommodate the child with special learning needs:

Interactive writing. This shared pen activity was designed to scaffold the emergent writer as she attempts to record her oral language. Suggested accommodations for this activity included creating a rebus for the English language learner as well as using word processing for the writing of the story. The interactive writing observation sheet was presented in Chapter 6 as the assessment instrument for this activity.

The interactive writing observation sheet may be changed to accommodate the child with special needs (see Figure 10.22).

Scaffolded writing. This additional emergent writing activity uses the language experience approach and integrates it with phonological processing. By providing the emergent writer with blanks instead of words, the child is gradually pushed

Interactive Writing Observation Sheet		
Interactive Writing Behaviors	***Observed—Date***	***Not Observed—Date***
Participates in group discussion about experience		
Retells or summarizes story or news		
Verbalizes thoughts and feelings about an experience		
Writes letter, word, or sentence when called upon		

Timing of Assessment	*Setting of Assessment*	*Presentation of Materials*	*Student Response*
Once teachers have a sense of the child's daily rhythm of behaviors, they should plan assessment tasks at the child's peak performance period.	This assessment can be completed as the child engages in the class activity. If the child is unable to focus, the teacher may have to administer the instrument at the study carrel.	As mentioned in the activity, allowing the child to use electronic software such as Richard Scarry's World of Reading would help the English language learner or child with learning disabilities.	Children using the Richard Scarry software might print out their electronic story as their product. Also, teachers might use the English language learner's drawing as their story product.

Figure 10.21
Ways to Adapt the Emergent Writing Rubrics

Timing of Assessment	*Setting of Assessment*	*Presentation of Materials*	*Student Response*
Teachers may ask aides to record assessment data during the classroom activity. This might help the children to focus on the task rather than the assessment instrument.	This assessment can be completed as the child engages in the class activity. If the child is unable to focus, the teacher may have to administer the instrument at the study carrel.	For children who are English language learners, the teacher might want to use the rebus modification that was discussed earlier in the chapter.	The English language learner might use drawings to record the story. Children who need a more tactile approach might use a word processor to type out the story.

Figure 10.22
Ways to Adapt the Interactive Writing Observation Sheet

Table 10.3
Emergent Writing Rubrics

Emergent Writing Behaviors	Target	Acceptable	Needs Improvement
Writes uppercase and lowercase letters	Uses both uppercase and lowercase letters	Sometimes uses uppercase and lowercase letters	Uses only uppercase letters
Writes consonants and vowel sounds in words	Writes both consonants and vowel sounds	Writes some vowel and consonant sounds	Writes only consonant sounds
Begins to write sentences and use punctuation	Writes sentences with punctuation	Sometimes writes sentences and uses punctuation	Does not write sentences or use punctuation

Timing of Assessment	*Setting of Assessment*	*Presentation of Materials*	*Student Response*
Once teachers have a sense of the child's daily rhythm of behaviors, they should plan assessment tasks at the child's peak performance period.	This assessment can be completed as the child engages in the class activity. If the child is unable to focus, the teacher may have to administer the instrument at the study carrel.	If children are having difficulty writing the words for the sounds, magnetic letters or picture cards might be used as concrete prompts to help them recall the sounds for each letter.	Children using the Richard Scarry software might print out their electronic story as their product. Also, teachers might use the English language learner's drawing as their story product.

Figure 10.23
Ways to Adapt the Emergent Writing Rubrics

toward encoding the spoken word. Modifications for this activity include using electronic software as well as the rebus method for English language learners. The emergent writing rubrics (Table 10.3) are used as a developmental assessment for the emergent writer. The same assessment tool is suggested for the language experience approach.

The emergent writing rubrics may be modified as shown in Figure 10.23 to accommodate the child with special learning needs.

Storyboards. The storyboards instructional strategy is designed as an independent emergent literacy activity. The emergent reader and writer illustrates her own version of the story and presents it to the class. Accommodations for the inclusive classroom included using stick puppets as well as photocopied pictures from the actual book to act as prompts. The concepts about books rubrics (Table 10.4) were provided as an example of an assessment instrument for this activity in Chapter 6.

This assessment tool may be changed to fit the needs of the inclusive classroom (see Figure 10.24).

Table 10.4
Concepts About Books Rubrics

Concepts About Books	Target	Acceptable	Needs Improvement
Makes predictions based upon cover and title	Uses cover and title to make predictions	Sometimes uses cover and title to make predictions	Never uses cover and title to make predictions
Shares background knowledge related to text	Shares prior knowledge in story discussions	Sometimes uses prior knowledge about text	Never uses prior knowledge about text
Gives responses to text that show comprehension	Responds to text with comprehension	Sometimes demonstrates comprehension through story response	Never or seldom demonstrates comprehension

Timing of Assessment	*Setting of Assessment*	*Presentation of Materials*	*Student Response*
This activity should be assessed as the child is presenting. If the child is an English language learner and is too shy to present orally in front of peers, the teacher may assess the student privately.	This assessment should be conducted while the child performs the storyboard for peers in the classroom.	As discussed previously in the chapter, some students may need photocopied pictures from the storybook to act as prompts for the script.	The child may use stick puppets instead of pictures to tell the story. Also, the child might use an electronic drawing software program to illustrate the storyboard.

Figure 10.24
Ways to Adapt the Concept About Books Rubrics

Differentiated Assessment for Early Literacy Activities

The child at the early literacy level is gradually mastering the printed word but still needs instructional support. This section describes how to individualize assessment for the child at the early literacy level. Differentiated instruction assessment instruments that were discussed in the previous pages will be used to illustrate this process.

Directed Listening Thinking Activity

This activity was designed to help children at the early literacy level to improve their ability to generate predictions. Accommodations for the inclusive classroom included using CD-ROMs of the presented stories as well as selected pictures from the storybooks as concrete prompts. The concepts about books rubrics (Table 10.5) were used as a developmental checklist to record the child's progress from the emergent literacy stage.

Table 10.5
Concepts About Books Rubrics

Concepts About Books	Target	Acceptable	Needs Improvement
Makes predictions based upon cover and title	Uses cover and title to make predictions	Sometimes uses cover and title to make predictions	Never uses cover and title to make predictions
Shares background knowledge related to text	Shares prior knowledge in story discussions	Sometimes uses prior knowledge about text	Never uses prior knowledge about text
Gives responses to text that show comprehension	Responds to text with comprehension	Sometimes demonstrates comprehension through story response	Never or seldom demonstrates comprehension

Timing of Assessment	*Setting of Assessment*	*Presentation of Materials*	*Student Response*
This activity should be implemented at the time when the child with special needs will perform at peak level.	This activity should be conducted in class. However, if the child with ADHD cannot focus, she should be taken to the study carrel or to another room.	As discussed previously in the chapter, some students may need the CD-ROM or audiotape version of the story to perform this task.	The child may illustrate her predictions regarding the story or type her responses on a word processor.

Figure 10.25
Ways to Adapt the Concepts About Books Rubrics

The concepts about books rubrics may be changed to best record the performance of the child with special needs (see Figure 10.25).

Wall Story

The wall story instructional strategy is designed to help the child at the early literacy stage to compose informational text. As discussed previously, the activity can be modified by providing the child with background information or by allowing her to create a diorama instead of printed text. The early writing checklist was presented in Chapter 7 as an example of an assessment instrument for this activity.

The early writing checklist may be modified to differentiate assessment for the writer at the early literacy stage (see Figure 10.26).

Biography Maps

Biography maps are designed to help the young child process informational text. The child at the early literacy stage is shown how to select the highlights of a famous

Early Writing Checklist		
Early Writing Behaviors	***Observed—Date***	***Not Observed—Date***
Writes a bank of high-frequency words		
Segments sounds in words heard		
Uses word patterns to write words		
Writes stories with a beginning, middle, and end		
Composes stories using familiar text as models		
Begins to write paragraphs		
Uses punctuation and capital letters		
Writing is close to conventional		

Timing of Assessment	*Setting of Assessment*	*Presentation of Materials*	*Student Response*
Once teachers have a sense of the child's daily rhythm of behaviors, they should plan assessment tasks at the child's peak performance period.	The child with ADHD may be unable to focus on this task in a large group. Therefore, the teacher might want to administer this task individually or with a small group.	The child with special needs might need concrete prompts such as pictures from textbooks to generate text for the wall story.	As discussed previously, a portable wall story might help the child with ADHD to focus on the printed word. Also, creating a model or diorama could substitute for the wall story as the child's product.

Figure 10.26
Ways to Adapt the Early Writing Checklist

person's life as well as their major contributions to society. Modifications for the inclusive classroom discussed previously in this chapter included using electronic software to create the biography maps as well as providing background information for the English language learner. The biography map observation sheet was presented in Chapter 7 as a useful assessment tool for this instructional strategy.

The chart shown in Figure 10.27 illustrates how to modify the assessment process for this activity.

Strategy for Inflected Endings

The strategy for inflected endings is intended to help the child at the early literacy stage to build upon their spelling vocabularies and knowledge of word patterns.

Biography Map Observation Sheet		
Early Literacy Behaviors	***Observed—Date***	***Not Observed—Date***
Participates in group discussion about content		
Retells or summarizes story or news		
Verbalizes thoughts and feelings about a concept or person		
Selects key vocabulary words regarding concept or famous person		
Selects key events in person's life to create a biography map		

Timing of Assessment	*Setting of Assessment*	*Presentation of Materials*	*Student Response*
Teachers should not assess the child doing this activity until they are certain that the child has acquired enough background knowledge to complete the biography map.	This assessment can be completed as the child engages in the class activity. If the child is unable to focus, the teacher may have to administer the instrument at the study carrel.	For children who are English language learners or who have a learning disability, the teacher might have pictures from the person's life to generate the timeline or key concepts for the biography map.	The second language learner might use drawings to record the biography map. Children with ADHD might prefer to use Kidspiration to create their biography map.

Figure 10.27
Ways to Adapt the Biography Map Observation Sheet

Modifications for this activity included Grammar Games software or role playing the inflections. The spelling behavior rubrics (Table 10.6) were presented in Chapter 7 as a developmental assessment tool to track spelling development from the emergent to fluent literacy levels.

The assessment procedures for the spelling behavior rubrics can be changed to help the child with special needs (Figure 10.28).

Differentiated Assessment for the Fluent Reader and Writer

The fluent reader and writer is now reading to learn and uses her ability to decode text to engage in critical thinking. In the inclusive classroom, children who have

Table 10.6
Spelling Behavior Rubrics

Spelling Behavior	Level 3	Level 2	Level 1
Uses knowledge of phonics to encode words	Spells words based upon knowledge of phonics	Sometimes uses phonics to spell words	Does not use phonics to spell words
Compares unknown words with familiar words	Uses knowledge of words to spell unknown words	Sometimes uses word knowledge to spell	Does not use knowledge of known words to spell
Uses word wall as a reference	Uses word wall as reference	Sometimes uses word wall to spell	Never uses word wall to spell
Spells words based upon knowledge of syllabication	Uses knowledge of syllabication to spell	Sometimes uses syllabication to spell	Does not spell using syllabication

Timing of Assessment	*Setting of Assessment*	*Presentation of Materials*	*Student Response*
Children with attention-deficit disorder should be assessed at their most attentive time. For most children, this is the morning period.	The spelling behavior rubrics may be administered during the instructional activity or at a study carrel for a child with ADHD.	Children with learning disabilities may need magnetic letters with raised bumps to feel the word endings. In addition, color-coded letter cards would also help children to focus on the task.	A substitute assessment product for this activity might be the printout from the Grammar Games software.

Figure 10.28
Ways to Adapt the Spelling Behavior Rubrics

attained this high literacy level but have special learning needs still require modifications during the assessment process. This section discusses the assessment processes for the differentiated instructional strategies for the fluent reader and writer that were discussed previously.

Questioning the Author

Questioning the author is an instructional strategy designed to help the fluent reader critique informational text. The suggested changes for the inclusive classroom were to provide the child with a hearing disability with a scribe or a buddy reader to help with the difficult vocabulary. The questioning the author observation sheet was discussed in Chapter 8 as a possible evaluative tool for this activity.

The assessment process for the questioning the author observation sheet may be individualized to meet the needs of the child with special needs (see Figure 10.29).

Questioning the Author Observation Sheet

Book Title

Fluent Literacy Behaviors	***Very Effective (++)***	***Effective(+)***	***Needs Improvement(−)***	***Not Observed (No)***
Makes predictions based upon cover and title				
Shares background knowledge related to text				
Challenges the story and text content				
Questions the author's assumptions				

Timing of Assessment	***Setting of Assessment***	***Presentation of Materials***	***Student Response***
This activity should be implemented at the time when the child with special needs will perform at peak level.	This activity should be conducted in class. However, if the child with ADHD cannot focus, she should be placed in a smaller group or the group should be moved to an adjoining quiet room.	As discussed previously in the chapter, some students may need the CD-ROM or audiotape version of the story to perform this task. Children with visual disabilities might also need copies of the text in Braille.	The child with special needs may need to complete this activity with her buddy reader. If the whole text is too difficult, she might be assessed on a few paragraphs instead.

Figure 10.29
Ways to Adapt the Questioning the Author Observation Sheet

Word Maps

This instructional strategy is designed to help fluent readers generate their background knowledge regarding a concept and to create a word map based upon it. Suggested modifications for this activity that were discussed previously include providing the child with supplemental background knowledge or allowing her to illustrate her word map. The word map observation sheet was presented in Chapter 8 as a possible tool for evaluating students during this task.

Word Map Observation Sheet

Fluent Literacy Behaviors	*Observed—Date*	*Not Observed—Date*
Participates in group discussion about content		
Relates concept to background knowledge		
Verbalizes thoughts and feelings about a concept		
Selects key vocabulary words regarding concept		
Creates graphic organizer to reflect key concepts and vocabulary		

Timing of Assessment	*Setting of Assessment*	*Presentation of Materials*	*Student Response*
Teachers should not assess the child doing this activity until they are certain that the child has acquired enough background knowledge to complete the word map.	This assessment can be completed as the child engages in the class activity. If the child is unable to focus, the teacher may have to administer the instrument at the study carrel.	For children who are English language learners or who have a learning disability, the teacher might use manipulatives or pictures to generate vocabulary to create the word map.	The second language learner might use drawings to create the word map. Children with ADHD might also use Kidspiration software to create the word map.

Figure 10.30
Ways to Adapt the Word Map Observation Sheet

The word map observation sheet may be used in the inclusive classroom if the assessment process includes the modifications shown in Figure 10.30.

Inquiry Charts (I-Charts)

One of the teacher's tasks when working with the fluent reader is to prepare them for the research reports they will be required to write in middle school and beyond. Inquiry charts, or I-Charts, help to introduce a strategy for research that the fluent reader may use to generate a research report. This is a difficult activity for the child with special needs; however, modifications such as segmenting the activity into smaller tasks or using computer software to generate concept webs would help the child complete the assignment. The inquiry charts checklist was presented in Chapter 8 as an assessment instrument for this activity.

This activity is extremely difficult for the child with special needs. Therefore, it is recommended that the child be assessed at varying points throughout the process. The rationale for this segmented assessment process is that the child with special needs may not be able to focus for long periods and therefore may have to complete this task over several days. The chart shown in Figure 10.31 suggests additional accommodations for assessing this strategy.

Inquiry Charts Checklist

Inquiry Charts Checklist

Research Topic:

Fluent Literacy Behaviors	***Target (++)***	***Acceptable (+)***	***Needs Improvement (–)***	***Not Observed (No)***
Generates questions based upon background knowledge				
Shares background knowledge related to text				
Uses a variety of strategies when confronted by text not understood				
Generates answers to queries from text and multiple sources				
Composes paragraphs based upon I-Chart				

Timing of Assessment	***Setting of Assessment***	***Presentation of Materials***	***Student Response***
This activity should be implemented at the time when the child with special needs will perform at peak level. It is best to record the behavior in class as the activity progresses, but at segmented intervals over a period of days.	This activity should be conducted in class. However, if the child with ADHD cannot focus, she should be placed in a smaller group or the group should be moved to an adjoining quiet room.	As discussed previously in the chapter, some students may need the CD-ROM or audiotape version of the informational text in order to process. If none is available, it may have to be read to them.	The child with special needs may need to complete this activity with a buddy reader. She may also create her I-Chart using software such as Kidspiration.

Figure 10.31
Ways to Adapt the Inquiry Charts Checklist

Reporting and Using Information

In order for assessment to promote learning, the information about the student's performance must be shared with other teachers, the student, and her parents. It is also important that new information about the child with special needs is shared with the child study team at the school. Child study teams vary across the nation, but they mainly consist of the classroom teacher, special education teacher, occupational therapist, school psychologist, and a school administrator. It is imperative that assessment data be shared because ongoing authentic assessment may change the team's goals for the child. Ongoing evaluation of the child may create changes in the child's individualized education plan (IEP) which is mandated by law. The child study team creates the IEP and seeks the necessary resources and materials to help meet the instructional goals for the child. In order to keep instruction aligned with assessment, the child study team has to work as a unit, sharing assessment data and brainstorming the next instructional cycle for the child with special needs.

Portrait of Differentiated Instruction for All Children

It is Friday morning in Ms. Gonzalez's third-grade class and typically, it is humming with activity. John is in the study carrel finishing his spelling worksheet. Because John has attention-deficit hyperactivity disorder, he needs to wear noise buffer headsets as well as work in an isolated partition. This helps John to focus on the task before him and not on the myriad activities in the room. Ms. Gonzalez is working on a wall story about the rain forest. To help the English language learners with the science content, Ms. Gonzalez has placed the "Magic Schoolbus Visit to the Rainforest" CD-ROM in the computer center. Joaquin and Marta are watching the Spanish version of the story, which will help them to participate in the discussion.

Discussion Questions and Activities

1. Visit an early childhood classroom and identify a student with special needs. Design an instructional strategy for this child and describe how you would accommodate his or her special needs.
2. Today's classroom is highly diverse. Choose a book from the recommended list and design an instructional strategy and assessment that addresses cultural or linguistic diversity.
3. Interview the members of a child study team at your field school and identify how they work together to meet the needs of children with special needs.

Additional Web Sites

The Assessment Reform Group
http://www.assessment-reform-group.org.uk
The Assessment Reform Group is a British educational organization that provides publications on assessment for learning.

Center for the Improvement of Early Reading Achievement
http://www.ciera.org
This site has excellent resources and publications concerning literacy in early childhood.

International Reading Association
http://www.ira.org
This international literacy organization offers books and online articles on literacy across age groups.

Learning Disabilities Online
http://www.ldonline.org
This site offers teachers myriad links and activities for children with special needs.

National Council of Teachers of English
http://www.ncte.org
This organization publishes the journal *Language Arts* and has numerous links for educators.

Additional Children's Literature

Aardema, V. (1991). *Pedro and the padre.* New York: Dial.

Bardot, D. (1991). *A bicycle for Rosaura.* Brooklyn: Kane/Miller.

Betancourt, J. (1993). *My name is Brain/Brian.* New York: Scholastic.

Booth, B. (1991). *Mandy.* New York: Lothrop, Lee & Shepard.

Brown, T. (1982). *Someone special just like you.* New York: Holt.

Daly, N. (1985). *Not so fast Songololo.* New York: Viking Penguin.

Havill, J. (1989). *Jamaica tag-along.* Boston: Houghton Mifflin.

Palacios, A. (1993). *A Christmas surprise for Chabelita.* New York: Troll.

Polacco, P. (1998). *Thank you, Mr. Falker.* New York: Philomel.

Riggio, A. (1997). *Secret signs along the underground railroad.* Honesdale, PA: Boyds Mills Press.

Children's Literature References

McCloskey, R. (1941). *Make way for ducklings.* New York: Viking Press.

Seuss, Dr. (1957). *The cat in the hat.* New York: Random House.

Seuss, Dr. (1988). *Green eggs and ham.* New York: Random House.

CHAPTER 11

Portfolio Assessment

Portrait of a Balanced Literacy Classroom

Ms. Nagori's fourth-grade class is busily preparing for their portfolio celebration that is scheduled for Thursday. The students have completed their first semester of work and are eagerly awaiting their parents' reactions to their work. Julio is putting the finishing touches to his concept map about Gandhi, while his friend Jorge is fixing his diorama of The Lion, the Witch and the Wardrobe *by C. S. Lewis (1950). The students have rehearsed their presentations and will describe the work samples in their portfolios to their parents.*

To a novice teacher, assembling a literacy portfolio for every one of the students can be a daunting task. However, with an assessment framework and organizational skills, every teacher can achieve this goal. This chapter will describe how to organize a literacy portfolio system across the grades. It will also include samples from emergent, early, and fluent readers' literacy portfolios and how they were evaluated.

As you read this chapter, think of the following questions:

- What is a literacy portfolio?
- How do I organize a literacy portfolio?
- How do I evaluate the child's work samples?
- How do I prepare for a parent conference?

Defining Portfolio Assessment

Portfolio assessment looks at the child from a developmental perspective.

The concept of using a portfolio for assessment was borrowed from the art world. For several generations, art students have been required to assemble a collection of critical work to demonstrate their developmental progress. This concept was developed into authentic assessment of literacy progress that could be used to offer teachers another perspective of students' development.

A literacy portfolio can be defined as a purposeful collection of students' literacy work that shows effort and achievement (Arter & Spandel, 1992). In order to develop a valid literacy portfolio, the following three requirements must be addressed:

- **Representativeness:** The teacher must be clear about the skills and strategies that are being assessed. The use of benchmarks throughout this book are to help guide the portfolio assessment process.
- **Rubrics:** In order to alleviate instructor bias, assessment criteria should be clearly stated.
- **Relevance:** The skills and strategies required of the students to complete their portfolios should be developmentally appropriate and rooted in a literacy curriculum. The benchmarks presented in this book are aligned with national standards and the National Association for the Education of Young Children (NAEYC) guidelines (Tombari & Borich, 1999).

What Are the Benefits of Using Benchmarks?

Unlike many standardized tests, literacy portfolios allow teachers to view students through a different lens (Soderman, Gregory, & O'Neill, 1999). Portfolios also help teachers to become decision makers as they assess students' abilities to reach state and district mandates. As teachers analyze student samples, they are able to see the young reader's ability to problem solve, use strategies, and construct knowledge (Tombari & Borich, 1999; Wiener & Cohen, 1997).

Involving Parents: If you are not able to get parents to keep a home literacy portfolio, encourage them to send home literacy artifacts to include in the school portfolio.

Therefore, as the teacher analyzes samples, decisions are made about which instructional strategies should be implemented or what grouping changes are needed. Portfolio assessment is the agent for instructional change and catalyst toward student-centered literacy instruction.

In addition, portfolio assessment creates student ownership and increases motivation for literacy (Tompkins, 2002). During conferences, teachers and students discuss their progress and together outline future goals. This collaborative planning helps to facilitate the young reader's **metacognition.** Metacognition is the ability to reflect on one's own thinking processes. To become a self-regulated learner, young children have to be able to reflect on their performance.

How to Organize the Literacy Portfolio

The literacy portfolio can be constructed of two separate components: reading assessments and writing assessments. In the reading component, the assessment tools should combine both reading process and product entries. The chart shown in Figure 11.1 outlines sample entries for both components (Wiener & Cohen, 1997).

Portfolios enable teachers and students to collaborate.

Process	Product
✓ Metacognitive interviews	✓ Reading logs
✓ Think-alouds	✓ Photos of reading projects
✓ Self-assessment sheets	✓ Retellings of stories
✓ Tapes of oral reading	✓ Reactions to readings
✓ Reading discussions	

Figure 11.1
Process and Product Components for Reading Portfolio

The writing component of the literacy portfolio would also be subdivided into the same categories (Wiener & Cohen, 1997). Figure 11.2 features the process and product components of the writing portfolio.

Included in the portfolio might be parents' responses to portfolio samples as well as samples from resource room activities for children with special learning needs.

Organizing the Classroom for Literacy Assessment

The list of contents for literacy portfolios can be accumulated through daily instruction. The instructional strategies that have been presented in this text have been linked to benchmarks and assessment tools. This basic framework is the starting point for organizing a primary-grade classroom for assessment.

Process	Product
✓ Brainstorming webs	✓ Published story
✓ List of topics	✓ Poems
✓ Drafts of work	✓ All about books
✓ Tapes of conferences	✓ Writing self-assessment

Figure 11.2
Process and Product Components for Writing Portfolio

In September, when students first enter the primary classroom, teachers begin their assessment. Through observations of children's oral language and listening skills, early childhood teachers can begin to ascertain the child's grasp of concepts and vocabulary. As the weeks pass in September, the teacher also begins to collect samples of the child's listening, speaking, reading, and writing. The following list outlines this process:

Getting Started With Assessment

- Collect samples of students' listening, reading, writing, and speaking.
- Determine the child's literacy level by comparing samples to benchmarks for emergent, early, and fluent literacy levels.
- Based upon determination of child's literacy level, implement instructional strategies for literacy needs (Cooper & Kiser, 2001).

Once teachers have a sense of their students' literacy levels, they can begin scaffolded instruction. Scaffolded instruction occurs in the following sequence: *modeled, shared, guided, and independent practice.* The strategies are a primary starting point for instructional planning, thus this text has been organized according to the four phases. In addition, once teachers grasp the patterns of literacy needs and levels, flexible grouping may begin.

What Is Flexible Grouping?

Flexible grouping usually occurs during the *guided reading phase* of scaffolded instruction. However, it can also occur during other phases if the teacher wants to highlight a skill or strategy with a certain group.

Flexible grouping is based upon ongoing assessment. The teacher gathers data and places children in groups according to their literacy needs. They are called flexible groups because children should move in and out of groups as their literacy performance changes (Opitz, 1998) based upon data from running records, checklists, or other assessment tools.

How to Group Students

There are several different ways to group students for flexible grouping. In one model, students are grouped according to a necessary skill or strategy that may be taught. Children can also be categorized according to reading level so that all children in the group can read the book on their instructional level. These types of ability groups are also called guided reading groups (Fountas & Pinnell, 1996). Another possibility is to group children according to their interests in a particular book or author. Figure 11.3 outlines several ways to form flexible groups in a literacy program (Opitz, 1998).

The length of time spent in each group depends upon the assessment data. When the teacher ascertains that students have mastered a particular skill or strategy, it is time to reformulate the groups. Therefore, the length of time spent in a group will vary from 3 days to 4 weeks for an author study group.

Flexible grouping is based upon ongoing assessment..

Category	*Description*
Random	Students are chosen by random in order to form smaller reading groups.
Achievement	Students are placed in groups according to their reading level.
Interest	Groups are formed based upon data from an interest survey. They could focus on favorite authors or characters or hobbies.
Tasks	This grouping category is to place students according to their learning modality. For example, students who learn through tactile tasks would be placed together.
Skill or Strategy	Students are placed in groups according to their learning needs. For example, students who need reinforcement in decoding strategies would form one group.
Student Choice	Students are allowed to form their own reading groups. This is used most often for literature response groups.

Figure 11.3
Categories of Reading Groups

How to Manage Groups

Flexible groups are one strand of a balanced literacy program. A typical primary-grade classroom should have a 2-hour language block daily. This daily "time on task" helps to immerse the young reader and writer in the world of print. The 2-hour block can be divided into the following schedule:

Scheduled Activity	Allotted Time
Modeled reading or read-aloud	20 minutes
Shared reading	30 minutes
Guided reading (groups)	60 minutes
Independent reading	10 minutes

The time for independent reading should increase as the child gains fluency. Shared or modeled reading can decrease to allow more time for independent reading. As children enter the early and fluency stages, teachers may also choose reading and writing workshops as an alternative format (Tompkins, 2002).

Reading and Writing Workshops

Reading and writing workshops follow a similar design in that literacy instruction occurs within a block period. In addition, children may be placed in small groups for mini-lessons or in whole-class instruction. The major difference between this design and others is that children select the books they would like to read (Atwell, 1987).

Reading Workshop

In order to implement reading workshop, teachers should have a diverse, large classroom library to accommodate students' interests and reading levels. If reading materials are not abundant, one possibility is the sharing of texts among teachers of the same grade level on a rotating basis.

A sample schedule for reading workshop may be the following:

Scheduled Activity	Allotted Time
Reading aloud and modeling of strategies	30 minutes
Independent reading	40 minutes
Responding through activities and groups	40 minutes
Whole-class sharing	20 minutes

This sample schedule allows for the students and teacher to meet together to set goals and then conclude the reading workshop by discussing their progress (Tompkins, 2002). Figure 11.4 describes the four components of reading workshop.

Writing Workshop

The procedures for writing workshop are very similar. The major difference is that during writing workshop, the focus is on the five steps of the writing process. However, the teacher's role remains one of a coach, guiding the students through the creative process.

Component	Description
Reading	Students select books or magazines for their activities. Teachers can introduce students to topics or books through a preview discussion that will help children to vary their reading interests. Teachers should also go over the procedures for reading workshop and post classroom rules for everyone to see.
Sharing	As a response to literature, students may choose an activity from an available list of choices. For example, the teacher might post the following chart: After the story you may 1. Make a rolled story 2. Make a character puppet 3. Retell a story into a tape recorder All of the activities focus on the literal comprehension skill of retelling, yet are differentiated to accommodate students' learning styles and reading levels. Students also share their responses in grand conversations that are usually done with the whole class. In a grand conversation, students first write or draw their response to the story and share it with their peers. The teacher acts as a facilitator and guides the students to discuss the literary elements such as characterization or setting.
Mini-lessons	As with guided reading groups, mini-lessons during reading workshop are based upon the data the teacher has gathered observing students. These mini-lessons may be for small groups or for whole-class instruction based upon the data. The mini-lessons focus on skills or strategies that the students need to master.
Reading aloud	As with any balanced literacy program, a critical component is the modeling of reading. In reading workshop, the teacher reads aloud every day. The choice of text is also rooted in assessment. The teacher may choose to read a slightly more challenging text or choose a book that has complex sentence structures. Another option is to choose a certain text in order to model a specific comprehension strategy.

Figure 11.4
Components of Reading Workshop
Source: Adapted from Tompkins (2002).

The five stages of the writing process are the following:

- **Brainstorming**—Students and teacher generate story ideas or concepts. Students may use a graphic organizer to create their stories or informational text.
- **Drafting**—During this phase, the students write without focusing on grammar or spelling. The key is to get ideas on paper during this stage.
- **Revising**—This critical stage should include sharing their text with peers and the teacher. Based upon this feedback, students radically change their text. This might include moving sections or adding missing plot elements.
- **Editing**—This is a critical stage before publication. The student corrects any grammatical or spelling errors and makes final revisions.
- **Publishing**—The final stage is a public sharing of their written work. The students may decide to share their text in a newsletter, on a Web site, or in a published book. The venues for publication should vary throughout the year (Tompkins, 2002).

Category	Description
Mini-lessons	Using data from student work, the teacher focuses on a writing strategy, an aspect of grammar or spelling, or brainstorming.
Workshop session	During this component, the teacher may do the following: • Write with the class • Hold individual conferences • Hold group conferences
Group share	Students discuss their work samples and how they worked through the writing process.

Figure 11.5
Components of Writing Workshop
Source: Adapted from Vacca, Gove, Burkey, Lenhart, & McKeon (2003).

Using Technology: Kathy Schrock's *Guide for Educators* contains many teaching tips (http://www.school.discovery.com/schrockguide).

During the components of writing workshop, the teacher guides the students through the five stages of the writing process (Vacca et al., 2003) shown in Figure 11.5.

The length of time spent in each group depends upon the assessment data. When the teacher ascertains that students have mastered a particular skill or strategy, it is time to reformulate the groups. Therefore, the length of time spent in a group will vary from 3 days to 4 weeks for an author study group.

Linking Instruction and Assessment

The portraits of literacy text has attempted to address this topic in every chapter. In order to link instruction and assessment, assessment should be embedded in instruction. When teachers plan instructional strategies based upon developmental benchmarks for literacy, they are already attuned to their students' literacy behaviors.

Linking instruction and assessment promotes a dialogue between teacher and student when teachers plan based upon ongoing data collection. They are implementing *assessment for learning* which is the single most powerful tool for raising educational standards (Assessment Reform Group, 2002). When assessment *of* learning occurs, the emphasis is placed on standardized text scores, which focus on the products of learning rather than the process.

Instead of teaching to a specific standardized test, assessment *for* learning has the following characteristics:

- Embeds assessment in instructional strategies
- Creates dialogue with students on learning goals and standards to be met
- Promotes self-assessment as students develop ownership of their work
- Provides specific feedback to the students in what they have to do to meet the standards
- Focuses on the belief that every student can learn and meet the standards
- Creates a partnership between teachers and students in meeting the goals (Assessment Reform Group, 2002).

The partnership between teacher and student is strengthened as they reflect and dialogue about the work samples. Even young children can identify how their writing samples have developed when presented with examples. Fostering this self-assessment at an early age will increase intrinsic motivation and academic achievement.

In order to begin this process of integrating instruction and assessment, the teacher should use the following methods:

Focused Observations

✔ *Using guiding questions, the teacher observes specific behaviors based upon the instructional strategy. For example, in the story map instructional strategy, the teacher focused on the following behaviors:*

Was the student able to identify the main character?

Was the student able to identify the setting?

Was the student able to identify the problem?

Was the student able to identify the solution?

Students struggling with certain story elements can be grouped for assistance in identifying the setting, plot, and so on.

Open-Ended Questions

✔ *Asking open-ended questions allows the teacher to see the child's reasoning and cognitive processes. For example, the following dialogue is an example of open-ended questioning:*

The class is discussing *The Lion, the Witch and the Wardrobe* by C. S. Lewis. The teacher asks, "What do you think will happen next?" The student responds, "I think when Lucy goes through the door she will enter the Land of Oz because this story reminds me of the movie *The Wizard of Oz.*"

The teacher noted on her anecdotal record sheet for Emily that she was using her knowledge about previous stories to figure out the plots of new books. This is an important reading behavior because it shows that the child is developing a schema for story elements such as plot and setting.

Open-Mind Portraits

✔ *Open-mind portraits entail creating instructional activities that require the child to use certain tasks or skills.*

This teacher used the instructional strategy open-mind portrait (Figure 11.6) to see how the child inferred the character's feelings in Patricia Polacco's Thank You, Mr. Falker *(1998). The teacher noted that James was able to identify the character's emotions. However, his spelling strategies needed to be developed.*

Story Quilts

✔ *Story quilts facilitate student communication of ideas through artifacts, graphic organizers, concept maps, and writing.*

Figure 11.6
Open-Mind Portrait

Figure 11.7
Story Quilt

In this activity, the student was asked to visualize the setting of Bridge to Terabithia by Katharine Paterson (1977) and to recreate it in a quilt (see Figure 11.7). The teacher rated Sam on his ability to defend his visualization of the setting by citing evidence from the story.

Story Elements	Target	Acceptable	Needs Improvement
Setting	Student uses text to recreate setting on quilt patch. Student presentation includes evidence.	Student has some elements of the setting in his quilt patch. Presentation is partly text based.	Quilt does not represent text setting or use evidence from book.

This instructional activity integrated critical thinking and the language arts through visual representation.

Picture Dictionary

✔ *The picture dictionary promotes word study and is another method for linking assessment and instruction. Through activities that explore multisyllabic words or create picture dictionaries, teachers evaluate a child's conceptual knowledge base as well as decoding ability.*

This teacher used a picture dictionary (see Figure 11.8) to help Jorge, a recent Mexican immigrant, to learn English. Conversations about each picture were used to help the child gain confidence and facility with English. The rubrics below focused on the child's use of the picture dictionary as a reference for their oral language and writing tasks.

Oral Language Ability	Target	Acceptable	Needs Improvement
	Child names object in dictionary and describes it.	Child names some objects in dictionary.	Child was not able to identify pictures.

Figure 11.8
Picture Dictionary

Using Data to Inform Instruction

Linking instruction to assessment occurs when teachers use their data to create lesson objectives. This section illustrates how several teachers used developmental benchmarks to determine a child's literacy level. The data from instructional activities helped the teacher to determine the child's literacy level and then to design appropriate lessons. This can seem an overwhelming task to a novice teacher. However, if teachers focus on patterns across student data, they can get a clearer idea of how to proceed. For example, if a majority of children had difficulty with rhyming words on a phonemic awareness screening, that would be the starting point for instruction.

The scenarios presented in this section illustrate this process. The teachers demonstrate how they used ongoing literacy data to inform practice.

Using Running Record Data to Develop Word-Solving Strategies

Ms. Gonzalez used a running record of her second grader Maria's oral reading of *Ruby the Copycat* by Peggy Rathmann (1997). The running record is shown in Figure 11.9.

Figure 11.9
Running Record Example

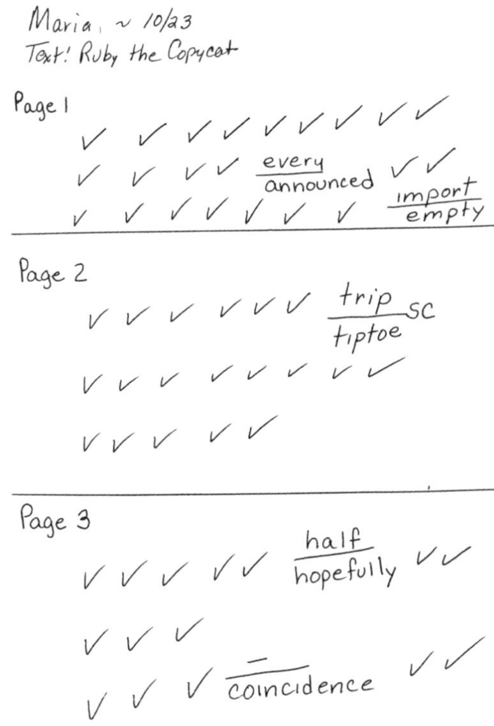

Ms. Gonzalez decided to focus on decoding multisyllabic words. She used clapping to help Maria divide the words into syllables. After the child had broken down the words into syllables, they were traced by using cornmeal. This tactile, multisensory instructional activity helps the child to process multisyllabic words.

Notes on Running Record

Strengths	*Areas in Need of Improvement*
✓ Has core bank of sight words	✓ Blending of sounds
✓ Is beginning self-correcting behavior	✓ Decoding multisyllabic words
✓ Reads with expression	✓ Using cross-checking strategies

Using the Language Experience Approach to Help English Language Learners

Ms. Harron had a number of students who were second language learners. One of the first activities of the year was to write their own version of Cinderella (see Figure 11.10). The class had heard a read-aloud of the story and Ms. Harron decided that this activity would give the students the opportunity to demonstrate their knowledge of vocabulary and syntax.

After evaluating the data from the Cinderella story, Ms. Harron decided to focus on verb tense which was a significant problem for many students. After modeling how to conjugate verbs, students were given the verb tense tutorial sheet shown on page 419.

*Cinderella

Cinderella wanted to be a fairy Princess. She lived with her evil Step mother. Suddenly a god mother appeared and send her to the ball. She dresed Cinderella in a dress and turned 6 mouse into horses and pumkin into a coch.

When Cinderella entered in the castle the prince told her if she wanted to dance. So she was dancing with the prince The bell rang and Cinderella had to run.

The prince got in love Wit the girl he was dancing wit. He found a shoe. The next day we went to look who was the girl that the shoe fit on that person so he could marry her.

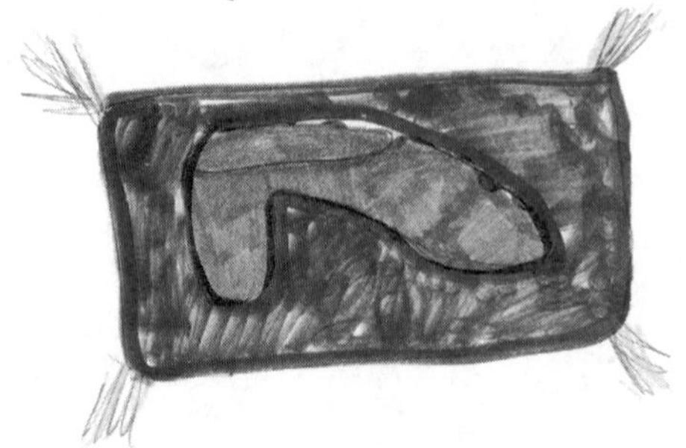

After months the
prince went to
Cinderella's house He
reconised her and tried
on the shoe It fit her.
Then the price and
Cinderella lived happily
ever after
THE END

Figure 11.10
Example of Cinderella Story

Working on Tenses

1. I will ___________ (rode/ride) on my bicycle.
2. The girl ___________ (ate/eat) the sandwich.
3. My cat ___________ (drink/drank) all the milk.

This instructional activity also assessed the children's comprehension of the new words.

Working on Tenses

4. I will ___________ (rode/ride) on my bicycle.
5. The girl ___________ (ate/eat) the sandwich.
6. My cat ___________ (drink/drank) all the milk.

This instructional activity also assessed the children's comprehension of the new words.

Facilitating Emergent Literacy

Assessment for learning may also be implemented in the primary grades and in preschool. The example shown in Figure 11.11 is from Mr. Kern's nursery school class. Evan, a 4-year-old boy, demonstrated the need for oral language enrichment during a dictated story assessment.

Halloween

I am a ct for Halloween

I see a ct.

Look at the ct

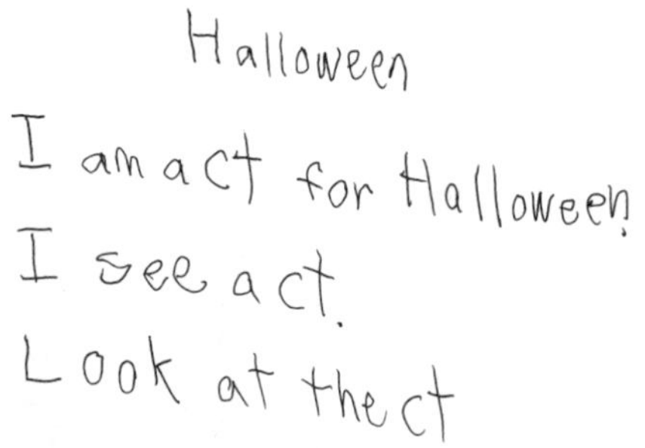

Figure 11.11
Dictated Story Assessment Example

After analyzing Evan's dictated story data, Mr. Kern decided to use environmental print and toy catalog pictures to stimulate conversations with Evan, as shown in Figure 11.12.

Use of descriptive words	Target	Acceptable	Needs Improvement
	Uses several adjectives to describe toy objects or pictures.	Uses some adjectives to describe toy objects or pictures.	Did not use any adjectives.

Mr. Kern used toy catalogs and other familiar objects to improve Evan's use of descriptive words. By working on Evan's oral language, Mr. Kern helped to build the necessary foundation for future literacy achievement.

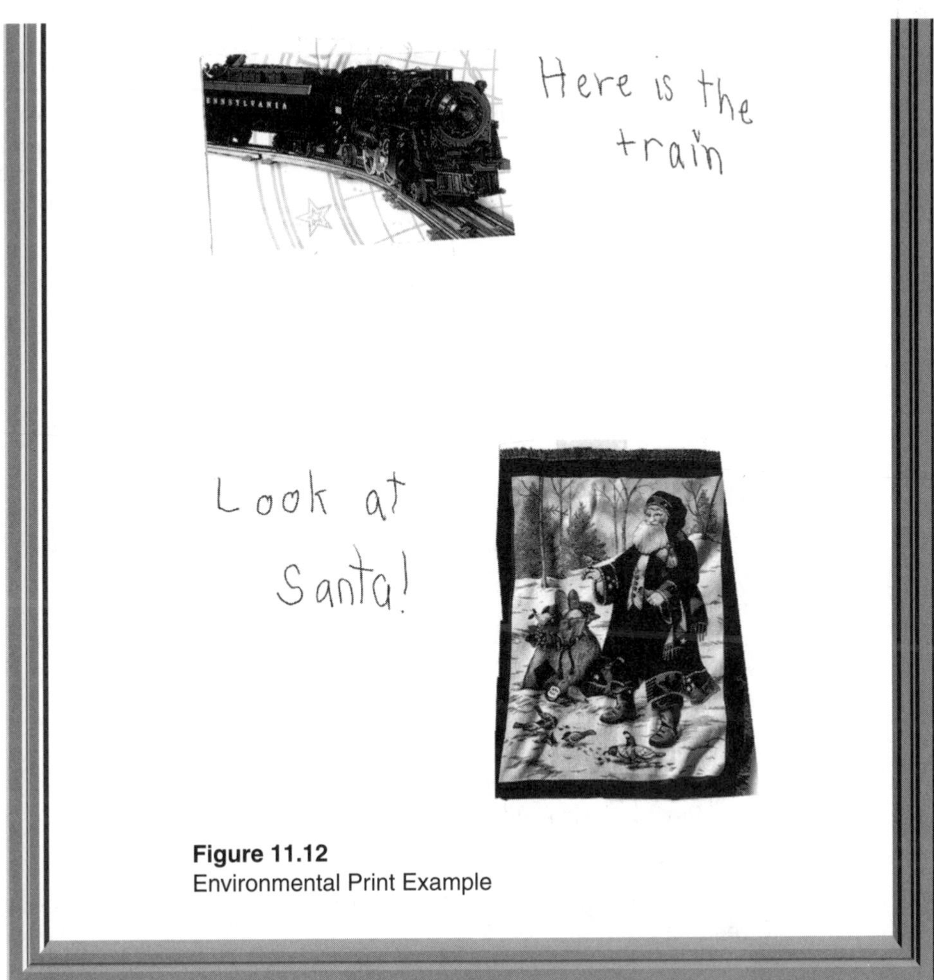

Figure 11.12
Environmental Print Example

Evaluating Assessment Results

In the previous section, we illustrated how assessment for learning is linked to ongoing instructional strategies. As teachers collect data from running records or retellings, it is important to highlight how to evaluate assessment results.

Teachers often use the words *assessment* and *evaluation* interchangeably. However, the two words represent different processes. *Assessment* refers to collecting data to record students' literacy progress. *Evaluation* is the judgment based upon the assessment results such as determining a child's literacy level.

Evaluation of assessment data depends upon the questions teachers are seeking to answer about their students. There are three main types of assessment questions, as presented in Figure 11.13.

These three categories of questions will be used to evaluate the assessment data.

Diagnostic	Formative	Summative
✓ Are my students prepared for literacy learning? ✓ Do they have the necessary skills to acquire literacy?	✓ Did the student master the strategy or skill presented in the lesson? ✓ Did the student comprehend the story? ✓ Did the student use decoding strategies to read new words?	✓ What progress has the student shown? ✓ Has the student changed his attitude toward reading?

Figure 11.13
Types of Assessment Questions

Diagnostic Questions

Early in the year, before teaching new material, teachers want to find out what skills, strategies, or knowledge the child is bringing to the task. The language experience approach is an instructional strategy that can be used to answer these diagnostic questions (Figure 11.14).

Based upon the results of this diagnostic task, Ms. Harron concluded that Evan needed to

- Work on punctuation
- Focus on word endings and verb tense
- Review basic sight words such as *went*

The evaluation of diagnostic tasks helps teachers organize and plan their literacy instruction. Information from diagnostic tasks can also be used to formulate reading groups.

Formative Questions

Formative assessment tasks help the teacher to ascertain if students are grasping the content of the lesson. It can also be used to discover if students are using the strategies or skills that were modeled in shared reading or guided reading.

Running records are effective formative assessment tools. From the running record shown in Figure 11.15, Ms. Gonzalez was able to identify the following behaviors about her student, Jennifer:

- She is reading for meaning.
- She is beginning to self-correct.
- She primarily uses her graphophonic cueing system.
- She is not using cross-checking strategies.

Based upon this evaluation, Ms. Gonzalez planned her next shared reading lesson to model cross-checking strategies. Formative assessment tools guide and change the teacher's literacy instruction.

Figure 11.14
Language Experience Story Example

Figure 11.15
Running Record Example

Page 1
✓ ✓ ✓ ✓ ✓ ✓
✓ ✓ ✓
✓ ✓ ✓ $\frac{\text{jump}}{\text{gum}}$ sc

Page 2
✓ ✓ ✓ ✓ ✓
✓ ✓ ✓ ✓ ✓
✓ ✓ ✓ ✓ ✓

Page 3
✓ ✓ ✓ $\frac{\text{hop}}{\text{hopped}}$
✓ ✓ ✓ $\frac{\text{run}}{\text{running}}$ sc

Figure 11.16
Concept Map Example

Summative Questions

After completing an author study or thematic unit, the teacher uses summative assessment to check the child's literacy achievement. Summative assessment tools can be unit tests, class plays, books, or concept maps, as shown in Figure 11.16.

Ms. Nagori used a summative assessment tool to determine the extent of the children's knowledge about Gandhi after completing a unit of informational books about the slain leader. The concept map required the children to create symbolic representations for Gandhi's teachings. Ms. Nagori evaluated her student Mary Anne as follows:

- She comprehended Gandhi's main teaching of nonviolence.
- She was able to associate Gandhi with India's independence movement.
- She used symbolic representation to describe Gandhi's teachings that demonstrated critical thinking.

Therefore, the evaluation of assessment data depends upon the purposes of the assessment tools. The use of the assessment data is also determined by its purpose, as the chart in Figure 11.17 illustrates.

Determining Literacy Level

When teachers evaluate assessment data, one of their major goals is to determine the child's literacy level. In order to decide the child's reading level, the teacher must use

Diagnostic	Formative	Summative
Tools: Language experience story Phonemic awareness tasks Concepts about print tasks Running records	*Tools:* Running records Graphic organizers Story retellings	*Tools:* Unit tests Retellings Essays Plays Projects Dioramas
Evaluation From Data: What skills and strategies do I have to model? What is the child's literacy level? What are the child's strengths? What are the child's interests?	*Evaluation Decisions:* Literacy level Skills and strategies mastered Strategies and skills needed for review Mastery of vocabulary and comprehension of story	*Evaluation Decisions:* Content mastered Skills and strategies mastered or needed for review Connections to prior knowledge

Figure 11.17
Use of Assessment Data

developmental benchmarks as guideposts. In this process, the teacher refers to the literacy behaviors categorized for a particular level and compares the child's progress against those benchmarks.

Using Developmental Benchmarks

Ms. Perez was evaluating a language experience story assessment for Mario, a second grader who had been struggling since first grade. According to the data, Mario did not have fluency in decoding but was able to recognize a few sight words:

- He recognized the words *look, the, went, have.*
- He is still spelling phonetically rather than using knowledge of word patterns.
- He read his story with a pointer.
- He read from left to write and was able to point to the beginning and end of the sentence.

Mario also demonstrated concepts about print such as the concept of a word or sentence. Ms. Perez compared Mario's data with developmental benchmarks and began to focus on behaviors of the emergent reader (see Figure 11.18).

After comparing the language experience story assessment data with the emergent literacy benchmarks, Ms. Perez hypothesized that Mario was probably an emergent reader. Ms. Perez decided to confirm her evaluation with further observations and data collection.

Using Running Records to Determine Literacy Level

Mr. Oldham used running records data to assess Shannon's literacy progress. Shannon, a first grader, was tackling the story *How Much Is That Doggie in the Window?*

✓ Sees self as reader and writer
✓ Reads a bank of core words
✓ Recognizes own name
✓ Participates during book introductions and picture walks
✓ Begins to make predictions based upon picture clues
✓ Demonstrates reading for meaning
✓ Uses pictures to recall unknown words
✓ Points to words when reading
✓ Reads to the end of the story
✓ Participates during story discussions

Figure 11.18
Emergent Literacy Behaviors

(Trapini, 2001). As Mr. Oldham reviewed and studied the data, he noticed that Shannon was demonstrating the following literacy behaviors:

- Attempts to decode words
- Recognizes sight words such as *see, the, and*
- Reads for meaning by self-correcting mistakes
- Uses picture clues to identify unknown words

Using Technology: Cast eReader (http://www.cast.org) helps readers who are struggling or children with special needs to read text.

Mr. Oldham compared Shannon's observed literacy behaviors with the developmental benchmarks; he began to focus on the behaviors of the early literacy stage (see Figure 11.19).

Mr. Oldham's evaluation was that Shannon was in the early stage of literacy. He used his evaluation to plan lessons that would strengthen Shannon's shift toward decoding of print.

✓ Actively participates in book discussions
✓ Actively participates during book introductions, and begins to initiate questions and to respond to the story
✓ Reads left to right with a fast sweeping return to the next line
✓ Increases rate of reading and writing
✓ Begins to set purposes for reading and writing
✓ Visibly matches word to word while reading
✓ Begins to use multiple sources of information, including picture clues to decode unknown words
✓ Reads using letter–sound relationships

Figure 11.19
Early Literacy Benchmarks

Stage	Description
Drawing	The child's illustration is the story.
Scribbling	The child may write a series of letters or squiggly lines.
Letterlike forms	This is similar to the previous stage; however, the child separates the letters.
Prephonemic spelling	These are conventional letters, but no phonemes are attached.
Copying	The child copies from environmental print.
Invented spelling	The child is spelling phonetically but may be missing a few letters.

Figure 11.20
Stages of Emergent Writing

Using Writing Samples to Determine Literacy Level

Mr. Kern was working with Evan on a language experience story. Evan was excited about Halloween and wrote the following story:

Halloween
My pupkin is bg.
My pupkin is oranj.
I luv Halloween.

Figure 11.20 shows a comparison of Evan's writing sample with the stages of emergent writing (Sulzby, 1989).

After comparing Evan's performance to the stages of emergent writing chart, Mr. Kern determined that Evan was in the final stage, *invented spelling.* The next step in the instructional process will be to focus on word families with Evan to develop his growing lexicon.

As teachers refer often to developmental benchmarks for literacy, they will begin to internalize their content. This will help to facilitate the evaluation process and assist the teacher in easily determining the child's literacy level. Another advantage of constant reference to the developmental benchmarks is to help guide the child to the next literacy level. For example, when Ms. Perez determined that Maria was at the emergent literacy level, her lessons focused on recognizing word patterns and manipulating onsets and rimes. These instructional activities will help Maria move toward decoding print and the early stage of literacy.

In summary, evaluations of assessment data help the teacher to answer questions about their students' literacy behaviors and progress. Primarily, evaluative decisions regarding data help to determine the students' literacy levels and the goals of future instruction. Therefore, evaluation of assessment data completes the instructional cycle and brings the teacher back to its beginning stage—deciding goals and outcomes for the children. Figure 11.21 illustrate the model of assessment for learning.

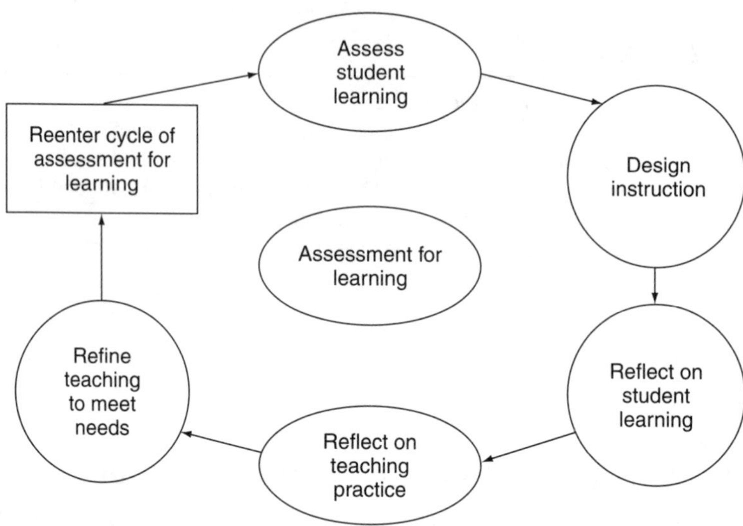

Figure 11.21
Model of Assessment for Learning

Planning the Portfolio Conference

The first step for teachers in planning for portfolio conferences is to decide which type of conference is to be held. There are three types of portfolio conferences: *teacher-student, teacher-parent-student,* and *portfolio celebrations.*

- **Teacher-student:** This type of conference may be held individually or with a group of students. The students decide which pieces reflect their work and should be included in their portfolio. The teacher's primary role in the teacher-student conference is to listen as the students answer the following questions:
  1. Which work are you the most proud of?
  2. Which activity or project was the easiest for you? The most difficult?
  3. What can you do well now in reading and writing?
  4. What do you have to work on? (Wiener & Cohen, 1997)

  The teacher jots down the student's responses and analyzes them for patterns. The purpose of the conference is to jointly determine the student's areas of literacy strengths and skills and strategies to develop further. The conference also helps the child to develop self-awareness in regard to his literacy progress.
- **Teacher-parent-student:** The purpose of this type of conference is to create a dialogue among the three major stakeholders in education. The student explains his work to the parents and the teacher acts as a facilitator. In addition, the teacher informs the parent of the literacy continuum and provides the professional knowledge base to help the parents evaluate their child's literacy portfolio.
- **Portfolio celebrations:** Portfolio celebrations generally occur at the end of a unit or marking period. Some teachers also end their school year with a portfolio celebration that is open to other classes as well as children's families. The

purpose of the portfolio celebration is for communal rejoicing of the child's literacy growth and self-knowledge. The portfolio celebration resembles the opening of an art exhibit at a gallery as each child stands by the portfolio display and discusses the major pieces of his collection. A portfolio celebration is a wonderful strategy for building self-esteem and intrinsic motivation for literacy among children who have struggled academically.

Preparing for the Teacher-Parent-Student Conference

An effective technique to prepare students for the teacher-parent-student conference is role playing (Soderman et al., 1999). Students who are well prepared can report on their work to parents and actually lead the conference.

A few days before the conference, the teacher prepares the students by providing them with a graphic organizer to review their work.

What I know I do well . . .	***What I want to work on . . .***	***What I love to do . . .***	***Strategies I used . . .***	***Skills I have improved on . . .***

The next day after completing the graphic organizer, the child is paired with an older student from another grade. The older student acts as the parent and the child uses the graphic organizer to report on the major categories of the think sheet, such as *What I know I do well.*

The role playing also helps the child make any necessary changes to his portfolio or to include pieces that may be missing. The older student offers suggestions and feedback to the younger classmate.

Conference Time

The scheduling of conferences often depends upon the school's timetable for parent night. Some schools allocate 15 minutes for each parent group or a block of time for all primary-grade classes. If teachers are given a block of time, they might choose a portfolio celebration, with the children sharing their work with parents at separate tables. The teacher facilitates the session and walks around the room responding to questions from parents.

Whether the conferences are individual or group or student led, parents should leave with a clear understanding of their child's literacy progress. Hopefully, parents were given copies of the developmental benchmarks at the beginning of the academic year. Parents would then use the benchmarks as they listen to their child share the literacy portfolio. Portfolio conferences should report to the parents how their child has demonstrated key literacy behaviors or strategies such as concepts about print.

After the Conference

One of the purposes of portfolio assessment is to foster collaboration between home and school. Portfolios become primary tools for assessment conversations as parents, students, and teachers dialogue about stories children have written or running records that illustrate reading behaviors.

When parents leave the conference, teachers should ask them to reflect on their child's portfolio and respond. There are several ways for busy parents to comment on their child's progress:

- **Graphic Organizer.** The parents could complete the think sheet below that parallels the one that their child completed prior to the conference.

I am proud of . . .	*I will help you with . . .*	*I want to know more about. . .*

- **Dialogue Journal.** Several teachers develop ongoing conversations with their students through dialogue journals. In this type of journal, the student writes to the teacher and the instructor responds. This can easily be modified to allow the parent to respond as well. Another possibility is to create a separate dialogue journal for parents that would allow them to respond to conference night or other areas of concern. The teacher would then respond to parents' queries.

- **E-mail.** In this age of telecommunication, e-mailing the teacher might be the easiest way for parents to respond to their child's work. Teachers might want to post the graphic organizer on their class Web site. Parents would then fill it out at work or on the commuter train and e-mail it back to the teacher.

The purpose of these different types of communication is to keep the parents involved and conversing about their child. Parents who are recent immigrants to this country may feel hesitant about coming to school. A portfolio celebration led by their child who could translate for them might be more inviting than a teacher-parent conference. Some schools have used other parents of the same culture to assist them on parent night. When parents feel that their culture is valued and respected at their child's school, they will feel more comfortable being there. Therefore, schools might want to have food available or translators to ease the fears of parents who are new to this country (Wiener & Cohen, 1997).

Grading the Portfolio

One of the difficult aspects of portfolio assessment is grading. District and school policy may mandate the use of letter or numerical grades that are often difficult for teachers to use with portfolio assessment.

Across the country, many early childhood programs are using narrative reports that resemble a case study on each individual child. The teacher describes the physical, socioemotional, cognitive, and language development of the young child. However, teachers with many students may not be able to write in detail about their students. Therefore, districts with large populations still rely upon numerical or letter grades.

Creating a Grading Policy

It is very important for the novice teacher to consult district school policy on assigning grades or reporting to parents. Teachers might be required to use standard performance rankings that have been outlined by the district. However, even if the district has a mandated policy, each teacher should reflect before the school year begins on her own grading policy.

In constructing a grading philosophy, it is important for the teacher to reflect on her responses to the following questions:

- What will be my purpose for giving a grade?
- How will I distribute grades across the class?
- What components of performance will I consider for the final grade?
- How will I weigh the importance of each component?
- Will I give extra opportunities to raise a grade?
- Will my grade be absolute or relative measures of achievement? (Tombari & Borich, 1999)

The most important aspect of this process is to reflect on the objectives for each component of the literacy portfolio. Depending upon the objectives, the teacher determines the numerical score. Teachers of older students such as third and fourth graders might include them in creating a numerical rating for literacy tasks.

Literacy Task	Percentage
Language experience story	20%
Rolled story	20%
Arguing a point	20%
Wall story	10%
Book discussion	10%
Spelling activity	10%
Reflection on portfolio	10%

Figure 11.22
Scoring the Literacy Portfolio

Scoring the Literacy Portfolio

Once teachers have developed their grading philosophy, they are ready to score the different components of the literacy portfolio. Ms. Perez has reflected on the various literacy tasks in her students' portfolios. She has decided that the language experience story, rolled story, and arguing a point activities were the major pieces of the portfolio. Therefore, they will be more heavily weighted in the final scoring of the portfolio.

The students are shown the scoring rubrics (see Figure 11.22 for an example) before undertaking the literacy tasks. Including students in the assessment dialogue allows them to set goals and become self-regulated learners (Assessment Reform Group, 2002). The students should also be given a table that connects the numerical score to a letter grade such as the following:

100–90	89–80	79–70	69–60	Below 60
A	B	C	D	F

Children can monitor their grade throughout the semester or marking period as they add up the scores on their various tasks. In addition, rubrics for each task should be given out before each assignment so that students are aware of the assessment criteria before they complete the task, as shown in the sample below.

A successful grading system is one in which there are no surprises for students or their parents. It must be clear and discussed prior to the completion of the activity. Many teachers include the children in the creation of the rubrics and the numerical value for each component. However, the report card policy should be consistent with the grading philosophy constructed by the teacher.

Rolled Story

Includes major events and details	10%
Narration of rolled story	5%
Participation in group	5%

Portrait of Assessment for Learning

Mr. Kern is completing his first year as a nursery school teacher. He is eager to share the results of his year-long efforts to facilitate literacy development among his 4-year-old students. Mr. Kern has devoted a great deal of instructional time to Evan, who struggled at the beginning of the year. In September, Mr. Kern noted on his anecdotal records that Evan did not have phonemic awareness and was inconsistent with his letter recognition. Therefore, Mr. Kern designed an intensive instructional program using environmental print to build phonemic awareness.

Now in June, Mr. Kern can see the results of his strategy as Evan has progressed to the inventive stage of spelling. Mr. Kern designed an intensive instructional program using environmental print and the language experience approach to improve Evan's letter–sound recognition and identification. Evan is well on his way to becoming a successful reader in kindergarten.

Discussion Questions and Activities

1. Observe an early childhood classroom and record how the teacher schedules literacy instruction. Interview the teacher and ask why he or she designed the schedule and grouped for instruction in a certain way.
2. Obtain a sample of a running record. Analyze the child's miscues and design an instructional strategy to meet the child's needs.
3. Obtain a literacy portfolio from an early childhood classroom. Record your observations of the child's development and identify whether the child is in the emergent, early, or fluent stage of literacy.
4. Design your own literacy program. How would you ensure that it integrates assessment and learning?

Additional Web Sites

Children's Literature Web Guide
http://www.acs.ucalgary.ca/~dkbrown/index.html
This site offers teachers a rich database of possible books for children to explore.

ERIC Clearinghouse on Assessment and Evaluation
http://www.ericae.net/
This government database offers teachers thousands of articles and assessment instruments.

ERIC Clearinghouse on Elementary and Early Childhood Education
http://www.ericeece.org
This one site will offer teachers myriad articles, publications as well as lesson plans.

Chicago Public Schools Performance Assessment Ideas and Rubrics
http://intranet.cps.k12.il.us/Assessments/Ideas_and_Rubrics/ideas_and_rubrics.html

This site offers teachers a wide variety of rubrics and assessment tools.

Log on to Literacy
http://www.tdd.nsw.edu.au/logon/index.htm

National Center for Research on Evaluation, Standards, and Student Testing
http://www.cresst96.cse.ucla.edu/index.htm

Teachers.Net
http://www.teachers.net

Additional Children's Literature

Emergent Literacy Level

Asch, F. (1992). *Little fish, big fish.* New York: Scholastic.

Barton, B. (1990). *Bones, bones, dinosaur bones.* New York: Crowell.

Carle, E. (1995). *The very lonely firefly.* New York: Philomel.

Wong, H. (1992). *Eek! There's a mouse in the house.* New York: Houghton Mifflin.

Early Literacy Level

Burton, V. (1942). *The little house.* New York: Houghton Mifflin.

Cazet, D. (1991). *Born in the gravy.* New York: Orchard.

Cole, J. (1986). *Hungry, hungry sharks.* New York: Random House.

Sendak, M. (1964). *Where the wild things are.* New York: HarperCollins.

Fluent Literacy Level

Adler, D. (1997). *Lou Gehrig: The luckiest man.* New York: Harcourt Brace.

Dahl, R. (1961). *James and the giant peach.* London: Puffin.

Giff, P. (1994). *Shark in school.* New York: Delacorte.

O'Connor, J. (1989). *Jackie Robinson and the story of all black baseball.* New York: Random House.

Children's Literature References

Lewis, C. S. (1950). *The lion, the witch and the wardrobe.* New York: HarperCollins.

Paterson, K. (1977). *Bridge to Terabithia.* New York: Crowell.

Polacco, P. (1998). *Thank you, Mr. Falker.* New York: Philomel.

Rathmann, P. (1997). *Ruby the copycat.* New York: Scholastic.

Trapani, I. (2001). *How much is that doggie in the window?* Watertown, MA: Charlesbridge.

Appendix

Included in the Appendix are selected figures and tables appearing throughout the book that are organized by chapter order. Most figures are forms to manage assessment of student learning. The figures are reproducible for use in the classroom by our readers as they implement the assessment strategies.

Chapter 2

IRA/NCTE
Standards For the English Language Arts

The vision guiding these standards is that all students must have the opportunities and resources to develop the language skills they need to pursue life's goals and to participate fully as informed, productive members of society. These standards assume that literacy growth begins before children enter school as they experience and experiment with literacy activities—reading and writing, and associating spoken words with their graphic representations. Recognizing this fact, these standards encourage the development of curriculum and instruction that make productive use of the emerging literacy abilities that children bring to school. Furthermore, the standards provide ample room for the innovation and creativity essential to teaching and learning. They are not prescriptions for particular curriculum or instruction.

Although we present these standards as a list, we want to emphasize that they are not distinct and separable; they are, in fact, interrelated and should be considered as a whole.

1. Students read a wide range of print and nonprint texts to build an understanding of texts, of themselves, and of the cultures of the United States and the world; to acquire new information to respond to the needs and demands of society and the workplace; and for personal fulfillment. Among these texts are fiction and nonfiction, classic and contemporary works.
2. Students read a wide range of literature from many genres to build an understanding of the many dimensions (e.g., philosophical, ethical, aesthetic) of human experience.
3. Students apply a wide range of strategies to comprehend, interpret, evaluate, and appreciate texts. They draw on their prior experience, their interactions with other readers and writers, their knowledge of word meaning and of other texts, their word identification, and their understanding of textual features (e.g., sound-letter correspondence, sentence structure, context, graphics).

4. Students adjust their use of spoken, written, and visual language (e.g., conventions, style, vocabulary) to communicate effectively with a variety of audiences and for different purposes.
5. Students employ a wide range of strategies as they write and use different writing process elements appropriately to communicate with different audiences for a variety of purposes.
6. Students apply knowledge of language structure, language conventions (e.g., spelling and punctuation), media techniques, figurative language, and genre to create, critique, and discuss print and nonprint texts.
7. Students conduct research on issues and interests by generating ideas and questions and by posing problems. They gather, evaluate, and synthesize data from a variety of sources (e.g., print and nonprint texts, artifacts, people) to communicate their discoveries in ways that suit their purpose and audience.
8. Students use a variety of technological and informational resources (e.g., libraries, databases, computer networks, video) to gather and synthesize information to create and communicate knowledge.
9. Students develop an understanding of and respect for diversity in language use, patterns, and dialects across cultures, ethnic groups, geographic regions, and social roles.
10. Students whose first language is not English make use of their first language to develop competency in the English language arts and to develop understanding of content across the curriculum.
11. Students participate as knowledgeable, reflective, creative, and critical members of a variety of literacy communities.
12. Students use spoken, written, and visual language to accomplish their own purposes (e.g., for learning, enjoyment, persuasion, and the exchange of information).

Source: From the *Standards for the English Language Arts* (p. 13), by the International Reading Association and the National Council of Teachers of English, 1996, Newark, DE: International Reading Association. Reprinted with permission of the International Reading Association.

Chapters 3, 4, and 5

Checklist for Finger Plays

Benchmarks for Oral Language	Target	Acceptable	Needs Improvement
Enjoys tongue twisters	Engages in and enjoys tongue twisters	Enjoys tongue twisters but does not participate	Does not participate or enjoy this activity
Repeats and uses new words	Is able to identify new words and use them orally in a sentence	Is able to identify new words but only sometimes uses them in a sentence	Cannot identify new words and does not use them in oral language
Identifies rhymes	Is able to identify rhymes	Sometimes is able to identify rhymes	Is still unable to identify rhyming words

Directions: Place check mark next to observed behavior.

Name ____

CHECKLIST FOR DIALOGIC STORYTELLING

Benchmark Behaviors					
Can be understood by peers when talking					
Asks questions					
Follows rules for conversations					
Participates during discussions					
Uses book language heard from storybooks					
Tells a story to go with pictures					
Talks about favorite picture					
Can restate what others have said in discussion					

Checklist for Modeling Activities

Benchmarks for Oral Language	Target	Acceptable	Needs Improvement
Conversational skills	Participates in discussions and asks questions; can also summarize information from books	Sometimes participates in discussions and partially summarizes information	Is not able to participate in discussions or to summarize text
Enjoyment of language	Continues to learn new vocabulary words and enjoys riddles	Sometimes uses new vocabulary words and enjoys jokes	Does not use new vocabulary words and does not enjoy riddles or jokes

Name ____________________

Checklist for Book Talk

Benchmarks for Oral Language	Target	Acceptable	Needs Improvement
Language habits	Asks questions and sustains conversations	Sometimes questions and converses, does not begin conversations	Does not ask questions or start conversations
Use of literary language	Elaborates on story elements and critiques text with evidence	Is beginning to elaborate on story elements and to critique text	Does not elaborate on story or critique it

Chapter 6

Name ____________________

Emergent Writing Rubrics

Emergent Writing Behaviors	Target	Acceptable	Needs Improvement
Writes uppercase and lowercase letters	Uses both uppercase and lowercase letters	Sometimes uses uppercase and lowercase letters	Uses only uppercase letters
Writes consonants and vowel sounds in words	Writes both consonants and vowel sounds	Writes some vowel and consonant sounds	Writes only consonant sounds
Begins to write sentences and use punctuation	Writes sentences with punctuation	Sometimes writes sentences and uses punctuation	Does not write sentences or use punctuation

Spelling Behavior Rubrics

Spelling Behavior	Level 3	Level 2	Level 1
Uses knowledge of phonics to encode word	Spells based upon knowledge of phonics	Sometimes uses phonics to spell words	Does not use phonics to spell words
Compares unknown words with familiar words	Uses knowledge of words to spell unknown words	Sometimes uses word knowledge to spell	Does not use knowledge of known words to spell
Uses word wall as a reference	Uses word wall as a reference	Sometimes uses word wall as a reference	Never uses word wall as a reference
Spells words based upon knowledge of syllabication	Uses knowledge of syllabication to spell	Sometimes uses syllabication to spell	Does not use syllabication to spell

Name ______________________________

Concepts About Books Rubrics

Concepts About Books	Target	Acceptable	Needs Improvement
Makes predictions based upon cover and title	Uses cover and title to make predictions	Sometimes uses cover and title to make predictions	Never uses cover and title to make predictions
Shares background knowledge related to text	Shares prior knowledge in story discussions	Sometimes uses prior knowledge about text	Never uses prior knowledge about text
Gives responses to text that show comprehension	Responds to text with comprehension	Sometimes demonstrates comprehension through story response	Never or seldom demonstrates comprehension

Name ______________________________

Spelling Behavior Rubrics

Spelling Behavior	Level 3	Level 2	Level 1
Uses knowledge of phonics to encode word	Spells based upon knowledge of phonics	Sometimes uses phonics to spell words	Does not use phonics to spell words
Compares unknown words with familiar words	Uses knowledge of words to spell unknown words	Sometimes uses word knowledge to spell	Does not use knowledge of known words to spell
Uses word wall as a reference	Uses word wall as a reference	Sometimes uses word wall as a reference	Never uses word wall as a reference
Spells words based upon knowledge of syllabication	Uses knowledge of syllabication to spell	Sometimes uses syllabication to spell	Does not use syllabication to spell

PHONOLOGICAL AWARENESS CHECKLIST

Word-Solving Behavior	Demonstrates	Needs Improvement	Not Observed
Has mastery of core frequency words			
Manipulates onsets and rhymes			
Sorts words according to pattern			
Is able to chunk words			
Uses structural analysis (of prefixes and suffixes, for example) to identify words			

Chapter 7

Name: ____________________________

Listening			
Student talk focused on question			
Student talk showed an understanding of the text			
Practiced good listening behaviors and turn taking			
Demonstrated an interest in the story through engaged discussion			

KEY

H	**High** level of engagement	L	**Low** level of engagement
M	**Moderate** level of engagement	NO	**No** level of engagement

Assessing Guided Listening and Discussion of a Read Aloud

Name: ____________________________ Date: ______________

Key Y = Yes N = No	Childhood			Youth			Adulthood			Person's Contribution		
	Fact			Fact			Fact			Fact		
	#1	#2	#3	#1	#2	#3	#1	#2	#3	#1	#2	#3
Accurate												
Clearly Expressed												
Significant Event												

Assessment Checklist of the Biography Map

Name: ______________________________

Name	*Participates in Discussion*	*Contributes Ideas for Composing the Story*	*Shares Pen During Writing of the Story*	*Reads Story Back to Group Upon Request*

KEY

H	**High** level of engagement	L	**Low** level of engagement
M	**Moderate** level of engagement	NO	**No** level of engagement

Annotated Checklist for Shared Writing: The Group Experience Story

Name ______________________________ **Date of Birth** ________

Prephonetic Stage of Spelling Development—Random Letters

Date:

__________ Scribbles and draws shapes that look like letters

__________ Makes random letters and shapes

__________ Uses no spaces between words

__________ Draws pictures to express meaning

Grade____

Early Phonetic Stage of Spelling Development—Consonants

Date:

__________ Begins to show letter–sound relationships

__________ Uses invented spelling

__________ Uses initial consonants

__________ Spells words with consonants

__________ Uses spaces between words

Grade____

Advanced Phonetic Stage of Spelling Development—Letter Sounds

Date:

__________ Spells words using letter–sound relationships

__________ Spells words based on how they look

__________ Begins to use long vowels in spelling words

Grade_____

Transitional Stage of Spelling Development—Vowel and Consonant Combinations in Words

Date:

__________ Spells words using more standard forms of spelling

__________ Relies more on visual memory, how words look, to spell words

__________ Spells more sight words correctly

__________ Spells words using familiar letter patterns

__________ At the end of the stage, words are spelled representing all syllables

Grade____

Standard Stage of Spelling Development—Correct Spelling

Date:

__________ Spells most words using standard or correct spelling

__________ Begins to spells words that have multiple spellings (e.g., *their*, *there*, *they're*) correctly

__________ Relies on meaning and syntax as well as phonics to spell words

Grade____

Student Profile of Spelling Development

Running Record Assessment Form

Name ______________________ Date ______________ Grade ________

Literacy Level ________________ Teacher ____________________

Text Title ______________________________ Level ______________

Quantitative Analysis

\# Running Words _____ # Correct Words _____ # Errors _____ # Self-Corrections _____

Accuracy Rate _________ Error Rate _________ Self-Correction Rate ___________

Qualitative Analysis

Page	*Coding of Child's Reading*	*# Words*	*# Errors*	*# Self-Corrections*	*Cue Used for Attempt Error/Self-Correction*		
					M	*S*	*G*

Name: ______________________________ Grade: _______

Language Context	*Date*	*Ratings and Comments*		
Conversations Context of conversation		1 Very limited vocabulary; frequently uses words incorrectly.	3 Developing vocabulary; attempts to use new words.	5 Developed vocabulary; uses idioms; uses new words correctly.
		Rate student's growth and give examples of vocabulary used in conversations.		
Book Discussion Title of book Type of discussion		1 Very limited vocabulary; frequently uses words incorrectly.	3 Developing vocabulary; attempts to use new words.	5 Developed vocabulary; uses idioms; uses new words correctly.
		Provide examples of vocabulary used during the book discussion. Did the child appropriate the language of the book discussed? What new and interesting words from the story were used?		
Informal Writing • Journals • Reading logs • Letters and messages to friends • E-mail		1 Very limited vocabulary; frequently uses words incorrectly.	3 Developing vocabulary; attempts to use new words.	5 Developed vocabulary; uses idioms; uses new words correctly.
		Cite examples of new and interesting words found in the child's writing.		

Documenting Observations of Vocabulary Growth

Name ______________________ Grade ________

Observer ______________________

Date	**Rate of Reading**	**Automatic Word Recognition** Accuracy Level: # of Words Correct Out of 100	**Stage of Oral Reading: Proficient, Developing, and Beginning**	**Additional Comments**

Comprehensive Assessment of Children's Fluency in Oral Reading

Name ________________________ Grade ________
Beginning Date ________________________ Ending Date ________________________

Number of Readings and Reading Rate (WPM)

# of Words	0	1st	2nd	3rd	4th	5th	6th	7th	8th	9th
150										
145										
140										
135										
130										
125										
120										
115										
110										
105										
100										
95										
90										
85										
80										
75										
70										
65										
60										
55										
50										
45										
40										
35										
30										
25										
20										
15										
10										
	0	1st	2nd	3rd	4th	5th	6th	7th	8th	9th

Number of Readings

Summary of Readings

Date	Reading	WPM	Date	Reading	WPM	Date	Reading	WPM

Assessing Children's Reading Rate—Timed Reading Chart

Chapter 9

Name ______ ***Grade*** ______ ***Age*** ______
Teacher ______ ***Examiner*** ______ ***Date*** ______

Rhyming Words: Examiner: Today we will rhyme words. Remember, when words rhyme they sound like each other. *Cat* and *sat* rhyme, so I will say, "Yes." Say the word *yes* to any two words you think rhyme, and say the word *no* to two words you think do not rhyme.

tan, ran (yes)	______	**plate, late (yes)**	______
sock, tock (yes)	______	**clap, clock (no)**	______
help, flood (no)	______	**let, met (yes)**	______
Jill, hill (yes)	______	**said, jump (no)**	______
		Total # Correct	______

Segmenting Words in Sentences: Examiner: You will listen to words in sentences. Each time I say a word, tap the pencil only once. Listen to me: "Today is Monday." (3 taps).

______ **I ride on the bus. (5 taps)**
______ **I have one brother and one sister. (7 taps)**
______ **My name is very long. (5 taps)**
______ **Today we will play in the gym. (7 taps)**
______ **I can jump rope. (4 taps)**
______ **How old are you? (4 taps)**

Total # Correct ______

Segmenting Compound Words: Examiner: I will say long words that have two parts. Please say each part of the words. Listen while I say a word: *firehouse.* Now tell the two parts: *fire house.*

Superman	______	***goldfish***	______
doghouse	______	***beehive***	______
hairbrush	______	***anything***	______
firefly	______	***bluebird***	______
bedroom	______	***backpack***	______
		Total # Correct	______

Student Profile of Phonemic Awareness Development

Segmenting Syllables: Examiner: I will say long words that have one or more parts or syllables. This time listen to each word and then say and clap each part of the word. Listen while I say a word: *baby.* Now say and clap the parts you hear in the word *ba-by* (2 claps).

candle (2 claps) ____________
boy (1 clap) ____________
father (2 claps) ____________
elephant (3 claps) ____________
yellow (2 claps) ____________

strawberry (3 claps) ____________
peanut (2 claps) ____________
man (1 clap) ____________
lady (2 claps) ____________
mountain (2 claps) ____________

Total # Correct ____________

Segmenting First and Last Sounds: Examiner: I will say a word. Listen to the word and say only the first sound. Listen while I say *cat.* The first sound is /c/. When the child has finished identifying the first sounds in words, continue to the last sounds. Now listen to the word for the last sound. The word is *cat.* The last sound is /t/.

First Sounds:

1. **sat (/s/)** ____________
2. **big (/b/)** ____________
3. **not (/n/)** ____________
4. **fun (/f/)** ____________
5. **candle (/c/)** ____________
6. **yellow (/y/)** ____________

Total # Correct ____________

Last Sounds:

1. **met (/t/)** ____________
2. **ran (/n/)** ____________
3. **sad (/d/)** ____________
4. **miss (/s/)** ____________
5. **hope (/p/)** ____________
6. **leaf (/f/)** ____________

Total # Correct ____________

Segmenting All the Sounds Within a Word: Examiner: I will say a word. Listen to the word and to each sound in the word. Then say each sound you hear. Listen while I say *cat.* I hear /c/, /a/, and /t/.

1. **me (/m/ /e/)** ____________
2. **sit (/s/ /i/ /t/)** ____________
3. **bike (/b/ /i/ /k/)** ____________
4. **so (/s/ /o/)** ____________
5. **pet (/p/ /e/ /t/)** ____________
6. **game (/g/ /a/ /m/)** ____________

Total # Correct ____________

Name ______________________________

Blending Compound Words and Syllables: Examiner: I will say parts of a word. Listen to each word part. Then put the parts together to say one word. Listen while I say it: *Fruit cake. Fruitcake.*

Compound Words		***Syllables in Words***	
1. air plane	______	***1. can dle***	______
2. dog house	______	***2. bak ing***	______
3. door bell	______	***3. fas ter***	______
4. blue berry	______	***4. mo ther***	______
5. base ball	______	***5. boys***	______
6. bull dog	______	***6. child ren***	______
Total # Correct ______		**Total # Correct** ______	

Blending Phonemes: Examiner: I will say some sounds. When you put them together they make a word. Listen to each sound, and then put them together to make a word. Listen: /c/ /a/ /t/. The word is *cat.*

1. b–e (be)	______	**4. m–o–p (mop)**	______
2. g–e–t (get)	______	**5. h–u–g (hug)**	______
3. h–a–nd (hand)	______	**6. b–u–n–ch (bunch)**	______
		Total # Correct ______	

Phoneme Deletion: Examiner: I will say a word. Then I will say it without part of the word: *baking.* Now I will say it without *-ing. Bake.*

1. Say the word *carried.* Now say it without *–ed.* (carry) ______
2. Say the word *happy.* Now say it without *–py.* (hap) ______
3. Say the word *mat.* Now say it without *–t.* (ma) ______
4. Say the word *lamp.* Now say it without *–l.* (amp) ______
5. Say the word *boat.* Now say it without *–b* (oat) ______
6. Say the word *return.* Now say it without *–turn.* (re) ______

Total # Correct ______

Directions: Write the date the child has demonstrated the performance of each skill in the appropriate column next to the letter mastered. Under the Summary section, indicate the total numbers of letters known by skill area with the summary date.

Name ______________________ ***Grade*** ________ ***Age*** ________
Teacher ______________________ ***Examiner*** ______________________
Can recite the alphabet or sing the ABC song: Date ______________________

Letters	Recognizes Uppercase Letters	Recognizes Lowercase Letters	Knows the Letter Sounds	Writes the Uppercase Letters	Writes the Lowercase Letters
Aa					
Bb					
Cc					
Dd					
Ee					
Ff					
Gg					
Hh					
Ii					
Jj					
Kk					
Ll					
Mm					
Nn					
Oo					
Pp					
Qq					
Rr					
Ss					
Tt					
Uu					
Vv					
Ww					
Xx					
Yy					
Zz					

Summary of Alphabet Knowledge

Date					
Total Score					

Profile Chart of Child's Alphabet Knowledge

Directions: Have the child read each word. Place a "+" in the first column, *R*, if the child recognizes the word, and place a "+" in the second column, *A*, if the child can say the word automatically—that is, before the lapse of 4 to 5 seconds.

Name ______________________ Grade ________ Age ________ Date ________

Teacher ______________________ Examiner ______________________

Group I			Group II			Group III		
	R	A		R	A		R	A
1. the			1. give			1. city		
2. have			2. sound			2. country		
3. was			3. work			3. earth		
4. you			4. sentence			4. saw		
5. they			5. know			5. thought		
6. were			6. where			6. few		
7. your			7. through			7. group		
8. their			8. around			8. might		
9. each			9. follow			9. always		
10. said			10. show			10. important		
11. would			11. another			11. children		
12. about			12. large			12. white		
13. them			13. because			13. river		
14. time			14. went			14. carry		
15. write			15. move			15. second		
16. people			16. picture			16. enough		
17. water			17. play			17. almost		
18. who			18. animal			18. mountain		
19. down			19. mother			19. young		
20. over			20. America			20. family		
Total			Total			Total		

Child's Profile of Automatic Recognition of Sight Words
Source: Adapted from Rasinsky & Padak (2001, p. 191).

Directions: Indicate the correct response only. Use a "+" to code a correct response and indicate the date of testing.

Name ______________________ Grade __________ Age __________ Date __________

Teacher ______________________ Examiner ______________________

Matching Word With Same Rimes	Date	Producing Another Word Within the Word Family	Date	Substitution: Initial Letter—Onset	Date	Substitution: Final Letter in Rime	Date	Substitution: Medial Letter in Rime	Date
boy		-ell		pot (got)		cat (can)		cat (cut)	
cat		-ake		sun (fun)		but (bud)		but (bat)	
top		-in		cat (rat)		set (sell)		set (sit)	
pit		-ot		net (pet)		pin (pit)		pit (put)	
bun		-ook		will (sill)		pod (pot)		pod (pad)	
pet		-un		them (hem)		them (then)		hem (him)	
TOTAL		TOTAL		TOTAL		TOTAL		TOTAL	

A Student's Profile of Knowledge and Skills Using Word Families

References

Aaron, P. G., & Joshi, R. M. (1992). *Reading problems: Consultation and remediation.* New York: Guilford Press.

Adams, M. J. (1990). *Beginning to read: Thinking and learning about print.* Cambridge, MA: MIT Press.

Adams, M. J., & Bruck, M. (1995). Resolving the "great debate." *American Educator, 19*(2), 7, 10–20.

Adams, M. J., & Henry, M. K. (1997). Myths and realities about words and literacy. *School Psychology Review, 26,* 425–436.

Alexander, D. (1999). Keys to successful learning: A national summit on research in learning disabilities. Retrieved from http://www.ldonline.org/ld_indepth/reading/ncld_summit99.html

Allen, R. V. (1976). *Language experience in communication.* Boston: Houghton Mifflin.

Allington, R. L. (1983). The reading instruction provided readers of differing ability. *Elementary School Journal, 83,* 255–265.

Allington, R. L., & Cunningham, P. M. (1996). *Schools that work: Where all children read and write.* New York: Longman.

Allington, R. L., & Cunningham, P. (2002). *Schools that work: Where all children read and write* (2nd ed.). Boston: Allyn & Bacon.

Alvermann, D. E. (1991). The discussion web: A graphic aid for learning across the curriculum. *The Reading Teacher,* 45(2), 92–99.

Anderson, R. C., Fielding, L. G., & Wilson, P. T. (1988). Growth in reading and how children spend their time outside of school. *Reading Research Quarterly, 23,* 285–303.

Anderson, R. C., & Freebody, P. (1981). Vocabulary knowledge. In J. T. Guthrie (Ed.), *Comprehension and teaching: Research reviews.* Newark, DE: International Research Association.

Anderson, R. C., & Pearson, P. D. (1984). A schema-theoretic view of basic processes in reading comprehension. In P. D. Pearson (Ed.), *Handbook of reading research* (pp. 255–291). New York: Longman.

Anderson, R. C., Hiebert, E. H., Scott, J. A., & Wilkinson, I. A. G. (1985). *Becoming a nation of readers: The report of the Commission on Reading.* Washington, DC: National Institute of Education.

Antonacci, P. (2000). Reading in the zone of proximal development: Mediating literacy development in beginner readers through guided reading. *Reading Horizons, 41*(1), 19–34.

Armbruster, B. B., Lehr, T., & Osborn, J. M., (Eds.). (2001). *Putting reading first: The research building blocks for teaching children to read.* Washington, DC: National Institute for Literacy.

Arter, J., & Spandel, V. (1992). Using portfolios of student work in instruction and assessment. *Educational Measurement: Issues and Practice,* 12, pp. 36–44.

Assessment Reform Group. (2002). *Assessment for learning: 10 principles.* Retrieved from http://www.assessment-reform-group.co.uk

Association for Supervision and Curriculum Development. (2002). *Differentiating instruction.* Retrieved from http://www.ascd.org/pdi/demo/diffinstu/11esex.html

Atwell, N. (1987). *In the middle: Writing, reading and learning with adolescents.* Portsmouth, NH: Heinemann.

Bakhtin, M. M. (1981). *The dialogic imagination: Four essays by M. M. Bakhtin* (C. Emerson & M. Holoquist, Trans.; M. Holoquist, Ed.). Austin: University of Texas Press.

Baron, N. (1992). *Growing up with language: How children learn to talk.* New York: Addison-Wesley.

Bartolome, L. I. (1998). *The misteaching of academic discourses: The politics of language in the classroom.* Boulder, CO: Westview Press.

Beach, R. W. (1993). *A teacher's introduction to reader-response theories.* Urbana, IL: National Council of Teachers of English.

Bean, W., & Bouffler, C. (1997). *Read, write, spell.* York, ME: Stenhouse.

Beck, I. L., & Juel, C. (1995). The role of decoding in learning to read. *American Educator, 19*(2), 8, 21–25, 39–42.

Beck, I. L., & McKeown, M. G. (1991). Conditions of vocabulary acquisition. In R. Barr, M. L. Kamil, P. Mosenthal, & P. D. Pearson (Eds.), *Handbook of reading research* (Vol. 2, pp. 789–814). New York: Longman.

Beck, I. L., & McKeown, M. G. (1999). Comprehension: The sine qua non of reading. *Teaching and Change, 6,* 197–211.

Beck, I. L., & McKeown, M. G. (2001). Text talk: Capturing the benefits of read aloud experiences for young children. *The Reading Teacher, 55*(1), 10–20.

Beck, I. L., McKeown, M. G., Hamilton, R., & Kucan, L. (1997). *Questioning the author: An approach for enhancing student engagement with text.* Newark, DE: International Reading Association.

Bell, H. (1999). Spotlight on New Zealand. *Reading Today, 17(1),* 37.

Bensen, V., & Cummins, C. (2000). *The power of retelling: Developmental steps for building comprehension.* Bothell, WA: The Wright Group.

Bereiter, C. & Scardamalia, M. (1982). From conversation to composition: The role of instruction in a developmental process. In R. Glass (Ed.). *Advances in Instructional Psychology, Vol.2, pp. 1–64.* Hillsdale, NJ: Erlbaum.

Berk, L. E., & Winsler, A. (1995). *Scaffolding children's learning: Vygotsky and early childhood education.* Washington, DC: National Association for the Education of Young Children.

Birnbaum, J., & Emig, J. (1983). Creating minds: Creating texts. In R. Parker & F. Davis (Eds.), *Developing literacy: Young children's use of language.* Newark, DE: International Reading Association.

Bissex, G. (1980). *GNYS AT WRK: A child learns to read and write.* Cambridge, MA: Harvard University Press.

Blackman (1999). Phonological awareness. In M. Kamil, P. B. Mosenthal, P. O. Pearson, & R. Barr (Eds.), *Handbook of reading research* (Vol. 3). Mahwah, NJ: Erlbaum.

Bloom, L., & Lahey, M. (1978). *Language development and language disorders.* New York: John Wiley & Sons.

Bloome, D. (1991). Anthropology and research on teaching the English language arts. In J. Flood, J. M. Jensen, D. Lapp, & J. R. Squire (Eds.), *Handbook of research on teaching the English language arts* (pp. 45–56). New York: Macmillan.

Bond, G. L., & Dykstra, R. (1967). The cooperative program in first grade reading instruction. *Reading Research Quarterly, 2,* 5–142.

Borgstein, J. (2001). A sense of language. *Lancet, 357,* 2.

Bowman, B. T., Donovan, M. S., & Burns, M. S. (2000). *Eager to learn: Educating our preschoolers.* Washington, DC: National Academy Press.

Bredekamp, S., & Copple, C. (Eds.). (1997). *Developmentally appropriate practice in early childhood programs* (Rev. ed.). Washington, DC: National Association for the Education of Young Children.

Britton, J. (1993). *Language and learning: The importance of speech in children's development* (2nd ed.). Portsmouth, NH: Heinemann-Boynton/Cook.

Bromley, K. D. (1995). *Webbing with literature: Creating story maps with children's books.* Boston: Allyn & Bacon.

Brown, H., & Cambourne, B. (1990). *Read and retell: A strategy for the whole-language/natural learning classroom.* Portsmouth, NH: Heinemann.

Bruck, M. (1992). Persistence of dyslexics' phonological awareness deficits. *Developmental Psychology, 28,* 874–886.

Bruner, J. (1978). The role of dialogue in language learning. In A. Sinclair, R. J. Jarvella, & W. J. M. Levelt (Eds.), *The child's conception of language.* Berlin, Germany: Springer-Verlag.

Bruner, J. (1983). *Child's talk: Learning to use language.* New York: Norton.

Brunn, M. (2002). The four square strategy. *The Reading Teacher, 55*(6), 522–525.

Bryant, P. (1974). *Perception and understanding of young children.* London: Methuen.

Buehl, D. (2001). *Classroom strategies for interactive learning* (2nd ed.). Newark, DE: International Reading Association.

Burgess, S. R., & Lonigan, C. J. (1998). Bidirectional relations of phonological sensitivity and prereading abilities: Evidence from a preschool sample. *Journal of Experimental Child Psychology, 70,* 117–141.

Burns, M., & Snow, C. (Eds.). (1999). *Starting out right: A guide to promoting children's reading success.* Washington, DC: National Academy Press.

Bus, A. G., & van Ijzendoorn, M. H. (1999). Phonological awareness and early reading: A Meta-analysis of experimental training studies. *Journal of Educational Psychology, 77,* 349–361.

Bus, A. G., van Ijzendoorn, M. H., & Pellegrini, A. D. (1995). Storybook reading makes for success in learning to read: A meta-analysis on the intergenerational transmission of literacy. *Review of Educational Research, 65,* 1–21.

Byrne, B., & Fielding-Barnsley, R. (1995). Evaluation of a program to teach phonemic awareness to young children: A 2- and 3-year follow-up and a new preschool trial. *Journal of Educational Psychology, 87,* 488–503.

Byrne, B., & Fielding-Barnsley, R. F. (1991). Evaluation of a program to teach phonemic awareness in young children. *Journal of Educational Psychology, 82,* 805–812.

Calkins, L. M. (1983). *Lessons from a child on the teaching and learning of writing.* Exeter, NH: Heinemann.

Calkins, L. M. (1994). *The art of teaching writing.* New Edition. Portsmouth, NH: Heinemann.

Calkins, L. M. (2001). *The art of teaching reading.* New York: Pearson.

Cambourne, B. (1988). *The whole story.* Auckland, New Zealand: Ashton Scholastic.

Cecil, N. L. (1999). *Striking a balance: Positive practices for early literacy.* Scottsdale, AZ: Holcomb Hathaway.

Chall, J. (1983). *Stages of reading development.* New York: McGraw-Hill.

Chall, J. (1989). Learning to read: The great debate many years later. A response to "Debunking the great phonics myth." *Phi Delta Kappan, 71,* 521–538.

Chall, J. S. (1987). Two vocabularies for reading: Recognition and meaning. In M. G. McKeown & M. E. Curtis (Eds.), *The nature of vocabulary acquisition* (pp. 7–17). Hillsdale, NJ: Erlbaum.

Chaney, J. H. (1993). Alphabet books: Resources for learning. *The Reading Teacher, 47,* 96–104.

Ching, D. C. (1976). *Reading and the bilingual child.* Newark, DE: International Reading Association.

Chinn, C. A., & Brewer, W. F. (1993). The role of anomalous data in knowledge acquisition: A theoretical framework and implications for science instruction. *Review of Educational Research, 63,* 1–49.

Chomsky, C. (1979). Approaching reading through invented spelling. In L. B. Resnick & P. A. Weaver (Eds.), *Theory and practice of early reading* (pp. 43–65). Hillsdale, NJ: Erlbaum.

Chomsky, N. (1965). *Aspect of the theory of syntax.* Cambridge, MA: MIT Press.

Chomsky, N. (1975). *Reflections on language.* New York: Pantheon.

Clark, M. M. (1976). *Young fluent readers.* Portsmouth, NH: Heinemann.

Clay, M. (1972). *Sand—"concepts about print" tests.* Auckland, NZ: Heinemann.

Clay, M. (1991). *Becoming literate: The construction of inner control.* Portsmouth, NH: Heinemann.

Clay, M. (1993). *An observation survey of early literacy achievement.* Portsmouth, NH: Heinemann.

Clay, M. (1998). *By different paths to common outcomes.* Portland, ME: Stenhouse.

Clay, M. M. (1975). *What did I write?* Portsmouth, NH: Heinemann.

Clay, M. M. (1982). *Observing young readers.* Portsmouth, NH: Heinemann.

Clay, M. M. (1985). *The early detection of reading difficulties: A diagnostic survey with recovery procedures.* Portsmouth, NH: Heinemann.

Clay, M. M. (1993a). *An observation survey of early literacy achievement.* Portsmouth, NH: Heinemann.

Clay, M. M. (1993b). *Reading recovery: A guidebook for teachers in training.* Portsmouth, NH: Heinemann.

Clay, M. M. (1998). *By different paths to common outcomes.* York, ME: Stenhouse.

Cochran-Smith, M. (1984). *The making of a reader.* Norwood, NJ: Ablex.

Cooper, J. D., & Kiger, N. D. (2001). *Literacy assessment: Helping teachers plan instruction.* Boston: Houghton Mifflin.

Cooper, J. D. (2000). *Literacy: Helping children construct meaning* (4th ed.). Boston: Houghton Mifflin.

Copenhaver, J. (1993). Instances of inquiry. *Primary Voices* K–3, *1*(1), 6–12.

Crawford, P. A. (1995). Early literacy: Emerging perspectives. *Journal of Research in Childhood Education, 10*(1), 75–81.

Cullinan, B., Scala, M., & Schroeder, V. (1995). *Three voices: An invitation to poetry across the curriculum.* York, ME: Stenhouse.

Cummins, J. (1979). Cognitive/academic language proficiency, linguistic interdependence, the optimal age question and other matters. *Working Papers on Bilingualism, 19,* 197–205.

Cunningham, A., & Stanovich, K. (1997). Early reading acquisition and its relation to reading experience and ability 10 years later. *Developmental Psychology, 33,* 934–945.

Cunningham, A., & Stanovich, K. (1998). What reading does for the mind. *American Educator,* Spring/Summer, 1–8.

Cunningham, P. (1990). The names test: A quick assessment of decoding ability. *The Reading Teacher, 44,* 124–129.

Cunningham, P. M. (2000). *Phonics they use: Words for reading and writing* (3rd ed.). New York: Longman.

Cunningham, P. M., & Cunningham, J. W. (1992). Making words: Enhancing the invented spelling-decoding connection. *The Reading Teacher, 46,* 106–107.

D'Alessandro, M. (1990). Accommodating emotionally handicapped children through a literature based reading program. *The Reading Teacher, 44*(4), 288–293.

Dahl, K., & Farnan, N. (1988). *Children's writing: Perspectives from research.* Newark, DE: International Reading Association.

Daniels, H. (2002). Literature circles: Voice and choice in book clubs and reading groups. (2nd ed.). York, ME: Stenhouse.

Dewey, J. (1990). *The school and society. The child and the curriculum: An expanded edition with a new introduction by Philip W. Jackson.* Chicago: University of Chicago Press.

Dixon-Krauss, L. (1996). *Vygotsky in the classroom: Mediated literacy and assessment in the classroom.* White Plains, NY: Longman.

Doake, D. (1981). *Book experience and emergent reading behavior in preschool children.* Unpublished dissertation, University of Alberta, Edmonton, Alberta, Canada.

Doake, D. (1985). Reading-like behavior: Its role in learning to read. In A. Jaggar & M. Trika Smith-Burke (Eds.), *Observing the language learner.* Newark, DE: International Reading Association.

Doake, D. (1986). Learning to read: It starts in the home. In D. R. Tovey & J. E. Kerber (Eds.), *Roles in literacy learning* (pp. 2–9). Newark, DE: International Reading Association.

Dole, J. S., Duffy, G. G., Roehler, L. R., & Pearson, P. D. (1991). Moving from the old to the new: Research on reading comprehension. *Review of Educational Research, 61,* 239–264.

Durkin, D. (1966). *Children who read early.* New York: Teachers College Press.

Dye, G. (2000). Graphic organizers to the rescue! Helping children link—and remember—information. *Teaching Exceptional Children, 32,* 72–76.

Dyson, A. H. (1989). *Multiple worlds of child writers: Friends learning to write.* New York: Teachers College Press.

Edelsky, C., Altwerger, B., & Flores, B. (1991). *Whole language: What's the difference?* Portsmouth, NH: Heinemann.

Ehri, L. (1994). Development of the ability to read words: Update. In R. B. Ruddell, M. R. Ruddell, & H. Singer (Eds.), *Theoretical models and processes of reading* (4th ed., pp. 323–358). Newark, DE: International Reading Association.

Ehri, L. C., & McCormick, S. (1998). Phases of word learning: Implications for instruction with delayed and disabled readers. *Reading and Writing Quarterly: Overcoming Learning Disabilities, 14,* 135–163.

Elley, W. B. (1989). Vocabulary acquisition from listening to stories. *Reading Research Quarterly, 24,* 174–187.

Erikson, E. (1963). *Childhood and society.* New York: Norton.

Farris, P. (2001). *Language arts: Process, product and assessment* (3rd ed.). New York: McGraw-Hill.

Ferreiro, E. (1986). The interplay between information and assimilation in beginning literacy. In W. H. Teale & E. Sulzby (Eds.), *Emergent literacy* (pp. 15–49). Norwood, NJ: Ablex.

Ferreiro, E. (1988). L'ecriture avant la letre. In H. Sinclair (Ed.), *The production of notations in the young child* (pp. 18–69). Paris: Presses Universitaires de France.

Fletcher, R. (1993). *What a writer needs.* Portsmouth, NH: Heinemann.

Flynn, P. A. H. (2002). *Dialogic approaches toward developing third graders' comprehension using questioning the author and its influence on teacher change.* Unpublished doctoral dissertation. Fordham University, New York.

Foorman, B. R. (1995). Research on "The great debate": Code-oriented versus whole language approaches to reading instruction. *School Psychology Review, 24,* 376–392.

Fountas, I. C., & Pinnell, G. S. (1996). *Guided reading: Good first teaching for all children.* Portsmouth, NH: Heinemann.

Fountas, I. C., & Pinnell, G. S. (2001). *Guiding readers and writers: Grades 3–6.* Portsmouth, NH: Heinemann.

Freeman, D., & Freeman, Y. (2000). *Teaching reading in multilingual classrooms.* Portsmouth, NH: Heinemann.

Freeman, E. B., & Hatch, J. A. (1989). Emergent literacy: Reconceptualizing kindergarten practice. *Childhood Education, 66*(1), 21–24.

Fries, C. (1962). *Linguistics and reading.* New York: Holt, Rinehart and Winston.

Fry, E. (1980). The new instant word list. *The Reading Teacher, 34,* 284–289.

Fry, E., Fountoukidis, D. L., & Polk, J. K. (1985). *The new reading teacher's book of lists.* Upper Saddle River, NJ: Merrill/Prentice Hall.

Galda, L., & Guice, S. (1997). Response-based reading instruction in the elementary grades. In S. A. Stahl & D. A. Hayes (Eds.), *Instructional models in reading* (pp. 311–330).

Galda, L., & West, J. (1995). Exploring literature through drama. In N. L. Roser & M. G. Martinez (Eds.), *Book talk and beyond: Children and teachers respond to literature.* Newark, DE: International Reading Association.

Galda, L., Cullinan, B., & Strickland, D. (1997). *Language, literacy and the child.* Fort Worth, TX: Harcourt Brace.

Garcia, E. E. (1997, March). The education of Hispanics in early childhood: Of roots and wings. *Young Children (52)*3, 5–14.

Gardner, H. (1993). *Multiple intelligences: The theory in practice.* New York: Basic Books Inc.

Gasparro, M., & Falletta, B. (1994). *Creating drama with poetry: Teaching English as a second language through dramatization and improvisation.* Washington, DC: ERIC Clearinghouse on Languages and Linguistics. (ERIC Document Reproduction Service No. ED368214)

Gee, J. P. (2001). A sociocultural perspective on early literacy development. In S.B. Neuman & D. K. Dickinson (Eds.), *Handbook of early literacy research* (pp. 30–43). New York: Guilford Press.

Genishi, C. (1987). Acquiring oral language and communicative competence. In C. Seefeldt (Ed.), *The early childhood curriculum: A review of the current research.* New York: Teachers College Press.

Genishi, C. (1988). Children's language: Learning words from experience. *Young Children, 44,* 16–23.

Gentry, J. R. (1982). An analysis of developmental spelling in GNYS AT WRK. *The Reading Teacher, 36,* 192–200.

Gentry, R. (1985). You can analyze developmental spelling. *Teaching K–8, (15)*9, 44–45.

Gentry, R. (1999). The literacy map: Guiding children to where they need to be (K–3). Mondo Publishers.

George, P. S. (1988). *What's the truth about tracking and ability grouping?* Gainesville, FL: Teacher Education Resources.

Gessell, A. (1925). *The mental growth of the preschool child.* New York: Macmillan.

Gipe, J. (1998). *Multiple paths to literacy* (pp. 168–205). Upper Saddle River, NJ: Merrill/ Prentice Hall.

Goodman, K. (1996). *On reading: A common-sense look at the nature of language and the science of reading.* Portsmouth, NH: Heinemann.

Goodman, K. S. (1986). *What's whole in whole language.* Portsmouth, NH: Heinemann.

Goodman, Y. (1985). Kidwatching: Observing children in the classroom. In A. Jaggar & M. T. Smith-Burke (Eds.), *Observing the language learner.* Newark, DE: International Reading Association.

Grant, C. (2001). Teachers and linking literacies of yesterday and today with literacies of tomorrow: The need for education that is multicultural and reconstructionist. *National Reading Conference Yearbook, 50,* 63–81.

Graves, D. (1994). *A fresh look at writing.* Portsmouth, NH: Heinemann.

Graves, D. H. (1983). *Teaching writing.* Portsmouth, NH: Heinemann.

Graves, M. (1994). Vocabulary knowledge. In C. Purves (Ed.), *Encyclopedia of English studies and language arts* (Vol. 2, pp. 1246–1248). Urbana, IL: National Council of Teachers of English.

Griffin, M. (2001). Social contexts of beginning reading. *Language Arts, 78,* 371–378.

Griffin, M. L. (2002). Why don't you use your finger? Paired reading in the first grade. *The Reading Teacher, 55*(8), 766–774.

Gunning, T. (1999). *Building literacy.* Newington, CT: Galvin.

Gunning, T. (2000). *Creating literacy instruction for all children,* 3rd ed. Needham Heights, MA: Allyn & Bacon.

Gunning, T. (2001). *Building words: A resource manual for teaching word analysis and spelling strategies.* Boston: Allyn & Bacon

Gunning, T. (2003). *Creating literacy instruction for all children,* 4th ed. Needham Heights, MA: Allyn & Bacon.

Hadaway, N. L., Vardell, S. M., & Young, T. A. (2001). Scaffolding oral language development through poetry for students learning English. *The Reading Teacher, 54*(8), 786–804.

Halliday, M. (1973). *Explorations in the functions of language.* London: Edward Arnold.

Halliday, M. (1975). *Learning how to mean: Exploration in the development of language.* London: Edward Arnold.

Halliday, M. (1982). Three aspects of children's language development: Learning language, learning through language, learning about language. In Y. Goodman, N. Haussler, & D. Strickland (Eds.), *Oral and written language development research: Impact on the schools.* Urbana, IL: National Council of Teachers of English.

Halliday, M. A. K. (1975). *Learning how to mean: Explorations in the development of language.* London: Edward Arnold.

Harris, A. J., & Jacobson, M. D. (1972). *Basic elementary reading vocabularies.* New York: Macmillan.

Harris, T. L, & Hodges, R. E. (Eds.). (1995). *The literacy dictionary: The vocabulary of reading and writing.* Newark, DE: International Reading Association.

Harste, J. D., Short, K. G., & Burke, C. (1988). *Creating classrooms for authors: The reading-writing connection.* Portsmouth, NH: Heinemann.

Hartle-Schutte, D. (1993). Literacy development in Navajo homes: Does it lead to success in school? *Language Arts, 70,* 642–654.

Harvey, S. (2002). Nonfiction inquiry: Using real reading and writing to explore the world. *Language Arts, 80*(1), 12–22.

Harvey, S., & Goudvis, A. (2000). *Strategies that work: Teaching comprehension to enhance understanding.* York, ME: Stenhouse.

Harvey, S., & Goudvis, A. (2000). *Strategies that work: Teaching comprehension to enhance understanding.* York, ME: Stenhouse.

Head, M. H., & Readence, J. E. (1992). Anticipation guides: Using prediction to promote learning from text. In E. K. Dishner, T. W. Bean, J. E. Readence, & D. W. Moore (Eds.), *Reading in the content areas: Improving classroom instruction,* 3rd ed. (pp. 227–233). Dubuque, IA: Kendall/Hunt.

Heath, S. B. (1983). *Ways with words.* Cambridge, MA: Cambridge University Press.

Heilman, A. W. (2002). *Phonics in proper perspective* (9th ed.). Upper Saddle River, NJ: Merrill/Prentice Hall.

Heimlich, J. E., & Pittelman, S. D. (1986). *Semantic mapping: Classroom applications.* Newark, DE: International Reading Association.

Hennings, D. (2001). *Communication in action.* Boston: Allyn & Bacon.

Herber, H. (1978). *Teaching reading in the content area* (2nd ed.). Upper Saddle River, NJ: Merrill/Prentice Hall.

Hiebert, E. H. (1986). Using environmental print in beginning reading instruction. In M. R. Samson (Ed.), *The pursuit of literacy: Early reading and writing.* Dubuque, IA: Kendall/Hunt.

Hiebert, E. H., Pearson, P. D., Taylor, B. M., Richardson, V., & Paris, S. G. (1998). *Every child a reader: Applying reading research in the classroom.* Topic 1: Oral Language and Reading. University of Michigan, Ann Arbor, Michigan: Center for the Improvement of Early Reading Achievement (CIERA).

Hoffman, J. V. (1992). Critical reading/thinking across the curriculum: Using I charts to support learning. *Language Arts, 69,* 121–127.

Holdaway, D. (1979). *The foundations of literacy.* Sydney, Australia: Ashton Scholastic.

Holdaway, D. (1986). The structure of natural language as a basis for literacy instruction. In M. L. Sampson (Ed.), *The pursuit of literacy: Early reading and writing.* Dubuque, IA: Kendall/Hunt.

Holquist, M. (1990). *Dialogism: Bakhtin and his world.* New York: Routledge.

Howard, S., Shaughnessy, A., Sanger, D., & Hux, K. (1998). Let's talk: Facilitating language in early elementary classrooms. *Young Children, 53*(3), 34–39.

Hu, H. (1995). Bringing written retelling into an ESL, English as a second language, writing class. *Journal of Developmental Education, 19*(1), 12–14.

Hurley, S. R., & Tinajero, J. V. (2001). *Literacy assessment of second language learners.* Boston: Allyn & Bacon.

International Reading Association & National Association for the Education of Young Children. (1998). Learning to read and write: Developmentally appropriate practice for young children. *The Reading Teacher, 52,* 193–216.

International Reading Association and National Council of Teachers of English. (1994). *Standards for the assessment of reading and writing.* Newark, DE: International Reading Association.

Iversen, S., & Reeder, T. (1998). *Organizing for a literacy hour: Quality learning and teaching time.* Bothell, WA: The Wright Group.

Jaggar, A. (1985). On observing the language learner: Introduction and overview. In A. Jaggar & M. T. Burke-Smith (Eds.), *Observing the language learner* (pp. 1–7). Newark, DE: International Reading Association.

Janongo, M. R. (2000). *Early childhood language arts* (2nd ed.). Boston: Allyn & Bacon.

John-Steiner, V., & Souberman, E. (1978). Afterword. In L. S. Vygotsky, *Mind in society: The development of higher psychological processes.* Cambridge, MA: Harvard University Press.

Johnston, P. (1981). *Prior knowledge and reading comprehension test bias.* Unpublished doctoral dissertation. University of Illinois, Champaign.

Joseph, L. (2002). Helping children link sound to print: Phonics procedures for small-group and whole-class settings. *Intervention in School & Clinic, 37,* 217–222.

Juel, C. (1988). Learning to read and write: A longitudinal study of fifty-four children from first through fourth grade. *Journal of Educational Psychology, 80,* 437–447.

Juel, C., & Minden-Cupp, C. (2000). One down and 80,000 to go: Word recognition instruction in the primary grades. *The Reading Teacher, 53*(4), 332–336.

Juel, C., Griffith, P., & Gough, P. (1986). Acquisition of literacy: A longitudinal study of children in first and second grade. *Journal of Educational Psychology, 75,* 243–255.

Kaderavek, J. N., & Sulzby, E. (1999, April 1). *Issues in emergent literacy for children with language impairments.* Ann Arbor, MI: Center for the Improvement of Early Reading Achievement. (CIERA Report #2-002)

Kagan, S. (1994). *Cooperative learning.* San Juan Capistrano, CA: Kagan Cooperative Learning.

Kasten, W. C. (1997). Learning is noisy: The myth of silence in the reading-writing classroom. In J. R. Paratone & R. L. McCarrick (Eds.), *Peer talk in the classroom: Learning from research* (pp. 147–170). Newark, DE: International Reading Association.

Katz, L. (1995). Dispositions in early childhood education. In L. G. Katz (Ed.), *Talks with teachers of young children. A collection.* Norwood, NJ: Ablex.

Katz, L. (1999). Curriculum disputes in early childhood education. Champaign, IL: *ERIC Clearinghouse on Elementary and Early Childhood Education.* (EDO-PS-99-13)

Kohn, A. (1993). Punished by rewards: The trouble with gold stars, incentive plans, A's, praise, and other bribes. Boston, MA: Houghton Mifflin.

Krashen, S. (1988). *Second language acquisition and second language learning.* Oxford: Pergamon Press.

Krashen, S., & Biber, D. (1988). *On course: Bilingual education's success in California.* Sacramento: California Association for Bilingual Educators.

Kuhn, M. R., & Stahl, S. (2000). *Fluency: A review of developmental and remedial practices.* Ann Arbor, MI: Center for the Improvement of Early Reading Achievement. (CIERA Report # 2-008)

LaBerge, D., & Samuels, S. J. (1974). Toward a theory of automatic information processing in reading. *Cognitive Psychology, 6*(2), 293–323.

LaBerge, D., & Samuels, S. J. (1985). Toward a theory of automatic information processing in reading. In H. Singer & R. B. Ruddell (Eds.), *Theoretical models and processes of reading.* Third edition. Newark, DE: International Reading Association.

Landau, J. K., Vohs, J., & Romano, C. (2002). Examples of accommodations from state assessment policies. Retrieved from http://www.ldonline.org/ld_indepth/special_education/peer_accommodation.html

Levy, B. A., & Carr, T. H. (1990). Component process analysis: Conclusions and challenges. In T. H. Carr & B. A. Levy (Eds.), *Reading and its development: Component skills approaches* (pp. 460–468). New York: Academic Press.

Lionetti, J. (1992). An author study: Tomie dePaola. In B. E. Cullinan (Ed)., *Invitation to read: More children's literature in the reading program* (pp. 64–71). Newark, DE: International Reading Association.

Loban, W. (1963). *The language of elementary school children.* Urbana, IL: National Council of Teachers of English.

Loban, W. (1976). *Language development: Kindergarten through grade twelve.* Urbana, IL: National Council of Teachers of English.

Lombardi, T. P. (1994). Responsible inclusion of students with disabilities: Fastback 373. ERIC document Reproduction Service No. ED 376634

Lonigan, C. J., Anthony, J. L., Bloomfield, B. G., Dyer, S., & Samwel, C. S. (1999). Effects of two preschool shared reading interventions on the emergent literacy skills of children from low-income families. *Journal of Early Intervention, 22,* 306–322.

Lonigan, C. J., Burgess, S. R., & Anthony, J. L. (2000). Development of emergent literacy and early literacy skills in preschool children: Evidence from a latent variable longitudinal study. *Developmental Psychology, 36,* 596–613.

Lyle, S. (1993). An investigation into the ways in which children talk themselves into meaning. *Language Education, 7*(3), 181–187.

Maclean, M., Bryant, P., & Bradley, L. (1987). Rhymes, nursery rhymes, and reading in early childhood. *Merrill-Palmer Quarterly, 33,* 255–281.

Mandler, J., & Johnson, N. (1977). Remembrance of things parsed: Story structure and recall. *Cognitive Psychology, 9.*

Maxim, G. (1989). *The very young: Guiding children from infancy through the early years* (3rd ed.). Upper Saddle River, NJ: Merrill/Prentice Hall.

McCarrier, A., Pinnell, G. S., & Fountas, I. C. (2000). *Interactive writing: How language and literacy come together, K–2.* Portsmouth, NH: Heinemann.

McConaughy, S. (1980). Using story structure in the classroom. *Language Arts, 57,* 157–165.

McCormick, L., Loeb, D. F., & Schiefelbusch, R. L. (1997). *Supporting children with communication difficulties in inclusive settings: School-based language intervention.* Boston: Allyn & Bacon.

McNeil, J. D. (1992). *Reading comprehension: New Directions for classroom practice.* New York: HarperCollins.

Meek, M. (1992). *On being literate.* Portsmouth, NH: Heinemann.

Meyer, B. (1975). *The organization of prose and its effects on memory.* New York: American Elsevier.

Meyer, B., Brandt, D. M., & Bluth, G. J. (1980). Use of top-level structure in text for reading comprehension of ninth-grade students. *Reading Research Quarterly, 16,* 72–103.

Miller, W. (2000). *Strategies for developing emergent literacy.* Boston: McGraw-Hill.

Monson, D. L. (1992). Realistic fiction and the real world. In B. E. Cullinan (Ed.), *Invitation to read: More children's literature in the reading program.* Newark, DE: International Reading Association.

Morrow, L. M. (1989). New perspectives in early literacy. *The Reading Instruction Journal, 32,* 8–15.

Morrow, L. M. (1997). *Literacy development in the early years: Helping children read and write.* Boston: Allyn & Bacon.

Morrow, L. M. (1997). *The literacy center.* York, ME: Stenhouse.

Morrow, L. M., Barnhart, S., & Rooyakkers, D. (2002). Integrating technology with the teaching of an early literacy course. *The Reading Teacher, 56*(3), 218–230.

Morrow, L., Pressley, M., Smith, J., & Smith, M. (1997). The effect of a literature based program integrated with literacy and science instruction with children from diverse backgrounds. *Reading Research Quarterly, 32*(1), 54–76.

Moss, B., Leone, S., & Dipillo, M. L. (1997). Exploring the literature of fact: Linking reading and writing through information trade books. *Language Arts, 74*(6), 148–158.

Moya, S. S., & O'Malley, J. M. (1994). A portfolio assessment model for ESL. *The Journal of Educational Issues for Language Minority Students, 13,* 13–36.

Nagy, W., & Herman, P. (1987). Breadth and depth of vocabulary knowledge: Implications for acquisition and instruction. In M. M. McKeown & M. Curtis (Eds.), *The nature of vocabulary acquisition.* (pp. 19–35). Hillsdale, NJ: Erlbaum.

Nagy, W. E., & Anderson, R. C. (1984). How many words are there in printed school English? *Reading Research Quarterly, 19,* 304–330.

Nathan, R. G., & Stanovich, K. E. (1991). The causes and consequences of differences in reading fluency. *Theory Into Practice, 30,* 176–184.

National Council of Teachers of English & International Reading Association. (1996). *Standards for the English language arts.* Urbana, IL: National Council of Teachers of English, and Newark, DE: International Reading Association.

National Education Goals Panel. (1996). *Executive summary: Commonly asked questions about standards and assessments.* Washington, DC: National Education Goals Panel.

National Research Council. (2001). *Eager to learn: Educating our nation's preschoolers.* Washington, DC: National Academy Press.

National Research Council. (2002). *Achieving high standards for all children.* Washington, DC: National Academy Press.

Neumann, S. B., & Bredekamp, S. (2000). Becoming a reader: A developmentally appropriate approach. In D. S. Strickland & L. M. Morrow (Eds.), *Beginning reading and writing* (pp. 22–34). Newark, DE: International Reading Association.

Neumann, S. B., & Dickinson, D. K. (Eds.). (2001). *Handbook of early literacy research.* New York: Guilford Press.

New Standards Speaking and Listening Committee. (2001). *Speaking and listening for preschool through grade three.* Pittsburgh: National Center on Education and the Economy and the University of Pittsburgh.

Newberger, J. J. (1997). New brain development research: A wonderful window of opportunity to build public support for early childhood education. *Young Children, 52*(4) 4–9.

Norton, D. A. (1993). *The effective teaching of language arts* (4th ed.). Upper Saddle River, NJ: Merrill/Prentice Hall.

Opitz, M. F. (1998). *Flexible grouping in reading: Practical ways to help all students become better readers.* New York: Scholastic.

Opitz, M. F., & Rasinski, T. V. (1998). *Good-bye round robin: 25 effective oral reading strategies.* Portsmouth, NH: Heinemann.

Owens, R. F., Hester, J. L., & Teale, W. H. (2002). Where do you want to go today? Inquiry-based learning and technology integration. *The Reading Teacher, 56,* 616–625.

Palinscar, A., & Brown, A. (1986). *Reciprocal teaching of comprehension strategies: Anatural history of one program for enhancing learning.* Champaign: University of Illinois Center for the Study of Reading.

Papalia, D. E., & Olds, S. W. (1998). *A child's world: Infancy through adolescence* (7th ed.). New York: McGraw-Hill.

Pappas, C. (1993). Is narrative "primary"? Some insights from kindergartens' pretend reading of stories and information books. *Journal of Reading Behavior, 25,* 97–129.

Pappas, C. (1998). The role of genres in the psycholinguistic guessing game of reading. *Language Arts, 75*(1), 36–44.

Paratore, J. R., Melzi, G., & Krol-Sinclair, B. (2003). Learning about the literate lives of Latino families. In D. M. Barone & L. M. Morrow (Eds.), *Literacy and young children: Research based practices* (pp. 101–121). New York: Guilford Press.

Pearson, P. D., & Johnson, D. D. (1978). *Teaching reading comprehension.* New York: Holt, Rinehart and Winston.

Perry, N., & Drummond, L. (2002). Helping young students become self-regulated researchers and writers. *The Reading Teacher, 56*(3), 298–310.

Piaget, J. (1948). *The language and thought of the child* (2nd ed.). London: Routledge & Kegan Paul.

Pinnell, G. S. (1985). Ways to look at the functions of children's language. In A. Jaggar & M. T. Smith-Burke (Eds.), *Observing the language learner.* Newark, DE: International Reading Association.

Pinnell, G. S., & Fountas, I. C. (1998). *Word matters: Teaching phonics and spelling in a reading/writing classroom.* Portsmouth, NH: Heinemann.

Piper, T. (1998). *Language and learning: The home and school years.* (2nd ed.). Upper Saddle River, NJ: Merrill/Prentice Hall.

Purcell-Gates, V. (1996). Stories, coupons, and the "TV Guide": Relationships between home literacy experiences and emergent literacy knowledge. *Reading Research Quarterly, 31,* 406–428.

Purves, A., Rogers, T., & Soter, A. (1995). *How porcupines make love III: Readers, text, culture in the response-based literature classroom.* White Plains, NY: Longman.

Raban, B. (2001). Talking to think, learn and teach. In P. G. Smith (Ed.), *Talking classrooms: Shaping children's learning through oral instruction* (pp. 27–42). Newark, DE: International Reading Association.

Rasinski, T. V. (1985). *A study of factors involved in reader-text interactions that contribute to fluency in reading.* Unpublished doctoral dissertation. Ohio State University, Columbus.

Rasinski, T. V., & Padak, N. D. (2001). *From phonics to fluency: Effective teaching of decoding and reading fluency in the elementary school.* New York: Longman.

Rasinski, T. V., & Zutell, J. B. (1996). Is fluency yet a goal of the reading curriculum? In E. V. Sturtevant and W. Linek (Eds.), *Growing Literacy, The Eighteenth Yearbook of the College* Reading Association, (pp. 237–246). Harrisonburg, VA: College Reading Association.

Read, C. (1971). Preschool children's knowledge of English phonology. *Harvard Educational Review, 41,* 1–34.

Readence, J. E., Bean, T. W., & Baldwin, S. W. (2000). *Content area literacy: An integrated approach* (7th ed.). Dubuque, IA: Kendall/Hunt.

Reutzel, D. R., & Cooter, R. B. (2000). *Teaching children to read: Putting the pieces together.* Upper Saddle River, NJ: Merrill/Prentice Hall.

Ricci, G., & Wahlgren, C. (1998, May). *The key to know PAINE know gain.* Paper presented at the 43rd Annual Convention of the International Reading Association, Orlando, FL.

Rinsland, H. D. (1945). *A basic vocabulary of elementary school children.* New York: Macmillan.

Robinson, D. (1998). Graphic organizers as aids to text in learning. *Reading Research and Instruction, 37,* 85–105.

Roehler, L. R., & Duffy, G. G. (1991). Teacher's instructional actions. In R. Barr, M. L. Kamil, P. Mosenthal, & P. D. Pearson (Eds.), *Handbook of reading research* (Vol. 2, pp. 861–883). New York: Longman.

Rogoff, B. (1990). *Apprenticeship in thinking: Cognitive development in social context.* New York: Oxford University Press.

Rosenblatt, L. (1938). *Literature as exploration.* New York: Modern Language Association.

Rosenblatt, L. (1991). Literature—S.O.S.! *Language Arts, 68,* 444–448.

Rosenblatt, L. M. (1978). *The reader, the text, the poem: The transactional theory of the literary work.* Carbondale: Southern Illinois University Press.

Rossetti, C. (1986). Wind. In M. Daniel (Ed.), *A child's treasury of poems.* New York: Dial Books.

Routman, R. (2000). *Conversations: Strategies for teaching, learning, and evaluating.* Portsmouth, NH: Heinemann.

Rubin, D. (2002). *Diagnosis and correction in reading instruction* (4th ed.). Boston: Allyn & Bacon.

Rumelhart, D. E. (1980). Schemata: The building blocks of cognition. In R. J. Spiro, B. C. Bruce, & W. F. Brewer (Eds.), *Theoretical issues in reading comprehension* (pp. 35–58). Hillsdale, NJ: Erlbaum.

Samway, K. D., Whang, G., Cade, C., Gamil, M., Lubandina, M. A., & Phommachanh, K. (1991). Reading the skeleton, the heart, and the brains of a book. Students' perspectives on literature study circles. *The Reading Teacher, 45*(3), 196–205.

Sawyer, W. E., & Sawyer, J. C. (1993). *Integrated language arts for emergent literacy.* Albany, NY: Delmar.

Schwartz, R., & Raphael, T. (1985). Concept of definition: A key to improving students' vocabulary. *The Reading Teacher, 39,* 198–205.

Sedgwick, F. (1999). *Thinking about literacy: Young children and their language.* London, England: Routledge.

Shiel, G. (2002). Kindergarten children's involvement in early literacy activities: Perspectives from Europe. *The Reading Teacher, 56*(3), 282–284.

Silva, C., & Alves-Martin, M. (2002). Phonological skills and writing of presyllabic children. *Reading Research Quarterly, 37*(4), 466–485.

Skinner, B. F. (1957). *Verbal behavior.* Upper Saddle River, NJ: Merrill/Prentice Hall.

Smith, P. G. (Ed.) (2001). *Talking classrooms: Shaping children's learning through oral instruction.* Newark, DE: International Reading Association.

Snow, C. (1983). Literacy and language: Relationships during the preschool years. *Harvard Educational Review, 53*(2), 165–189.

Snow, C. (1994). Enhancing literacy development: Programs and research perspectives. In D. Dickinson (Ed.), *Bridges to literacy* (pp. 267–272). Cambridge, MA: Basil Blackwell.

Snow, C. E. (1999). Why the home is so important to read. Paper presented at the George Graham Lecture in Reading, Charlottesville, VA.

Snow, C. E., & Ninio, A. (1986). The contracts of literacy: What children learn from learning to read books. In W. H. Teale & E. Sulzby (Eds.), *Emergent literacy: Writing and reading* (pp. 116–138). Portsmouth, NH: Heinemann.

Snow, C. E., Burns, M. S., & Griffin, P. (Eds.). (1998). *Preventing reading difficulties in young children.* Washington, DC: National Academy Press, National Research Council.

Snow, C., Burns, M. S., & Griffin, P. (1999). *Language and literacy environments in preschools.* Champaign, IL: ERIC Clearinghouse on Elementary and Early Childhood Education.

Snow, C., & Goldfield, B. A. (1983). Turn the page please: Situation-specific language acquisition. *Journal of Child Language, 10,* 551–569.

Soderman, A. K., Gregory, K. M., & O'Neil, L. T. (1999). *Scaffolding emergent literacy: A child-centered approach for preschool through Grade 5.* Boston: Allyn & Bacon.

Spear-Swerling, L., & Sternberg, R. J. (1996). *Off track: When poor readers become "learning disabled."* Boulder, CO: Westview Press.

Spivey, N. N. (1997). *The constructivist metaphor.* New York: Ablex.

Stahl, S. A. (1998). Teaching children with reading problems to decode: Phonics and "not-phonics" instruction. *Reading and Writing Quarterly: Overcoming Learning Difficulties, 14,* 165–188.

Stanovich, K. (1986). Matthew effects in reading: Some consequences of individual differences in the acquisition of literacy. *Reading Research Quarterly, 21,* 360–406.

Stanovich, K. (1991). Word recognition: Changing perspectives. In R. Barr, M. L. Kamil, P. Mosenthal, & P. D. Pearson (Eds.), *Handbook of Reading Research* (Vol. 2, pp. 418–452). New York: Longman.

Stanovich, K. (1992). Speculations on the causes and consequences of individual differences in early reading acquisition. In P. B. Gough, L. C. Ehri, & R. Treiman (Eds.), *Reading acquisition* (pp. 307–342). Hillsdale, NJ: Erlbaum.

Stauffer, R. (1980). *The language experience approach to the teaching of reading* (2nd ed.). New York: Harper & Row.

Stauffer, R. G. (1975). Directing the reading thinking process. New York: HarperCollins.

Sternberg, R. J. (1987). Most words are learned from context. In M. G. McKeown & M. E. Curtis (Eds.), *The acquisition of word meanings* (pp. 89–106). Hillsdale, NJ: Erlbaum.

Stevens, S. (1997). Adjustments in classroom management. Retrieved from http://www.ldonline.org/ld_indepth/teaching_techniques/class_manage.html

Sticht, T. G., & McDonald, B. A. (1989). *Making the nation smarter: The intergenerational transfer of cognitive ability.* San Diego, CA: Applied Behavioral and Cognitive Sciences.

Strickland, D. (1998). *Teaching phonics today: A primer for educators.* Newark, DE: International Reading Association.

Strickland, D. S. (1990). Emergent literacy: How young children learn to read and write. *Educational Leadership, 47*(6), 18–23.

Strickland, D. S. (2000). Classroom intervention strategies: Supporting the literacy development of young learners at risk. In D. S. Strickland & L. M. Morrow (Eds.), *Beginning reading and writing* (pp. 99–110). Newark, DE: International Reading Association.

Strickland, D. S., & Morrow, L. M. (1989). Interactive experiences with storybook reading. *The Reading Teacher, 42*(41), 322–324.

Strickland, D. S., & Morrow, L. M. (1989). *Emerging literacy: Young children learn to read and write.* Newark, DE: International Reading Association.

Strickland, D., Ganske, K., & Monroe, J. K. (2002). *Supporting struggling readers and writers.* Portland, ME: Stenhouse & International Reading Association.

Sulzby, E. (1985). Children's emergent reading of favorite storybooks. *Reading Research Quarterly, 20,* 458–481.

Sulzby, E. (1986). Kindergarteners as writers and readers. In M. Farr (Ed.), *Advances in writing research.* Vol. 1: *Children's early writing.* Norwood, NJ: Ablex.

Sulzby, E. (1989). Assessment of writing and children's language while writing. In L. Morrow & J. Smith (Eds.), *The role of assessment and measurement in early literacy instruction* (pp. 83–109). Upper Saddle River, NJ: Merrill/Prentice Hall.

Sulzby, E., & Teale, W. H. (1991). Emergent literacy. In P. D. Pearson, R. Barr, M. L. Kamil, & P. Mosenthal (Eds.), *Handbook of reading research* (Vol. 2). New York: Longman.

Swan, E. A. (2003). *Concept oriented reading instruction: Engaging classrooms, lifelong learners.* New York: Guilford Press.

Taberski, S. (2000). *On solid ground: Strategies for teaching reading K–3.* Portsmouth, NH: Heinemann.

Taylor, D. (1980). *Family literacy: Young children learning to read and write.* Exeter, NH: Heinemann.

Taylor, D., & Dorsey-Gaines, C. (1988). *Growing up literate.* Portsmouth, NH: Heinemann.

Taylor, G. (2002). Who's who? Engaging biography study. *The Reading Teacher, 56*(4), 342–344.

Tchudi, S. (1997). *Alternatives to grading student writing.* Urbana, IL: National Council of Teachers of English.

Teale, W. H. (1984). Reading to young children: Its significance for literacy development. In H. Goelman, A. Oberg, & F. Smith (Eds.), *Awakening to literacy.* Portsmouth, NH: Heinemann.

Teale, W. H. (1986). The beginning of reading and writing: Written language development during preschool and kindergarten years. In M. Sampson (Ed.), *The pursuit of literacy: Early reading and writing.* Dubuque, IA: Kendall/Hunt.

Teale, W. H. (1987). Emergent literacy: Reading and writing development in early childhood. In J. Readance & R. S. Baldwin (Eds.), *36th yearbook of the National Reading Conference.* Rochester, NY: National Reading Conference.

Teale, W. H., & Sulzby, E. (1986). Emergent literacy as a perspective for examining how young children become readers and writers. In W. H. Teale & E. Sulzby (Eds.), *Emergent literacy: Writing and reading* (pp. vii–xxv). Norwood, NJ: Ablex.

Tharp, R., & Gallimore, R. (1988). *Rousing minds to life: Teaching, learning and schooling in social context.* New York: Cambridge University Press.

Thorndyke, P. (1977). Cognitive structures in comprehension and memory of narrative discourse. *Cognitive Psychology, 9,* 97–110.

Thurlow, M. (2002). Assessment: A key component of education reform. Retrieved from http://www.ldonline.org/ld_indepth/special_education/thurlow_assessment.html

Tinajero, J., & Schifini, A. (1993). *ESL theme links program guide.* Carmel, CA: Hampton-Brown Books.

Tombari, M., & Borich, G. (1999). *Authentic assessment in the classroom: Applications & Practice.* Upper Saddle River NJ: Merrill.

Tomlinson, C. A. (2000). Differentiation of instruction in elementary grades. Retrieved from http://www.ed.gov/databases/ERIC_Digests/ed443572.html

Tomlinson, C. A. (2001). *How to differentiate instruction in mixed ability classrooms.* Alexandria, VA: Association for Supervision and Curriculum Development.

Tomlinson, C. A. (2002). Basics of differentiation. Retrieved from http://www.readingrockets.org/wfyi/article.php?ID=154

Tomlinson, C. A., & Kalbfliesch, M. L. (1998). Teach me, teach my brain: A call for differentiated classroom. Retrieved from http://www.ascd.org/pdl/demo/diffinstru/tomlinson.html

Tompkins, G. (2002). *Language arts.* Upper Saddle River, NJ: Merrill/Prentice Hall.

The University of the State of New York. (1998, July 16). *Regents Task Force on Teaching: Teaching to high standards.* Albany, NY: The State Department of Education.

Vacca, J., Vacca, R., Gove, M., Burkey, L., Lenhart, L., & McKeon, C. (2003). *Reading and learning to read* (5th ed.). New York: Allyn & Bacon.

Valdes, G. (1997). Dual language immersion programs: A cautionary note concerning the education of language minority students. *Harvard Educational Review, 67*(3), 391–429.

van Dijk, T., & Kintsch, W. (1977). Cognitive psychology and discourse: Recalling and summarizing stories. In W. U. Dressler (Ed.), *Current trends in text linguistics.* Berlin, Germany: De Gruyter.

Vaughan, J., & Estes, T. (1986). *Reading and reasoning beyond the primary grades.* Boston: Allyn & Bacon.

Veatch, J. (1978). *Reading in the elementary school.* (2nd ed.) New York: Wiley.

Veatch, J., Sawicki, F., Elliott, G., Barnette, E., & Blakey, J. (1973). *Key words to reading: The language experience approach begins.* Upper Saddle River, NJ: Merrill/Prentice Hall.

Vukelich, C., Christie, J., & Enz, B. (2002). *Helping young children learn language and literacy.* Boston: Allyn & Bacon.

Vygotsky, L. S. (1978). *Mind in society: The development of higher mental processes* (M. Cole, V. John-Steiner, S. Scribner, & E. Souberman, Eds. & Trans.). Cambridge, MA: Harvard University Press.

Vygotsky, L. S. (1986). *Thought and language.* Cambridge, MA: Harvard University Press.

Wagstaff, J. M. (1999). *Teaching reading and writing with word walls.* New York: Scholastic.

Walmsley, S. A., & Walp, T. (1990). Integrating literature and composing into the language arts curriculum: Philosophy and practice. *Elementary School Journal, 90*(3), 251–274.

Watson, R. (2001). Literacy and oral language: Implications for early literacy acquisition. In S. B. Neuman & D. K. Dickinson (Eds.), *Handbook of early literacy research* (pp. 43–54). New York: Guilford Press.

Wells, G. (1981). *Learning through interaction: The study of language development.* Cambridge, England: Cambridge University Press.

Wells, G. (1986). *The meaning makers: Children learning language and using language to learn.* Portsmouth, NH: Heinemann.

Wells, G. (1987). The negotiation of meaning: Talking and learning at home and at school. In B. Fillion, C. Hedley, & E. DiMartino (Eds.), *Home and school: Early language and reading:* Norwood, NJ: Ablex.

Wells, G. (1990). Creating the conditions to encourage literate thinking. *Educational Leadership, 47*(6), 15–17.

Wells, G., & Chang-Wells, G. L. (1992). *Constructing knowledge together: Classrooms as centers of inquiry and literacy.* Portsmouth, NH: Heinemann.

Wells, G., & Chang-Wells, G. L. (1993). Dynamics of discourse: Literacy and the construction of knowledge. In E. A. Forman, N. Minick, & C. A. Stone (Eds.), *Contexts for learning: Sociocultural dynamics in children's development* (pp. 58–90). New York: Oxford University Press.

White, T., Sowell, J., & Yanagihara, A. (1989). Teaching elementary students to use word part clues. *The Reading Teacher, 42,* 302–308.

Whitehurst, G. J., & Lonigan, C. J. (2001). Emergent literacy: Development from prereaders to readers. In S. B. Neuman & D. K. Dickinson (Eds.), *Handbook of early literacy research* (pp. 11–30). New York: Guilford Press.

Whitin, P. E. (1996). *Sketching stories, stretching minds.* Portsmouth, NH: Heinemann.

Wiener, R. B., & Cohen, J. H. (1997). *Literacy portfolios: Using assessment to guide instruction.* Upper Saddle River, NJ: Merrill/Prentice Hall.

Wood, J. D. (2002). *Adapting instruction to accommodate students in inclusive settings.* Upper Saddle River, NJ: Merrill/Prentice Hall.

Wood, K. (2001). *Literacy strategies across the subject areas.* Boston: Allyn & Bacon.

Wylie, R. E., & Durrell, D. D. (1970). Teaching vowels through phonograms. *Elementary English, 47,* 787–791.

Xu, H. (1999). Re-examining continuities and discontinuities: Language minority children's home and school literacy experiences. *National Reading Conference Yearbook, 48,* 224–237.

Xu, S. H. (2003). The learner, the teacher, the text and the context: Sociocultural approaches to early literacy instruction for English language learners. In D. M. Barone & L. M. Morrow (Eds.), *Literacy and young children: Research based practices* (pp. 61–83). New York: Guilford Press.

Yopp, H. K. (1988). The validity and reliability of phonemic awareness tests. *Reading Research Quarterly, 23,* 159–177.

Yopp, H. K. (1992). Developing phonemic awareness in young children. *The Reading Teacher, 45*(9), 696–703.

Yopp, H. K. (1995). A test for assessing phonemic awareness in young children. *The Reading Teacher, 49,* 20–22.

Name Index

Subject Index